Alien Kind

Foxes and Late Imperial Chinese Narrative

Harvard East Asian Monographs, 222

Alien Kind

Foxes and Late Imperial Chinese Narrative

{ Rania Huntington }

Published by the Harvard University Asia Center
and distributed by Harvard University Press
Cambridge (Massachusetts) and London, 2003

Printed in the United States of America

The Harvard University Asia Center publishes a monograph series and, in coordination with the Fairbank Center for East Asian Research, the Korea Institute, the Reischauer Institute of Japanese Studies, and other faculties and institutes, administers research projects designed to further scholarly understanding of China, Japan, Vietnam, Korea, and other Asian countries. The Center also sponsors projects addressing multidisciplinary and regional issues in Asia.

Library of Congress Cataloging-in-Publication Data

Huntington, Rania.
Alien kind : foxes and late imperial Chinese narrative / Rania Huntington.
p. cm. — (Harvard East Asian monographs : 222) Includes bibliographical references and index.
ISBN 0-674-01094-9 (alk. paper)
1. Chinese literature—Qing dynasty, 1644–1912—History and criticism. 2. Foxes in literature. I. Title. II. Series.
PL2327.H85 2003
895.1'093629775—dc22 2003016274

Index by the author

♾ Printed on acid-free paper

Last figure below indicated year of this printing
08 07 06 05 04 03

To Alan, for reading it
and
to Dipesh, for not reading it

Acknowledgments

I owe a great debt of gratitude first to a trio of advisers: Judith Zeitlin, Li Jianguo of Nankai University, and Patrick Hanan. Without their tireless guidance, this book would neither have been begun nor finished.

Paul Katz gave insightful commentary on the fox worship chapter, and two of my colleagues at Illinois, Emanuel Pastreich and Gang Xu, helped me with Chapter 7. Many Harvard classmates at various times helped me through difficult sections.

My initial trip to China to work with Li Jianguo was made possible through a Sheldon Travelling Fellowship. A subsequent trip in 1999 was supported by the University of Illinois exchange program with Beijing University, sponsored by the Freeman Foundation. A semester of Humanities Release Time from the University of Illinois allowed me to complete the manuscript.

Chapter 5 has previously appeared as an article in *Nannü* 2:1.

I am grateful for the help of John Ziemer, and two anonymous readers from the Press, for their helpful comments.

During my illness, when I despaired of (among other things) ever finishing this book, an incredible number of friends stood by me and helped me through. I cannot name you all here, but I remain eternally grateful.

Finally, my old roommate Alan Boudreau read this book not once but twice, once as a dissertation and once as a manuscript. He literally carried it around the world. And without Dipesh at home, none of this would have been possible.

Acknowledgments

Contents

List of Illustrations

List of Abbreviations

BJXSDG	*Biji xiaoshuo daguan* 筆記小說大觀
LZ	*Liaozhai zhiyi* 聊齋志異
TPGJ	*Taiping guangji* 太平廣記
YTSL	*Yetan suilu* 夜譚隨錄
YWCT	*Yuewei caotang biji* 閱微草堂筆記

Alien Kind

Foxes and Late Imperial Chinese Narrative

Introduction

狐五十歲能變化为婦人，百歲为美人，爲神巫。或爲丈夫與女人交接，能知千里外事，善蠱魅，使人迷惑失智。千歲，即與天通，爲天狐。When a fox is fifty years old, it can transform itself into a woman. When it is one hundred, it becomes a beautiful woman or a shaman; some become men and have sex with women. They can know events from more than a thousand *li* away and are good at witchcraft, beguiling people and making them lose their senses. When they are a thousand years old, they can commune with the heavens and become heavenly foxes.[1]

人物異類，狐則在人物之間。幽明異路，狐則在幽明之間。仙妖殊途，狐則在仙妖之間。故謂遇狐爲怪可。謂遇狐爲常亦可。
Humans and beasts are different species, but foxes are between humans and beasts. The dead and the living walk different roads, but foxes are between the dead and the living. Transcendents and monsters travel different paths, but foxes are between transcendents and monsters. Therefore one could say to meet a fox is strange; one could also say it is ordinary.[2]

---

1. Under the title "Shuo hu" 說狐, with *Xuanzhong ji* 玄中記 listed as the source; in Li Fang et al., comp., *Taiping guangji* (hereafter *TPGJ*) 447. 3652. *Xuanzhong ji* does not survive; for a reconstructed version, see Lu Xun, *Gudai xiaoshuo gouchen*, p. 239. The attribution to Guo Pu is contested. The earliest extant mention appears in the Song work *Taiping yulan* 太平御覽 attributed to an unspecified Mr. Guo. Robert Campany (*Strange Writing*, p. 93) doubts the attribution; Li Jianguo (*Tangqian zhiguai xiaoshuo shi*, pp. 270–71) argues in its favor.

2. Ji Yun, *Yuewei caotang biji zhuyi* (hereafter *YWCT*) 10.503–4, story 229. *Yuewei caotang biji* is composed of five collections, *Luanyang xiaoxia lu* 灤陽消夏錄, *Rushi wowen* 如是我聞, *Huaixi zazhi* 槐西雜志, *Guwang tingzhi* 姑妄聽之, and

These two quotations, fifteen hundred years apart, are among the most famous definitions of the fox in the Chinese literary tradition. The first focuses on the fox's transgressive abilities; the second on its transgression of categories. The first depicts a creature in a progressive state of change; the second a creature suspended in the middle. This book deals with the world of late imperial China, in which the first quotation represents ancient, established lore about foxes and the second a creative man's synthesis of the contemporary narrative tradition. It is a study of an age in which the rare thousand-year-old fox has become the most ordinary strange creature a man might meet.

To talk of the "supernatural" in China is, in one common phrase, to *tanhu shuogui* 談狐說怪 "talk of foxes and speak of ghosts."[3] Indeed, in certain periods, ghosts only barely outnumbered foxes as the most common denizen of the Chinese imagination. Every culture has to contend with the dead, thus ghosts are a familiar, cross-cultural category for dealing with mortality as a limit of humanity. But what is this other category? What limits do foxes define? This book attempts to answer these questions.

Foxes matter because an extraordinary range of people of all ages and both sexes in late imperial China—peasants, officials, servants, professional spirit mediums, flower vendors—talked about them. A more limited section of the population, literate, elite, and apparently all male, recorded stories about them, and a somewhat larger portion of the literate read those stories. Yet few of these raconteurs, listeners, authors, or readers, with the exception of the mediums, would have described foxes as central to their lives. Rather, foxes appeared at the edges—a strange noise in the attic, a desperate treatment for an illness, a curious tale told after dinner, a bit of light reading, or an

---

Luanyang xulu 灤陽續錄. The numbering of the stories, which begins anew at the beginning of each of the sub-collections, is based on the 1994 Zhongguo huaqiao chubanshe edition.

3. Leo Tak-Hong Chan alludes to this phrase in his book title: *The Discourse of Foxes and Ghosts: Ji Yun and Eighteenth-Century Chinese Storytelling*. Use of the term "supernatural" in the Chinese context is problematic, because foxes and ghosts were not seen as distinct from the natural world.

avowedly casual composition. This study explores the interests that made foxes at the same time ubiquitous and marginal.

Recent interest in cultural studies, with its border crossing between literary and non-literary texts, seems to have increased interest in the fox. Ylva Monschein's *Der Zauber der Fuchsfee: Entstehung und Wandel eines "Femme-Fatale" Motivs in der chinesischen Literatur* (The magic of the fox fairy: the formation and transformation of a "femme fatale" theme in Chinese literature) traces the theme from its earliest beginnings to the modern era, focusing on the fox as femme fatale. It is primarily a literary study; although she tries to introduce the popular tradition of fox beliefs at the beginning of each historical segment, she admits she has not been able to pursue that aspect of the tradition in depth. In Chinese, Li Jianguo's *Zhongguo hu wenhua* 中國狐文化 (China's fox culture) surveys the history of the fox from the pre-Qin period through the Qing. As the title indicates, he places particular emphasis on the popular tradition and its influence on the literary tradition. In Taiwan, Li Shouju's *Huxian xinyang yu hulijing gushi* 狐仙信仰與狐狸精故事 (Beliefs in fox immortals and stories of fox spirits) is a historical survey of both the literary and the popular religious traditions from the earliest records to modern times. Recently, Xiaofei Kang completed a dissertation studying the fox from the earliest times through the present day from the perspective of popular religion. And Steven Heine's detailed study of a particular textual case, the fox koan, uses the fox tradition to explore the intersection between folklore and philosophy.[4]

4. Other studies include Fatima Wu, "Foxes in Chinese Supernatural Tales"; Gu Meigao, "Tan hu"; and Nishioka Haruoka, "Jinshi to Einei no aida: koyō im ji no henyo." The current publishing vogue in mainland China for topical anthologies of classical tales, often with vernacular translation, has proved useful in my search for references. The popularity of such works is interesting in its own right: it provides an interesting parallel with the Ming vogue for topical anthologies and proves that fox stories are once again marketable in a time of rapid changes in popular culture. Although some of these publications were edited by scholars, these are not scholarly works. I have used them to direct me to the original texts but have not otherwise relied on them. Some examples I have consulted are: Ma Guojun, ed., *Lidai huxian chuanqi quanshu;* Miao Zhuang, ed., *Qinghu zhuan;* Lu Lin, ed., *Qingdai biji xiaoshuo leibian jingguai juan;* and Li Jianguo, ed., *Huli jing de gushi.*

Building on the efforts of these broad historical surveys, I chose to focus on the past three or four centuries of the narrative tradition on foxes, the period from the sixteenth through the nineteenth centuries. This decision is justified on both quantitative and qualitative grounds: the Tang and the Qing are the two high points in the fox's popularity, but both the growth in publishing and the higher survival rate of recent books ensure that late imperial foxes far outnumber their Tang ancestors. Focusing on a narrower historical period has allowed me to pursue a thematic, rather than a chronological, organization and to explore those themes in more depth. Finally, as I hope to show, because of external changes in publishing and literary history and internal changes in the fox tradition, the fox stories of the Ming and Qing form a distinct body of texts.

In contrast to studies that concentrate on popular religion, this is primarily a literary study. Because the fox is as transgressive of our contemporary disciplinary divisions as it was of Ji Yun's 紀昀 (1724–1805) categories, the textual tradition on foxes is inextricably linked to popular religion and other extra-textual traditions. Nonetheless, the focuses of this study are the fox in narrative and how a textual tradition contends with those other traditions. This leads to exclusions which I regret: I have not, for example, carried out anthropological fieldwork on contemporary practitioners of fox belief. There remains a great deal of work for those in other fields, but I hope to make a contribution to the interdisciplinary understanding of the fox.

This book is an investigation of one particular society's conception of one kind of alien, and as such, I hope it will contribute to our understanding of the general human capacity for, and interest in, imagining the alien. By imagining the alien, we establish the boundaries of the human. As the most ubiquitous and ambiguous alien in the Chinese imagination from the sixteenth through the nineteenth centuries, the shape-changing fox helped to establish the boundaries around the human and the ordinary. Its frequent violations of these boundaries reveal the anxieties of late imperial culture. The borders it crossed were the most jealously guarded ones.

Each section of this thematically arranged study traces a particular boundary violated by the fox. I examine how maneuvers across that border change, both between earlier periods and the late imperial era and over the course of the Ming and Qing. I will not, however, be offering a single unified answer about the meaning of the fox. I am inspired here by Gail Hershatter's work on prostitutes (a category, as we will see, closely related to foxes). She divides concepts of prostitutes in Shanghai into a series of "approximations," an approach perhaps even more appropriate to an entirely imagined and thus even more flexible subject.[5] Although there is not a single Fox, there are a finite number of distinct traditions of talking about foxes. The traits of an imaginary species recombine and mutate with a flexibility impossible for a biological species, but the need to be recognizable demands some constants over time even as the novelty required to replenish our sense of wonder leads to constant change.

Just as the fox crosses boundaries, the genre in which most fox stories appear, *wenyan xiaoshuo* 文言小說 (the classical tale) is a liminal one, crossing boundaries between fiction and nonfiction, folklore and literary invention, oral and written, and popular and elite. Each of the thematic chapters explores problems of the genre as it explores foxes as a species. Consideration of *wenyan xiaoshuo* enriches a comparative discussion involving folktales, legends, literary fairy tales, and fantasy.

Chapter 1 introduces the narrative tradition of the fox before the Ming and Qing and the history of the *wenyan xiaoshuo* and its subgenres, particularly the *zhiguai* 志怪 (records of the strange) during the Ming and Qing. Chapter 2 examines the narrative practice and theory of the high Qing fox story through close readings of two sets of stories against their authors' theoretical statements on the fox. The intent of these two chapters is to introduce foxes as they appear and examine the gaps between a discussion of a particular fox and discussions about foxes in general.

Chapter 3 begins the thematic treatment of foxes and their violation of boundaries, in this case their crossing of the boundary between domesticity and the outside world by intruding into the human home. Chapter 4 explores the shapes fox worship takes in

5. Hershatter, "Modernizing Sex, Sexing Modernity."

narrative and thus the relation between tales of the strange and popular religion. Chapter 5 discusses vulpine sexuality as a violation of the boundaries of the human self. Chapter 6, in contrast, shows how the romance, by curbing sexual peril, creates vixens who as ideal lovers are on the brink of erasing their difference from humanity and thus effacing their own marvel. Chapter 7 examines two of foxes' contrasting roles: *xian* 仙 (transcendents), who improve themselves, and *yao* 妖 (monsters), who are stirred up by human misbehavior. The Conclusion compares the fox with the most familiar and proximate alien creatures in other cultures, particularly the fairies of the Western European tradition.

Throughout, I am concerned with several categories of question. One is the changes in the representation of the fox over time, both between the pre-Ming period and the Ming and Qing, and over the course of the Ming and Qing. Do foxes as a species evolve, their boundaries with humanity shifting? What can these shifts tell us about changes in the concerns of the human authors and narrators of fox tales? A second group of questions relates to the generic forms in which fox stories are narrated. Over the period of interest in this book, foxes appeared in a variety of forums, from the traditional collections of *zhiguai* 志怪 (records of the strange) and *chuanqi* 傳奇 (tales of the marvelous) to the more modern media of newspapers and illustrated journals. How do different genres shape the portrayal of the fox? How do the genres in which a culture describes nonhuman species affect its conception of species? A third set of questions revolves around the role of the fox in narratives. What human anxieties, concerns, and desires were foxes used to express? Through the fox I wish to explore the human project of imagining the alien and its limitations.

As much as the fox reveals about the people and society who fashioned it, I do not want to reduce the fox to these social meanings and lose sight of its inherent fascination. I wish to reaffirm the fox's place between the explicable and the mysterious, between imagination's habits and its innovations. My title, *Alien Kind*, from *yilei* 異類, has a double resonance. A relatively polite way for foxes to allude to their own status as an alien species, it also implies Ji Yun's observation that they are a different and strange category.

{1}
Species History, Genre History

One of the interesting features of late imperial fox narrative is the presence of a long textual history, some of it consciously remembered and some forgotten. The history of the fox as a culturally constructed species is intertwined with the history of the classical tale as a genre, and fox stories read in published books intersected in complex ways with oral accounts of fox encounters. The following is not an exhaustive history of the pre-Ming literary tradition, but a brief summary, with emphasis on those parts of the tradition still relevant to Ming and Qing authors.

Why did foxes become first magical animals and then a magical people? The idea of the fox as a tricky creature is shared by many cultures, suggesting some link between the natural and the cultural fox.[1] As a small predator, it is neither deadly nor innocuous. Since it is no threat to human life, it cannot play the awe-inspiring role of the wolf or tiger, but yet it can prey on domestic livestock or compete with humans for small game. Foxes hunt alone, not as members of a pack. They are nocturnal, but often glimpsed in the transitional hours of dawn or twilight. Dwelling easily on the edges of human habitation as well as in the wilderness gives them a marginal place. They are burrowers in the earth, passing between this world and the one below, and like to take up residence in existing hollows,

---

1. Compare the role the fox plays in Aesop's fables, or the figure of Renard, liar, thief, and brazen adulterer, in the medieval verse narrative (see, e.g., Terry, *Renard the Fox*).

including tombs. Above all, they are extremely adaptable—they eat sweet fruit as well as small rodents and dwell as readily in an abandoned badger's burrow as in a bombed-out building. The red fox has the largest natural range of any large terrestrial mammal, save humans.[2] All these observations resonate with Ji Yun's characterization of the fox as both ubiquitous and mysterious.

These zoological aspects of human-fox interaction provided only the most rudimentary foundations for the development of the cultural fox in China. As humans developed new conceptions of the relationship between themselves and other creatures, impressions of individual species were fit into that framework. When a complex system of animals as omens developed in the Han, the fox took its place among them.[3] But more important, beginning in the Han and becoming more prominent in the Six Dynasties, was the development of ideas of interspecies transformation. The fox becoming human was part of a larger concept of mysterious transformation by long-lived animals and men. As men went into the mountains to seek to become other than human, they met creatures there who were also becoming other than what they were.[4]

In the Ming and Qing, the most influential body of earlier fox lore was indisputably the nine *juan* of fox stories in the Song compendium of story, lore, and anecdote, *Taiping guangji* 太平廣記 (Broad gleanings of the era of Great Peace). The references in this book to the "earlier fox tradition" are primarily to this body of stories, scarcely less rich and various than their more numerous descendants. No other body of earlier fox stories was so accessible to the authors of the Ming and Qing.[5] *Taiping guangji* includes some Six Dynasties

2. For a discussion of the link between the cultural fox and the zoological fox in the Japanese context, see Smyers, *The Fox and the Jewel*, pp. 87–89; and Grambo, *The World of the Fox*, pp. 3–12, 29–33, 103.

3. For a discussion of the fox omen tradition, see Li Jianguo, *Zhongguo hu wenhua*, pp. 40–53.

4. See "Deng she pian" 登涉篇, in Ge Hong, *Baopu zi neipian xiaoshi*, 17.300.

5. Outside *Taiping guangji*, only a few famous tales from *Soushen ji* that are not included in the Song compendium have comparable influence. One measure of *TPGJ*'s influence is the extent it was used as a source from which to create forged works; see the addendum on forgeries in Li Jianguo, *Tang wudai zhiguai chuanqi*

zhiguai, but the greater part of its material dates to the Tang. Later authors commonly did not conceptualize the Six Dynasties and Tang as distinct periods of fox lore; instead the *Taiping guangji* assembly was regarded as a whole.[6] The stories collected in *Taiping guangji* represent a high point of interest in foxes unequaled until the Qing. My emphasis on Tang material is not to deny that the fox tradition evolved and changed between *Taiping guangji*'s completion in 981 and its republication in 1566. However, foxes do not seem to have been as important a subject from the Song to the early Ming, and stories from that period do not seem to have nearly as much influence on later authors as these Tang tales did. The late Ming *Humei congtan* 狐媚叢談 (Complete tales of fox seduction), the only collection in Chinese literary history exclusively devoted to foxes, drew most of its material from *Taiping guangji,* and its bias toward the compendium over later material was widely shared in Ming-Qing anthologies.[7]

The most enduring legacy of the earlier tradition was the fox's capacity for transformation. The idea that non-human creatures could, with advancing age, assume human form is presented in Wang Chong's 王充 (27–91) *Lun heng* 論衡. He suggested that the ghosts seen by sick men might be the spirits of venerable plants and animals in human guise. These spirits come into contact with humans and cause afflictions and illusions.[8] According to the fourth-century philosophical work *Baopu zi* 抱扑子, 萬物之老者，其精悉能假托人形，以眩人目，而常試人。"When any one of the myriad creatures grows old, its spirit can assume human shape in order to dazzle

xulu; and Feng Menglong's complaints on this subject in the preface to Feng, *Taiping guangji chao.*

6. Ji Yun (*YWCT,* 10.216–7, story 229) did refer to the Tang as a period of intense interest in fox spirits.

7. Mo Chizi, *Humei congtan.* Another example of heavy reliance on *Taiping guangji* is *Gujin tushu jicheng* 古今圖書集成, which includes nearly all the fox stories of *Taiping guangji* in the *waipian* section of its definition of foxes but few later stories and no contemporary ones. Feng Menglong's compendium *Qingshi* also shares this preference.

8. "Dinggui pian" 訂鬼篇, in Wang Chong, *Lunheng xiaoshi,* 4:22.934–35.

humans' eyes and frequently test men."[9] Transformation is not simply a natural anomaly; rather, its intent is to deceive and toy with human beings.

Wang Chong described the transformations of animals in general, and other Han and earlier texts portrayed the fox as either an auspicious or an uncanny animal,[10] but it was not until the Six Dynasties that the tradition of the transforming fox in particular began. Transformations were one of the central themes of the young *zhiguai* genre. The most frequently quoted early statement of foxes' unearthly abilities is found in *Xuanzhong ji* (quoted at the beginning of the introduction), "When a fox is fifty years old, it can transform itself into a woman. When it is one hundred, it becomes a beautiful woman or a shaman; some become men and have sex with women. They can know events from more than a thousand *li* away and are good at witchcraft, causing people to be beguiled and lose their senses. When they are a thousand years old, they can commune with the heavens and become heavenly foxes."[11] This theoretical treatise introduces many elements developed in the later fox tradition: sexual parasitism, the association with spirit mediums, steady progress, and the possibility of transcendence.

However, the bulk of the fox tradition consists of specific narrative examples rather than theoretical statements. Close analysis of the foxes of *Taiping guangji* is a worthy topic in itself.[12] Here I will provide only a simplified, composite portrait, and in the following chapters I will make reference to examples that remained influential in the treatment of specific topics. Like any composite portrait drawn from several individual stories, it is inherently inaccurate; the features I describe are never all present at the same time.

One of the most ancient ways of understanding strange animals is

---

9. "Deng she pian," in Ge Hong, *Baopu zi*, 17.300. *Baopu zi*'s close kinship with *zhiguai* works should be noted; Ge Hong was also the author of the *zhiguai* collection *Shenxian zhuan* 神仙傳. For Ge Hong, the fox was not yet the leader among marvelous creatures. Its longevity, at 800 years, was not the longest, but like wolves and jackals, it was "good at changing to human shape"; see "Dui su" 對俗, *Baopu zi* 3.48.

10. For an introduction, see Li Jianguo, *Tangqian zhiguai xiaoshuo shi*, p. 277.

11. *TPGJ*, 447.3652.

12. See Xiaofei Kang, "The Fox and the Barbarian."

to interpret them as portents. Foxes could be both positive and, more usually, negative omens.[13] In contrast with the rest of the narrative tradition, foxes as omens appear in their original shapes. But since only a small minority of tales depicts foxes in their own shape, transformation became the fox's identifying trait. For other beasts in *Taiping guangji*, the proportion of shape-changers to those appearing in their natural forms is more even.

In the Tang, the link between foxes and the netherworld was closer than in later stories, since the tomb is a common lair. One piece of lore makes the charnel-house associations particularly vivid: foxes assume human form by wearing a human skull and praying to the moon.[14]

Campany describes the exposure of the true forms of transformed creatures as one of the principal modes of anomaly;[15] the pattern of illusion followed by exposure dominates pre-Ming fox tales. The illusion is not limited to foxes' physical bodies but extends to everything they use and touch: their opulent mansions are revealed as tombs, their clothing and gifts prove to be leaves, their wine turns back to urine.[16] Foxes do not merely pass as human but imitate specific people. Sexual stories present the fox as a stranger, but in other tales foxes often take the shape of familiar people, particularly those who have just died, which suggests a link with the netherworld.[17] The darkest and most psychologically suggestive tales of this type exploit the fox's role as doppelgänger to incite family members to slay one another in the conviction that a father or a sister is in reality a fox.[18]

As the most sensitive violation of human boundaries, sexual illusion aroused the most anxiety and exerted the greatest fascination. The crucial term is *mei* 媚, seduction, which carries strong connotations of deception and loss of will. Foxes could accost both men and

---

13. Negative examples include "Bei qi hou zhu" 北齊後主, *TPGJ*, 447.3656; and "Li Linfu" 李林甫, 451.3688. A positive example is "Li Kui" 李揆, 451.3690.

14. "Seng Yan" 僧晏通, *TPGJ*, 451.3691.

15. Campany, *Strange Writing*, pp. 253–55.

16. "Weishi zi" 韋氏子, *TPGJ*, 454 .3712.

17. "Shen Dongmei" 沈東美, *TPGJ*, 448.3663; "Yan Jian" 嚴諫, 450.3680; "Xin tifou" 辛替否, 450.3682.

18. "Zhang Jian" 張簡, *TPGJ*, 447.3658.

women sexually, and the affliction was often depicted as demonic possession or madness.[19] The ability to possess humans was shared by all uncanny beings and was not directly linked to the assumption of human shape. The distinction between sexual possession and spirit possession could be extremely vague. Madness was especially typical of tales of seduced women: a fox asks a woman's father asking for her hand; when refused, he claims her anyway. As a consequence, the chosen woman goes mad and speaks with the voice of the fox. Although there was no romanticization of a woman's relationship to a male fox, these women had a broader range of experience than their later counterparts.[20] For men, the scorned fox might cut her victim's hair, with implications of loss of life force and vitality.[21] In general, however, the danger of involvement with foxes was not rendered physically concrete.

A small number of stories strive to create a positive vision of the vixen lover, but the plots usually close with the death of the fox woman.[22] By far the most influential and complex of these is Shen Jiji's 沈既濟 (?–ca..797) "Renshi zhuan" 任氏傳 (Miss Ren's story, 781). Although Miss Ren's lover is willing to ignore her species for love's sake, she still dies as a beast in the maws of hunting hounds.[23]

Foxes sometimes exploit their skill at deception by taking the

---

19. For examples of men's affairs with vixens, see "Chen Xian" 陳羨, *TPGJ*, 447.3653; "Sun Yan" 孫嚴, 447.3655; "Li canjun" 李參軍, 448.3666; "Wang Bao" 王苞, 450.3677; "Xue Jiong" 薛迥, 450.3682; "Helan jin ming" 賀蘭進明, 451.3684; and "Wang An" 王黯 451.3686. For fox relations with humans of both sexes in a single story, see "Wei Mingfu" 韋明府, 449.3674.

20. For examples of male fox–human woman liaisons, see "Shangguan yi" 上官翼, *TPGJ*, 447.3659; "Yang Bocheng" 楊伯成, 448.3664; "Liu Jia" 劉甲, 448.3666; "Li Yuangong" 李元恭, 449.3672; "Li shi" 李氏, 449.3673; "Xu An" 徐安, 450.3679; "Daizhou min" 代州民, 450.3682; and "Zhang Liben" 張立本, 454.3709.

21. "Sun Yan" 孫巖, *TPGJ*, 447.3655.

22. "Wang xuan" 王璿 (*TPGJ*, 451.3689) includes a relatively sympathetic portrayal of a man's vixen lover, who, however, still has to leave when her lover achieves high office. Tales of doomed vixens include "Li Nuo" 李麐, *TPGJ*, 451.3689; and "Ji Zhen" 計眞, 452.3707–9. "Yao Kun" 姚坤 (454.3710) is a very early case of what later became the common story type of a vixen lover as a reward for saving a fox's life.

23. *TPGJ*, 452.3692–97.

forms of bodhisattvas and hoodwinking the devout.[24] In these stories, spectacular displays of Buddhist proselytizing are blended with demonic deception. Some stories of this type express Tang ambivalence about Buddhism even more explicitly by linking religious and sexual deception, as male foxes in the guise of bodhisattvas seduce human women.

In the Tang, there was some overlap between *hu* 狐, "fox," and *hu* 胡, "barbarian." Foxes were strongly identified with the north. In some cases, the link was overt: foxes became "foreign" bodhisattvas, or a fox bride was purchased from a barbarian vendor. In other cases, there was a more subtle parallel with the different kinds of others who could infiltrate human society.[25]

The *Xuanzhong ji* alluded to foxes' uncanny knowledge. Scholarly male foxes appeared as early as the Six Dynasties, their animal cleverness translated into erudition. The most accomplished heavenly foxes could be masters of arcane knowledge[26] and possess magical books in illegible, Sanskrit-like script that humans tried to steal at their peril.[27] A show of learning, however, provided no defense against violence when their species identity was exposed.[28]

Regardless of the precise nature of the deception, human relations with foxes often end in the violence of the hunt and the fatal exposure of the foxes' deceptions. Structural necessity apparently dictated that sexual intoxication, madness, and trickery lead to the same end.

There is one tantalizing description of popular fox worship. A text entitled "Hu Shen" 狐神 (Fox gods) reads: 唐初以來， 百姓

---

24. "Seng fu li" 僧服禮, *TPGJ*, 447.3658; "Da'an heshang" 大安和尚, 447.3660; "Ye Fashan" 葉法善, 448.3665; "Pingyang ling" 汫陽令, 449.3670; "Daizhou min" 代州民, 450.3683; "Changsun Jia" 長孫甲, 451.3685.

25. See Xiaofei Kang, "The Fox and the Barbarian."

26. An example of a female fox as Daoist adept (and later false immortal) is "Jiao lianshi" 焦練師, *TPGJ*, 449.3672. For a discussion of the fox scholar tradition, see Li Jiangao, *Zhongguo hu wenhua*, pp. 74–76.

27. "He Rangzhi" 何讓之, *TPGJ*, 448.3661; "Lin Jingxuan" 林景玄, 449.3675; "Sun Zengsheng" 孫甑生, 451.3688; "Wang Sheng" 王生, 453.3699; "Li Ziliang" 李自良, 453.3700–701; "Zhang Jianlou" 張簡棲, 454.3706.

28. "Cui Chang" 崔昌 (*TPGJ*, 451.3685) is a good example of the tensions between foxes' scholarly aspirations and animal nature. In "Yin Yuan" 尹瑗 (454.3711), a scholarly fox exposes his true form when drunk and is slain by his human friend.

多事狐神，房中祭祀以乞恩，飲食與人同之。事者非一主。當時有諺曰無狐魅，不成村。"Since the beginning of the Tang, many commoners have worshiped fox spirits. They make offerings in their bedchambers to beg for their favor. The foxes share people's food and drink. They do not serve a single master. At the time there was a figure of speech saying, 'Where there is no fox demon, no village can be established.'"[29] This text suggests widespread domestic practices of religious worship, but since it is the only record of its kind, one can only speculate as to the relationship between these beliefs and the other narratives recorded in *Taiping guangji*.

No Tang author attempted to assemble all these varied images of foxes into a coherent picture; nor did any Ming or Qing author make an overt comparison between the Tang fox tales and those of his own time. Nevertheless, this body of tales is enlightening both as a textual history on which Ming and Qing authors consciously embroidered and as an attic of themes forgotten and neglected as the fox changed.

GENRE HISTORY AND GENRE PROBLEMS

Genre is important to the study of the fox for two reasons: first, the vast majority of fox material appears in a single genre. The career of the fox as a literary character is inextricably tied to this genre, *wenyan xiaoshuo* 文言小說, the classical tale, which is almost as promiscuous a border-crosser as the fox itself. The prominence of the fox in this genre, in contrast to its relative obscurity in vernacular fiction and drama, raises the question of what binds species and genre to each another. Second, and more important, judgments about the genre used for fox tales determine how we read the fox. Facing textual depictions of any imaginary being, we ask whose imagination is at work, and whether invention occurs during the writing or before. Thus the crucial questions are whether the fox is the product of shared lore or individual imagination, and whether these tales are records of oral narratives or literary fabrications. Three layers of generic terms are relevant to discussion of the Ming and Qing fox story: first, terms used at the time; second, terms used by modern scholars of Chinese

---

29. *TPGJ*, 447.3658. For a different translation, see Xiaofei Kang, "Power at the Margins," p. 33.

literature; and third, international generic terms that originated outside of China.

These questions of orality and fictionality are central to both the Chinese and the international generic terms applicable to the fox story. Throughout its history, the Chinese concept of *xiaoshuo,* now accepted as the translation for "fiction" and "the novel," was exceedingly broad. Originally defined as petty talk of the streets and alleys, the genre seems to have included almost anything brief in form and miscellaneous in content. Later bibliographers included both records of conversation and narratives that, for various reasons, could not be accepted as official history under this rubric. Fictional invention is present in pre-Ming definitions of the genre only as a flaw: unreliability condemned *xiaoshuo* to be a petty art, excluded from history. *Xiaoshuo*'s generic nature is amorphous: the Ming bibliographer and literary theorist Hu Yinglin 胡應麟 (1551–1602) observed that although *xiaoshuo* 白話小說 belongs to the *zi* 子, philosophers, category of traditional bibliography, it also shares traits with the other categories, classics, history, and literary collections.[30] The boundaries between the tale and philosopher's anecdotes invented for didactic purposes and between the tale and historiography were particularly blurry. At the time of the genre's beginning, all *xiaoshuo* were in the literary language; when vernacular narratives developed, the term was also applied to them. Modern literary historians have endeavored to narrow the definition to exclude non-narrative material.[31] *Wenyan xiaoshuo* is a modern descriptive term, invented as a counterpart to *baihua xiaoshuo*, vernacular fiction.

The generic subdivisions of the classical tale most often used in modern histories, and most useful to discussions of the fox, are *zhiguai* 志怪, "records of the strange," and *chuanqi* 傳奇, "tales of the

30. Hu Yinglin, "Jiuliu zhulun xia" 九流諸論下, in idem, *Shaoshi shanfang bicong,* 29.374.

31. This discussion largely follows the summary given in Li Jianguo, *Tangqian zhiguai xiaoshuo shi*, p. 4. Hu Yinglin's categorization of *xiaoshuo* still contains several categories not considered *xiaoshuo* by contemporary scholars. On the changing definitions of the genre as narrative becomes more important, see Chen Wenxin, *Zhongguo wenyan xiaoshuo liupai yanjiu*, pp. 2–10.

marvelous."[32] These terms are not a modern invention, but nor were they standard usage as generic terms in the Ming and Qing. Both were used in book titles before they were used as generic distinctions. Hu Yinglin was the first to present them as clear subdivisions of *xiaoshuo*,[33] and they became firmly established only in the twentieth century when Lu Xun used them in *Zhongguo xiaoshuo shilüe* (A brief history of Chinese fiction).[34]

The *zhiguai*, brief narrative records of the strange, flourished in the Six Dynasties, and shape-changing animals were one characteristic topic during this period.[35] I translate the term "classical tale" rather than "classical fiction" primarily because application of the term "fiction" to *zhiguai* is problematic. From the genre's inception, authors and compilers claimed, like Confucius, to be "transmitting but not creating."[36] *Zhiguai* prefaces and titles routinely assert that they are records of events the authors had witnessed, or more commonly, heard about. *Jianwen* 見聞, "that which is seen and heard," is one of the standard definitions of the genre and is often used in the titles of collections. Initially *zhiguai* were often treated as supplements to official histories, preserving information and incidents not recorded elsewhere because of their weird subject matter. In the preface to *Soushen ji* 搜神記 (In search of the supernatural), the most famous of the Six Dynasties collections, Gan Bao 干寶 (fl. 320) adopted a defensive tone, saying that all historians confronted the possibility of error and inaccuracies. The fact that they did not aban-

---

32. These translations of the two terms are based on Zeitlin, *Historian of the Strange*. To give one recent example, Hou Zhongyi and Liu Shilin's *Zhongguo wenyan xiaoshuo shigao* uses these two categories as well as a third, *yishi* 軼事, "historical anecdotes."

33. On the usage of the term *zhiguai*, see Li Jianguo, *Tangqian zhiguai xiaoshuo shi*, pp. 10–11. See also Hu Yinglin, *Shaoshi shanfang bicong*, 29. 374. For Hu, however, *zhiguai* and *chuanqi* were only two of six categories of *xiaoshuo*. Although Hu predates the bulk of the works I examine closely in this book, he astutely captured the condition of the classical tale immediately before the period I cover.

34. Lu Xun, *Zhongguo xiaoshuo shilüe*, chaps. 5–10.

35. The major English-language works on the Six Dynasties *zhiguai* are Kenneth Dewoskin, "The *Sou-shen chi* and the *chih kuai* Tradition"; Karl Kao, *Classical Chinese Tales of the Supernatural and the Fantastic*; and Campany, *Strange Writing*.

36. *Analects* 7.1, 述而不作.

don their task on this account must mean that their errors were insignificant in comparison with their successes. If he erred, he was in good company.[37] Gan Bao was a historian by profession and even in this work aligned himself with more credible histories,[38] but he was not alone in this approach. Throughout its history, *zhiguai*'s focus remained the recording of events or hearsay.

The second term, *chuanqi*, is more problematic, again because of the issues of orality, writing, and fictionality. The term *chuanqi* has retroactively been applied to classical-language narratives longer than *zhiguai*, with more convoluted plots and ornamental language, especially a group of Tang stories that *Taiping guangji* groups under *zazhuan* 雜傳, "miscellaneous biographies/chronicles."[39] Literary historians, beginning with Hu Yinglin, saw them as a crucial turning point in the history of Chinese fiction.[40] Hu Yinglin regarded *chuanqi* as intentional fictional inventions; in contrast *zhiguai*, although they may be false records, were not intended to be creative.[41] Some contemporary scholars have accepted Hu's characterization of Tang *chuanqi;* others have seen him as projecting a Ming idea of fictionality back in time.[42] Despite critics' perception of intentional invention, the authorial personae in Tang *chuanqi* continue to insist that they were merely transmitting accounts of actual events and oral narratives.

As Hu Yinglin noted, no absolute line can be drawn between *zhiguai* and *chuanqi*. When discussing Ming and Qing fox stories, *chuanqi* and *zhiguai* are instead useful as opposite ends of a spectrum. Since there is no litmus test for intentional fictionality, formal and stylistic differences serve to place individual anecdotes

---

37. Gan Bao, *Soushen ji*, preface.

38. In terms of bibliographic classification, as of the early Tang, *xiaoshuo* was moved out of the philosophy category and into history.

39. Most Western-language studies of *chuanqi* deal with individual tales. See especially Dudbridge, *The Tale of Li Wa*. On the relationship of history, allegory, and fantasy in Tang fiction, see Sheldon Lu, *From Historicity to Fictionality*, pp. 93–128.

40. See Cheng Yizhong's 程毅中 entry on "Chuanqi" in Liu Shide, ed., *Zhonguo gudai xiaoshuo baike quanshu*, pp. 37–38.

41. Hu Yinglin, *Shaoshi shanfang bicong*, 37.486.

42. Chan, *The Discourse on Foxes and Ghosts*, pp. 45–50; Dudbridge, *Religious Experience and Lay Society*, p. 17.

along that spectrum. The influence of historiography remains very important in *chuanqi*, but there is a shift from the model of a simple record of events to a complete biography of a character, more elaborate in both structure and description. *Chuanqi* take a creative approach to language, striving to be marvelous in style as well as content. They are often self-conscious displays of individual literary talent and include as many different types of writing as possible within a single piece.[43] Content alone cannot distinguish between the two forms of the classical tale, since both can describe the strange and supernatural, but the stylistic differences lead to a difference in emphasis between the *guai* (bizarreness) of incident and the *qi* (marvel) of character and relations between characters. This generic distinction is made on the level of the individual story; the nature of collections is more complex. Some collections contain primarily stories at one end of the spectrum, but many are mixtures of both.

Although Qing authors and critics were inconsistent in their use of terminology, some did recognize a difference between the two kinds of writing. What we now call *chuanqi*, Ji Yun called *zhuanji*, a choice that placed more emphasis on their biographical nature. Even so, he considered the distinction with *zhiguai* as crucial.[44] Lu Xun divided the classical tales of the Qing into two large groups, those which imitated the tales of the Jin and those that imitated those of the Tang, which is another way of phrasing the same distinction.[45] Although I will argue that in the Ming and Qing both *zhiguai* and *chuanqi* differ considerably from their predecessors, the difference between the two subgenres raises important issues of fictionality, verisimilitude, and literary style. These differences between the two forms are clearly apparent in fox narratives: *zhiguai* treat them as phenomena, and *chuanqi* as characters.

The task of defining *xiaoshuo* seems unproblematic in compari-

---

43. This argument in principle agrees with that made in the preface of Li Jianguo, *Tang Wudai zhiguai chuanqi xulu*.

44. Hu Yinglin, *Shaoshi shanfang bicong*, 29.374–75; Sheng Shiyan, colophon to *Guwang tingzhi*, *YWCT*, 18, following story 215, pp. 471–74.

45. Lu Xun, *Zhongguo xiaoshuo shilüe*, chap. 22.

son with the difficulties we confront in defining *biji* 筆記,[46] the works left behind when *xiaoshuo* is restricted to narratives. *Biji,* the "notation book," is the most miscellaneous of genres, defined by the brevity of the entries and the casualness of composition.[47] Their contents can range from *zhiguai* and *chuanqi* to personal reminiscences, historical information, and scholarly notes. So broad is the term that many of the classical tale collections consulted for this book could be called *biji,* and some of the most celebrated examples even include *biji* in their title (e.g., *Yuewei caotang biji, Youtai xianguan biji*). Some contemporary scholars use the combined term *biji xiaoshuo* to describe all categories of *wenyan xiaoshuo* other than *chuanqi,* including *zhiguai,* historical miscellanies, and records of conversation.[48] Fox stories included in *biji* appear in the context of a broad range of narratives, observations, and information, rather than among strange narratives alone.

Contemporary Western terms for literature describing imaginary beings are also divided by concepts of belief and fictionality. The location of tales in time and space is also important. Among genres presumed to have oral origins, "folktales" are timeless, placeless, and are not presented as true; "myths" are presented as true and located in time and space, but in an earlier or different world, and "legends" are presented as true, with precise details of space and time that place them in our world.[49] Among written genres, *Kunstmärchen,* or literary fairy tales, are literary inventions in imitation of a popular, originally oral genre. To use these definitions, nearly all *zhiguai* are legends: they claim plausibility, with concrete place-names and

---

46. Liu Yeqiu, *Biji gailun.* On some of the philosophical underpinnings of the Song *biji,* see Bol, "A Literati Miscellany and Sung Intellectual History."

47. Here I am following Y. W. Ma's definition in Nienhauser, ed., *The Indiana Companion to Traditional Chinese Literature,* pp. 650–651.

48. These are the three categories of *xiaoshuo* in the *Siku quanshu congmu tiyao,* which excluded *chuanqi* along with vernacular fiction; see Chan, *The Discourse of Foxes and Ghosts,* p. 170. The term *biji xiaoshuo* is represented by the large compendium *Biji xiaoshuo daguan* 筆記小說大觀, published by the Shanghai jinbu shuju in 1912 (hereafter *BJXSDG*). Recently several histories of *biji xiaoshuo* have been published: see, e.g., Chen Wenxin, *Zhongguo biji xiaoshuo shi*; and Miao Zhuang, *Biji xiaoshuo shi.*

49. See Bascom, "The Forms of Folklore," pp. 1–7.

historical periods that locate them firmly in this world.[50] Because of the immense quantity of *biji* and the early development of publishing, the corpus of preserved legends may be larger in China than anywhere else in the world. By analogy, the late imperial *chuanqi*, especially *Liaozhai zhiyi* 聊齋誌異 (*Liaozhai*'s record of marvels) and its followers, might, borrowing European terms, be called *Kunstlegende*, with a relation to the *zhiguai* similar to that of *Kunstmärchen* to *Märchen*.[51] *Chuanqi* wed the form of records of oral narrative, situated in this world, with invention.

What are the consequences for our reading of the problems of orality and fictionality in the classical tale? Ever since Ban Gu 班固 (32–92) described *xiaoshuo* as talk gathered from the streets in the *Yiwen zhi* 藝文志 (Bibliography of Arts and Letters) of the *Han shu* 漢書 (Han History), the genre has been strongly associated with the recording of oral material. Tak-hung Leo Chan argues that the common trait of the three subdivisions of *xiaoshuo* in *Siku quanshu congshu tiyao* 四庫全書總目題要 (Summaries and general catalog of works in the Complete Collection of the Four Treasuries) is orality rather than fictionality.[52] Classical tales commonly claim to be records of oral narratives and meticulously note their sources. Moreover, the prefaces to tale collections present their contents as "material for conversation," thus circulating the stories back into the realm of orality. Claims of transcription allow authors and compilers to elide the question of fictional invention: by noting the circumstances of a story's narration, authors insist that it originated outside their own imagination, even if the truth of its content cannot be proven. In the late imperial and modern periods, the desire to grant all stories an oral provenance remains powerful and potentially deceptive; the popularity of the legend that Pu Songling traded tea in exchange for stories at the Liuquan seems based on this desire.[53]

---

50. Bascom (ibid., p. 10) also admits anecdotes and personal reminiscences, which are also included among *zhiguai*, as "proto-legends."

51. See Meyer and Tismar, *Kunstmärchen*.

52. Chan, *The Discourse of Foxes and Ghosts*, p. 170.

53. When Xu Kun, the author of *Liuya waibian*, claimed in his preface to be the reincarnation of Pu Songling, he adduced as proof that his father had seen in a dream before he was born a man telling stories by a stream lined with willows (*liuquan*). The Liuquan image seems to have become a standard symbol by Ji Yun's

The language in which classical tales were written is crucial to their relationship with the oral. Classical Chinese was the language of education but no one's mother tongue; it was the language in which one wrote poems, memorials to the throne, letters, diaries, scholarly works—everything except for certain popular entertainment genres often dismissed as frivolous. Since classical Chinese was no longer a spoken language, no classical tale could be an exact transcription of what someone said; the written accounts are inevitably translations. The vernacular was used precisely for those genres in which capturing someone's exact spoken words was key.[54] We should not, however, make the mistake of equating the classical language with the erudite and the inaccessible and the vernacular with the popular and the comprehensible. A simple classical writing with a limited vocabulary and regular sentence structure could, for someone with a rudimentary classical language education, be easier to read than the more verbose vernacular, with its wider range of vocabulary, sentence structures, and colloquialisms. As a genre, the classical tale (and *zhiguai* in particular) was the most economical and direct means to transcribe oral narratives from a wide range of informants; in contrast, vernacular fiction was often a means for literati authors to imitate the form of the popular. The classical tale preserved the content of oral narrative while stripping away many aspects of performance.

This combination of purported oral sources and known literati authorship raises a question: Should classical tales be considered records of oral folklore or products of individual authorship? Addressing the relationship of oral narrative to written literature in the premodern era is rendered difficult by the fact that the written alone survives. Furthermore, the relationship between oral and written transmission in an age of popular publishing is complicated even for illiterate and semi-literate groups, let alone for the highly literate men who authored these collections. The classical tale's relationship to oral narrative is highly mediated, but how can one tell where mediation ends?

Individual fictional invention, although problematic in all genres

generation. See also the later account of the story in "Pu Liuxian" 蒲留仙, in Zou Tao 鄒弢, *Sanjie lu bitan* 三借廬筆談, in *BJXSDG*, 13: 6.15b–16a.

54. Hanan, *The Chinese Vernacular Story*, pp. 1–5.

throughout the Chinese literary tradition, flourished and attained more respectability than ever before in vernacular fiction and drama during the Ming and Qing. Yet despite this vastly transformed literary landscape, in which the classical tale coexisted with genres in which invention could be celebrated, the problem of fictionality was far from resolved. On the one hand, *Liaozhai zhiyi* was the first collection of classical tales to be written by an individual author to be accepted and read in the same way as some vernacular fiction: it acquired commentaries in the style of Jin Shengtan, praising the author's inventiveness and use of language.[55] Even though they were fictional, its characters were admired for their genuine emotions. On the other hand, this victory of fictional invention was not uncontested. Although Ji Yun represents only one side of the argument, he made the clearest statement of the problem. Ji's views on the role of *xiaoshuo* were quoted in his disciple Sheng Shiyan's 盛時彥 colophon to *Guwang tingzhi* 姑妄聽之 (Just listen to it), one of the installments of *Yuewei caotang biji* 閱微草堂筆記 (Notebook from the cottage of close scrutiny). Ji describes *Liaozhai* as being written in 才子之筆， 非著書人之筆, "the style of a talented man, not that of an author of books." Ji acknowledged Pu's talent but seemed to feel that a display of virtuosity and personal sentiment appropriate to other genres has been mistakenly devoted to the classical tale. 小說既述見聞，即屬敘事，不比戲場關目，隨意裝點。"*Xiaoshuo*, being an account of what one has seen or heard, is a narrative of events; it is not like the plot of a play, which one can freely embellish."[56] Ji denied literary invention in the case of the most famous Tang *chuanqi* as well and thought their elaborate details were based on the authors' personal experience.[57] He objected that Pu, on the other hand, recorded detailed, intimate conversations that he could not possibly

55. Judith Zeitlin (*Historian of the Strange*, pp. 34–41) calls this response to *Liaozhai* the "third wave" of defense of the strange. The first wave was just fiction of the strange, and the second allegorical interpretation and self-expression.

56. *YWCT*, 18, following story 215, pp. 471–73. For a long discussion of Ji's theory of fiction as revealed in the *Siku quanshu tiyao*, comparing him to Jin Shengtan, see Maeno Naoaki, *Chūgoku shōsetsu shikō*, pp. 357–93.

57. His two examples are *Yingying zhuan* 鶯鶯傳, which was often considered to have been based on Yuan Zhen's personal experience, and *Zhao feiyan waishi* 趙飛燕外史, whose author supposedly had heard the tale from palace women.

have heard. Ji wished to keep *xiaoshuo* free of the contemporary attitudes toward invention prevalent in other genres, and in *Liaozhai* he saw signs of dangerous generic confusion. For him fictional invention was related to literary talent and emotional self-indulgence. Pu Songling and Ji Yun framed the debate about fiction and the nature of the classical tale for the rest of the Qing.

In my view, the surviving corpus of classical tales is a mixture of records of actual oral stories, transformed to an unknowable extent by authorial choice and memory, and inventions in the same mode.[58] There is no filter that will separate the diverse elements of the classical tale. My approach to the problem is close reading and comparison of a large range of stories to find shared and differing elements across space and time. The similarities reflect shared lore, and the differences reveal, if not necessarily invention, the space for differences in authorial interest. I also pay close attention to the positioning of tales at different removes from the narrators' own experience and social circles. If we read stories both with and against the grain, the classical tale can reveal both popular lore and literati attitudes toward it.

I am persuaded by the work of those scholars, like Robert Campany, Glen Dudbridge, and Leo Chan, who wish to extract *zhiguai* from an anachronistic definition of fiction, but my concerns lie with both records and fabrications. Ji's arguments in the face of *Liaozhai*'s popularity reveal the issue of fictionality was more contested in this period than ever before. The border-crossing aspects of the classical tale, and the fox, again seem crucial: the possibilities of accuracy and fabrication existed side by side. Foxes were both everyday experience and a tempting subject for invention. Jean-Claude Schmitt's argument, from his work on medieval ghosts, that belief is not something that exists independently of the making and reproducing of narratives is very useful. He emphasizes the social functions that narratives served for those who told them rather than on the gap between a world with and one without ghosts.[59] The acceptance of

---

58. For examples of Pu Songling's playful use of the conventions of claiming oral sources, see Barr, "Pu Songling and *Liaozhai zhiyi*," pp. 252–54. For a discussion that takes Ji's claims of the oral origins of his stories seriously, see Chan, *The Discourse of Foxes and Ghosts*, pp. 50–76.

59. Schmitt, *Ghosts in the Middle Ages*, pp. 7–9.

ghosts and spirits as part of the same level of reality does not exclude the possibility that they can be deployed in imaginative or subversive ways.

One way in which collections of classical tales differ from the folklore collectors of nineteenth-century Europe is the different distance between the collector and his informants. Folklore studies, as they emerged in early modern Europe, seemed to be premised on loss and distance: the folk knowledge of the peasants would be lost, unless more educated, urbanized people recorded it. Folk culture was someone else's culture, or one's own true culture that one had to rediscover. Some of the earlier works of *zhiguai,* in the *fengsu zhi* 風俗志, "recording of customs" subgenre, shared some of this flavor, as did the association of *xiaoshuo* with gossip on the streets. But the authors of the Ming and Qing recorded stories related by their educated equals as well as by illiterate servants and peasants. The stories were in danger of being lost because they were ephemeral and minor, but not because they were potentially part of a whole culture of lost knowledge. This proximity of authors to oral lore makes the "artificial (or artistic) legend" of the *chuanqi* end of the spectrum much closer to the "natural legend" than was the case with the literary fairy tale and its antecedents: they not only took place in the same world but were often recorded by the same authors, in the same books.

THE LITERARY TERRITORY OF THE LATE IMPERIAL FOX

Although this book is not chronologically arranged, a chronological framework may help as background.[60] Here I first discuss the classical tale, my principal subject of interest, before turning to vernacular

60. For the period up to *Liaozhai,* Alan Barr's "Pu Songling and *Liaozhai zhiyi*" is indispensable. For the Qing up through Ji Yun's generation, Maeno Naoaki's *Chūgoku shōsetsu shikō* provides a useful summary. Chan's *The Discourse of Foxes and Ghosts* also has useful bibliography on Ji Yun's contemporaries and predecessors. Hou Zhongyi and Liu Shilin's *Zhongguo wenyan xiaoshuo shigao* provides a survey of selected collections throughout the period. Chen Wenxin's *Zhongguo biji xiaoshuo shi* also provides introductions to selected collections. Useful reference works include Liu Shide, ed., *Zhongguo gudai xiaoshuo baike quanshu*; and Ning Jiayu, *Zhongguo wenyan xiaoshuo congmu tiyao.*

fiction, which I use for comparison. The divisions of *zhiguai*, *chuanqi*, and *biji* are useful in constructing this history. Four broadly conceived eras are the most important: the Wanli (late sixteenth–early seventeenth century), the Kangxi (late seventeenth–early eighteenth century), the Qianlong (second half of the eighteenth century), and the Guangxu (late nineteenth century).

Foxes were not a frequent topic in the long poetic romances of the early Ming, the most famous collection of which was *Jiandeng xinhua* 剪燈新話 (New stories told while trimming the wick, 1378).[61] Their numbers increase with the revival of short, unadorned *zhiguai* beginning in the early sixteenth century. There is scattered material on foxes in a group of sixteenth-century collections, but the material is too sparse to make any firm judgments.[62] I will occasionally refer to these stories for comparison.

In the Ming, expanded interest in the classical tale prompted both the composition of original works and the reprinting and editing of earlier material. The reprinting of *Taiping guangji* in 1566 provides a symbolic starting date, given that compendium's importance as a repository of the earlier fox tradition.[63] This period is distinguished by an obsession with anthologizing and categorizing earlier material that resulted in the proliferation of thematic collections about particular topics such as women, ghosts, or knights-errant.[64] Not surprisingly there was also a specialized collection devoted exclusively to foxes, the Wanli work *Humei congtan*.

As for original collections, a cluster of works belong roughly to the

61. For a summary of this tradition, see Barr, "Pu Songling and *Liaozhai zhiyi*," pp. 203–5. See also Richard Wang, "Creating Artifacts." The one fox story in *Jiandeng xinhua* and its sequels is "Hu meiniang zhuan" 狐媚娘傳 in Li Changqi, *Jiandeng yuhua*.

62. Barr, "Pu Songling and *Liaozhai zhiyi*," pp. 205–8. The collections I consider in this category are Lu Can's 陸粲 *Gengsi bian* 庚巳編, Zhu Yunming's 祝允明 *Zhiguai lu* 志怪錄 (A record of accounts of the strange), Lu Yanzhi's 陸延枝 *Shuoting* 說聽 (Tales told and heard), and Du Mu's 都穆 *Tan zuan* 談纂 (A collection of conversation). For an introduction to *Gengsi bian*, see Hou Zhongyi and Liu Shilin, *Zhongguo wenyan xiaoshuo shigao*, pp. 142–44.

63. Barr, "Pu Songling and *Liaozhai zhiyi*," p. 198.

64. Ibid., pp. 199–203.

Wanli period and can be considered together: *Ertan* 耳談 (Tales overheard; 1602) (and its categorized expansion *Ertan leizeng* 耳談類增; 1603), *Yanshan conglu* 燕山叢錄 (Complete records of Yanshan; 1602), *Wuza zu* 五雜俎 (Five assorted notes, earliest dated edition 1616), and *Kuai yuan* 獪園 (The garden of cleverness; 1613).[65] They form the chronological beginning of this book and introduce many of the distinct themes of the late imperial fox tale. Although these approximate contemporaries share some ideas about foxes, they represent different categories of the classical tale tradition. *Ertan leizeng* and *Yanshan conglu* are categorized collections of relatively unornamented anecdotes; *Yanshan conglu* has a geographic focus on the Beijing area. *Wuza zu* is also arranged by topic, but it more closely resembles a *biji* collection of natural-historical information and personal observations than a collection of tales. *Kuai yuan* is a very distinctive, personal collection which includes more elaborate tales in the Tang style.[66] Feng Menglong 馮夢龍 (1574–1646) is chronologically close to this generation but distinguished from it by his work in multiple genres, both as an editor and author. In his classical tale works, foxes are included both in a history of passion, *Qingshi leilüe* 情史類略 (Anatomy of passion), and a collection of humorous anecdotes, *Gujin tangai* 古今譚概 (Anecdotes old and new).

The compendium *Shuoling* 說鈴 (The bell of stories; preface dated 1705) preserves many early Qing *zhiguai*, with heavy emphasis on tales of karmic retribution; only one of the collections in it, *Shuyi ji* 述異記 (Record of tales of the strange; 1703), contains a significant number of fox tales.[67] On the other side of the generic divide, *Yuchu xinzhi* 虞初新志 (The new records of Yuchu; ca. 1700) is an influential anthology of *chuanqi*-type narratives from the late Ming and early Qing, including two memorable tales of vixens.[68]

Pu Songling stands apart from his contemporaries. Although his

65. All but *Wu zazu* are discussed in ibid., p. 209.

66. Ibid., p. 209.

67. Ibid., p. 215. For a fairly thorough introduction to the collections included in *Shuoling*, see Maeno Naoaki, *Chūgoku shōsetsu shikō*, pp. 261–73. For an introduction to one of the collections focused on karmic retribution, *Ming bao lu*, see Hou Zhongyi and Liu Shilin, *Zhongguo wenyan xiaoshuo shigao*, p. 286–87.

68. Hou Zhongyi and Liu Shilin, *Zhongguo wenyan xiaoshuo shigao*, p. 186–201.

collection contains both *zhiguai* and *chuanqi*, it was the latter that made him famous. He combined highly elegant and allusive language, vivid description more typical of vernacular fiction, intricate plots, and fantastic content in an unprecedented way. *Liaozhai zhiyi* has received more scholarly attention than all other works of the Qing classical tale tradition put together, and the history of late imperial *zhiguai* is often framed in terms of its predecessors and imitators. Although one of my goals in this book is to examine Pu's work in the context of other, more obscure collections, I do not deny his uniqueness.

Liaozhai was composed over the period roughly from 1675 to 1705 and circulated in manuscript for many decades; it was first published in 1766.[69] Although *Liaozhai* gained considerable popularity in manuscript, it was the generation writing after its formal publication that felt the full impact of its influence. In the second half of the eighteenth century, classical tales were published in unprecedented quantities.[70] Because of their numbers and the shared struggle of responding to *Liaozhai*, these authors fit together as a generation more than do any of their predecessors. Although they can roughly be divided between *Liaozhai* admirers and detractors,[71] another equally useful criterion for classifying them is the role of commentary and interpretation. Thus the Qianlong and later classical tale can be divided into long *chuanqi* tales with authorial commentary, modeled on *Liaozhai* to a greater or lesser extent; short *zhiguai* with extensive commentary and interpretation; and short *zhiguai* without such interpretation. The foremost author in this post-*Liaozhai* generation was Ji Yun, commonly considered the second most famous author of the classical tale in the Qing. He can also be considered representative of a backlash against *Liaozhai*'s innovations, although he was innovative himself in the areas of interpretation and theorizing about

---

69. For the dates of composition and textual transmission of *Liaozhai*, see Barr, "Pu Songling and *Liaozhai zhiyi*," pp. 5–104.

70. Noted by Chan, *The Discourse of Foxes and Ghosts*, pp. 12–17. I use his translations of collection titles, with some revisions.

71. Although in general Hou Zhongyi and Liu Shilin (*Zhongguo wenyan xiaoshuo shigao*, p. 224) categorize works according to *zhiguai/chuanqi*, in one passage they list works using this division.

the strange. He represents an extreme of the tendency to explicate the fox. In contrast, Yuan Mei's 袁枚 (1716–98) collection *Zi bu yu* 子不語 (What the Master would not speak of; 1788) differs drastically from both Pu's and Ji's. Although his tales are relatively simply narrated and firmly at the *zhiguai* end of the spectrum, his lack of concern with judgment and interpretation sets him apart from Ji.[72] A less famous example of tales of the strange for the sake of strangeness, unadorned by interpretation, is Wang Jian's 王椷 *Qiudeng conghua* 秋燈叢話 (Collected tales of the autumn lamp; preface completed in 1777, published 1791).[73] Liu Shoumei's 劉壽眉 *Chunquan wenjian lu* 春泉聞見錄 (Records of things seen and heard at Spring Stream; 1800) records weird tales from a relatively narrow social circle, with a strong autobiographical cast, and makes very little attempt at interpretation or elaboration. Liu included a great many simple tales of poltergeists and unexplained oddities. Zhang Jing-yun 's 張景運 *Qiuping xinyu* 秋坪新語 (New words on autumnal plains; 1792), by one of Ji's kinsmen by marriage, shares *Chunquan*'s lack of judgments and autobiographical tendency.

The imitators of *Liaozhai* are more numerous than the outspoken detractors, although perhaps not as numerous as those who recorded uninterpreted, unelaborated *zhiguai*. Two of the most famous imitations are *Yingchuang yicao* 螢窗異草 (Strange grasses of the firefly window; attributed to the Qianlong but published in the Guangxu) and He Bang'e's 和邦額 *Yetan suilu* 夜譚隨錄 (Occasional records of conversations at night; 1791).[74] Both include many romances that attempt to improve on *Liaozhai* with increased numbers of characters and added convolutions of plot. *Yingchuang yicao* in particular expands on *Liaozhai*'s fascination with supernatural women and includes a large number of fox stories. However, *Yetan suilu* has a strain

72. For a comparison of the three, see Fishman, *Tri kitaishi novellista.* Leo Chan (*The Discourse of Foxes and Ghosts*, pp. 224–25) considers Yuan Mei the only practioner of non-didactic *zhiguai* in the eighteenth century.

73. For a discussion, see Maeno Naoaki, *Chūgoku shōsetsu shikō*, pp. 291–99.

74. For discussions, see Hou Zhongyi and Liu Shilin, *Zhongguo wenyan xiaoshuo shigao*, pp. 225–28 and pp. 239–44, respectively. One important difference between the two was that *Yingchuang yicao* circulated in manuscript but was not published until the Guangxu period. On *Yetan suilu*, see Eberhard, *Die chinesische Novelle des 17–19. Jahrhundert*, pp. 47–54.

of bloodiness and scatological humor foreign to its model. *Xiao dou peng* 小豆棚 (The small bean-trellis; 1796) by Zeng Yandong 曾衍東 tends to more cloying imitation, with sexuality largely supplanted by sentimentality. Less well known is Xu Kun's 徐昆 *Liuya waibian* 柳崖外編 (Unauthorized compilation of the Willow Cliff; preface dated 1791). Xu took adulation of *Liaozhai* to an extreme, claiming in his preface to be Pu Songling's reincarnation. His collection also contains highly elaborate romances; however, his stories also favor repetition of dialogue and situations that recall folk narrative and include a large number of song lyrics. Another aspect of imitation found in all of these is the inclusion of authorial commentary on each story. Although Hou Zhongyi considers Yue Jun's 樂鈞 *Ershi lu* 耳食錄 (Hearsay accounts; published 1792) an imitation, his criterion for this judgment seems in large part to be a predominance of the *chuanqi* form.[75] Yue has a vivid style, as well as his own original ideas about foxes.

Tu Shen's 屠紳 (1744–1801) *Liuhe neiwai suoyan* 六合內外瑣言 (Scattered words from the six directions) does not resemble any other collection. Its language is elaborate but recalls the *guwen* movement of the Tang more than *Liaozhai*; its highly complex plots feature a vast cast of supernatural characters, often to the almost total exclusion of human characters, a characteristic reminiscent of vernacular fiction. Tu's stories resemble pure allegory, which is rare for classical fiction.[76]

General *biji* that contain a section of strange tales, such as the previously mentioned *Wuza zu*, *Lüyuan conghua* 履園叢話 (Collected tales of Lüyuan; 1839), and *Meng'an zazhu* 夢庵雜著 (Miscellaneous works from the Hut of Dreams; 1811) seem to stand apart from the rest of this literary history.[77] The portrayal of foxes in these contexts is often quite different from that found in sources focusing on tales of the strange; this may suggest a closer relationship to oral anecdote. In a separate category are collections that, with or without citing sources, exclusively copy works from other collec-

75. Hou Zhongyi and Liu Shilin, *Zhongguo wenyan xiaoshuo shigao*, pp. 235–39.

76. Ibid., pp. 306–8. Lu Xun, *Zhongguo xiaoshuo shilüe*, p. 138.

77. For a discussion of *Meng'an zazhu*, see Hou Zhongyi and Liu Shilin, *Zhongguo wenyan xiaoshuo shigao*, pp. 339–44.

tions. They offer a glimpse of what was being read at particular times.[78]

The generations after Ji Yun had two models, but Ji was not as obviously imitated as Pu. Although he seems to provide an alternative authority to *Liaozhai*, his influence was never as strong, and those who claimed to follow him could duplicate some of his moral attitudes but none of his investigative spirit. Although there was no lull in the publishing of classical tales in the first half of the nineteenth century, the next boom and cluster of authors important to my topic are found in the second half, especially in the Guangxu reign (1875–1908). This generation can be still be divided by type of tale: there are collections that consist almost entirely of long, elaborate tales, and others have the occasional long *Liaozhai* imitation among a large number of short *zhiguai*. Some important collections made up almost exclusively of long *chuanqi* narratives are Xuan Ding's 宣鼎 (1833–80) *Yeyu qiudeng lu* 夜雨秋燈錄 (Records of the autumn lamp and night rain) and the works of Wang Tao 王韜 (1828–97), especially *Songyin manlu* 松隂漫錄 (Random jottings of a Wusong recluse; 1884). *Yeyu qiudeng lu* and its sequel include a considerable number of fox stories.[79]

As for mixed *zhiguai/chuanqi* collections, Li Qingchen 李慶辰 in *Zuicha zhiguai* 醉茶志怪 (Drunk on Tea's accounts of the strange; 1892) consciously alternates the models of Pu Songling and Ji Yun. Li had a sympathetic attitude toward popular material and recorded stories involving a wide social range of characters and narrators. Yu Yue 俞樾 (1821–1906) in his *Youtai xianguan biji* 右臺仙館筆記 (Miscellany from the Transcendent's Abode at Youtai) overtly stated that he was following Ji Yun's path, but his interpretations of the strange are not as extensive or original as Ji's.[80]

The persistence of the *zhiguai/chuanqi*, or Pu/Ji, divisions should not mask the fundamental transformations in the publishing world of the Guangxu era. This era could also be called the Shenbao guan 申

78. Examples include Deng Xuan 鄧晅, *Yitan kexin* 異談可信; Zhao Jishi 趙吉士 (*juren* 1651), *Jiyuan ji suoji* 寄園所寄; and Gao Chengxun 高承勛, *Songjun ge chaoyi* 松筠閣鈔異 (preface dated 1829).

79. Hou Zhongyi and Liu Shilin, *Zhongguo wenyan xiaoshuo shigao*, pp. 244–52.

80. Ibid., pp. 308–13.

報館 generation because of the importance of that publishing house to classical tale production and marketing. In addition to the Shenbao guan's production of classical tale collections, *zhiguai* material, including fox stories, were printed in the daily newspaper *Shenbao.* Wang Tao married the classical tale with the new media of the late nineteenth century; his *Songyin manlu* was published in installments in the pictorial *Dianshizhai huabao* 點石齊畫報.[81] *Hutian lu* 壺天錄 (Record of a pot as heaven; 1885) attempts to assemble anecdotes in a rational fashion, rather like an encyclopedia. Its content is quite miscellaneous, not predominantly fantastic, and drawn heavily from the pages of the *Shenbao.*[82]

Vernacular fiction here serves primarily as a source of comparison. Foxes are not a prevalent topic in the vernacular short story. The late Ming collections *Sanyan* 三言 and *Erpai* 二拍 each contain one fox story, but both are directly adapted from classical tales.[83]

One common way in which foxes appear in the vernacular novel is the supernatural frame, attached to the rest of the plot through the devices of reincarnation or possession. The first significant examples are a set of novels retelling the fall of the Shang and the rise of the Zhou dynasty, all of which depict the nation-destroying concubine Da Ji as a fox: *Wu wang fa Zhou pinghua* 武王伐紂評話 (Account of King Wu's attack on Zhou; also known as *Wu wang fa Zhou shu* 武王伐紂書; a published edition from 1322–23 survives); *Chunqiu lieguo zhi* 春秋列國志 (Records of the states; 1615 edition), and the most famous, *Fengshen yanyi* 封神演義 (Enfeoffment of the gods; probably completed in the late sixteenth century). *Zhaoyang qushi* 昭陽趣史 (The intriguing history of Zhaoyang Palace; Ming, before 1621) continues the tale, with the fox who had been Da Ji reborn as Hede, the sister of Zhao Feiyan. Feng Menglong's *Ping yao zhuan* 平妖傳

81. For a discussion of *Songyin manlu*, see ibid., pp. 252–260. On *Dunku lanyan*, see Eberhard, *Die chinesische Novelle*, pp. 63–72. For a full-length study of Wang Tao (which dismisses his classical tale efforts as a money-making venture), see Cohen, *Between Tradition and Modernity*.

82. Hou Zhongyi and Liu Shilin, *Zhongguo wenyan xiaoshuo shigao*, pp. 345–48.

83. See Feng Menglong, "Xiaoshui wan tianhu yi shu" 小水灣天狐詒書, in idem, *Xingshi hengyan* 醒世恒言 6; and Ling Mengchu, "Zeng zhima shipo jiaxing, xie caoyao qiao xie zhen'ou" 贈芝麻識破假形，擷草藥巧諧真偶, in idem, *Erke pai'an jingqi* 二刻拍案驚奇 29.

(Suppression of monsters; 1620) adapts an earlier novel by turning three leaders of a supernatural rebellion into a family of foxes. The shrew who is the main character of *Xingshi yinyuan zhuan* 醒世姻緣傳 (Marriage destines to awaken the world; early Qing) is a reborn fox taking revenge on the hunter who killed her.

Another common role for foxes in vernacular fiction is a representative of dangerous lust, one monster out of many. In a pair of religiously oriented Ming novels, *Sanjiao kaimi yanyi* 三教開迷演義 (Romance of the three teachings expelling delusion) and *Dong du ji* 東度記 (Deliverance to the east, 1635), foxes are both monsters for the protagonists to expel and commentators on the moral failings of humanity. Later examples include *Yesou puyan* 野叟曝言 (A country codger's words of exposure; Qianlong) and *Lüye xianzong* 綠野仙蹤 (Traces of the transcendent of the green wilds; completed 1753–62). Novels focusing on foxes are rare, but there are a few examples: *Yaohua zhuan* 瑤華傳 (The tale of Yaohua; 1803), the protagonist of which is a male fox reborn as a human woman; the pornographic *Yaohu yanshi* 妖狐艷史 (The voluptuous history of fox demons; Qing); and *Huli quanyuan* 狐狸全緣 (The complete destiny of a fox; 1876), a tale of the relationship between a parasitic fox and a human man, originally derived from a *tanci*.[84]

The period I describe both opens and closes with great changes in publishing. In the late Ming, the boom in publishing made earlier and contemporary classical tales more accessible than ever before; in the late Qing, the new media of newspapers and periodicals transformed the transmission of familiar classical tale material. By no means did the fox tradition come to a sudden end with the fall of the Qing dynasty. Occasional fox stories can still be found in collections from the early Republican period, and I shall make occasional reference to them. The fox theme has also been adapted in various ways by modern Chinese authors, but that is beyond the range of the present work.[85]

The guiding voice of this book is Ji Yun, whose deliberate consid-

---

84. Other examples of foxes in vernacular fiction include *Jintai quanzhuan* 金台全傳 (1895), described in *Zhongguo tongsu xiaoshuo congmu tiyao*, pp. 744–45; and *Jiaoye pa* 蕉葉帕 (Qing, date uncertain), pp. 642–43.

85. On these works, see Monschein, *Der Zauber der Fuchsfee*, pp. 329–56.

eration of foxes as a problem is unparalleled. He was extremely quirky and opinionated and cannot be taken as a "typical" voice in the discussion of foxes. But it is precisely the strength of his opinions and his conservatism that allow him to provide a vivid portrait of those forces that he omits and opposes, as well as those he includes and approves. He responded to the generations before him, and the generations since him continue to deal with the problems he raised.

{2}

The High Qing: Fox Practice and Theory

This chapter turns to the period at the chronological center of this book, the Qianlong reign, and two authors who both recorded fox stories and made general statements about the fox. Both Ji Yun and He Bang'e wrote down groups of fox stories, ostensibly told on a single night. In subsequent chapters, I divide stories into thematic categories; here I introduce the themes jumbled together, as they are in written practice and probably were in oral practice as well. Then I examine theoretical statements on foxes by these two authors and compare these theories to examples of their writings about foxes. I intentionally put the individual stories first, in the belief that theorizing was a distinct but secondary activity that synthesized views out of the stories. Of course, there was an interchange between the two, since the stories also cited theory, but the vast bulk of the fox tradition consists of individual, fragmented, often contradictory experiences.

"OCCASIONAL RECORDS OF CONVERSATIONS AT NIGHT"

In 1779 a Manchu, a holder of the *juren* degree and a onetime local magistrate, wrote of himself,

> This year I am 44 years old. Although I have never encountered the strange, I have always enjoyed, together with a few friends among the wine and teacups, blowing out the candle and talking of ghosts, and sitting in the

moonlight and speaking of foxes. Whenever a story strayed into the realm of the extraordinary, I would always write it down. As the days went by, I filled a volume, idly, for my own amusement.[1]

The title he gave his collection, *Occasional Records of Conversations at Night*, reflects this image of evening conversation and casual composition.

One particular occasion of storytelling is presented in greater detail. This was a gathering of classmates, perhaps He's companions in the school for Manchu and Chinese bannermen that he attended in Beijing, when he was fifteen–twenty years old. Thus the night of storytelling probably happened some decades before the publication of the book. He gave these stories the title "Zaji wuze" 雜記五則 (Five miscellaneous records), which distinguishes them from the bulk of his stories, many of which have as titles the names of their main characters.[2] By giving them a vague title, rather than a biographical one, he marked them as closer to the *zhiguai/biji* end of the spectrum.

In the following discussion, I refer to these stories as "He's work" or "Ji's work." I do this not to discredit the authors' attributions to their friends but to emphasize that the material has undergone an extensive process of selection, translation, and editing that gives the stories in each collection a distinctive cast. He's stories are not, in my opinion, masterpieces. But their limitations are revealing of the interests of the genre; stories of the second rank may in some ways be more representative than masterpieces.

I reserve his introductory comment on foxes for later discussion, but it is worth noting that he provided a theoretical introduction before launching into his stories. After the introduction, he continues,

---

1. He Bang'e, *Yetan suilu* (1988 ed.; hereafter *YTSL*), p. 6.

2. Elsewhere in the collection, He has other groups of stories arranged by topic, on strange events related to the examinations, revenants, oddities about corpses, and cat monsters. These are grouped together at the beginning of the sixth *juan*. They differ from the present example because they are not marked as products of a single night of storytelling, and they are given topical titles. It is interesting that He did not call this selection "foxes"; he seems to be putting emphasis on recording a night of miscellaneous stories.

I and all my classmates happened to talk of fox monsters; I chose five of the most outstanding stories and recorded them here.

Liu Zilai 劉紫來, style Yudong 昱東, from Guizhu 貴筑,[3] having completed his studies, acted as host at the Shandong natives' hall of Hu Huiyan 胡輝岩 from Chang'yi 昌邑.[4] At the midautumn festival, we gathered to drink in the southern building. Among the company were Ju Muzhou 鞠慕周, style Zhuangxing 莊行, from Haiyang 海陽;[5] Hu Daifeng 胡岱峰, style Ziyi 子翼; Wu Jingzhai 鄔敬齋, style Weisu 維肅, of Guiyang 貴陽;[6] Xue Luyuan 薛魯園, style Tingjie 廷楷; myself, and the host. As we spoke together of foxes, I presented the story of "The Red Girl," and they all thought it strange.

Recalling his friends' names and native places plainly matters; part of the point of remembering these stories is to recall a party. All these men are now more obscure than He Bang'e himself. "The Red Girl" ("Hong guniang" 紅姑娘) is not included with the other five miscellaneous records but appears elsewhere in the collection, an arrangement that suggests he had a repertoire of stories, both in written and oral form.

The Red Girl

In the inner and outer walls of the capital, there are altogether fifty guard towers. They are tall and deep and always inhabited by mice and foxes. In the tower at the northeast corner of the inner wall, there was one fox who would change into a sixteen- or seventeen-year-old girl in a red blouse and a green skirt, an outstanding beauty. The soldiers guarding the wall would always see her, and although they all knew she was not human, there was none who was not driven to distraction. Because of the color of her clothes, they called her the "Red Girl."

Among them were frivolous young men who often got drunk on fine evenings. Once their lustful thoughts were aroused, they would go below the tower to proposition her with impudent words. Then they heard a dulcet voice saying, "Don't be fresh!" When they went home, either they had unbearable headaches or their lips suddenly swelled up like peaches. Only

3. In Guizhou.

4. In Laizhou Fu, Shandong.

5. There are two cities called Haiyang, one in Shandong, one in Guangdong. Ju's name is also mentioned in *Qiudeng conghua*.

6. In Guizhou.

when they sincerely regretted their error would it stop. Because of this, everyone feared her, and no one dared to make playful remarks.

The foot soldier Xiao Xiase 校嚇色 was over sixty. One night when he was on night duty on the wall, sitting alone at his post, he longed for wine but had none. After the third watch, he heard the sound of fingers tapping on the door. He asked who it was, but there was no answer. When he opened the door to look, he saw a sixteen-year-old beauty. In her countenance all five colors coursed together in harmony;[7] her beauty could not be described in full. When one looked at her closely, she dazzled the eyes.[8] Behind her followed two maids with their hair in tufts. They stood in the moonlight holding wine and boxes of food.

Xiao had always had courage. Once he recovered from his surprise, he realized she was a fox. He asked her why she had come to this high wall in the middle of the night. She answered, "I am Miss Hong,[9] third in my family. Since I knew you were longing for wine, I have respectfully brought some of my family's brew to present to you." Xiao was very happy and invited her in. He took the wine and food she brought as comfort for his pains as a soldier away from home.

After he got drunk and his spirits were high, he asked, "Third sister, do you want anything from me?"

She said, "All those who use foxy wiles to beguile men want something from them. You are poor, ill, and old besides; what could I want from you? The reason I've come to you is because you have done me a great favor." Baffled, Xiao didn't know what she was talking about. She said, "Have you forgotten buying me at Songting 松亭 then?"[10] Only then did he understand, and sighed for a long time. He recognized her as a foster daughter.

From then on, every time he went on night duty, he would steal away from his fellows by various means and, leaning on his staff, go alone beneath the corner tower, announcing, "Inform Third Sister that I am on duty tonight." Late at night she would indeed appear, and the two maids served wine and food, arraying delicacies before him. Xiao feasted night after night. Whenever he desired something in his heart, she, knowing even before he said a word, would provide it in an instant. Once Xiao gave her a jade ring. She bowed repeatedly in thanks to accept it and wrapped it up to treasure it.

---

7. The five colors are *qing* (green/blue/black), red, white, black, and yellow.

8. There is a reference here to the "Gaotang fu," which may by this time have become more a standard means of describing beautiful women rather than a specific allusion.

9. Her surname, 洪, is a pun with "red" 紅.

10. Possibly Songting guan 松亭關 in Zunhua county, Hebei.

When Xiao spoke with her, he brooded on the fact he was a white-haired old man, who at any moment might die of the ravages of the fog and the dew. As he spoke, lines of tears trickled down. She said, "You are all right. When I look at you, I think you could live for thirty more years." She taught him the art of breathing exercises, which proved quite effective when he practiced it. There was nothing strange about her except that she loved to wash her face, as much as four or five times every night.

When Xiao's youngest son was taking a wife, Xiao worried about the lack of proper dishes. He was about to go rent them at the market when she said, "No need. I should borrow them for you, Father." When the day arrived, indeed there were gold and silver services arrayed in the room, and no one could guess where they came from. The family was amazed. Only when Xiao told them the truth were they all happy. Once the ceremony was over, all the dishes vanished.

Xiao's second son, a military officer, heard the woman was beautiful; so he secretly went up the wall to the post and peeked in through a crack in the window. But he saw nothing, only his father alone, talking, laughing, and drinking by himself.

Once, after Xiao had been drinking, he happened to pocket one of her jade wine vessels. When he got home, it had vanished. But if he really had an urgent need, she would amply provide for him with large ingots, all silver of the highest grade. It went on like this for ten years.

Suddenly one night she wept inconsolably, saying, "Our destined tie is already over. From now on we will be parted forever." Surprised, Xiao asked her why, but she didn't answer. After the fifth watch she left sobbing. Xiao was also devastated but didn't yet know what she meant by "parting forever." The next day the supervising officer applied to the court that Xiao be allowed to retire on account of his age. Then Xiao sighed in understanding.

Earlier, when Xiao had been in his prime, he went on expedition to subdue the Ge'erdan 葛爾丹 as a cavalry officer. When returning victorious, they reached Songting. His fellows caught a black fox and wanted to kill it for its hide. The fox cried piteously to Xiao. Moved, he bought it for two taels of silver and released it. That had been thirty years ago; he had never thought that he would be repaid now. Afterwards Xiao lived into his nineties and died without illness. The fox also left, and no one knew where she had gone.

Lanyan said, "As a member of an alien species, the fox still knew to repay favors and reward good deeds. She was chaste and guarded her virtue, taking no pleasure in seducing men with her charms. Alas, there are people in the world who use the seven spans of their body to stoop, grovel,[11] and smile fawningly in order to make requests of people, and don't think it strange in the least! Instead they think the people who hold to the straight and narrow without wavering are mediocrities, and in contrast consider themselves extraordinary talents who recognize the needs of the time. How could they compare with her? How deplorable!"[12]

For contemporary listeners and readers, no fox story ever existed in isolation; in contrast to the situation of many modern readers, perhaps even of readers of this book, no fox tale was ever the "first" such story the reader encountered. Other stories were in the background both as textual antecedents and as possibilities that this narrative rejects. The basic outlines of this narrative are, for example, found in an account in *Yanshan conglu*, composed at least 150 years earlier. In the earlier story, a soldier guarding the same city walls in Beijing had an affair with a fox who did him no harm. She would not give him money, telling him he was destined to be poor, but did provide him with food and wine. No one knows what became of the couple, because the soldier's superior officer (from whose perspective this story was evidently told) was transferred.[13]

As we shall see, Beijing is an important center for fox narratives. Both He's story and the earlier tale describe a habitat for foxes, a marginal space between the inside and the outside of the human city. It is at once a place both public and obscure: everyone would know of these guard towers, but only certain people would ever spend any time there, especially at night. The idea of foxes infesting city walls in their animal form is old, as seen in the phrase "the foxes in the walls and the mice in the altar," an expression for those who take advantage of their position to do mischief.[14] That foxes are mentioned in the same breath as mice implies mundane infestation, but the next

---

11. Literally, to raise the shoulders as a sign of respect.

12. *YTSL*, 2.37–39. Cf. the translation of Lanyan's comment in Chan, *The Discourse of Foxes and Ghosts*, p. 222.

13. *Yanshan conglu*, *juan* 8, story 3.

14. *Hanyu dacidian* 2:1096. For a story that reverses the meaning of this phrase by making foxes in the walls the guardians against human corruption, see "Chenghu ji" 城狐記, in Yang Fenghui, *Nan'gao biji* in *BJXSDG*, 14:4.15b–16a.

line suggests that vermin easily become haunts. (Foxes' occupation of human spaces is the subject of the next chapter.)

The story opens with a public, shared apparition and then shifts to private experience. In the shadows of both the recurring experience of the "frivolous young men" and the singular experience of Xiao Xiase is plainly another story about erotic involvement with a vixen, one who would respond positively to the young men's advances and with ulterior motives "use foxy wiles to beguile men." Male desire is controlled in the first case by supernatural revenge, and in the second case by delayed karmic reward, which leaves Xiao too old to make sexual demands of the grateful vixen. The young men's desire frames the chaste encounters with the old man. In this context, his name, "Teaching to scare away passion," is suggestive. Its allusive meaning would be more apparent to a reader, rather than a listener. His son's thwarted voyeurism reinforces the framing with young men's desire and even further underlines the private nature of this relationship.

Miss Hong is not a distinct individual; even the name she gives herself is a pun on that given her by the soldiers. She is an embodiment of restrained fantasy and karmic reward. With the possibility of a sexual liaison excluded, every moment in the story's progression is wish fulfillment kept within practical bounds: longevity and health but not immortality; wine, food, and companionship but not erotic bliss; and a short-term loan of tableware rather than untold riches. The end of the relationship is in keeping with this banality: they are parted not by death of the human or exposure of the fox body but by retirement.

The story is structured by karmic retribution in a double sense: karma provides both the motivation for the plot and the closing of the story. Just as hunters are the fox's traditional bane, a fox's rewarding of her rescuer is also a (later) convention. Although the vixen makes her karmic motivation clear to Xiao early in the story, the readers are enlightened only at the end. The fox body is exposed only in retrospect. The gap in time between rescue and recompense does suggest, as the commentary says, that she deliberately deferred repayment in order to avoid sexual demands.

The commentary by Lanyan belongs to a different stratum than the night of storytelling; all the stories in the collection end with similar remarks. Commentary, whether by the author himself or others, had become a common feature of the classical tale by the eighteenth century.[15] As a commentator, Lanyan sounds only one note: moral judgment of the fox as a means of moral judgment of the human world. This shift of focus might be taken to imply that foxes are not important in themselves but serve only as vehicles for discussing moral issues. I would argue instead that commentary is a genre in its own right, with its own conventions, and that the relationship between story and commentary is not one of absolute containment and restriction of meaning. After the mixed pleasures of the narrative, the commentary offers the more straightforward pleasure of moral righteousness. The commentary creates a world different from that of the story: it is more abstract, referring to anonymous representatives of moral failure, yet it has its own vividness in its depiction of moral monstrosities among the human race. As is often the case with this kind of allegorical comparison, the fox who is not present in the story, the skilled seductress, is projected onto the human world.

Then Zilai related that when he had been a guest in Shanxi, he heard of a rich family with many foxes in their home. The foxes constantly assumed illusory shapes to haunt them, terrifying the whole household. Sometimes a fox would appear as an old hunchback walking alone in the hall; sometimes as an old woman carrying a basket in and out of the kitchen and granary; or sometimes as a young, painted up woman leaning against the gate, looking out at the town, to turn the heads of the passerby. Sometimes at the top of the walls visions of towers, outer walls, and secondary walls would suddenly appear. Each successive manifestation grew stranger and stranger. Although they didn't harm anyone, the family really hated it.

The master of the house had a daughter. Next to her room there was a Buddhist shrine, in which there were tens of vats full of fermenting wine. The door was usually locked. One evening when the daughter and her maid were returning to sleep, they passed by the shrine and heard the sounds of wine being strained from within. They peeked in to see two hunchbacked old crones going to the vats to steal wine to drink, fighting as they drank. In a little while one of the crones got very drunk. The daughter found her besotted appearance hysterical and couldn't help breaking out in giggles. The

15. On this tradition, including the commentary of *Yetan suilu*, see Chan, *The Discourse of Foxes and Ghosts*, pp. 215–24.

crone heard her and said angrily, "What business is it of yours, maid, if we drink a few cups of wine? What is there to laugh at?"

The maid replied, "Seeing someone stealing wine and getting so drunk, how could we not laugh?"

The enraged crone cursed her loudly, "Don't you mess with your grandmother! I'll bite your daddy's black dick!" Hearing her dirty talk, the daughter immediately left to avoid her. But the maid couldn't stand her curses and stood below the window berating her soundly. Suddenly a flying tile hit home, hurting her lip and knocking out two teeth. As she ran away in pain, loud laughter was heard from within the shrine. The master heard it and warned the household not to talk about it. That night passed without incident.

When the master of the house woke up the next morning, he saw a black object beside his pillow. On closer examination, he saw it was a man's penis, with the color of blood still fresh. Greatly alarmed, and fearing the women might see it, he secretly picked it up with fire tongs and put it in the toilet. He gathered all the male servants to examine them, but none of them had been harmed.

At that time the maid's father, who had followed a district magistrate to Henan, was having an affair with a prostitute. One night the prostitute suddenly arrived, and they slept together. As he lay snoring, his private parts hurt as if cut by a knife. He cried out and fainted. When his companions got up startled and came to look, his penis was already missing. The prostitute wasn't at his side either. Everyone was mystified.

They reported it to the local magistrate. When the prostitute was taken in for interrogation, she said she had been gambling with all her female friends the night before and hadn't slept all night. She truly knew nothing of the matter. In the end it became an unsolved case. The victim was sent back home, and although he didn't die, he was already a eunuch. There was nothing his master could do except move away to avoid the foxes. Only then did he get to live in peace.

The time when the maid's father lost his member was exactly the time that the master of the house found one by his pillow. The maid's surname was Zhang. Her father had a dark complexion and was called "black Zhang." That's why the fox said, "Bite off the black dick."

Nizhai [He Bang'e himself] said: "I have heard that foxes' nature is extremely lustful, and therefore they are called "lustful foxes." In this case, since their revenge of wrongs also originated from lust, one may call this an extremely fitting name. Names are the guests of the truth. Foxes' lustfulness originates from their natures; the reality existed first, and afterwards the name was fitted to it. How could foxes be lustful on account of their reputation? However, those in the world whose reputations exceed the reality are not even the equals of lustful foxes."

Lanyan said: "They stole wine themselves but did harm to someone else's father. Not only was this fox not benevolent, it was brazen. This is probably a case of shame turning into rage!"[16]

The stories seem to alternate crudity and refinement, reward and revenge, demonstrating both the range of the fox and the range of different pleasures these young men could take from their narratives. Again, this story opens by establishing a shared set of apparitions before moving to a specific encounter. In a narrative of personal experience or from a source close to one's own family tradition, any of the initial apparitions could make a story on its own, but here they serve only as introductory elements for a crude joke held at considerable distance from its narrator.

A family's home is another possible habitat for a fox, and foxes' presence is more disturbing there than on city walls. The escalating strangeness of the manifestations suggests a situation much less stable than in the Red Girl's case. Yet for all their strangeness, the apparitions mirror human age and sex roles, especially in the ways in which female foxes violate the boundaries of the household: young women try to seduce passersby from the threshold, and old women pilfer the pantry. There is a tradition of stories of foxes stealing wine, although the culprits are more typically male foxes.[17]

There is a tense gender, age, and class structure to the confrontation. It is the young women of the household (walking, significantly, out of the inner chamber) who confront the other in the forms of older women. With drunkenness, laughter, and cursing, there is a loss of female decorum on all sides, but the upper-class daughter is spared the worst humiliation. Revenge for the confrontation among women is taken on men in the most sexually charged form of violence possible. One suspects this story might exist for the sake of the bloody image, since "black dick" is the phrase that links the middle of the story and the concluding explanation, in the same way as

16. *YTSL*, 4.102–4.

17. For example, "Jiuyou" 酒友, in *LZ*, 2.217–19.

"bought me at Songting" does in the Red Girl's story. As transgressive as the castration is, it reinforces certain hierarchies: the misbehaviors of women are men's responsibilities, and although servant households suffer for their own misdeeds, the message is delivered to masters. Violence is perpetrated by female foxes, but human women are sheltered from the signs of it. Class relations are further suggested by the fact it is the master's story that is told first, while the servant victim appears in a flashback.

Since the point of the story is shocking revenge, not the karmic neatness of the previous story, it ends with the master of the house defeated through no particular fault of his own. The castration is also grossly out of proportion to the crime that provoked it. There is an implication that the servant drew this disaster on himself with sexual indulgence; the link between foxes and prostitutes as equally dangerous females is seldom made in such violent terms. The story concludes by linking together the narrative threads involving the act of sexual violence rather than by invoking justice. If the stories were told in this order, this seems like an overwhelming rejection of the previous story's justice and chastity. For He, revenge and reward seem to be the virtues or vices of particular foxes, not the unvarying justice of the universe expressed through foxes.

He Bang'e's comment, under the pseudonym Nizhai, makes a move similar to Lanyan's previous comment by comparing foxes favorably to people in this world. The issue he raises, foxes' lustful reputation and lustful nature, is undercut by half of the stories presented in his work. As much as the foxes in Li Zilai's tale energetically live up to that reputation, Miss Hong refuted it. This raises the question: To what extent are foxes creatures with a single species nature, and to what extent are they varied individuals? We will return to this question later. The fox's reputation as the embodiment of lust is the subject of Chapter 5, and its negation is the subject of Chapter 6.

Lanyan uses the negative fox rather differently from the way he uses the positive fox. Its personality flaws are analyzed in their own right, and the insight provided is indeed helpful: the disproportionate scale of the foxes' revenge is explained by the ugliness of the initial scene of old women drinking and the young women's laughter.

He implies that the vices of flawed foxes are uniquely their own, whereas their virtues are the ones humans should have.

Hu Huiyan related that Juren Cai of Guiju was an erudite and refined gentleman. He once told Huiyan that Chu, twelfth in his family, from Cai's village followed his maternal grandfather, Senior Licentiate Gu, to travel in Sichuan, where they lodged with the Luo family in Linqiong 臨邛. The Luos were a great family who had been prominent officials for generations. Although in later generations they had gradually declined, their large, deep mansions and their splendid, secluded garden and pavilions were still the finest in the locality. The Luo family had two sons and three nephews, all of whom were instructed by Gu. Chu also studied along with them. Chu and the Luo's nephew, young Qin, were close friends, setting up their beds side by side in the west pavilion of the garden.

After they had lived there half a year, in the autumn months, it came time for the Luo's second son to marry. Gu was exhausted by the daily feasts, and Qin was also busy taking care of things, so Chu walked alone in the pavilion. Feeling very lonely, he took out his books to relieve his boredom.

After the second watch, Qin brought a box with wine to drink a bit with Chu, saying, "These days I've been so busy, with no time to meet you. Tonight I've got a bit of leisure to share a cup of wine and talk heart to heart." With that they sent away the servants, locked the garden gates, cut the lampwick and poured the wine, feeling quite at ease.

Chu drank a cup of wine and said, "With pleasures like these in life, when would one need wealth or glory?"

Qin laughed, "When a mole drinks from a river, it just fills its belly![18] [i.e., You are too easily satisfied.] How can mere drinking be considered pleasure? I know a splendid person. If you saw her, you would wish to grow old in this town." Chu asked what kind of person it was. Qin hemmed and hawed and wouldn't give a straight answer. Only when Chu pressed him did Qin say quietly, "I've been sleeping in this garden for a year. I got to know a beauty, seventeen years old. After you arrived, she's made herself scarce. But on every night of moonlight and flowers, or when you are dreaming drunk, we always embrace. Since you have been good to me, I dare to reveal this intimate secret. I hope you'll reveal it to no one else."

Chu said, "I think you're making fun of me. If it's really so, then if she's not a ghost, she's a fox, and you can't be intimate with her."

---

18. A reference to Zhuangzi, "Xiaoyao you" 逍遙遊; see Chen Guying, ed. *Zhuangzi jinzhu jinyi*, p. 18.

Qin said, "She is truly a fox, and no ghost. She's a vixen more beautiful than Consort Fu and just as talented as Miss Xie.[19] Why can't I be intimate with her?" Chu was after all a young man, and his blood was still unsettled; moreover, he was in high spirits from the wine. So he demanded to meet her once. When Qin looked troubled, Chu begged him, to the point of going down on his knees. Qin smiled faintly, "There should be nothing wrong with seeing her, but I haven't asked yet whether she will permit it. Let's try it, and see if you are destined to meet her." With that he got up and went out the winding corridor. Under the miniature mountains by the lake, he quietly called "Lianjie" three times.

Then a woman appeared among the flowers, approaching slowly, walking in the moonlight. Her demeanor was charming, her beauty exceptional, the like of which Chu had not seen before. She wore a green brocade blouse and a trailing silk skirt. Her glance radiated intelligence, and a flush ran across her lotus-like face. Demurely she looked sideways at Chu and rebuked Qin, "Little pedant (*suanzi* 酸子), are you saying I dare not meet this bookworm?" Chu blushed and stuttered, forcing himself to bow to her.

Qin said, "Chu Twelve is bashful. Don't laugh at him, Lianjie."

Lianjie suddenly laughed and said, "This isn't bashfulness, but a display of his good nature. How could he be like you, with your natural goodness all spent, knowing no shame?" Then she entered the pavilion with them. When she saw the wine cups, she laughed, "You two pedants! Their son is taking a bride, and at this very moment they must be groping around for these things. But you have taken the leftovers, slurping them down and gobbling them up. I congratulate you on getting these two measures to fill your gullets tonight."

Qin said, "If you can't be our host, how can you mock us?"

She said, "You truly are the fleas in the inn, plotting to eat the guests! But I just happen to be coming from eating peaches at my Sixth Sister's place. I saved several. How about if I present them to you?"

Qin said, "Splendid!" So she took out a gold-rimmed coconut dipper filled with five foreign peaches, fresh as if newly picked. Sichuan had no such fruit, and they could not guess where they came from. The two young men split them and found them very sweet. Then she brought out rare delicacies and fragrant wine, all from the same ladle, and arranged them to fill the table. As they were growing tipsy with drink, she suddenly looked at Chu and said, "From your fragrant countenance and pure quality, I can see

---

19. Consort Fu 宓妃 is the legendary goddess of the Luo river. Xie Daoyun 謝道韞, the Jin poetess, was a standard representative of women with literary talent.

that you will be able to outdo your father. But the flowers of the thousand-leaved peach bloom early and fall early, blossoming without ever bearing fruit. This principle is foreordained. We must seize the moment for our enjoyment. How could we wait in vain for such a chance to come again?" From then on her laughter and conversation were in perfect accord with him, and her playful words gradually grew intimate. Chu was bewitched and could not control himself. Watching from the side, Qin's face bore a jealous expression.

She glanced sideways at him and laughed, "Little pedant, you really are a gourd full of vinegar. When two people meet like duckweed on the water and enjoy themselves together at the place they meet, how is that worth getting upset about? For example, look at what is about to happen to the new bride—how could the young groom of the Luo family bear it [if he took things as seriously as you do]?"

Qin asked, "What is about to happen to the new bride?"

She said, "Wait and you'll see for yourself."

A bit later, they suddenly heard a hubbub of human voices, and all the trees in the garden were red. When people went out to look, they found a fire had broken out in the kitchen and spread to the nuptial chamber. All the local official troops came to extinguish the fire and save the victims. Relatives and neighbors gradually gathered, teeming like ants or fleas. The entire family of tens of people fortunately hadn't gone to sleep yet. Only the bride and the son of the Luo family were stark naked, trembling before the hall, the finest hair visible to everyone in the reflected firelight. The two young men couldn't look directly at them. But Lianjie went forward, took off her gauze robe, wrapped it around them, and led them back to another room. All the aunts and sisters came in succession to comfort them, and in the confusion they lost track of where the woman who had covered them was. Everyone thought it was a neighbor's daughter who had gone back to her boudoir. Only Chu and Qin knew her, but they kept the secret and said nothing.

From this time on Chu talked with her every night, and although they thoroughly enjoyed each other's company, they never reached the point of sexual intimacy, for Chu was bashful and she was chaste, just like Wei Yin and Miss Ren.

When it came time for Qin to return to Chengdu with his father, Lianjie wept as she bade him farewell and never appeared again. Two years later, Gu died, and Chu returned to his native place with the coffin. Not long after he took part in the examinations. The following year he became a *jinshi* and worked as a supervisor in the Ministry of Works. He died before he got married, only 24 years old.

Nizhai said: "The reason why a penniless scholar 酸子 is often jealous is no other than his poverty and career frustration. If a man could lock his door, tend to his wife and children, and spend the rest of his life that way, then he never had far-reaching ambitions. The chaste fox and Chu only strayed into the realm of intimacy in their talk and facial expressions, but the bookworm Qin revealed his jealousy on his face. How could he be so small-minded?" Lanyan said, "She preserved her body's chastity, she perceived principle clearly, she spoke eloquently—such a fox is hard to find."[20]

These stories preserve alleged chains of transmission, with two named informants between He Bang'e and the young man who talked with a vixen. Although we have no way of testing their accuracy, these opening notes are traces of a real or imagined social world, with stories transmitted along lines of shared native place, literati friendship, and the trajectory of travel. This story in particular is equipped with specifics of name, both of the informant and the participants, that are unnecessary to the plot but might fulfill other, social needs.

The alternation of violence and restraint continues. The bulk of the story describes the first encounter with the vixen, which serves as a miniature of the entire relationship. The fox offers a perfect interlude in an enchanted bubble of space and time, demarcated by her foreknowledge. A relatively uneventful idyll of conversation with a fox is another story type that had been established in the late Ming.[21] Recalling the Red Girl, she offers nothing more dramatic than charming conversation, exotic fruits out of season,[22] and a bottomless dipper of food. Food and drink seem more indispensable to this fantasy than sex.

The story sketches a portrait of another kind of man, besides the old soldier, who might need a vixen: the tutor's grandson, studying along with the sons of his grandfather's employer, a poor relation who isn't even related. This young man away from home finds no place in another family's celebration. The first part of the fantasy is

---

20. *YTSL*, 4.104–6.

21. See Qian Xiyan, *Kuai yuan zhiyi*, 14, story 10.

22. For other stories of foxes providing fresh fruits out of season, see Jin Liang, *Guayuan shuyi*, *xia*, 47b; and Xu ? (pseud. Qingliang daoren), *Ting yu xuan biji* in *BJXSDG*, 12:1.10.

to have a friend at all: it is Qin who shows up with wine when Chu is lonely, just as the Red Girl did for the old soldier, and then the vixen follows. Chu will die a virgin, or at least unwed, but not without having had a beautiful woman appreciate him. The equivalent of the Red Girl at the other end of the life cycle, she is the most important woman in his short life. The human men can enjoy a timeless idyll in her company, but she is entirely aware of its limitations; her plea of "carpe diem" is based on clear-eyed knowledge. Similarly, her platonic appreciation of Chu is based on her knowledge of his vulnerability. The young man who dies without sexual experience is a much rarer topic than the young woman in the same situation. Perhaps this explains the gender reversals created in Lianjie's banter: one man is mocked for jealousy, and another is described as bashful and shy. Overall Chu is figured as extremely feminine and virtually silent.

The sexual affair with a vixen is both at the margin and crucial. At this point in the history of the fox romance, other possibilities are more interesting than consummation; fascination with intimacy shy of consummation is explored in a more graphic way in the next story. Lianjie creates a charmed space by sustaining a love triangle without destroying the friendship between two young men of different characters, who will later be separated by the vicissitudes of family and career. The comparison to Miss Ren reveals some of the crucial differences between the Tang and Qing fox story: Miss Ren's platonic friendship with Wei began with an attempted rape (see Chapter 6). We have already seen what happens, in the eighteenth century, to men who harass, let alone rape, fox spirits. Far from being "bashful" like Chu, Wei was an adult man with many lovers, on whom Ren's lover was dependent. That relationship of dependency has been reversed here, with only the general impression of the triangle remaining.

The argument between the two young men over whether one can be intimate with a vixen captures two ways of looking at foxes: Should the vixen be judged by her species or by her individual merits? In this story, and in this collection and its era, it is no longer much of a debate, but the tension between the exceptional individual and the general assumption of lust is illustrated in this series of stories and their commentary.

This interlude is placed very specifically in space and time, not only at a particular point in a young man's geographical trajectory as he follows his grandfather but in the middle of someone else's wedding party. The moment of exposure on a wedding night seems to represent another kind of story, jokes about mishaps at charged ritual moments. This time the fox draws a silk coverlet over a moment of human embarrassment, rather than being its cause. Foxes are often associated with fires, and a wedding night disaster is precisely what one might expect of one of her mischievous sisters. Reversal of mischief is a common trope in tales of benign foxes.

As He Bang'e's comment reveals, the unconventional position of the vixen allows exploration of a subject, male jealousy, which would not be possible in a romance with human women. This is another aspect of the feminization of both young men. As much as a story about vixens, this is a story about young literati, the impoverished and stodgy *suanzi*, as both Lianjie and He Bang'e call them.

Ju Muzhou of Haiyang was the best at telling fox stories; I cannot record them all. Among them some were strange enough to make one laugh out loud. He said that when he was a traveler in Shaanxi, he went on business to Fufeng.[23] Among his acquaintances was Juren Ding, who was almost forty and widowed, with his young children crying at his knees. Since he had no patience for living as a widower, he tried to seek another wife, but many times his hopes were disappointed.

Ding had long studied the way of spirits and immortals and was good at Daoist meditation. Whenever he purified his heart and sat in meditation, exhaling the old and inhaling the new, he would see a black fox crouching across from him, facing him with staring eyes. When Ding yelled at it, it would immediately run away. After several times, he grew accustomed to this and no longer thought it strange.

One night just as he was sitting in meditation, he felt someone climb on the bed and sit shoulder to shoulder with him. The scent of her clothes was intoxicating. Ding thought to himself, "All of this has been summoned by my wayward thoughts. If my heart were unmoved, how could a demon arise? I can withstand this." With that he lowered his eyes, calmed his heart, and steadfastly refused to move. Soon this person leaned her cheek against his cheek, and tried to kiss him. Her powder was fragrant, her rouge cloying, her skin smooth as cream. Ding, unable to bear it any more, opened his eyes

23. West of Xi'an.

and glared at her. He saw a sixteen-year-old girl of dazzling beauty looking at him and smiling. He said, "I know you are the fox from the other day. Why should you disturb someone's exercises? Go away quickly, or else you will enrage my old fists, which won't be pleasant acquaintances." She covered her mouth and giggled, still lingering. Extremely agitated, Ding kicked her, sending her tumbling off the bed.

Immediately she stood up, straightened her clothes and said, "How could such crudity be the behavior of an educated man? If I leave and never return, won't you regret it?"

He clasped his hands in gratitude, "I am deeply moved by your kindness [in leaving]. Dare I speak of regret?"

She said, "After this, even if you were to burn incense and kowtow, begging me to come back, I fear it couldn't happen."

Ding laughed, "I would never dare do such a thing." She left without looking back.

One evening several days later, when Ding was bathing in his room, he saw her rolling up the bamboo shades and coming in. She smiled and said, "I've come again to see you bathing naked." Ding didn't reply. She crouched beside him and stroked him with her hand, saying, "You have two inches of dirt on your back; may I scrub it away for you?" Ding was very aroused, and that thing in his pants rose erect. She laughed without stopping. She playfully pinched his cheek with a small noise and said, "What a bookish fool! You are so impertinent! Don't you fear insulting the eyes of another man's daughter?"

Ding secretly thought to himself, "How could someone who studies the Way indulge in desire? Especially when I plainly already know she is a fox, why is my heart moved?" So he glared at her in rage and struck her in the nose with his fist. She rolled on the ground in pain, crying piteously, then charged through the shades and fled. From then on she did not appear again.

Ding's household finances had always been prosperous. Although his children were taken care of by nursemaids, he still felt that he lacked a helpmeet to take care of food, clothing, and the household accounts. Again he summoned a matchmaker to search for a fine match. One day an old matchmaker came, saying "There is a great family with the surname Bian, with a fortune of a hundred thousand. Their daughter is eighteen, lovely, bright, and virtuous; there are few like her in the world. Since you are an educated man, who doubts much and believes little, you usually think of matchmakers as liars. But send a female relative to look at her. That will serve to prove that my words are not false." Ding agreed with this, and sent his paternal aunt and his elder brother's widow to call on the Bian household. Inspecting her demeanor, they found she really was a divine beauty. They returned delighted and extravagantly praised her beauty. Both said they'd seen many women but had never seen her equal. "She stands alone not only in our locality but in the entire world." Ding was very pleased and immediately accepted the betrothal gifts.

It came time for the presentation of the goose. Relatives and old friends filled the hall, hoping to catch a glimpse of her. When the couple entered the chamber to share the nuptial cup, Ding suddenly looked at the beauty. Upon close examination she was no other than the vixen from before. He was very alarmed. When he interrogated her, she laughed, "I am not without benefit to you. Your Daoist ambitions are already strong, and you have hope of success. But there is still a necessary secret formula, without which you are a bit confused. I will come and be a good teacher, and we will ascend to the registry of transcendents together. Won't that be acceptable?"

The matchmaker interrupted from the side, "Marriages are determined by heaven. Groom, don't be stubborn any longer." Ding was furious, and raised the bar of the door and struck her. The matchmaker and the bride broke through the window and fled. Ding ran out the door in pursuit, but they had already vanished. He immediately called for torches and searched for them. When they were found in the latrine, Ding's men cried out loudly and began to strike them forcefully. The two women in the latrine pulled up their pants, cried out in alarm, and fell to the ground. When examined by torchlight, they proved not to be the fox and matchmaker, but Ding's nephew's wife and his older brother's widow, covered in filth and with wounds all over their bodies. Everyone present, disheartened, picked the two women up and took them home.

The next day they all went together to the Bian household. There were no longer any buildings but only many *wutong* trees and the ruins of ancient tombs. From then on the fox-haunting ceased. Ju was good friends with Ding when he was in Qin, and heard this from his own account.

Lanyan said, "People say that Confucian scholars are often foolish, but since Ding in the end maintained the Way through his folly, in truth it wasn't real folly!"

The opening comments about Ju's gift for telling fox stories make it clear that He Bang'e is most interested in the strange as it overlaps with the comic. Oral narrative can be an entertaining performance, and commenting on a particular man's gift suggests the possibility of fictionalizing and fabrication.

The fox observing a man meditating seems to evoke the Buddhist image of a fox in disguise listening to sutras and gaining redemption.[24] There is a suggestion that the vixen attains her ability to assume human shape through her initial proximity to him by absorbing his spiritual attainments.[25] However, whereas a fox listening to a Buddhist preacher assumes the role of disciple, who can transcend the fox shape only through human magnanimity, it may be capable of teaching men Daoist self-cultivation. This is the only one of He's story series in which the body of the fox appears in the main timeline rather than in the past, as in the Red Girl's story, placing emphasis on the fox's upward mobility, a theme which will be discussed further in Chapter 7.

Despite all his aspirations to spiritual self-sufficiency, Ding's need for a woman is his weakness. The stated reasons for this need are practical rather than sexual, but the saucy fox embodies the repressed part of that need. One cause of Ding's anger is the realization that he is neither self-sufficient nor fully in control of himself. The stories in this cycle provide an interesting range of stages in the male life-cycle, with a vixen fulfilling different needs each time: she is the foster daughter of a sick old man, the platonic companion of a callow youth, and the torment of a man who should be at the height of his maturity and powers.

Ding's story is almost a parody of the common argument that because monsters such as foxes arise from the human heart, the man without desire will not be troubled by them. Both Ding and the persistent fox are comic figures. The narrative exists for the sake of the titillating details of unwilling arousal and Ding's absurd outbursts of violence. Again, the interest lies in alternatives to consummation, and as I will discuss later in my treatment of the relationship of the fox story to pornography, the description of the alternatives grows more graphic than any tale of intercourse with a vixen. The tension between seduction and denial is captured perfectly in the description of her first appearance in human form, with all the sensual details

24. For an extensive study of this group of texts, see Heine, *Shifting Shape, Shaping Text*.

25. There are other texts that describe foxes as initially gleaning human *qi* in order to become capable of transformation; see, e.g., Lang Ying, *Qixu leigao*, 48.9b.

perceived by man with his eyes tightly closed. The focus of the story is on the will of a man who can refuse a vixen who offers him everything, in contrast to the old soldier or the young scholar who wish for more than their vixens would grant. Thus Lanyan's comment focuses on him and ignores the fox. Because of the centrality of Ding's will, her desire for him is never explained. Supernatural romances often feature sexually aggressive females, but this extreme case again puts a man in an unusual position.

The fox finally exploits the more official side of Ding's need for a woman. Again, the confrontation ends with a swoop into violence and crudity and the comedy of important ritual events gone awry, with a touch of the scatological interest typical of this collection. In contrast to the "black penis" story, here it is the women of the family who pay for the man's intransigence. Ending the story with exposure of the foxes' lair is an old motif. This story has a punchline rather than a conclusion: neither the fox nor Ding get what they want.

Xue Luyuan said that none of these stories was strange at all. Nothing was stranger than the fox in Wanqiu 宛邱 [in Henan]. The magistrate of Wanqiu, Master Li, had a daughter who had just reached adulthood, a girl of uncommon grace and style. She was possessed by a fox, to the deep distress of her mother.

At the time in the region there was a female medium skilled at exorcising evil influences. It happened that Master Li had gone to the provincial capital, and so the lady of the house invited the medium to the official residence. She told her of her daughter's suffering and bid her to drive it away. The medium boasted, "What's hard about that? All it requires is the outlay of several tens of strings of cash. Please allow me to drive it out for you this very night. I'll make the little fox demon suffer bitterly!" The mistress was delighted, and the medium left richly rewarded.

That evening she returned with both of her disciples, carrying a drum and sack. They set up an altar in the garden. The mistress led all her maids and female servants to peek at the proceedings, hidden behind a screen. Just as the medium was stepping her ritual paces, a great wind rose up. Dust clouded their eyes, but the candles were not extinguished. Suddenly they saw four or five young men carrying staves approaching the altar table. They threw the medium and her two disciples to the ground, ripped their pants down, and stuffed the wooden staves in their private parts. The men clapped their hands and laughed, "Please suffer bitterly first!"

The mistress was terrified and commanded her servants to rescue the medium. The medium removed the wooden staff herself and got up quickly. The mistress comforted her, "Divine teacher, you have suffered bitterly for nothing."

The medium came forward painfully and uneasily but forced herself to smile and say, "This is indeed a very happy event. How can you call it bitter?" The two disciples were still exhausted, with bright red blood covering their clothes. They came forward supported by several maids. The medium looked back and commanded them, "This bloody clothing is most rare. After we go back we must save it as a treasure."

The mistress asked, "What are you saving it for?"

The medium replied, "If I save it, we can repel monsters!" The mistress laughed loudly and dismissed her.

Lanyan said, "Some might say that the medium was a shameless big talker, and thus suffered this retribution. They don't know that foolish men and women aren't worth stern rebuke. What is incomprehensible is that literati and scholars also can never avoid [the same failing]. I regret I don't have a wooden staff to stuff them with!"[26]

Xue outdoes Ju's tale of the insistent fox and the impervious man with a sex-reversed version of the violent castration story. His introductory comment raises the question of what "strange" means for this group: here, it seems to be a combination of shock and humor.

Here we see the sexual inversion of all the stories of men and their vixen lovers. The word used to describe the daughter's possession, *ju* 据, is the same that would be used if a fox had claimed a building in the house. In marked contrast to the focus on the male will in tales of men's sexual experience with foxes, the possessed girl fades into the background as the narration focuses on the confrontation between the exorcist and the possessing fox. In this case the daughter virtually vanishes, and older women dominate the action.

Even more strongly than in the previous story, the lack of resolution of the daughter's situation makes it clear this story is working toward a punchline rather than toward closure. The joke has more to do with humiliation of an old female medium, a subject of particular contempt and anxiety in the works of upper-class male authors, than with foxes. It is conspicuous that this incident can take place only

26. *YTSL*, 4.108–9.

while the man of the house is away; the implication is that he would never have allowed the medium to be summoned in the first place. In a case like this, foxes can, through putting such types in their places, be seen as the allies of the elite. The old medium is the butt of the joke, but key to the joke is her shameless resourcefulness, which has some basis in magical practice: items traditionally regarded as polluted, such as urine or menstrual blood, were thought to thwart black magic. Lanyan appropriates the violence of the story for his own purposes; for him at least, humans of other classes are, like foxes, not the primary focus of his attention but resources for comparative purposes. He wants elite male readers, who have just laughed at this story, with the butt of the joke so different from themselves, to stop to ask if they are in any way similar.

Muzhou slapped his thigh and said, "This is truly a strange story, but the story I've heard of a certain instructor is also a rare encounter. A certain friend of mine was the teacher in a certain village. There had always been a lot of foxes in the school. When he had been at his post for several days, someone sent in his name card, on which was written, 'Your servant Hu Wanling respectfully greets you.' When he received the guest, it proved to be a white-haired old man, more than three *chi* tall, with a tranquil air, free as a transcendent. He faced the instructor and paid his respects. He introduced himself, 'I am originally from Jin, and have lodged here for almost a hundred years. Now because of a certain matter I am traveling to Chu. Because of your virtue, I dare to entrust my family to you.' The instructor knew he was a fox, but still agreed. The old man bowed in thanks and left.

"The entire clan, probably about twenty of them, arrived in the evening. The instructor invited them to the inner rooms and treated them with impeccable hospitality. The old man was deeply grateful for his kindness and lifted a cup to entrust him with his family, 'The tens of us, young and old, all rely on the auspicious clouds of your virtuous protection. When I return on another day, you can surely expect a generous repayment.'

"The instructor was chivalrous and unrestrained by nature. He rubbed his whiskers and laughed, 'Just go without worries, old man; your precious kin will surely not get lost.' The old man's expression of gratitude was plain enough to touch. The next day he put on his clothes and headed out on the road.

"The instructor had little work, and his salary was a pittance; now that he had done this good deed, the supply of firewood and water to the kitchen was interrupted. But he paid it no heed.

"The old man had two sons and three daughters, all of bewitching beauty. Sometimes they would come to spend the night in the instructor's quarters, and the teacher and they grew as intimate as parents and children. The instructor's family had never come to his official post; only his second son had followed him. He had just reached adulthood, and his appearance and quality were out of the ordinary. Whenever he saw the three girls, he would avoid them and wouldn't speak a word with them. One of the girls once addressed the instructor with flirtatious words, and he scolded her with a serious expression. She apologized in embarrassment and left, not daring to come again for several days. Once when the instructor's son happened to be passing through the inner quarters, he happened upon the youngest of the girls peeing beneath the steps. She laughed and tried to flirt with him, but he lowered his head and avoided her, pretending not to have seen or heard. It went on like this for more than a year, the time passing as quickly as a single day.

"When the old man returned, he bowed in thanks, saying, 'Your virtue is truly unlike other people's. I have no way to repay you. I'll just respectfully present you with a painting for your birthday.' The instructor accepted it happily. After several more days, the old man bid them farewell and took his family away, never to be seen again. The instructor looked at the painting and found it was extremely ordinary, merely depicting an old man and old woman facing forward, sitting side by side. It looked like someone's ancestral portrait, not worthy of aesthetic appreciation, and so the instructor just put it aside.

"It came to the time of the triennial exam. The assigned examiners ordered the instructor to retire on account of his age. Since his money was embarrassingly exhausted, he lived as a sojourner and couldn't go home. Unexpectedly, one day as he sat talking idly in the incense shop, he glimpsed a man stopping his carriage and entering the shop. He was fat and heavy jowled, his clothing clean and proper, followed by a throng of servants like a cloud. The owner of the shop received him very politely. The instructor wanted to avoid him, but since the stranger kept urging him to stay, they sat down in the proper places and introduced themselves. The newcomer bowed and said, 'I am Scholar Zhang. My family have been salt merchants for generations. My son is in the schools; do you know him?' He said, 'Oh, that is your son? He is a well-known scholar.' Zhang was very happy and invited him home. When he came to the hall and greeted Zhang's father, the instructor looked at him carefully and found he resembled the old man in the painting exactly. Although he found this strange, he didn't give it much thought.

"More than ten days later, Zhang's father died and Zhang sought a painter to paint a portrait. Although he switched painters many times, there was none who could capture the slightest resemblance. Thus the instructor took out his painting to show Zhang. Zhang was amazed as he unrolled the scroll. He bowed and wept, telling him, 'Not only is this the exact likeness of my late father, my late mother has been dead for twenty years. How could she come to be depicted here, as she was in her life? May I dare to ask the reason for this?' The instructor told the complete story of the painting's origins. Zhang sighed, 'This fox borrowed my desire to richly reward you in order to repay your good deed for him. The fox has performed a great service for me; how could I fail to fulfill his intentions and repay you?' With that he took the painting and gave the instructor a thousand taels. Only then could he take his son and return home. Up to now they remain prosperous."

Nizhai said, "With just one picture, three people were all able to achieve their hearts' desire. The fox's art was indeed both clever and illusory. But this marvel did not harm righteousness; it is fitting that he should stay quietly in the school and not be driven out."

Lanyan said, "When his salary was cut off, the father was not in the least distressed; when tempted by bewitching beauty, the son never let himself go. The rich reward of this father and son was justified."

Muzhou demonstrates that he is capable of the opposite mode of fox stories, and the alternation of obscenity and decorum ends with decorum. It is interesting that this—the least embarrassing of the stories to its participants—is also the most anonymous, in both space and time.

Foxes are a known presence in the protagonist's workplace, but not a source of apparitions. Here, domestic intimacy with foxes, although in the beginning described in terms not dissimilar to those that might be used for a stubborn infestation of vermin, can be an entirely civil affair negotiated between the patriarchs of the two species. This type, the fox lodger, is discussed in the following chapter.

The story has two foci: a human's exemplary hospitality, accompanied by stringent avoidance of inappropriate intimacy, and the complications of the fox's reward. The erotic tradition remains at the margins, as both father and son rebuff vixens' advances. Here we have yet another stage of a man's life-cycle, the adult man as ruler of a household. The fox forcefully demonstrates the extent of its powers by inserting itself in relations between humans, both between friends and between a man and his parents. This story exhibits the familiar folktale logic of generosity, particularly to supernatural beings, lavishly rewarded in unexpected ways.

The comments reveal that such stories are open to judgment on both sides, of the foxes and of the humans. He's comment points to the challenge of the late fox story: to make the fox as clever, artful, and marvelous as possible while staying within boundaries. The stilted quality of some of the stories testifies to the difficulties of this undertaking.

That a Manchu would record such a rich variety of fox stories belies the simplistic equation of *hu*, fox, with *hu*, Northern barbarian. By the Qianlong period, foxes were the shared cultural legacy of Han and Manchu alike, which both encountered in the same Chinese cities.

These friends told their stories in order to compete in strangeness, and we can try to discern which parts of these stories were strange, and which formed the ordinary backdrop of relations with foxes. For foxes to live in the city walls, someone's home, or a school bordered on the ordinary. For a fox to be a lover, to fulfill some men's wishes and frustrate others, and to reward good deeds or punish insults belonged to the expected. The precise means of repayment or punishment and the possibilities other than erotic consummation were the sources of surprise.

"MISCELLANEOUS RECORDS FROM WEST OF THE LOCUST TREE"

Some years after He wrote his preface, another man, of greater fame and stature, also made a record of a night of fox stories. Ji Yun was Han Chinese and one of the most prominent literati of his day. At 69, when he wrote the preface to *Miscellaneous Records from West of the Locust Tree*, he was completing the work of his life: he had spent the fourth month of that year checking the text of the *Siku quanshu* 四庫全書 (Complete collection of the four treasuries), the massive compendium of all works in the realm deemed worthy of record. Ji included this night of storytelling in a collection of stories he wrote at his lodgings, the Old Hut West of the Locust Tree, west of

Beijing and near the old summer palace, where he stayed while working as a censor when he needed to consult with other officials in his investigations. Few guests disturbed him in this remote place, and he had ample spare time. Ever since he had attained a reputation as a recorder of bizarre tales with the unauthorized publication of his earlier collections, his friends had gone out of their way to tell him weird events. Thus he left a notebook here and, whenever he was on duty, would while away the time by recording the stories people had told him. "Without knowing it," he filled three scrolls.[27]

The actual night of storytelling had occurred thirty years before, when he was 29, in the same decade when He's night of storytelling might have taken place. I present Ji's stories after He's both because He's book was published earlier and because He's stories represent literary tendencies that Ji vehemently rejected.

In the seventh month of 1752, a small group of us were gathered in the home of Song Mengquan 宋蒙泉[28] and happened to talk about foxes. Nie Songyan 聶松岩[29] said, "Do you know about the incident in your clan? In the past when I was in Ji'nan for the village exam, I heard there was a scholar Ji, I forget whether he was from Shouguang 壽光 or Jiaozhou 膠州.[30]

"One night he met a girl walking alone. She slipped in the mud and leaned on him for support. Thinking that this must be a vixen, he resolved to try being intimate with her for a while, so that he might know the nature and condition of demons. Therefore he said to her, 'I recognize you, so don't lie to me. But to get a woman like you is wonderful in its own right. Once everyone's asleep, you can come to my study. Let's not flirt here and bring needless trouble.' The vixen laughed and left.

"In the middle of the night she arrived as expected. After they had indulged in intimacy for several nights, he felt that he was gradually becoming bewitched, and so he turned her away, telling her to come no more. The vixen cursed him resentfully, unwilling to go.

---

27. Preface to *Huaixi zazhi*, *YWCT*, 11.531.

28. Song Bi 宋弼, *zi* Mengquan (1703–68).

29. Nie Jimao 聶際茂, *zi* Songyan, from Changshan 長山. He came to the capital that year, invited by Song Bi, and he and Ji became fast friends, and he often lodged at Ji's home. He was a carver of seals. See Ji Yun, *Ji Xiaolan wenji* 3:291.

30. Both in Shandong.

"With a stern face, he told her, 'Don't be like this. In affairs between men and women, the power is with the man. When a man pursues a woman, if the woman is unwilling, he can still force her. When a woman pursues a man, if the man is unwilling, then his heart is like cold iron, and even forcing him is futile. Furthermore, since you came to steal my essence, not to unite with me for passion's sake, I am not betraying your love. Since you have known many men, it would be hard for you to speak of chastity; so I haven't ruined your chastity either. All gentlemen despise the man who first seduces a woman and then abandons her, but this refers to humans and not to the likes of you. Why must you be so clinging? It does you no good.' At a loss for words, the fox left."

From this story we learn that those who, once bewitched, remain entangled to the point of death with spirits that amulets and charms cannot exorcise, are enchained by their own passions, unable to cut themselves free. If one is utterly unmoved, won't they, with nothing to gain, leave?[31]

The difference between Ji's style and He's style is already evident from this first example. Most obvious is Ji's brevity: the tale is shorter than He's shortest joke. What is missing here, which He might have added? We assume the vixen is beautiful, but there are no conventional phrases telling us that. Young Ji is evidently a man of courage and self-control, but he is not characterized. The bulk of the story is not event but argument: first the discussion within the story, as her erstwhile lover spells out why the vixen has no right to protest her rejection, and then the comment from the outside, as this story is used for general analysis of the nature of enchantment by foxes. Leo Chan accurately describes Ji Yun's stories as a combination of narrative and argument.[32]

As with many of He's stories, this story is framed by assumptions about sexual liaisons with foxes: a girl walking alone is likely to be a fox; a man who makes love to a fox risks bewitchment; foxes make love to men to steal their essence. Based on those premises, it raises the question: Can a human man resist a vixen with his own

31. *YWCT*, 12.627–28, story 94. I have consulted the translations of both Keenan, *Shadows in a Chinese Landscape*, p. 88; and Chan, *The Discourse of Foxes and Ghosts*, p. 70, but still differ from them on several points. The last paragraph is indebted to Chan.

32. Chan, *The Discourse of Foxes and Ghosts*, p. 246.

willpower? What is the basis of enchantment by foxes, vixens' power or male desire? Both Ji's voice within the story and the voice outside answer that a man is trapped by his own desire, not by a fox. This story can be read alongside He's story of the Juren Ding, which answers the same question about the male will. But Ji's success is much less ambiguous than Ding's; he remains in control the entire time, in contrast with Ding's arousal and violence. This vixen has nothing more to say, whereas Ding's vixen, although unsuccessful, got the last laugh. The story of consummation and rejection is less sexual than the story of thwarted seduction.

Young Ji's language, addressing the fox, delineates the complicated boundaries of species and gender: even though he knows she is a fox, "to get a woman like you is wonderful in its own right." A fox is not human, *fei ren* 非人, but she can be a woman *nü*, 女 (vixens are referred to with words for female animals only when they remain in animal form). In his argument, a vixen is both like and unlike a woman: like in that hers is the passive role in a sexual relationship, but unlike a woman she cannot claim the status of victim, either for love or virtue.[33]

The jocular tone with which Nie opens the story suggests that this man may, at whatever lighthearted level, be seen as reflecting on his distant kinsman, Ji Yun. To pursue a relationship with a fox spirit as a detached scientific investigation is in some way a parody of Ji Yun's own rational attitude toward the strange.

Fa Nanye 法南埜[34] also told a story, "In my village there were several evil young men. They heard that there were foxes in a certain family's ruined tomb who could change their shapes and seduce people. At night they took a net, blocked the mouth of the burrow, and actually captured two vixens. To prevent them from transforming or playing tricks, the men quickly stabbed their legs with an awl and strung a rope through them to tie them up. They threatened them, wielding knives, 'Since you can change your forms to become human, serve wine for us, and you will buy your lives. If

33. Cf. the account of Qing rape law, according to which forced sexual intercourse with an unchaste woman was not punished with the full penalty for rape, or even not considered rape at all, in Sommer, *Sex, Law, and Society in Late Imperial China*, pp. 73–75.

34. All the information about him is from *YWCT*. He is from Jiaozhou 膠州.

not, we will butcher you immediately.' The foxes barked and hopped as if they did not understand. The evil young men were enraged and stabbed one of them to death. The other then spoke in human language, 'I have no clothes or shoes. If I assume human form, how will that look?' Again they pressed the knife to her neck. She turned into a fine woman, stark naked. The mob was delighted and took turns dishonoring her without restraint. After that, they embraced her and forced her to pour wine for them but never let the ropes leave their hands. With sweet and tender words, the vixen begged them to untie her. The instant they loosened their grasp, she vanished.

"Heading home, they already saw the glow of fire in the distance before they reached the gate. Many homes had been burned to ashes, and a daughter of the man who had killed the fox had been incinerated. They knew it was the foxes' revenge. When foxes don't disturb men, but men disturb foxes, doing so many wrongs, this revenge is fitting."[35]

The correspondences with the former story are powerful enough to suggest this is a direct response, an exploration of similar issues with a reversal of sympathy and a transformation of tone. In He's series, the alternation was between decorum and obscenity; here, it is instead between human self-control and its failure. This is a contrasting case of men deliberately pursuing a fox. Such deliberate pursuit is a by-product of the late fox tradition: earlier, foxes had been an unexpected mischance that happened to men who wanted women; now, foxes themselves can be the object of desire. A wide range of men, from an articulate, elite young man like Ji to the nameless local toughs in a village, were familiar with the sexual promise of the fox tradition.

This story can be read as a vivid illustration of men's sexual power and sexual culpability, which were expounded in the previous story. Yes, men have the power to force women; but this story seems to contend that, despite her species and dubious moral status, a fox can be raped.[36] At the same time, the story investigates the power and vulnerability of the fox. In this case, that vulnerability is shown in two layers, in the body of the fox and in the naked body of the

35. *YWCT,* 12, story 95.629. Keenan, *Shadows in a Chinese Landscape*, pp. 89–90.

36. In Qing legal terms, this might not be considered rape because she gave in to violence rather than struggling continually. See Sommer, *Sex, Law, and Society in Late Imperial China*, pp. 73–75.

woman. The fox is more vulnerable than human women because she can be trapped as a beast. Since clothing seldom presents a problem when a fox assumes human form, the vixen's nudity here is dictated by the need to demonstrate her degradation, rather than received lore.[37] In contrast with the previous story in which the human man dominates language, the vixen protests her nakedness in a direct quotation. The fox is vulnerable in physical particularity but regains power as an unseen force setting fires. The equation of karmic retribution pays for female death with female death, rather than striking the molester directly. In contrast with He's stories, sexual violence here is the crime rather than the punishment. The final comment agrees with the previous story's judgment that men are responsible for the harm that accrues to them in relationships with foxes.

Tian Baiyan 田白岩 told this story, "A certain man's young and lovely second wife was seduced by a fox. Interrogation and punishment had no effect [in driving it out].

"Later, a Daoist of impeccable conduct summoned spirits to bind the fox and bring it before the altar. He commanded the fox to confess. Everyone heard the fox say, 'I am from Henan. Once I happened to hit my wife, and she secretly fled here and had an affair with this man. I hated him in my very bones and did this as revenge.' The man remembered that when he was young, this had actually happened, but it had been more than ten years ago.

"The Daoist said, 'If resentment is deep, naturally it is fitting to take revenge, but why did you delay until now? Is it not the case that you found out about this event and are taking it as an excuse?'

"The fox said, 'His former wife was a chaste woman. Fearing heaven's punishment, I dared not approach her. This woman is fickle and loose, so I could seduce her. Since the gods and ghosts do not consider karmic retribution a crime, why do you rebuke me for it?'

"The Daoist thought silently for a long while, then asked, 'For how many days was he with your wife?'

"The fox replied, 'More than a year.'

"'And for how many days were you with his wife?'

"'More than three years.'

37. In contrast, when a fox reverts from human shape to her true form, there are sometimes descriptions of the clothing left behind, most influentially in "Renshi zhuan."

"The Daoist said angrily, "Since your revenge was excessive, the fault again lies with you. If you don't leave, I'll report you to the Bureau of Thunder.' The fox admitted its crime and left."

Qingyuan (the father of Song Mengquan) said, "From this one can see that demons and monsters know all righteous or wicked thoughts, and that ghosts and gods cannot overcome the principles of retribution."[38]

In response to the conflagration that ends the previous story, this story continues the topic of the regulation of fox revenge, merging it with sexuality. A story of karmic revenge is contained within a story of exorcism. As in the story of the humiliated medium, a woman's relationship with a fox provides an occasion for a drama of exorcism rather than a narrative about the relationship itself. Once again, the victim's voice is inaudible, as her husband hires the exorcist, and the exorcist and the fox converse.

Exorcism of a possessed victim provides a precise framing structure: an illness that has been resistant to both explanation and control when viewed from the outside is made to speak intelligibly in the context of ritual practice. Explanation is the first crucial step in expulsion. In Ji's stories the substance of the exorcism becomes an argument. If we interpret spirit possession as the weapon of the weak, we could imagine exorcism not as an absolute expulsion, but as a negotiation over the terms under which the spirit would leave.[39] Here the woman gets the worst of the argument: not only is the proposed equivalence between her husband's sexual history and her own rejected, but her reputation is tarnished.

The contrast with He's account of failed exorcism and the differing treatments of a male practitioner "of impeccable conduct" who relies on moral reasoning and a boastful female medium who depends on the theatrical trappings of ritual are instructive. He Bang'e's physical confrontation and his resort to a joke rather than arguments reveals the differences between his interests and Ji Yun's.

The story has two points: first, the idea of human moral responsibility for sexual relationships with foxes is applied to human women but in different terms. Rather than describing a woman who

38. *YWCT,* 12.630, story 96; Keenan, *Shadows in a Chinese Landscape,* p. 90.
39. See Lewis, *Ecstatic Religion.*

remained unmoved in the face of the blandishments of the fox, the story depicts a male fox intimidated by the prospect of heavenly revenge if he approaches a chaste woman. The conclusion, that women seduced by foxes are probably wanton by nature, is similar to the judgment of men, but emphasis on will is lacking.

Second, the limitations on fox revenge are spelled out in precise equivalencies. The interaction between Daoist and fox, as well as the final comment, reveals the place of foxes in a moral cosmos: they enforce moral order and are aware of human moral violations, but at the same time they are restrained (if belatedly) by justice. Revenge is controlled in two ways, by human virtue and by the precise accounting of the moral balance sheet.

Song Qingyuan 宋清遠 also told a story, "There was a man named Zhu who had a maid of crude quality. As she grew older, she gradually grew more quick-witted, and her eyes and glance grew more fetching, and so he took her as his concubine. She was astute, managing the household in perfect order. No one in the household dared cheat her of even the slightest amount of rice or salt; if anyone did, she would surely expose it. She was also good at saving. Whatever she bought was bound to fetch a higher price the following year. Zhu, as he grew gradually more prosperous on her account, favored her exclusively.

"One day she suddenly said to him, 'Do you know who I am?'

"Zhu laughed, 'Are you crazy?' He playfully brought up her childhood name, saying, 'Are you not she?'

"She said, 'I am not. She ran away long ago and is now married to such-and-such a person in such-and-such a place; the son she bore is already seven or eight years old. I am actually a vixen. Nine lives ago you were a great merchant, and I was your accountant. You treated me well, but I embezzled more than 3,000 coins of your money. The infernal courts condemned me to fall to a fox's body. After refining my form for several hundred years, fortunately I attained the Way, but bearing this karmic debt, I could not become a transcendent. Therefore when this maid ran away I took on her appearance in order to serve you. I calculate the amount I have gained in these more than ten years is enough to make up for what I took. Now I am going to shed my corpse. After I have gone, my fox form must be revealed. You can make a certain servant bury me. When he buries me, he will butcher my corpse to take my skin. Do not blame him. Once, four lives ago, when he died of hunger, I had not yet achieved the way, and I gnawed his corpse. When I hear him tearing me asunder, there will be hope that this wrong will be atoned.'

"Suddenly she turned into a fox and fell to the floor. A beautiful woman a few inches tall emerged from the top of the fox's head and slowly departed. Her face was that of someone else. Zhu could not stand it and buried the corpse himself. In the end the servant secretly dug it up and cut off and sold the pelt. Zhu knew this was destiny and could only sigh."[40]

Following the discussion of karmic punishment, this story turns to karmic reward. The structure is basically similar to the previous story: a brief introduction of the situation is followed by a lengthy explanation, which provides the fox with means of exit.

A vixen enters a man's household by the same path as other women of dubious origins, as a serving maid who is promoted to the status of concubine. How common might the apparent miraculous transformation of a crude, lower-class girl into a clever and charming beauty as she matured in her master's household have been, even for human women? The human woman's escape and the vixen's substitution underline the upper-class man's uncertainty facing this class of females. They do his work, share his bed, and perhaps even bear his children, but does he ever really know who they are? The previous story also, in a different way, reveals the previously undisclosed sexual susceptibilities of a wife.

The vixen as a sexual fantasy is almost as marginal to this story as it was in the case of the Red Girl. Contrary to her origins as either maid or vixen, this woman plays the part of a primary wife, an astute household manager, with the less practical aspect of the relationship repressed. The karmic explanation further supplants desire with money.

In this story the two possible trajectories for foxes, self-improvement and the workings of karma are woven together. These two trajectories bind foxes to us in different ways. The self-improvement trajectory has foxes begin below us, approach us asymptotically, and eventually transcend us. The karmic entanglements link foxes to human stories, as for this fox, who must make recompense for her wrongs both as a man and as a beast. Her explanation here entangles both the past and the future and different classes in the household. The relationship

40. *YWCT*, 12.631, story 97; Keenan, *Shadows in a Chinese Landscape*, pp. 90–91.

with the master is couched in monetary terms, with the servant in terms of dead flesh.

Karmic explanation and transcendence provide a double justification for the vixen's exit. Her controlled and legitimized departure stands in stark contrast to her double's truancy. In later chapters I will discuss this feature of the fox story, as vixens are allowed to exit domesticity in ways that would be impossible for human women.

Like karmic explanation, the body of the fox is a means of exit from the narrative. In "Miss Ren's Story," the clothing cast off by a vixen reverting to her fox form is compared to a cicada's molted shell, but here that relationship has been reversed, revealing a tiny core of a woman in a fox shell. There are multiple layers of deception and identity here: the semblance of the maid conceals the corpse of a beast concealing this soul; and, on the karmic level, an embezzling male accountant becomes a female beast, who rises to become first a sentient fox spirit and then a transcendent. The contradiction between a past in which the vixen had identities of both sexes and this female achiever of immortality reveals the different needs of the two different trajectories, karmic debt and Daoist transcendence. In one gender identity is mutable but in the other it is essential. The fox body remains behind to repay the last debt; it becomes a beast and a commodity.

CONCLUSIONS: FOX PRACTICE

What knowledge of and interest in foxes do these two sets of stories reveal as a whole? What are the accepted assumptions, and what the innovations and tensions? Ji and He reveal distinct treatments of common interests and shared lore. The themes of most of the following chapters are touched on in these two nights of stories.

The stylistic differences between the two reveal different concepts of the classical tale. He's stories are several times the length of Ji's, primarily because he is interested in plot details, especially the sensual detail of a fox's charms or tricks, entertainment and banter. Ji's stories have a dialogic rather than a descriptive core.

The identity "fox" is highly independent of the creature recognized by zoology. We learn from these stories that the physical body of the fox is optional in a fox narrative, which makes its presence, when it does appear, all the more significant. It often appears at a point of vulnerability, transition, or closure.

Foxes intersect with human lives in multiple places and along multiple vectors, whether through possession, sexual advances, haunting, or tenancy. They can be, as in the Tang, encountered on the roads at night or in old tombs at the outskirts of the city; they can also dwell in homes, schools, or the city walls. These intrusions, whatever form they take, reveal the gender and class structures of a human household. I discuss fox haunting and intrusion into human homes in the following chapter.

For both authors, the most interesting problems, and the ones that demand containment, are desire and retribution. We learn that foxes can possess women sexually, and men resist affairs with them only with difficulty. Yet sometimes they thwart men's sexual expectations. Neither author is particularly interested in sexual or romantic consummation, although it is understated for the opposed purposes of control and arousal. The issues of vulpine sexuality and the fox romance are discussed in Chapters 5 and 6, respectively.

The fox's righteous vengeance is swift and violent, and its repayment of debts prolonged and elaborate. For Ji the most dramatic violence comes from human sources, but He is interested in shocking fox violence. For Ji Yun relations between human and fox are resolved by logical argument; in He Bang'e the confrontation is more physical. The possibility of wish fulfillment by a fox deliverer is both treasured and controlled: He restricts it to the pleasures of fruit out of season, wine on demand, and a healthy old age. For Ji, the vixen's activities as the perfect wife have a clear monetary limit. For both authors karmic justice is not only a structuring device but also a means of exit from both intimacy and the narrative. The form this karmic structure often takes in the narrative is foreknowledge; foxes seemingly manage their own departure.

Chapter 7 examines the ways in which fox stories are made to provide meaning. As Chan has pointed out, both authors are interested in moral interpretation of the stories and application of their implications to the human world.[41] The differing structure, of

41. Chan, *The Discourse of Foxes and Ghosts*, pp. 220–24.

commentary set apart in He's work as "so and so says" and comments either in Ji Yun's anonymous voice or in the voice of participants of the night of storytelling, creates a different relationship between tale and meaning. Ji's commentary is closer in form to the arguments in the body of the stories, whereas there is more of a generic disjunction between He's stories and his comments. Ji would surely have found a contradiction between the purported message of He's commentary and the stories themselves.

Ji and He's Theories on Foxes

Ji and He's theoretical statements on the nature and behavior of fox spirits in general, as opposed to narratives about individual fox spirits, give rise to such questions as, When addressing an audience familiar with fox tales, what needed to be said? How do these statements supplement the stories?

He Bang'e placed his theoretical statement before "Five Miscellaneous Records" as a general introduction to the topic.

There is more than one kind of fox[42]: the varieties include grass foxes, sand foxes, black foxes, fire foxes, white foxes, gray foxes, and snow foxes.[43] Some say that when the yelping kind are old, they become monsters. They wear a dry skull on their heads, clothe themselves with oak leaves, and assume a human guise. These creatures do harm in countless ways. People set fire to the mountains and dig up their burrows, grasping arrows and driving their hounds, thinking if fox kind is eradicated, monstrosity will cease.

They do not know that although foxes can become monsters, they do not necessarily do so. Once in a while one becomes a monster, but they do not all become monsters. Moreover, the monsters among foxes are limited in number, and the monsters among all other creatures are inexhaustible. Hairless creatures, those with scales, and those in shells, flowers, trees, the idols in temples, and the gold in the storehouse—all can become monsters. When creatures commit monstrosities, they do so by night; but humans commit monstrosities by day. All those who grovel and flatter, all those who assume the majesty of tigers and perch on the city walls to make trouble

42. Some textual variants open with the summarizing comment: 狐靈物也。亦妖物也 "The fox is an enchanted creature, and also a monstrous one," followed by "I have heard . . . ." See, e.g., the 1884 Hongbaozhai 鴻寶齋 edition.

43. The 1789 edition has 雲狐, "cloud foxes."

> [those who take advantage of their associations with powerful people or their position to misuse their power],[44] young women with dark brows and red skirts, or young men with crimson clothes and white faces, are monsters without exception. Why should one exterminate only the fox tribe? The *Zuo zhuan* says, "Monsters arise from humanity" (*yao you ren xing* 妖由人興). When human affairs are exhausted, monsters will also cease. How could foxes be to blame?
>
> Some say that those who get old and become monsters are called *pi* 狴 foxes or "spirit" foxes. They look like cats and are black. There are a lot of them in the north. They are probably another variety.[45]

He opened with a typological introduction such as might have appeared in an encyclopedia. He begins, apparently, with the biological rather than the cultural fox. Yet in the second sentence he immediately shifts to the fox as monster. The lore of the fox wearing a skull to assume human guise, using leaves to conjure illusory clothing, is more current in this period in expository introductions to the fox than in individual narratives.[46] Storytellers are no longer particularly interested in how foxes transform; transformation is taken for granted and often occurs offstage, as we have seen in Ji and He's stories. As transformation becomes a vulpine birthright, the physical apparatus of the skull and leaves is discarded as awkward. In the same way, the violent eradication campaigns against which he protested seem a rhetorical straw man rather than an actual or narrative practice. Some Tang stories ended with the destruction of fox burrows, but in Qing stories those victorious over foxes usually ignore rather than annihilate them. There are two explanations for He's use of images in his introduction that he does not use in his narratives. First, in this kind of formal statement, older textual sources tend to

---

44. The first part of this phrase is an allusion to the story of the fox who "borrowed the tiger's might" 狐假虎威 and tricked the tiger into believing that the animals fleeing before the two of them were fleeing the fox, not the tiger; see "Jingxuan Wang wen qunchen" 荆宣王問群臣, Chu ce 1, in Liu Xiang, *Zhan guo ce*, 2:14.482. The second alludes to the phrase 城狐社鼠, "the foxes in the walls and the mice in the altar," which refers to those who take advantage of their position to make trouble.

45. *YTSL*, 4.102.

46. One of the latest stories to make prominent use of this piece of lore is "Hu meiniang zhuan" 胡美娘傳, in Li Changqi, *Jiandeng yuhua*, 7.238. See also the discussion in the next chapter of Qian Xiyan, *Kuai yuan zhiyi*, 14.8a.

be preferred to more recent oral or written sources. Second, he needed to heighten the sense of a violent opposition between foxes and men to frame his apology.

This introduction to biology and lore then turns to a defense of the fox. Although mass eradications of foxes were probably a rhetorical exaggeration, He still seemed compelled to reply to a categorical association of foxes and monstrosity. Reading *zhiguai*, one could be forgiven for assuming that absolutely all foxes became monsters, but He insisted that, despite appearances, not all foxes are monsters, and not all monsters are foxes. Examples of each of the creatures on his list can be found in *zhiguai*. His apology works at two levels: after placing foxes among other creatures, He, in a very common move, reverses monstrosity back onto humanity, using language linked with the fox's traditional deceptions. The formula "monsters arise from humanity" was a mantra in this period and meant different things in different contexts; here it shifts the moral blame to humanity. He's introduction makes the same rhetorical move as the commentary to the tales and is generically closer to the commentary than to the narratives themselves. With this conclusion, the apology for the fox seems less an expression of sympathy for a wronged monster than a means of exposing the greater monstrosity of man.

The shift back to taxonomy after the apology is abrupt. In a piece of lore that is not widely shared, monstrosity is reduced to species variation. The shift from zoological catalog to apology and back may seem jarring, but it is typical of the mixed nature of the fox.

There is more of a disjunction between He's theoretical statement and his stories than one finds in Ji. Two of He's examples, the vixens involved in castration and the male foxes who rape the medium, are trouble-making monsters in the fullest sense, and attempts to assign human moral responsibility to their acts are strained. The acts of sexual violence can be justified as repayment for a maid's excessive cursing and her father's sexual indulgence or for a medium's boasting, but the initial haunting and possession are never justified. The decorous stories, on the other hand, support the forgiving tone of the introduction. The relationship of introduction to the stories is like that between the stories and the commentary: the paratext provides a distinct way of thinking about the fox, with an aesthetic and rhetorical pleasure of its own independent of the stories.

Ji's statement on foxes takes the form not of an introduction to a story but a story in its own right. In the collection he completed about a year earlier than the one that records the night of fox stories, Ji made the most systematic and prolonged statement in Chinese literary history on the nature and career of foxes. To repeat the passage that serves as epigraph for the Introduction to this book:

> Humans and beasts *Wu* 物 are different species, but foxes are between humans and beasts. The dead and the living walk different roads, but foxes are between the dead and the living. Transcendents and monsters travel different paths, but foxes are between transcendents and monsters. Therefore one could say to meet a fox is strange; one could also say it is ordinary.

Here Ji began a specific anecdote with a theoretical introduction, as He had introduced his group of stories. The division of the universe into different realms is one of the central assumptions of *zhiguai*. These divisions are often evoked in bodies of stories, both by human and inhuman beings, either as a warning to keep one's distance or a simple statement of fact.[47] Foxes violate each of these divisions, touching every category in the universe but belonging fully to none. This passage evokes the definitions found in folklore studies of Trickster figures, who establish the boundaries between categories by violating them.[48] Other authors in traditional China had observed the contradictions, but none had stated them so thoroughly or made the final leap: foxes are ubiquitous enough to fall out of even the one category to which they surely belong, the strange. As such, they are the principal challenge to a man who feels compelled to order the strange. Foxes both embody Ji Yun's system perfectly and stand poised on every pivot of uncertainty.[49]

Although a generic trickster is a critically useful concept, it should not distract attention from the precise substance of the categories a

---

47. For example, the division between the quick and the dead is evoked in *Soushen ji* 15, story 359; and 16, story 394.

48. Hyde, *Trickster Made this World*, pp. 7–8.

49. See Chan's discussion and translation of this opening passage, *The Discourse of Foxes and Ghosts*, p. 144.

fox strays between. Each of the categories in this statement is worthy of its own introduction. *Wu* can refer to the myriad things, inanimate and animate, of this world, but it can also refer specifically to monsters.[50] Humans are distinguished from all the myriad things by being the most *ling* 靈 "sentient" or "conscious," but this is often seen as a difference of degree rather than of kind. Foxes both are, and are not, animals, for they have this capacity for becoming, as He pointed out, *ling*, and in Ji's time seemed to spend more time in human form and human society than otherwise. He Bang'e also contrasted foxes, somewhat ambivalently, with all other creatures.

Foxes were associated with the dead by proximity—they, too, dwelled in tombs—and by categorical association—the two principal groups of non-humans, foxes and ghosts, shared traits. Relative to humans' world of *yang* and light, foxes were, like ghosts, *yin* and dark, yet they were still living beings.

The distinction between *xian* 仙 and *yao* 妖 is different from the other two divisions, because instead of balancing the human against something else, it contrasts two non-human categories. *Xian* and *yao* are both transgressive categories and imply motion between different categories of being. *Xian* are Daoist transcendents or immortals. *Yao* in its earliest usages referred to ill omens, anomalies of the animal kingdom and human society as opposed to natural disasters, *zai* 災. After the Qin, it began to refer to anomalous animals, especially those who could assume human forms.[51] Ji's word "path" tu 途 is even more suggestive: *xian* and *yao* are two different means of advancement, one approved and one forbidden. As we will see in Ji's discussion, foxes are between the two in the sense that they can choose either of the two paths. Those who flatter foxes call them *xian*, and those who criticize them call them *yao*. (The fox's split identity between *xian* and *yao* is discussed further in Chapter 7.)

Following these general statements, Ji traced the textual history of foxes. In his reconstruction, there is no evidence of them before the Han, but by the Han they had attained the ability to assume human form. He supported his arguments with references to a *Shi ji* story in

---

50. *Hanyu dacidian (HYDCD)*, vol. 6, 物 (s.v.), definition 12, p. 249.

51. For a brief discussion of the history of these terms, see the introduction to Li Jianguo's *Tangqian zhiguai xiaoshuo shi*, pp. 12–13.

which a fox is already seen as a creature of ill omen, and a story in *Xijing zaji* 西京雜記 (Miscellaneous records of the western capital) in which a man dreams that a fox he has killed appears to him in human form.[52] By the Tang, they had become overwhelmingly common, and Ji cited as proof the reference to fox worship discussed in the previous chapter and the large numbers of fox stories in *Taiping guangji*. His textual references are fairly standard. Ji's chronological treatment of the textual evidence followed the standard practice of an argumentative essay.[53] The conclusion of this chronology with *Taiping guangji* reflects a common conservative assessment of the classical tale tradition.

Then Ji's reasoning takes a more startling turn, "The records in all the various books are contradictory. The story that Liu Shitui[54] told explains their origins and evolution in the most detail." Ji himself admits the incoherence of the image of the fox in the written tradition and offers a tale from a contemporary as the most convincing account. Ji uses *kaozheng*-like procedure to define the fox but reverses its standards by giving contemporary oral material priority over the written tradition.[55] The conviction that his generation can resolve any inherited contradictions is, however, characteristic of the *kaozheng* scholar's ambitions. Within the anecdote Liu's motives are much the same as Ji's; he knows someone who has a fox friend, and he calls on the fox in the hope that the fox will explain some confusing points about foxes in *xiaoshuo*. This situation—one man acquainted with a fox pressured by his acquaintances to let them consult with the fox—is related to the popular religious practice of people who could commune with fox spirits holding séances at their homes. Since the fox is an old man who resembles a Daoist, he has

52. *Shi ji*, "Chenshi shijia," 6:48.1950. *Xijing zaji* collects anecdotes of the Western Han. Its authorship is disputed; it probably dates from circa A.D. 500. Actually, even animals who otherwise cannot assume human form often appear in human form to communicate with humans in dreams.

53. On the use of evidence in arguments about the existence or non-existence of ghosts, see Chan, *The Discourse of Foxes and Ghosts*, pp. 93–94.

54. Liu Guoshi 劉果實, *zi* 師退; *jinshi* in 1679.

55. On the comparison between Ji's approach to the strange and *kaozheng*, see Chan, *The Discourse of Foxes and Ghosts*, pp. 113–29.

the authority granted to a patriarch, in a form associated with esoteric wisdom. Liu opens politely:

"The accounts of human beings' contact with your kind vary, and there are things in them that are not clear to me. I have heard that you are frank and honest and do not conceal your identity;[56] therefore I beg you to clear up my misunderstandings."[57]

The fox laughed, "When heaven gave birth to the myriad things, it commanded that each should have its name. That foxes are named 'foxes' is just like the fact that men are named 'men'; to call a fox a 'fox' is just like calling a man a 'man.' Why should I keep any secrets? My kind are not all alike in goodness or wickedness, just as among men there are distinctions between the noble and the mean. If men do not refuse to discuss the wickedness of men, why should a fox conceal the evils of foxes? I will speak without reserve."

Liu asked, "Are there divisions *bie* 別 among foxes?"

The fox replied, "All foxes can pursue the way, but the most sentient ones are called *pi*.[58] This is like the fact there are few peasants who read books, but many Confucians who do."

Liu asked, "Are *pi* foxes born sentient?"

The fox replied, "This depends on their kind. Foxes born to parents who have not achieved the Way are ordinary foxes, but those born to parents who have achieved the Way can transform themselves."

Here Ji Yun rationalized the confounding diversity of the fox tradition by dividing foxes into categories. Other authors like Pu Songling presented the variety unapologetically, simply concluding that there are many kinds of foxes, but Ji wished to forge a unified fox tradition that could contain a wide variety of stories. Although in different stories he may have chosen to emphasize

---

56. Note the assumption that a fox will be ashamed of its identity. This may also be related to the taboos of fox worship, which called foxes *xian* and avoided the word "fox"; see Li Shouju, *Huxian xinyang yu huli jing gushi*, pp. 82–85.

57. The word used for misunderstanding is *mei* 媚, with all of its implications of fox enchantment and seduction.

58. Besides He and Ji, one of the few references to *pi* as a variety of foxes most capable of change is "Maoguai" 貓怪 in Yu Rukang, *Kuaixin xingshui lu*, 1.9b. In general, a *pi* was considered another wild beast in the category of 狸, sometimes interchangeable with 貔. See *Hanyu dacidian*, vol. 5, p. 25.

different distinctions among foxes, all his stories fit somewhere in the total system he presented here.

This is a systematic attempt to explain the strange in ordinary terms. From the polite opening, which alludes to the popular avoidance of calling foxes by their name lest they be offended, this fox explains his world entirely in terms of the human world, debunking any mystery. This sort of comparison is a common mode for Ji Yun. Chan argues that such comparisons should be taken not as allegories on humanity but as sober statements of fact, based on the understanding that different sentient species were governed by the same principles.[59] Because he was interested in norms rather than marvels, Ji did not resort to a zoological introduction to the species or a "technical" treatise on the ages at which foxes can attain human capabilities and their methods of transformation and instead gave an introduction to a complex fox society. He Bang'e's statement on transformation used outdated lore, with one, fixed technical practice for transformation, but Ji's gives a sense of contemporary ideas, a whole project of self-improvement rather than a single act of becoming *yao*.

Individual difference is at the center of this argument: foxes have the same moral and social range as human beings. Yet although there is the potential for individual variation, most differences can be explained in class terms. Although the word, *bie* 別, is the same word that He Bang'e used for his list of foxes, instead of breeds of animals, Ji's distinctions among foxes are based on the same standards he would use to make distinctions among humans: social class, which is inextricably linked to levels of education, and individual effort, which is still largely dependent on inherited family tradition. In this particular anecdote, studying for humans is the equivalent of Daoist self-cultivation for foxes, but there are other anecdotes in which foxes literally study the same books as humans in order to advance. Self-cultivation has become the fox's defining trait, and individual fox stories are placed somewhere along the trajectory of self-improvement.

59. Chan, *The Discourse of Foxes and Ghosts*, p. 197.

Liu said, "If they have achieved the Way, they should be able to retain the appearance of youth, but in fiction there are accounts of old fox men and women. Why?"

The fox replied, "'To achieve the Way' means to achieve the human way; therefore in eating and drinking, sex and marriage, birth and aging, sickness and death, they are like humans."

The foxes people encounter, as we have seen in the stories summarized above, tend to be either isolated young women or older men, or a patriarchal family with particular emphasis on the patriarch and the young women, in a distorted reflection of the human family structure. Each of the ages and sexes of foxes have its own narrative roles: patriarchs for wisdom, young women for seduction, and young men for mischief and seduction of women. Thus there is a contradiction between foxes as transcendent beings and as members of sham human families. But why do foxes limit their potentially infinite capacity for transformation to specific gender and age roles?

The answer in this case seems more central to Ji's vision of foxes than the question that prompted it. A conventional understanding of "achieving the Way" would imply transcending human aging and frailties, but Ji transformed the concept into human ordinariness. Thereby he explained all the foxes in late imperial narratives who not only age like men but seem to live like humans in their daily life, even when the humans are not looking. Not only are foxes made a comparable species, with comparable social organization, but they almost become human. The idea of human form as a stepping-stone in foxes' pursuit of immortality is as old as the *Xuanzhong ji* passage describing their chronological advance, but here an internal as well as external approximation of the human is possible. Many scholars have noted an increasing humanization of foxes throughout history;[60] Ji's foxes who have achieved the human way are a culmination of this development. As was typical for him, Ji rationally explained a tendency other writers simply took for granted.

However, even for the most successful foxes, the barrier between the species cannot be entirely erased. Even Ji's most elevated foxes introduce themselves not as men who were once foxes but as foxes

60. For example, Gu Meigao, "Tan hu," p. 263.

who have shed their form. But this does not devalue humanity; rather, the fox's mobility underlines its centrality.

The fox continued: "Those who ascend to immortality are another matter, just as among thousands of people, there will be one or two who seek political office. Those who refine their forms and control their breath are like men studying in order to make a name for themselves. Those who seduce people to drain their energy are like men taking devious shortcuts in order to pass the exams. To travel to the fairy islands and ascend to heavenly office is possible only for those who refine their shapes and control their breath; if the ones who seduce and drain energy harm a lot of people, they will always violate heaven's laws."

Liu asked, "Who controls their laws and rewards and punishments?"

He replied, "Minor punishments and rewards are in the power of fox elders, whereas major punishments are the responsibility of the ghosts and gods of the earth. If there were no punishments, foxes able to come and go invisibly, to enter and exit without a trace, would be capable of anything."

Liu asked, "Since seduction and vampirism is not the rightful path, why is it not specifically forbidden? Why wait for foxes to harm people before they are punished?"

The fox replied, "This is like men who skillfully cheat others out of their wealth, making their victims happy to help them. Royal law does not forbid this. If it comes to the point of seizing property and killing people, they will be controlled. *Liexian zhuan* records the story of the old wine-selling woman; when did she ever violate the laws of the underworld?"[61]

After the claims of human ordinariness, the fox goes on to incorporate the exceptional fox into his system. Predictably enough, in a scheme in which achievement of the Way is equivalent to literacy, transcendence and success in the examinations are equated. Besides social class, Ji's other principal standard for dividing foxes is the legitimacy of their methods of advancement. In Ji's stories we saw one vixen who took the moral path, and another, the vixen who seduced the dispassionate scholar Ji, who apparently opted for the route of

---

61. "Nü wan" 女丸, in Liu Xiang, *Liexian zhuan*, xia, relates the story of a female wine vendor who is given a scroll by an immortal in payment for wine. The scroll reveals the secrets of sexual alchemy; she uses these techniques to remain young for decades. When the immortal passes by again, she sets off in pursuit of him. Apparently she either did the young men she seduced no harm, or Ji considered it their own fault, thus something of no concern to the infernal courts.

parasitism. Fox progress has become a deliberate act, rather than a trait accruing naturally with age. It is a free choice, like humans' moral choices, but the comparison of immortality to officialdom implies the chances of success are open to very few and are inseparable from questions of class. The contemporary situation of a burgeoning number of examination candidates competing for a constant number of positions is clearly captured in the comparison. The mirror held up to the human world is telling: the society drawn here consists of a tiny elite of transcendent foxes (the officials); a larger group of foxes living out their lives in human form and aspiring to the elite (the literati); and ordinary, four-footed foxes burrowing in the ground and eating poultry (the peasants). The great difference between vulpine and human society is that advancement, by means fair or foul, is open to foxes of both sexes.

If we place Ji's foxes in the bureaucratic hierarchy of the heavens, they are the students struggling for a place in that firmament, with a real chance of achieving it. Not only are foxes between categories, but they are mobile. It is precisely this that made them more human in Ji's eyes; for human beings, or at least for the literati, life was also a continuous process of education, self-refinement, and longed-for political advancement. For Ji, the foxes who appear in stories were the counterparts of his own class.

In the fox world, the possibility of immoral success is eliminated; one doubts that Ji could have felt so confident of the human world. Ji controlled the strange by limiting the harmful effects of foxes with laws and punishments, at the hands, initially, of responsible fox elders. Age is another standard by which Ji frequently divided foxes; mischief is attributed to the children, whom the stern fox patriarch reprimands and eventually gets under control.[62] Outside of Ji's work, a recurring type of story portrays a fox patriarch agreeing to punish his own kind for wrongs against humans with a beating or sometimes even an execution.[63] In these stories the division is clear; the fox

62. See, e.g., *YWCT*, 13.700–701, story 162.

63. I discuss this type in the following chapter. Examples include "Hu daoxue" 狐道學, in Yuan Mei, *Zi bu yu*, 22.447; "Zhangde shuhu" 彰德署狐, in Tang Yongzhong, *Yijiong baibian*, 32: 8.17b; and "Jiu wu hu" 僦屋狐, in Dong Han, *Zhuanxiang zhuibi*, xia, 39b.

patriarch remains in human form, and the one punished is revealed as a fox.

Ji raised the terrifying possibility of omnipotent foxes, but promptly dismissed it by placing foxes under heavenly jurisdiction. On the other hand, he did not rule out these dangers altogether. By comparing foxes to those who cheat people with the victim's own consent, as he did consistently in his tales, he displaced the horrors of vampirism from the foxes to the human world. Since both species have free will, vampirism requires moral failure on both sides, which has consequences for both. If no human is complicit in a fox's crimes, a higher moral law will intervene. In another anecdote, the comparison with human law also suggests that violations are possible; no matter how stringent the law, there are still those criminals who risk punishment.[64] With the issue of parasitism, the gender of the vulpine subject has shifted, as the comparison to *Liexian zhuan* makes clear.

Liu asked, "I have heard of foxes bearing humans' children, but I have never heard of humans bearing foxes' children. Why?"

The fox smiled slightly, "This is not worth discussing. Probably they take something and do not give anything."

Liu asked, "If the Weaving Maid gives her loom-weight to another, shouldn't she fear the jealousy of the Cowherd?" [i.e.,Won't fox husbands be jealous if their wives take other lovers?]

The fox smiled again, "You speak too freely and really don't know the truth of the matter. Most girls can chose their own mates, as in the case of Jiji and Zengzi.[65] A wife who already has a mate would not dare to overstep the bounds. Sometimes someone will happen to get involved in an affair and go beyond the rules of propriety. Since human feeling (*renqing* 人情) and the principle of things (*wuli* 物理) are not very different, you can understand by analogy."

Now Liu turns to that aspect of fox society most clearly different from human society, the sexual role of women. Despite Liu's observation, although it is much rarer than the opposite case, there are occasional stories of human women bearing the children of their

64. *YWCT*, 2.31, story 75.

65. *Chun qiu*, 14th year of Lu xigong; Jiji chose her own husband.

fox lovers.[66] This is partially a result of the disproportionate number of vixen lovers, but the fox's answer is based on a vision of foxes as the receptive (and potentially parasitic) partner in any sexual relations, and male seed as an active principle. Although vixens make use of male semen, male foxes do not contribute their own.[67] As we have seen from the sampling of stories in this chapter, procreation is seldom central to fox stories regardless of the sex of the partners; it is the depleting aspects of sexuality that are foregrounded.

The fox defuses the question of vixens' sexual morality by dividing them into categories, unmarried vixens who can choose their own mates and married vixens who would not dare to stray. This admission of female sexual license, even when cloaked in a classical reference, is striking in a society that in all other ways mirrors the human one, but foxes are granted monogamous free choice, not wantonness. Ji tamed the sexual aspects of the fox tradition as much as possible. At this point the fox stops spelling out comparisons between vulpine and human society and insists that Liu should reason by analogy himself. In this particular context the assertion of similarity is also an evasion; Ji did not allow the reader to imagine a vastly different sexual world. Monschein points out that this elevated fox leaves the interlocutor and the reader in a state of embarrassed and unsatisfied curiosity about the more risqué details of the fox world, the topic of most intense interest to men;[68] the highly allusive language may serve as another layer of concealment. This reticence also reveals a contradiction within the systematic explanation. Purposeful wantonness is acknowledged in the context of self-improvement, a section largely depending on analogies with male humans, but denied when the subject turns specifically to vixens and a comparison to female humans. In contrast with the vixen who had an affair with Ji's clans

---

66. One rare example is "Fu duan huwei" 斧斷狐尾, in Yuan Mei *Zi bu yu*, 5.89–90.

67. There seem to be more narratives about dragon pregnancies; see, e.g., "Tui wei long" 穨尾龍, in Yu Guolin, *Jiaoxuan zhilu*, 3.21a. Cf. medical ideas about ghost pregnancies; see Furth, *A Flourishing Yin*, p. 90. This issue is further discussed in Chapter 5, including the similar European view of the inability of incubi and succubi to sire children.

68. Monschein, *Der Zauber der Fuchsfee*, p. 309.

man, who was denied claims of chastity or passion, this passage gives vixens a life-course parallel to that of human women, including both romance and virtue.

The line stating that *renqing* 人情, "human feeling," and *wuli* 物理, "the principles of things," are essentially similar, allowing reasoning by analogy, goes to the heart of Ji Yun's approach to the strange. Here he exposed the mechanics by which he understood the strange: it is not secret knowledge, and anyone with common sense can duplicate his reasoning. In Ji Yun's stories the comparison goes both ways; the human world is used to explain the strange, and the strange is used to expose the human world.[69] Elsewhere he stated more directly that the dead and the living follow different paths but share a single principle.[70] Campany notes that the conviction of shared rational principles between worlds exists as early as some Six Dynasties *zhiguai*, but the tendency becomes particularly strong in the Qing.[71]

Liu asked, "Why do foxes sometimes live in people's houses and sometimes live in the wilderness?"

The fox replied, "Those who have not yet achieved the Way have not yet left the state of animals; it is to their advantage to stay away from people, thus mountain forests are the most convenient. Those who have achieved the Way are like humans in every respect; it is to their advantage to be near people, thus cities are the most convenient. Those whose achievement of the Way is advanced can dwell in either the woods or the cities. This is like great families; their power can obtain everything, and so for them living in a remote wasteland or a great city is all the same."

The arguments about geography address another kind of variety in the fox tradition, which has been amply illustrated in the stories presented above. Ming and Qing fox stories do not support the assertion that foxes in the wilderness are less evolved than foxes in homes: some of the foxes in homes are disembodied poltergeists, with little evidence of kinship to humans. This explanation,

69. Also noted in Chan, *The Discourse of Foxes and Ghosts*, p. 196

70. *YWCT*, 2.85, story 85. This is a variation of the Neo-Confucian paradigm: "Principle is one, and its manifestations are many."

71. Campany, *Strange Writing*, pp. 342–62.

however, fits another range of variation into the master narrative of fox progress.[72]

In the fox's wide-ranging conversation with Liu, his main intent was to urge people to study the Way. He said, "My kind obtains a human body only after a couple of hundred years of toil. Since the likes of you already have human bodies, you have already achieved half the task, but your lives are so brief, rotting as quickly as grass and wood. It is very regrettable."

Throughout this passage foxes' self-improvement has been the main means both of making distinctions among foxes and of making comparisons to human beings, but in the end the fox finally turns the comparison the other way around to examine the human world. The conclusion of Ji's anecdote emphasizes that humans should pursue immortality; this seems on the surface to contradict his Confucian values, but his moral interpretation of foxes' self-refinement overcomes the possible contradiction. This kind of final assertion of human superiority and the lament that humans squander their potential is common in anecdotes about foxes' self-improvement. In the end, self-improving foxes serve as a spur to human self-improvement.

Liu had studied the Tripitaka thoroughly and tried to lead the fox into a discussion of Zen. The fox declined, saying, "The position of Buddhism is very high. But sometimes when someone has not yet attained enlightenment, he then enters the wheel of reincarnation and loses his original identity. It is better instead to pursue immortality, so that one may have more assurance of success. I have often met noble monks, but still I dare not change my opinion upon encountering different ideas."

As he was about to leave Liu said, "That we were able to meet today was indeed a great heavenly favor. Do you have some parting words of wisdom to give me?"

The fox hesitated for a long time. "Since the Xia, Shang, and Zhou, I fear men have not sought after good reputation—this is said for lower-class people. Since ancient times the sages have, however, been even tempered, without the slightest affectation. But the two Zhengs of

72. For another anecdote about foxes' choice of residence with a somewhat different argument, see *YWCT* 15.897, story 49.

Luoyang and Zhu Xi of Fujian raised their brows and stared[73] and caused a great many entanglements. Please think on this!"

Liu was deflated and at a loss. Actually, he was too haughty and sometimes exceeded the bounds of what was appropriate.[74]

The closing passage has little to do with foxes directly, but it illustrates the multiple functions of a single anecdote. The anecdote has three levels: the explication of the fox tradition; reflections on humans and their philosophical schools; and a critical comment on Liu himself. This final level reveals the function of fox stories as fables, directed at specific figures in the author's social circle. The fox uses his superior perspective, gained over his long life, to make pronouncements on the limitations of human philosophical systems in general and Liu in particular. The contrast between the true sages and the Song Neo-Confucians is a recurring theme in Ji's stories. The single frame of conversation with an otherworldly being is made to fulfill multiple uses. Despite the anecdote's active construction of ordinariness in the fox world, it is the sense of marvel at interviewing a fox that adds spice to philosophical musings and personal critique.

This interview with a fox reveals some of the areas of curiosity about foxes: their variety, their sexual liaisons with men, and their relation to a system of cosmic order. For Ji self-improvement is the key to the explanation, although he attempts to avoid some topics.

How does the discussion of foxes change when the topic shifts from "a fox" to "the fox"? Besides the obvious difference in length, He's brief apology and Ji's thorough explanation are in different modes. Ji was responding to contradictions in the stories he told, whereas He seemed to be dealing with a general concept of "fox monster." Nevertheless, both explanation and apology seek to keep foxes' potential mischief under control more firmly than do the stories. In place of individual moments of contact between human and fox, theories endeavor to connect and equate the two realms systematically, although the means of connection are different for Ji and He.

---

73. The explanation for this phrase in *Hanyu da cidian*, 6:868, does seem to refer to Zhu Xi's work.

74. *YWCT*, 10.503–4, story 229. I have also consulted the German translation in Monschein (*Der Zauber der Fuchsfee*, pp. 305–8), although I part ways with her on some passages.

Foxes were not as central a locus for theorizing about the supernatural in contexts outside *zhiguai* as were ghosts, perhaps because the questions were more practical: not whether they exist, but how they change, and what their limits are.

Foxes were plainly an attractive subject for a series of stories. If Ji and He had been asked why they talked about foxes, I imagine both would have agreed that foxes are worth talking about because of their mixed divine and monstrous nature. Both would have admitted, to varying degrees, that they spoke of them because they were entertaining. As both common and exceptional, foxes both provide a rich supply of diverting narrative and expose the principles of the universe. They are not us, but they can make and suggest judgments because of their position as outsiders.

The gap between individual narrative practice and theorizing on foxes seen here is a caution for my own efforts to theorize about foxes. My topic is further complicated by presences almost as changeable as the foxes themselves—authors and books.

{3}
Haunting and Residence

The household of Reader Dong Moyan[1] was disturbed by a fox. Shingles and bricks suddenly fell like hail. All the members of his household, one after another, ran to hide, waiting for a brief respite; only then would they come out to do work.[2]

In the spring of 1767, I took my family to Beijing. Because we had not redeemed the mortgage on our old home by Tiger Alley Bridge, we went to live temporarily in the empty house of Mr. Qian Xiangshu. It was said there was also a fox living upstairs, but the upstairs was locked up as a storehouse for miscellaneous stuff, and people didn't casually go up there. I playfully pasted a poem on the wall, saying,

"In a rush I moved my household and met you by chance;
Upstairs, downstairs, we divided this home equally.
An obsession with poetry has always been a scholar's weakness;
Please do not be vexed as I chant all night."

One day, the maids unlocked the room to get things and yelled excitedly, "How strange!" I came to look, and the dust of the attic floor was covered with paintings of lotus flowers, with tall stems and leaves, all with exquisite brushwork. Thereupon I put paper and brush on the table and pasted another poem on the wall, saying,

"Oh Transcendent, you like living in a lofty place after all,
Your talent and flair I could not match.

---

1. According to the Lu annotations of *Liaozhai*, his name was Na 訥, and he came from Pingyuan; he took third place in the exams in 1667 and was secretary of the Ministry of War.

2. *LZ*, "Jiao Ming" 焦螟, 1.79.

I've recently acquired 30 sheets of Wu paper,
You may paint lotuses on every one."

After a few days had passed, I opened the room to look, but it hadn't lifted up the brush. I told Qiu Wenda about this; he laughed, "The fox in Qian Xiangshu's house would have to be very elegant."[3]

In these two stories, an alien presence in a human household is called a "fox" although one never sees paws, sharp nose, or full red tail. Plainly, neither is meant to be the first story of a fox in someone's house that the reader encounters; that a fox can disturb a home, or dwell there, is taken for granted as each narrative gives the details of the case. In the first case, the fox is an inexplicable torment, and these few lines of description represent a commonly recurring experience, recounted frequently in *zhiguai*, happening to a named historical character. In the second, a personal experience is a means of displaying the literary refinement of the author and his acquaintances. These two examples are drawn from the collections of the most famous Qing authors of stories of the strange in general, and foxes in particular, Pu Songling and Ji Yun. For both, these were apparently atypical moments. Pu is known for his elaborate romances involving non-human women, but here we see him in territory shared with other *zhiguai* authors. Ji is known for his use of ghosts and foxes for didactic and argumentative purposes, but the message of this more wistful anecdote has more to do with personalities than morality. The two men are often depicted as diametric opposites, but here they used shared ideas about the presence of foxes in people's homes. Two of He Bang'e's stories discussed in the previous chapter, the wine-stealing foxes and the genteel family of houseguests, also take part in this conversation. Not only were these concepts shared by Ji, Pu, and He, but they also shaped both popular experience and the narration of the strange.

The two stories quoted above, as well as He Bang'e's two stories, introduce the presence of the fox in contrasting ways: in the first, the fox disturbs a place, and in the second, it dwells in one. Rather than

---

3. *YWCT*, 3.100, story 102. Qian Xiangshu 錢香樹, from Jiaxing in Zhejiang, was a poet favored by the Qianlong emperor. Qiu Wenda is Qiu Yuexiu 裘曰修 (1712–73), like Ji, a director of the *Siku* project. See Keenan, *Shadows in a Chinese Landscape*, p. 56*n*36; and *Eminent Chinese of the Qing Period*, 1:172.

being manifested as man or beast, the fox is revealed in the traces it leaves in physical objects and places. Both unstable and stable intrusions of the strange reveal the contours of human normalcy. Haunting, which throws human space into disorder and renders it strange, reveals concepts of order. Both fox haunting and fox residence reveal a geography of human space, with the most sensitive center the home itself.

As I read large numbers of fox stories with shared elements against one another throughout this book, I will refer to individual bits of information about foxes, such as "foxes disturb men by throwing tiles from the rafters," as lore. In a study of Danish legends, Timothy Tangherlini posits a symbiotic relationship between legends and lore.[4] These stories are comprehensible and palatable to the listener/reader because they draw on familiar concepts of fox behavior; at the same time they circulate lore about the fox and may contribute to changes in that body of knowledge. To treat lore independently of a story is still somewhat misleading: it exists primarily within stories, although, as we have seen, some items of lore are also deployed in explanations of the species. "Lore" is a more flexible term than "belief," because knowledge and use of lore do not presume a specific attitude toward it. After lore, a useful larger unit of comparison is a pattern of events, for example, the narrative pattern of a fox disturbing a human home and being driven out in the end. These patterns are sequences of events, based on a sense of how things tend to happen. Classical folklore studies, both the Stith-Thompson indexes and the work of Vladimir Propp, have provided inspiration for my work, but my motivation differs: I am not trying to strip away the variations of individual anecdotes to find the underlying pattern and then trace literary manifestations back to an oral or international original. Rather, the individual variation, instead of being dross to be discarded, is of as much interest to me as the recurring elements.

Pieces of lore and patterns of events have careers that span the entire range of the classical tale, from accounts of personal experience to legends to literary tales. For example, the idea that foxes throw roof tiles at people, as with poor Dong Moyan, is almost never recorded

---

4. Tangherlini, *Interpreting Legend,* p. 16.

simply by itself. It is never stated as a novelty; rather, it is presented as assumed knowledge. Some tales record it in a relatively simple account of disturbance and exorcism; some include pelting with roof tiles as one step in the development of a human relationship with a fox;[5] some tales provide a moral interpretation and tell us why someone deserved to be pelted. This range from simple to complex use of lore is not necessarily a historical progression, although the simplest tales are more common in late Ming collections than they are later. Rather, all these possibilities of use exist diachronically.

This piece of lore reveals the contours of domesticity: flying roof tiles suggest that falling tiles were a common problem, a product of human inattention; that roofs, being between the inside and the outside, are at the edge of the human sphere of control, and that crossing through courtyards, and thus being exposed to the outer side of a building where one is usually inside, is potentially perilous. Yet since the lore is deployed in different contexts, those contours are further refined by the individual case; tiles come crashing down into different contexts, with different results.

Even as I take individual stories apart to yield lore and structure, I also join them to one another to form "metanarratives." A metanarrative assembles stories and their patterns into a larger pattern, of which the actual stories are the exposed portion. For example, this chapter revolves around a metanarrative of domestication: a fox that was outdoors comes indoors and sometimes stays. Literary history, by connecting moments within different narratives, is itself a metanarrative. Metanarratives are useful analytical tools, but it must be remembered that they are constructs, valuable because they reveal the inferred parts of the story that are never explicitly described.

In many ways, fox haunting is a logical place to begin. The proverbial "thing that goes bump in the night," the inexplicable sound, the household object falling when it should not fall, moving when it should not move, seems the most basic and common experience of the strange in any society that has acquired households and possessions. As we saw in Ji's example, and as is further illustrated below, this is one of the kinds of stories that plays out closest to an author's own

5. For example, the fox family in "Xin Shisiniang" 辛十四娘 (*LZ*, 4.547) pelts the protagonist with tiles for shamelessly demanding Shisiniang's hand in marriage.

experience and own household, markedly closer than fox friends, vixen lovers, or (in most cases) the active practice of fox worship. More haunting stories are about named, identifiable historical persons than are tales of other kinds of relationships with the fox. The idea of foxes' domestic presence seems to be shared relatively unproblematically by different classes, although the most violent and unpleasant interactions are still held at a distance.

Disturbances by foxes, the throwing of roof tiles and the setting of fires, are rarer in explanations of the fox than they are in actual narratives. They fit nowhere in Ji's seemly narrative of self-advancement and only vaguely in He Bang'e's general concept of *yao*. Haunting is a raw oddity, resistant to explanation and large theories.

RESIDENCE AND REGIONAL GEOGRAPHY

In early narratives, foxes tend to be encountered on the road or in the wilderness. In the Tang tales in *Taiping guangji*, there is a gradual movement inward from the periphery to areas of human habitation, and foxes can be encountered walking the streets of Chang'an.[6] Although in the Qing, as we saw in the stories in the previous chapter, foxes are still encountered on lonely roadsides, at the edge of the city, and among old tombs, the home or other human space has become an important site of encounter. By the Tang, I argue, foxes had already ceased to represent wild nature as such, and in the Qing they are even more strongly linked to the by-products of human culture.

When Tang foxes entered human homes, they came most often as suitors or possessing spirits (and as we shall see in Chapter 5, the line between those two was not always clear). Their immediate relationship was thus with the human body, rather than human space and material objects. Although possession stories continue to occur in the Ming and Qing, the shift from possession of bodies to possession of houses suggests a change in a perception of the most vulnerable boundaries for humans.

The cultural fox, taking up residence in homes, was initially associated with a particular region. In the late Ming, southerners travel-

6. A striking example of the semi-urbanized fox is "Renshi zhuan"; see Huntington, "Tigers, Foxes, and the Margins of Humanity in Tang *chuanqi* Fiction."

ing to north China, particularly Beijing, began to comment on the presence of foxes in people's homes. In the early seventeenth century Xie Zhaozhe 謝肇淛 (1567–1624; a native of Fujian), after observing that foxes are common in Qi, Jin, Yan, and Zhao (roughly the contemporary provinces of Shandong, Hebei, Shanxi, and Shaanxi), commented, "Out of every ten houses in the capital, six or seven have fox demons, but they do no harm and people are used to them, just as people from Lingnan live with snakes."[7] In this statement on foxes' domestic presence, humans are accustomed to their company, a process of mutual tolerance and domestication. Snakes have their own history of transformation and supernatural powers, and the parallel of "fox demons" to "snakes" suggests that we are in a blurry territory between biological animals and their cultural manifestations.

The first fox story in Qian Xiyan's 錢希言 *Kuai yuan* 獪園 (1613) serves as an introduction to foxes for southerners. The story's position at the beginning of the category of fox stories hardly seems accidental. Related by the author's uncle, who traveled to the north and lodged with a wealthy family, it begins, "There are many wild foxes' burrows under people's homes in the capital."[8] The narrator Ye relates that he once watched a fox in the courtyard wear a human skull and pray to the moon in order to achieve human form. "In the middle of the night, this fox would become a beautiful woman or a handsome youth, walking in space and treading on air, slipping through a crack in the wall, coming and going among the room's corners and the chickens' perches as if it were flying. By dawn it would resume its former shape." For all the fox's mutability and mobility, its wanderings are contained within a domestic space.

This passage presents a juxtaposition of an older means of transformation, which in earlier stories took place in forest clearings, with a new setting. That is only one of many ways in which this story is a

---

7. Xie Zhaozhe, *Wu zazu, Wu bu* 物部 9.14. Another good example of the outsider's attitude is found in *Qixiu leigao*, in which the author, having heard that fox demons are common in Shandong, asks the locals for details about them when he is posted there; see "Huli," in Lang Ying, *Qixiu leigao* 48.705–6. On the northern origins of the fox, see Li Jianguo, *Zhongguo hu wenhua*, pp. 16–18. On their link to the north in the Ming, ibid, pp. 156–165.

8. Qian Xiyan, *Kuai yuan zhiyi*, 14.8a.

pastiche. It interweaves different registers of language and different kinds of information about the strange, mixing the encyclopedic with personal experience. It is in an intermediate space between the theoretical treatises on foxes and individual narratives. The discontinuity with the setting (the use of the skull recalls foxes' associations with tombs, but where would a house fox get one?) suggests an attempt to reconcile lore from two different sources, one older and possibly textual with a newer, more local, and possibly oral one. Whereas older stories of spying on the skull ritual would always end with exposure of the fox that had so transformed itself, here the human merely observes the transformation.[9]

The fact that a fox assuming human form and careening through the household does not necessarily disturb the human world reveals a level of familiarity and comfort. As with Xie Zhaozhe's statement, part of what is strange in the story is northerners' blithe acceptance of this kind of marvel. "When members of the family [Ye's hosts] came and went, a fox would often accompany them. They didn't think it strange." Here again foxes stand on the borderline between the strange and the commonplace.

> Foxes hide all day and run around all night. Foxes love women's chambers, and when women in the capital have their period, they throw their dirty rags in the gutter, and the foxes come and lick up all the menstrual blood. No one sees them. This is probably the reason they turn into monsters. Since southerners don't do this [throw menstrual rags in the street], foxes are rare in the south. The old figure of speech, "In the south there

---

9. The textual history of foxes wearing human skulls to transform themselves can be traced back to the Tang; see, e.g., two anecdotes from *Youyang zazu* 酉陽雜俎 "Liu Yuanding" 劉元鼎, *TPGJ*, 454.3709; and "Seng Yantong" 僧晏通, *TPGJ*, 451.3691. This theme seems to have been somewhat popular in the Ming but to have fallen from favor in the Qing, when it was mentioned more often in theoretical discussion of foxes than in actual stories. The only fox story in the *Sandeng* series of three collections of early to mid-Ming *chuanqi* to use this theme is "Hu Meiniang zhuan" 狐媚娘傳 in Li Changqi, *Jiandeng yuhua*, 7.238. Feng Menglong also makes use of it in *Pingyao zhuan*; see *Xin pingyao zhuan*, 3.1b–2a. As we have seen, He Bang'e mentions this practice in his general introduction to the fox, but it never appears in any of his stories; see "Zaji wuze" 雜記五則, *YTSL*, 4.102. The exposure of the skull-wearing fox can be found in "Zeng Yantong," "Humei niang zhuan," and chap. 3 of *Pingyao zhuan*.

are no wild foxes; in the north there are no cuckoos," is not an unfounded fabrication.

The older lore about transformation is framed as personal experience, but this new idea is framed as speculation. This means of transformation is plainly linked to the most intimate domestic space and to the unsanctioned mixing of the women's chambers with the outside world. Foxes' transformations are linked not only to northern geography but also to northerners' (in the mind of a southerner unsavory) local customs.[10] The second story in *Kuai yuan*'s fox section makes the cultural connection even more directly; a southern narrator describes a group of foxes as dressing just like residents of the capital.[11] These first two stories are closer to ethnographic observations than to narratives, with the *zhiguai* author taking the role of a folklorist recording someone else's lore.

Qian Xiyan's theory aside, why are foxes associated with the north? Part of the answer lies in the relationship between the biological fox and the culturally constructed fox; actual foxes are more common north of the Yangtze. The observation that foxes were northern was made as early as the Tang and by Hong Mai in the Song; it is in itself an older piece of lore.[12] Although zoology did not determine the range of the culturally constructed fox, it was clearly a contributing factor.

Different kinds of fox stories have different kinds of ties to place. In the mid-seventeenth century, the domestic fox plot seems to

---

10. Ji Yun (*YWCT,* 6.263–64, story 264) later made the argument that it is human culture which prepares the way for fox transformations.

11. This geographic association becomes a convention; see, e.g., "Guanku huxian" 管庫狐仙, in Qian Yong, *Lüyuan conghua*, 16.13a, for a tale about a pair of vixens in Hangzhou who have a northern accent and are asked what they are doing in the south. Foxes usually assert they are from Shaanxi, Beijing, Tianjin, Hebei, or Shandong. Gu Meigao ("Tan hu," p. 254) observes that all the foxes in *Liaozhai* claim to come from Shaanxi.

12. See the *Taiping guangji* reference, "In the south there are no foxes, in the north there are no cuckoos." "Cang zhu min" 滄渚民, *TPGJ,* 455.3718. Hong Mai (*Yijian zhi, dingzhi* 19.695) also asserted the fox's northern origins. However, Hong Mai's own fox stories are largely set in Jiangnan. See Li Jianguo, *Zhongguo hu wenhua*, p. 140. At least one observer asserts that differences between northerners' and southerners' attitudes toward foxes continue to the present day; see Li Shouju, *Huxian xinyang yu huli jing de gushi*, p. 101.

maintain its close ties with the north, whereas other kinds of stories are far more portable. *Kuai yuan* also includes two fox stories that occur in the south, an account of a handsome fox youth who seduced the loose women of Hangzhou and a literatus's splendid interlude of poetry and feasting with an exiled divine fox youth.[13] Neither of these stories has particular ties to the domestic sphere. The closer tie of domestic haunting to place seems related to the relative newness of this kind of story and its ties to local oral narrative.

In subsequent generations, one seldom finds this sort of ethnographic record of the domestic fox. On the one hand, the mere presence of foxes in human homes ceases to be worthy of comment; the question instead becomes what they did there. At the same time, the geographical outsider's perspective becomes rare, because the domesticated fox achieves nationwide currency. Later in the Qing, every kind of fox story became geographically more widespread, to the point that any kind of story could happen anywhere. Nevertheless, a disproportionate number continue to be set in the central fox territory of Shaanxi, Shanxi, Shandong, Beijing, Hebei, and Tianjin, and foxes themselves often claim to be from this region. The Guangxu era author Dai Lianfen 戴連芬 could still relate a tale of his father's encounter with a fox while lodging in the capital as a tutor in a general's household. When his possessions begin moving of their own accord, his host laughingly placates his household fox, telling him, "Southerners are cowardly."[14] The fox has definitely colonized the major cities of Jiangnan by the end of the Qing, with Nanjing, Yangzhou, and Hangzhou particularly common as scenes of fox stories. A rare fox narrative is even set as far south as Taiwan.[15] A mid-nineteenth-century author, who published his works in Henan, gave this description of the general presence of foxes, "There are many foxes in empty rooms, and if they from time to time show their forms or make their voices audible, this isn't worth wondering at."[16] This geographic spread suggests a disassociation of the biological and

13. Qian Xiyan, *Kuai yuan zhiyi*, story 8, 14.14a; story 10, 14.15b.

14. Dai Lianfen, *Libian xuan zhiyan*, 1.17a.

15. On the geographic spread of fox worship, see Kang, "Power at the Margins," pp. 351–56.

16. Zhang Yun, *Suoshi xianlu*, 1.2a.

cultural fox. One could add yet another boundary to Ji Yun's list: the fox straddles the boundary between the regional and the national.

INFESTATION AND HAUNTING

In late imperial times the fox could be either an intruder into domestic space or an established inhabitant of the household. The fox's wavering status between the strange and the ordinary is apparent in the two basic patterns of domestic fox stories, the fox haunt and the fox resident. The two basic opening phrases are "So and so's household was haunted by a fox" (*you hu zuo sui* 有狐作祟) and "Such and such a room of so-and-so's house was inhabited by a fox" (*you hu ju* 有狐居). In a less innocuous version of the latter, a place is "monopolized or seized by a fox" (*wei hu suo ju*" 爲狐所据).[17]

From a literary-historical perspective, there are two movements here: foxes moved into the human home, and the spirits of domestic mischance became identified as foxes. Imaginary creatures are seldom perfectly distinct from one another. Speciation is not a matter of diverging evolution that eventually results in two groups that absolutely cannot crossbreed; rather, the traits (or lore) associated with these species recombine and separate as human cultural needs change from moment to moment, narrative to narrative. Thus the fox overlaps in function with ghosts and other monsters. The idea of a haunted place or a domestic disturbance predates the Ming and Qing, and there are late imperial haunted place stories that attribute the disturbance to other causes. Why did the fox assume this role, and what difference does it make if your house is infested by a fox as opposed to some other creature?

One partial answer to the first question is that foxes in their animal form were one of many wild creatures reputed to move into spaces humans had abandoned and allowed to go wild. This is based in part on biological observation; actual foxes prefer burrowing in pre-existing structures rather than digging their own. The figure of speech, "the foxes in the walls and the rats in the altar" mentioned in the previous chapter, reflects this observation. Foxes were creatures who could live in the interstices between the settled and the wild.

---

17. For example, see *YWCT*, 1.2, story 2.

"The wild" overstates the case: they were signs of neglect, rather than ruin. Some of the places where foxes are situated in narrative, such as woodpiles or heaps of straw outdoors, are biologically plausible; but others, like tower rooms, are less so. As the disturbing sense of an alien presence in any formerly human or contested space was given the name "fox," the habitats of the zoological and the cultural fox came to overlap, but they were not identical.

Because of the fox's uncanny reputation, an infestation of foxes was regarded differently from an infestation of rats. Interactions with the zoological fox predate the cultural fox's move indoors by millennia, suggesting zoology supplies some material for the cultural fox, but is never the only, and seldom the primary, source. The question, then, is at what moment interest focused on a certain kind of domestic disturbance, and how the idea of domestic disturbance influenced understanding of the fox, and vice versa.

The idea of infestation by an annoying but not deadly pest helps explain the tone of fox haunting. My translation of *sui* as "haunting" demands some justification. The dictionary definition of the word is "harm done by gods and ghosts," but the parameters of that harm seem changeable. In connection with foxes, it can be used to refer to possession, but in late imperial times it refers more often to disturbance of a household.[18] In English "haunting" is exclusively associated with ghosts and conveys a sense of spectral horror. *Zuo sui* 作祟 is actively making trouble, and many different creatures can do it. In this, foxes are closer to imps or gremlins than ghosts, and haunting by foxes can be considered an infestation of supernatural vermin. Their activities often arouse annoyance rather than horror, and there often seems as much humor as malice in the foxes' behavior.

The word "poltergeist" from the European context is useful in describing the fox as mischief-maker. Acts of mischief, such as throwing stones (in the Chinese context, nearly always roof tiles) or crockery and moving the furniture around, are found widely in both traditions. Loud noises or rapping are less central to fox hauntings

---

18. For *sui* in the sense of possession, see "Tianmo sui" 天魔祟, in Yuan Haowen, *Xu Yijian zhi*, 1.16. For examples in the sense of domestic disturbance, see "Hu ru pin" 狐入瓶, *LZ*, 1.75, which says a home is "祟於狐"; and "Hu sui" 狐祟, in Dongxuan zhuren, *Shuyi ji* 1.11a.

than to European poltergeists, but footsteps are sometimes heard. One crucial difference is that fox mischief is usually not associated with a particular poltergeist "agent" at the center of a flurry of activity, though we may speculate there is some young servant, almost invisible to his or her masters, in the margins of the story. Rather, an entire household, and any who pass through, are afflicted. Robert Kirk's (ca. 1651–92) characterization of poltergeists as acting "like buffoons or drolls," and thus likely to be fairies rather than malevolent demons, captures the resemblance of these experiences to practical jokes.[19]

Stories of poltergeist-type haunting of homes occurred in China in earlier periods.[20] There is one example in *Taiping guangji*, taken from *Guangyi ji* 廣異記 (The great book of marvels), of what later become the foxes' signature acts of mischief, throwing roof tiles, and tossing feces in a man's cup.[21] However, in contrast with most later fox hauntings, the place inhabited by foxes was rumored to be deadly to any who stay there. The conclusion of the story, however, in which the male protagonist drinks with an invisible fox patriarch, who provides him with the amulets to drive out the destructive fox, is similar to later stories. Other *Guangyi ji* tales reveal that in the Tang, an animal discovered within the walls of a house could be taken as an explanation for domestic apparitions and oddities.[22] The difference between these Tang stories and the later fox haunting stories is, first, the predominance of the "haunted house" frame: a tale opens with the deadly reputation of a place, and later creatures are rooted out as the cause. This structure remains common in late imperial collections, but there are also many more stories in which, in a case of fox

19. Kirk, *The Secret Commonwealthes of Elves, Fauns, and Fairies*, p. 59. Wilson, *Poltergeists*, pp.100–101; Gauld and Cornell, *Poltergeists*, pp. 176–78.

20. For a comparison of Tang cases from the *Guangyi ji* with the international literature on poltergeists, see Dudbridge, *Religious Experience and Lay Society*, pp. 133–35.

21. "Li Chang" 李萇, in *TPGJ*, 452.3697–98. Dudbridge, *Religious Experience and Lay Society*, p. 231.

22. For two snake stories, see "Xinzhou cishi" 忻州刺史 and "Yugan xianling" 餘干縣令, in *TPGJ*, 456.3731–32. Dudbridge, *Religious Experience and Lay Society*, p. 231.

haunting, a place becomes haunted during the course of a story.[23] Also, it becomes more common for the identity of the fox to be made plain in the first line of a story.

One crucial difference between these Tang examples and the Ming-Qing stories discussed below is the nature of the haunted, contested space. All the examples in *Guangyi ji* are played out at official residences of local officials, and it is the new arrival in office who contends with haunting. Such stories dramatize the confrontation between the representative of national political power and local religious forces and are discussed in more detail in the following chapter. Official residences are still a significant site of hauntings in late imperial stories,[24] but the proportion of civilian residences increases. The prominence of official residences is understandable, since most *zhiguai* are the products of the itinerant scholar-official class and focus disproportionately on their experience. But the shift of emphasis from a confrontation with the strange with public implications to one which is more purely private is significant.

Compared with Ming and Qing fox hauntings, the poltergeist stories in Hong Mai's 洪邁 (1123–1202) *Yijian zhi* 夷堅志 (Record of the Listener, 1161–98) seem more violent and unpredictable.[25] For example, the disturbances in "Dai Shirong" 戴世榮 seem similar to foxes' misdeeds: all the utensils are lined up on the floor, with the dogs standing beside them; fires break out inside locked chests, and the contents burned without the chests themselves being damaged; and the family is pelted with a limitless supply of crockery. Yet the creature responsible is revealed as an unrecognizable horse-headed monster. In the end the master of the house dies, and his family declines. The narrator comments that no one knew a moral or other cause for this affliction.[26] This domestic disturbance is much more drastic and uncontained than those found in the Ming and Qing

23. For an example of a late Ming fox story in the horror story mode, see "Guan Yang" 關揚, in Tan Rumu, *Zaolin zazu*, in *BJXSDG*, vol. 15, 和集 16a–b.

24. For example, "Zunhua shuhu," *LZ*, 2.244–46. On the fox in yamen offices, see Kang, "Power at the Margins," 265–75.

25. Other examples noted by Dudbridge include "Tingzhou shan xiao" 汀州山魈, in Hong Mai, *Yijian zhi* 乙志, yizhi 7.240; "Hu dafu" 胡大夫, in ibid., dingzhi 3.558; and "Haimen yanchang" 海門鹽場, in ibid., dingzhi 3.560.

26. *Yijian zhi*, dingzhi 4.11. All these examples were pointed out by Dudbridge.

fox story. Fox haunting, unlike an explained "evil house," seldom leads to, or foretells, the downfall of a household. Foxes are linked to household decline, be it physical or moral, which has already occurred, but in the late imperial tale they are seldom harbingers of doom.[27]

Creatures other than the fox acting as poltergeists are stronger omens of the decline of the household. A ghost as a poltergeist suggests that the fissure running through domestic space is that between the living and the dead, which is more threatening. The rise of the fox as poltergeist is a sign of increased interest in apparently petty rather than lethal confrontations with the strange. As haunts, ghosts and foxes differ in both their entrances and their exits. Souls of the dead do not simply come to roost in places humans have abandoned; there should be a cause for their presence, often related to the circumstances of their death.[28] A ghost may also be offered food to appease it, but once appeased, it should become a contented spirit and leave, rather than remaining as part of the household. Finally there remains a difference in tone: ghosts are usually not as playful as foxes. The novelty of the late imperial fox is both the limited nature of its torments and the possibility of its incorporation into the domestic routine itself.

This kind of domestic mischief reveals an emphasis on physical possessions and the expected patterns of everyday life: the inanimate should remain inanimate, and possessions should remain in their categories and places. Poltergeists are democratic: although they can appear in the halls of power, they are not the sole reserve of any class. Anyone with a kitchen or a storage room can be afflicted.

---

27. A few exceptions, in which foxes are harbingers of death: "Ciyuan si husui" 慈原寺狐祟, in Xu Kunguo, *Dunzhai oubi, xia*.26a. "Hu da yong" 狐打饔, in Dai Lianfen, *Libian xuan zhiyan*, 1.17b.

28. The general category "ghosts and foxes" 鬼狐 is more like foxes in this respect. See Dan Minglun's comment to the *Liaozhai* story "Shan xiao" 山魈: "Any house that has long been left empty will be inhabited by ghosts and foxes" (*LZ*, 1.19).

DISTURBANCE AND EXORCISM

The comments on foxes quoted above emphasize northerners' remarkable acceptance of them as neighbors and roommates. That perceived harmony seems to be a consequence of these records' character as ethnographic summaries rather than narratives of particular cases; they reveal the same gap between theory and practice we saw in the previous chapter. In contrast, individual cases are interested in anomaly and conflict.

Here is a fairly representative example of disturbance and exorcism from the Qianlong-era collection *Qiudeng conghua*:

Ji Yunhui from Anqiu was a man of religious cultivation. His home was suddenly afflicted with a haunting by a fox. Hats, shoes, and clothes would always move of their own accord, as if alive, and were sometimes torn and destroyed in an instant. He was extremely distressed by it, but there was nothing he could do.

One day when Ji returned from outside, there was a creature as big as a dog lying on the ceiling beam. He knew it was the fox, and so he struck it. It fell to the earth and vanished. From then on the fox was even more unruly. All of Ji's food and drink were mixed with filth. All the women's hairpins and ornaments were stolen, and their skirts were often hung on the tips of trees. In his rage Ji complained to all the gods, with no results. When a thunderstorm came, Ji knelt bare-chested in the water, looking up to heaven and calling, "If there are no gods, why does the sky rain and thunder? If there are, and I Ji must blamelessly suffer such monstrous molestation while you do not hear me, why are the gods called efficacious"? Suddenly a giant hand as big as a winnowing fan, with fingers as thick as bushel baskets, hung out of the sky. It groped back and forth, searching, and drew out a bottle, which it whirled about. It set the bottle in the middle of the courtyard, and the giant hand suddenly vanished. Ji ripped cloth, stopped up the mouth of the bottle, and placed it in boiling water. There was a whimpering sound. After a while it was silent. Then he buried it on the outskirts of the city. The haunting stopped then.[29]

The representativeness of this narrative, or any haunting story, is limited. Foxes' disturbances are relatively constant, but an "uneventful" story of exorcism, in which an exorcist simply came and the fox

29. Wang Jian, *Qiudeng conghua*, 1.8b.

left, would not have been appealing. The details of how the fox was expelled are interesting. Patterns like "disturbance/expulsion" require different levels of adornment, at different points, to attract the reader's attention. For example, the *Liaozhai* story that opens this chapter ends with an exorcist driving out the fox but not before the fox possesses and speaks through a serving maid.

Foxes become mysteries on the smallest possible scale—the misbehavior of household utensils and furniture, as here, or strange noises heard in the night. They become the explanation for any bizarre apparition or event in a household. Ji's torments are a fairly thorough survey of the range of fox mischief: household items, furniture, food, clothing, are thrown into disorder and polluted. Note the particular emphasis on the public display of women's clothing, which would frustrate the sexual segregation of a household.[30] Only the characteristic acts of throwing bricks and tiles or setting fires are omitted. These are such telltale signs of the fox that it is no longer necessary to see one; when any of these things happen, it is assumed a fox is present. *Yanshan conglu* includes a one-line account of a house haunted by some creature that threw bricks among the fox stories, even though the species of the creature is never exposed.[31] One typical petty example is a fox who causes a chicken to be cooked after the fire has been put out.[32]

The fox that torments Ji is glimpsed in its animal form. Interestingly enough, when this happens in haunting narratives, the creature is often described in terms of other animals, usually dogs or

30. For another example, see "Zhi hu" 治狐, in Yongna jushi, *Zhi wen lu*, 1.19b. A story in Ji Yun's collection reverses chaos and order. When a child leaves his mother's shoe in the garden, his father finds it and assumes this is proof of adultery and berates his wife. The family's fox then diverts suspicion from the wife by casting personal objects belonging to several women in the household outside; see *YWCT*, 13.695, story 155.

31. Xu Changzuo, *Yanshan conglu, juan* 8, story 5. This chapter also includes a few stories of creatures other than foxes, such as temple idols, that become animate. For another example of a destructive haunting, see "Hu Dagu" 狐大姑, *LZ*, 6.788. Another simple example of a vulpine furniture mover is "Lingxian hu" 陵縣狐, *LZ*, 9.1296.

32. "Huguai" 狐怪, in Yu Yue, *Youtai xianguan biji*, 6.4b.

cats.[33] This vagueness about the traits of the physical fox is seldom present in other kinds of tales. But this vagueness is at the same time descriptive: rather than saying a "fox," the stories supply details of color and size and make comparisons, suggesting observation. Rather than a single true animal shape that is revealed after illusion has been dispelled, there is a sense of indeterminacy and groping for a description. Had the people seeing "foxes" in their homes never seen foxes in the wild? It is suggestive, too, that the fox is imagined in terms of common domestic animals.[34] The indefinite animal form, glimpsed quickly, helps to reinforce the sense of infestation. However, the link between that animal form and its mischief is virtually never spelled out; the four-footed creature is not envisioned physically moving objects or engaging in destruction. The body of the fox can be a stage in the development of a haunting story, but it is not essential, and it is not an ending of the tale. It is simply another disturbing manifestation. This fox is glimpsed on the rafters, a fairly unlikely spot for a biological fox but a very common lair for the fox as monster, because it was just at the edges of human control and an apt place for strange noises and half-glimpsed movements.

The first part of the story is relatively common, but the second half is more unusual. The giant hand from the sky takes the role that would otherwise be played by an exorcist. Containing a fox in a bottle and then boiling it were common means of extermination.[35] Even the overdramatic restoration of cosmic order underlines the problems of this inexplicable haunting; as Ji himself protests, this is an unprovoked torment. The ending offers containment rather than explanation.

As discussed in the previous chapter, the idea of the fox as a disruptive creature that violated the boundaries distinguishing humans

---

33. Cf. He Bang'e's description of *pi* foxes as resembling cats in *YTSL*, 4.102; and Liu Shoumei's glimpse of a fox as a creature bigger than a cat (translated p. 106), *Chunquan wenjian lu*, *juan* 2, story 38. See also "Zhuo hu" 捉狐, *LZ*, 1.22.

34. In the international (but predominantly American and Western European) accounts of poltergeists, apparitions of strange animals, including dogs and cats, are sometimes associated with poltergeist phenomena and are seen particularly commonly by child witnesses; see Gauld and Cornell, *Poltergeists*, p. 112.

35. See, e.g., "Hu ru ping" and "Hu sijie" 胡四姐, *LZ*, 1.75 and 2.201–4.

from others was established by the Six Dynasties and Tang, but then the violation was imitation of the human form, and it was solved by exposure of the fox body. In late imperial times, violation focuses instead on space and disorder. Exposure, the predominant pattern of fox stories in the Tang and earlier, is replaced by driving out or quieting the fox as the conclusion of the story. There is a relationship between exorcism and exposure. In both cases, the creature is identified on the brink of its exit. Both are moments of knowledge and containment: in the case of exposure, all illusions are stripped away and only the fox body remains; and in the case of exorcism, all the diverse apparitions and torments are reduced to a single spatially contained manifestation. Visibility is not, however, necessarily crucial to exorcism, as we see in this story.

In general, in late imperial literature foxes become more human in two ways: the fox body fades from view, the human forms are regarded as increasingly real and substantial, and they are assimilated to human culture and moral values. Foxes as domestic haunts prove this was not a linear process: such foxes are close to humans only in terms of proximity and ubiquity. Until the end, the fox that torments Ji seems a pure source of chaos, with no motive for its depredations. Throughout the Qing there are a fair number of such straightforward accounts of bizarre events attributed to foxes, with no explanation of the fox's motives.[36]

However, foxes are in different narratives outfitted with different amounts of human form, human speech, or explicable motivations for their actions. Foxes of differing degrees of humanity coexisted in the same collections, a range Ji Yun and many others attributed to different levels of fox accomplishment. Each kind of story uses a different range of relative humanity, and the domestic fox has a broader range than nearly every other type of fox story.

HAUNTED PLACES

Stories of fox haunting and fox cohabitation with humans form a metanarrative about control of space. As foxes move indoors, relations between humans and foxes are determined by the clash of two forces trying to inhabit the same narrow space: foxes move into human space, and humans move into space claimed by foxes. Conflicts occur

36. *Yanshan conglu*, *juan* 8, stories 2 and 10.

in both situations. These conflicts are signs of an urban, mobile society; humans confront the unknown not when settling a wilderness but when moving around in old and crowded cities, or when experiencing internal change in their own households. Territorial conflicts are often resolved by one side moving out. Peaceful cohabitation is usually possible only when people clean out a room or space for the fox to claim as its own. Disruptive haunting and fox residence have somewhat different relations to space: haunting at its extreme disrupts the whole household without being localized; a resident fox is assigned a place, and its disturbances are confined there.

Foxes are in this period defined by the spaces they inhabit, which include not just homes, but all sorts of quiet places: abandoned gardens, small temples, city walls, government offices, and even the library at Beijing University.[37] They become particularly associated with high places, the eaves, rafters, and the *chengchen* 承塵, the piece of cloth that separates the ceiling from the room. When they reside in a building, they usually occupy the upper floors.[38] Within a household, they often lay claim to pavilions or small outbuildings in gardens, which are more obviously liminal spaces between inside and outside. Indoors, they claim storage closets or attics, and sometimes studies, but the fact that their presence in a bedroom, the kitchen, or a main hall is an unsettling haunting rather than an accepted fact reveals which parts of the house are central and which marginal to the human residents. Most spaces claimed by foxes are narrow, such as small outbuildings often made up of two rooms. Foxes are also associated with the old mansions of families whose numbers have declined, leaving many rooms empty. Thus they can be signs of decline, but at the same time, having

37. According to the Republican author Jin Liang (*Guapu shuyi*, xia, p. 23b), the library at Beijing University used to be a shrine for the worship of an unspecified spirit, perhaps even a 大仙, which suggests a fox. It continued to be haunted by a fox in the early Republican period. Jin Liang was *juren* in 1902, *jinshi* in 1904, and contributed to *Qingshi gao* (Xu Youchun et al., eds., *Minguo renwu da cidian*, p. 474).

38. Li Jianguo (pers. comm., May 1995) believes this is related to the tradition that *xian* live in the upper floors of buildings. A poem by Ji Yun addressing a fox who lives upstairs includes the line 仙人好樓居 "Immortals like to live in (storied) buildings" (*YWCT*, 3.100, story 102).

enough space for a fox to claim is itself a mark of affluence (past or present). In peasant households, outdoor lairs like a woodpile or a tree are more likely.

In the case of haunting, the fox is the source of instability and must be either driven out or placated for the story to end. In contrast, the fox in residence is part of a stable order. In a story of a resident fox, the fox is present at the beginning of the story, contained in a specific domestic space; some human action provokes the plot. It is tempting to think that the story of disruptive haunting is the basic pattern, and peaceful coexistence is one of its possible resolutions, but that seldom happens in the course of a story. The quiet fox provoked to action is more common. Different collections contain different proportions of the two types. *Yuewei caotang biji* contains a great number of resident foxes, but Ji's contemporary Liu Shoumei favored tales of haunting in his *Chunquan wenjian lu*.

A first-person account of coming to terms with a fox in one's new home from Liu's collection is conspicuous in its ordinariness.

> In 1777, I moved to a house outside Chongwen Gate, in Handkerchief Alley. On cleaning day, a servant reached the curtained space between the eaves and the ceiling. He found two circles of soft grass like sparrow's nests with a heap of chicken bones beside them. He thought it strange and threw them out. That night his head hurt as if it were about to split open. The old servant suspected it was a haunt and offered wine and sacrifices, which cured him. That night it was silent, but the heads of four chickens were bitten off. The next evening a thing white as snow and bigger than a cat was seen. It came out from behind the *kang*, went to the corner of the wall, and vanished. After the autumn examinations, I was summoned by a friend to go wait for the results. My relatives sat up waiting for news. In the middle of the night, they saw a white-clothed man come out of the left wing; he circled the courtyard with slow steps and then returned to his former location. A bench under the covered corridor had one foot that wasn't steady; it moved of its own accord on the earth, making a sound on the ground. Some said if it wasn't a ghost, it was a fox, and were terrified. I told them not to be alarmed; after this they saw nothing.[39]

Liu's household inherits this problem when they move to another home, and the first confrontation is caused when they try to claim

39. Liu Shoumei, *Chunquan wenjian lu*, *juan* 2, story 38.

the space for themselves.[40] This is a rather intricate series of signs and apparitions, with different levels of involvement by different members of the household. Liu himself never sees the creature, even though he is the one who puts the household story together. He constructs a metanarrative from these fragmentary apparitions to which he might give the name "fox" or more loosely *guai*, but he does not do much to digest possibly contradictory details. First, a servant finds traces of animals and gets a headache. The servant makes his own interpretation, responds accordingly, and has his interpretation confirmed by the easing of his headache. The next sign, the four maimed chickens, is not interpreted. It is not clear who sees the apparition of the white creature bigger than a cat. The next apparition, in human form, occurs at a highly tense time, when Liu is waiting to learn his fate in the civil service examination that will determine his career success. Men of his class were especially attentive to omens at this time, and the quantity of recorded anomalies follows the examination calendar. One assumes, given Liu's biography, that the news was bad, but the vision is not interpreted. Liu steps in the very end to control the reactions of his household, and with that control he brings this series of experiences to an end.

The fox (although Liu does not conclusively identify it as such, the chicken bones leave me with little doubt) is the creature with the flexibility to fit together all these fragments. Liu is the household authority on the strange and his servants' direct experience of it. The apparition is contained by the master's insistence that his servants should not be alarmed. He neither condones nor condemns his servants' private arrangements, but he implies that once their fears cease, the monster will also cease. But Liu's role is limited: he does not explain the creature. This feels like raw experience that has been shaped only to a limited extent, into the simplest *zhiguai* shape: an anomaly occurs, and then it ceases. Liu does not take this fox as a reflection on himself or his household. The sheer bulk of *zhiguai* material published in the Qing produces an apparent paradox: although there is unprecedented effort to interpret and explain the strange—Ji

40. In one account a man who intrudes on a fox's space is politely requested to leave; the exchange is used as a frame for a discussion of fox advancement; see "Hu Shengyuan" 狐生員, in Yuan Mei, *Zi bu yu*, 1.9.

Yun was one of the strongest representatives of this trend—more accounts of unexplained, banal weirdness survive than from any other time.

Liu was also capable of the more wordy, argumentative form of Qing *zhiguai*. A contrasting story of a confrontation with a resident fox happened to Liu's father when he arrived to take up a post as a local official. The official lodging was not yet ready, and he was forced to stay with a local family. He found the quarters too small and asked to move to a vacant building, which the locals warned was occupied by a fox. His father insisted on lodging there despite his host's objections and drove the fox out with rational argument:

"I am an official renting a commoner's house. How can your kind disturb me? Moreover, if you want to imitate humans, it is because you know humans are noble and want to be the same. If you want to be human, then you shouldn't disturb people. When you enter people's homes and cause people to be so afraid they dare not struggle with you, your motives are the same as bandits, or even worse than bandits. This is truly to have a human face and the heart of an animal. If you truly have understanding, you will surely quickly regret your error. If not, you must enjoy being an alien species and imitate the human form in vain."[41]

Liu Shoumei's father begins by invoking his official status, which should render him immune to supernatural disturbance, but then he turns to an argument based on the fox's motives. His reasoning points out one of the fundamental contradictions in the narrative tradition: foxes imitate humans but resort to the inhuman pattern of occupying homes. Liu's father is constructing his own metanarrative by bringing these contradictory story types together and giving the fox a single, explicable set of motives. Although it was commonly accepted that foxes envied humans and want to be human, such a forthright statement is relatively rare. Liu's father is essentially appealing to the fox's humanity. The fox is being chastised not only by being compared to a class of evil human beings, bandits, but also by being called the beast it originally was. Here the convention of referring to a "human face and the heart of a beast," which is more usually used to compare evil humans to virtuous foxes in order to shame the humans, is instead used to per-

41. Liu Shoumei, *Chunquan wenjian lu*, 13.12a.

suade the fox. The fox's decision to leave proves its susceptibility to moral reasoning. After this, Liu's father often commented that this fox was superior to the stupid and stubborn among human beings, since it could be taught. A fox tale is turned into an admonition for humans and a regular tool in conversation.

Ji Yun also included two stories in his collection describing men who stay in a haunted place and argue with the fox who occupies it. Interestingly, the two juxtaposed stories have opposite endings. In the first Liu Pu, an old Confucian who had served as a teacher to two of Ji's cousins, drove away a fox with the argument, "I am a poor Confucian forced to lodge here for a single night. Do you want to do me harm? I am not your enemy. Do you want to toy with me? I have never been intimate with you. Do you want to drive me out? I cannot leave tonight, but nor can I stay tomorrow morning; why must you make this disturbance?" Liu used this exemplary tale to persuade his students that when one meets unexpected difficulties, one should respond calmly, and perhaps a solution could be found. In the next story, however, a man who rents a haunted house is persuaded by the fox's reasoning: "If you were already living here and I came later to fight with you, the fault would lie with me. But I have lived here for fifty or sixty years, as everyone knows. You could rent a house anywhere, but you insisted on coming to live with me. This is deliberately insulting me; how could I be willing to yield to you?"

The juxtaposition of the two stories demonstrates that there is no predetermined result to an argument between man and fox. In both cases, using arguments based on necessity and choice, Ji pointed out the illogic in both standard story types, the fox who overreacts to an incursion, however brief, and the man who insists on unnecessarily provoking a resident fox. The appended comments of He Xiu 何琇 (*jinshi* 1723), one of Ji Yun's teachers, and his elder brother Ji Zhuo 紀晫 (1706–1777) reveal that the juxtaposition of these two stories was not Ji's invention but already existed in a conversational context. He Xiu simply stated the comparison: one fox could be defeated with reason and another could defeat a man with reason. Zhuo concluded that it is easy to persuade a fox, but hard to be persuaded by one,[42] a

42. *YWCT,* 10.245, story 245.

comment not supported by the highly articulate foxes in his brother's collection. Both foxes and men reason with each other based on common sense and courtesy. These stories' two nested layers of commentary, the first by Liu and the next by He and Zhuo, again demonstrate the use of fox stories in exchanges between Confucian tutors and their students. These tales were didactic in a very literal sense and used to educate young men of the same social class. Ji recorded the tales with all these interpretive layers intact; they have become part of the story. Making foxes' arrivals and departures equally explicable serves to control awe of both monsters and exorcists.

As we see in these two Qianlong collections, logical argument has become a means of exorcism. Starting with much older *zhiguai*, there is an intimate relationship between exorcism and explanation. Accurately identifying the source of a haunting was the key to driving it out. In Qing *zhiguai*, this relationship of exorcist as the possessor of knowledge and the exorcised creature as the object of knowledge breaks down, as exorcism becomes a relatively equal debate. Rather than explaining what the fox is, the exorcist must explain why the fox should leave. At the same time as the inherent moral inferiority of foxes has become questionable, the status of exorcists had slipped. This is especially true of professional exorcists who rely on esoteric arts to drive out foxes. These skills seem dangerously close to more sinister forms of sorcery, and such sorcerers may indeed be more frightening than foxes. In the Chinese concept, sorcery is an art anyone can learn, rather than an inherent gift;[43] that control of foxes should rely on such an amoral force would be a morally uncomfortable idea for many in the Qing. Many Qing tales develop instead the old idea of exorcism as a matter of moral superiority: "The evil cannot defeat the orthodox" (*xie bu sheng zheng* 邪不勝正). However, this moral superiority is articulated and defended in some Qing tales of exorcism, rather than simply being displayed through action. In these tales the literatus has conspicuously taken the place of the professional exorcist, and the emphasis on morality and reasoning, rather than arcane arts, follows directly from this substitution. This

43. See Kuhn, *Soulstealers*, pp. 95–96.

emphasis reflects both authorship and audience of the tales.[44] This tendency for exorcism to become a moral debate reaches its extreme in *Yuewei caotang biji*. Since these tales were used to make points in conversation, the content comes to mirror the argumentative context. This is an example of the use of the shared lore and patterns of foxes' residence and expulsion. In stories of haunting and avoidance, the fox reveals meaning about humans by either staying or leaving, but in these tales the fox speaks as it comes and goes.

OUR FAMILY'S FOXES

For an example on the other end of the spectrum of relative humanity, compare Ji Yunhui's torments to Ji Yun's experience:

> There is a small building on the artificial mountain in my family's garden; foxes have inhabited it for fifty years. People don't go up there and the foxes don't come down, but from time to time one sees the windows and doors opening and shutting when there is no wind. To the north of the building is a place called the Pavilion of Remembering the Green, densely shaded by old trees, a fitting place to cool off in the summer. In the seventh month of 1749, suddenly in the middle of the night the sounds of the *qin* and chess pieces were heard. The servants ran to tell my father. He knew it was the foxes' doing, and he was not bothered in the slightest. Instead he looked at the servants and said, "[The foxes' pastimes] are certainly better than your drinking and gambling." The next day, he said to me, "When the boy on the beach had no ulterior motives, he could befriend the gulls. We've already lived at peace for so long; it's best if we handle this by ignoring them." And to this day there have been no other anomalies.[45]

This story immediately precedes the tale of the elegant lotus-painting fox that opened this chapter. Ji's haunting foxes have taken on not just human but literati guise: they exhibit their refinement by playing the *qin* and chess. The location in which Ji's family foxes are housed is itself an expression of cultured refinement. The cause of disturbance here is not the foxes but lower-class humans' reactions to

---

44. Compare Tangherlini's observations about different proportions of different classes of exorcists in tales from different informants, *Interpreting Legend*, p. 149, 178.

45. *YWCT*, 3.99, story 101.

them. Ji presents an ideal of peaceful coexistence with the fox. Such peace is possible only when the boundary between worlds is respected despite extreme proximity: neither side intrudes on the other. The correct way of dealing with foxes is framed as an example of Ji's father's wisdom, speaking to his adult son. The elder Ji refers to the story of a boy to whom the seagulls came flying, until the day his father asked him to bring the gulls to him. When the boy returned to the beach, the gulls flew far away. In the ideal relationship with foxes, humans have no ulterior motives (as we will see in the next chapter, this conforms with Ji's attitude toward fox worship). The fox becomes an accepted, stable part of family history and lore and starts to cross the line between "us" and "them."

Yuewei caotang biji and *Qiudeng conghua* are contemporary collections. Like Wang Jian, Ji Yun also recorded tales of haunting, but they did not happen to him. Although men will admit to having foxes in their houses, I have not seen a first-person account of being tormented. In contrast, harmonious relations with foxes were part of a flattering self-image. Liu Shoumei, whose collection is extremely personal, allowed the negative consequences of fox haunting to fall on his servants and some of his relatives by marriage, but he and his father always overcame the challenge without any humiliating incident. Anxieties about the permeability of the domestic sphere were displaced onto others, whether men of the same class in other households or the servants within one's own household. In one's personal experiences with fox intruders, the strange reinforces order.

The tone of an account of resident foxes can range from wary respect to annoyance to fascination with the appearance of enchantment in banal surroundings. Examples from Jin Liang's 金梁 (1878–1962) *Guapu shuyi* 瓜圃述異 (Tales of the strange from the Melon Garden; published 1936) provide clear examples of foxes as charming enchantment and also demonstrate that the tradition does not come to an abrupt end in the late Qing. Jin defended the belief in foxes against modern skepticism with examples from his own experience. He recalled an encounter with a fox in his childhood, when he saw a woman leaning out the window of the allegedly haunted house next door, and she threw cherries, not then in season, into his mouth.

Everyone said he had encountered a fox.[46] Fruits out of season are, as we saw in the last chapter, a common, petty marvel, and this experience is sensually suggestive. In the mid-nineteenth century, an author quoted earlier recounted a similarly friendly vixen: "Empty rooms have many foxes, and if from time to time their forms are visible or their voices audible, that isn't worth marveling at. My late mother often said that when I was young, every evening an old woman would smile at me, and this became a regular habit. But I don't remember."[47] His mother related this tale of a kindly fairy godmother as a comforting vision of childhood. These visions of kindly female foxes contrast with the stern fox patriarch. Fox-infested rooms can take on the charm of a world of marvel close at hand, reminiscent in this case of nineteenth- and twentieth-century Western children's literature, which offered worlds of enchantment behind the wardrobe door.

THEME AND VARIATIONS: THE FOX LODGER

Among He Bang'e's stories discussed in the previous chapter was the fox who moves in, not as vermin but as a guest. The recurring plot elements in tales of fox lodgers are more complex than those found in the basic structures of haunting and residence: a mysterious figure asks to rent or borrow an unused building for his family; at some point the human hosts discover that their lodgers are foxes; there is often, but not always, a confrontation; and the tale inevitably ends with the foxes' departure. The guise of humanity is an essential trait, especially at the opening of the tale. Conceptually this tale occupies a place between haunting and residence in the metanarrative about claims to indoor space. Like tales of haunting, this story explores the fear of unclaimed space being claimed by alien forces, and the foxes also depart within the time frame of the tale. Yet like tales of residence, the foxes claim a relatively contained space. The fox lodger thus completes a discussion of negotiation with the fox at home at the same time as it allows for a closer focus on the uses and variations of a narrower tale type.

46. Jin Liang, *Guayuan shuyi*, xia, 47b.
47. Zhang Yun, *Suoshi xianlu*, shang, 2a.

As a supernatural intrusion is normalized as a relationship between host and guest or landlord and tenant, the underlying strangeness of economic and social interactions is exposed. This story is possible only in an urban, transient society, in which strangers can move into your house and you hardly suspect how strange they really are. Haunting is transformed into an apparently voluntary economic or social transaction; however, it is often unclear precisely how much choice the human landlord has. The overt presence of money varies from tale to tale. Although it is always a single fox, usually an old man, who negotiates the rental, when he moves in, he brings along an entire fox clan of both sexes and various ages; the line between tenancy and infestation is thin.

Given the range and quantity of occurrences, the figure of the fox lodger clearly seems to be the material of shared folklore. I am not positing a line of textual descent for the examples I discuss here, although textual influence cannot be ruled out in individual cases.

The opening and closing of the story are relatively constant. Explanations may be supplied for the foxes' arrival, and some of the reasons foxes seek lodging elsewhere—renovations of their own dwellings; flight from rebellions—incorporate them into the human world.[48] Between the relatively fixed forms of entrance and exit, relations with tenant foxes are highly variable. Sometimes the fox clan is a source of mischief, and the depiction of their haunting is the same as it might be without the pretense of tenancy. Sometimes the two families have an entirely pleasant and "human" relationship. The fox can also play the role of moral judge, putting the family in order.[49] Interest is either in the failure of domestic intimacy or in its success, particularly the clever rewards foxes can grant (as we saw in He Bang'e's story).

The exposure of the lodgers as foxes, although a fixed element, is

---

48. The same story of virtuous fox lodgers fleeing the Taipings appears in *Shenbao*; in the collection of stories from the *Shenbao, Jiwen leibian*; and in *Hutian lu*, which copies liberally from the newspaper; see "Jia hu ji" 佳狐記, *Jiwen leibian* 9.27b; and Baiyi jushi, *Hutian lu*, xia, 48a–b.

49. E.g., Yu Yue, *Youtai xianguan biji*, 6.28a; and "Shu shang" 蜀商, in Yue Jun, *Ershi lu*, 1.18.

not the climax of the story and does not dictate their exit. The host may indeed know from the outset that his guests are foxes. Regardless of the variations, the one constant in the stories is that the foxes leave when their "lease" expires. This distinguishes them from house foxes who can remain for generations; the fixed duration of these stories more closely resembles the finite destined tie of the fox romance. This limited term could also be related to the temporary favors bestowed by the fox as an object of popular worship, which I discuss in the next chapter. The restriction of the fox in time is a crucial element of this story: an intrusion of the strange is given not only an intelligible shape but also a limited span.

This story type also domesticates the fox by imagining foxes as families, headed by a patriarchal spokesman. The elder male fox appears as a highly articulate human male, whereas the rest of his clan, his inferiors in age and gender, may be more like animals and are often silent. Ji Yun's tendency to control foxes by dividing them into age cohorts, seen in his theoretical explanation discussed in the previous chapter, was widely shared. Other types of stories, like the sexual plot, often deal with the individual fox on a lonely road; or else other members of a fox family serve as matchmakers or obstacles to nubile young females. Foxes were often envisioned in groups in the Tang as well, but they were usually groups of beasts in their own burrows. In the Qing one deals with entire fox clans in human form and in human residences. Pu Songling was one of the first authors to depict entire fox clans made up of individual personalities; this is one aspect of his unique blending of the strange and the domestic. His depictions of the relations of fox families and human ones remained focused on the romance, which bound the families together.[50] The appearance of whole clans allows for the depiction of love triangles with sisters or cousins. Later collections develop this further to create pure fantasies of asexual domestic intimacy with foxes. The *Liaozhai* imitations offer the domestic ideal on the scale of whole families of foxes and humans living in harmony side

50. E.g., "Qingfeng" 青鳳, in *LZ*, 1.112; "Fengxian" 鳳仙, in ibid., 9.1177; and "Hu meng" 狐夢, in ibid., 5.618.

by side, exchanging pleasantries, and offering to betroth their children.[51]

One way of looking at this story type is as a test of human domestic management and hospitality. The protagonist of this story, in an even more pronounced way than in tales of haunting, is the male head of the human household. The particular challenge of a whole clan of fox lodgers is that all members of the household, male and female, young and old, masters and servants, have their own interactions, but it is the head of the household who must control them all. That the interaction with foxes reflects on the order of the household is constant, but the precise message varies: some stories seem to laud generosity to strangers, and others affirm policing of the boundaries between the human and the non-human. In either case it is significant that the fox lodger is a dignified man of the same class of his landlord, not a beggar. Transient lower-class individuals arouse a different set of fears.[52]

As with the domestic fox in general, the fox lodger seems to turn up first in late Ming collections, for example, the sixth fox story in *Kuai yuan*. A fox in the form of an old man arrives and his human landlord agrees to his tenancy. Their relationship is amicable enough until the fox asks for help in hosting a banquet. The landlord grows suspicious when he discovers that none of the neighbors can see any of the huge numbers of guests. He goes to various temples to pray to get rid of the fox, but everywhere he goes, the fox is there praying first. Then the fox proceeds to make so much trouble that the man begs that things return to the way they were. The fox leaves of his own accord after three years.[53] The man is determined to expel the fox simply because it is a fox, not because of any offense on its part, an attitude typical of earlier stories, all the way back to the Six Dynasties. The man's powerlessness and the apparent lack of concern

51. E.g., "Yu gongzi" 玉公子, *YTSL*, 10.278–84. This story proves that the domestic fantasy is not entirely opposed to the erotic fantasy; the master of the house is rewarded with three fox wives.

52. There is a frequent comparison of beggars and ghosts. Also, fears of sorcery and witchcraft often focused on these transient strangers; see Kuhn, *Soulstealers*, pp. 115–17.

53. *Kuai yuan*, *juan* 15, story 6. Another late Ming example is "Jingshi hu" 京氏狐, in Wang Tonggui, *Ertan leizeng*, 47.2b.

on the part of the heavenly powers would make Ji Yun and many other Qing authors uncomfortable; they would need some moral justification for allowing the fox's continued presence in the face of human opposition. Both the man's automatic hostility and this moral lack of definition mark this story as early. *Kuai yuan* is an important starting point, revealing the resident fox and the fox lodger emerging side by side, but it differs from later collections in depicting an equal, unresolved struggle between foxes and men.

Both a story in *Liaozhai* and one in *Meng'an zazhu* use this frame as an opening for a tale of a fox massacre and fox revenge. In *Meng'an zazhu*, after the usual opening, the fox patriarch goes away, leaving his family behind, and they begin to throw stones and make noise. The fox lodger opening leads to a tale of a fox haunting of a more conventional sort. The foxes' landlord peeks through the wall to discover that all his guests have tails and excess body hair. He has hunters come to destroy them.[54] In *Liaozhai*, the guests appear entirely human and even invite their host to a splendid feast, making his slaughter of the foxes more unprovoked.[55] The clever and clan-annihilating means of revenge take up the rest of both narratives. Although the plot elements of the two differ, they are linked by the implication that the human host has violated his side of the bargain. The usual pattern of fox tenants' leaving when the lease expires is not allowed to complete itself, with disastrous consequences.

In a frequent variant of the fox lodger story that offers an interesting blend of the civilized and wild aspects of the fox and again highlights the role of the fox patriarch, one of the younger members of the clan makes trouble until the fox patriarch punishes the recreant, sometimes fatally.[56] The foxes often depart after this confrontation. The foxes' containment and control of the violation, which often results form young male foxes' advances toward the women of the human family, makes peaceful coexistence possible. Yet many of the

---

54. "Hu bao" 狐報, in Yu Jiao, *Meng'an zazhu*, 8 2a.

55. "Jiu shan wang" 九山王, *LZ*, 2.240–46.

56. For an argument that the plot of foxes punishing their own is linked to observations of fox cannibalism in the wild, see Yoshino Hiroko, *Kitsune*, pp. 30–31. Given the remoteness of most of these examples from the natural fox, I find this somewhat dubious.

stories dwell on the bloodiness and harshness of the punishment; the discovery of the fox corpse is a second violent intrusion into the domestic scene, particularly when found next to the woman's dressing table.[57] The corpse serves to end the narrative as it did in older fox stories, even though it is not the first evidence of the foxes' true identity. The old, wild aspects of the fox tradition are veiled by the guise of tenancy and controlled by fox elders, but they remain the driving interest of the story.

One story from *Zi bu yu* cleverly combines various conventions of the fox story, in this case the haunted place and the fox lodger. A room in a man's house is haunted by a ghost who had died of hanging. The owner is secretly delighted when a fox youth comes demanding a place to stay, since he assumes the fox will be able to drive out the ghost. Instead, the next morning he finds a fox corpse hanging from the rafters.[58] This story is typical of *Zi bu yu* both in the clever twist in its conclusion and in the utter lack of interest in any explanation of this surprise. I am not sure whether Yuan Mei himself combined the two pieces of lore, but in any event such twists represent his taste in *zhiguai*.

A story first included in *Tingyu xuan biji* 聽雨軒筆記 (Notebook from the Listening to Rain Pavilion; 1791) presents the most civilized and sympathetic extreme of fox lodgers.[59] When Yu Yue, the author of *Youtai xianguan biji*, adapted this story, he commented that stories of foxes lodging in men's houses were common, and pointed to the overwhelmingly positive nature of this one as a justification for in-

57. Examples include: "Hu daoxue" 狐道學, in Yuan Mei, *Zi bu yu*, 22.447; "Zhangde shuhu" 彰德署狐, in Tang Yongzhong, *Yijiong baibian*, 8.17b; "Jiuwuhu" 僦屋狐 in Dong Han, *Zhuanxiang zhuibi*, xia, 39b; and "Jie yu" 借寓, in Qian Yong, *Lüyuan conghua*, 16.20a. A late Qing case of foxes controlling their own bureaucratizes the relationship. The father of a fox-afflicted son makes his suit to a supervising official of foxes and finds a beheaded fox hanging in a tree; see *Shenbao* 3/8/1876, 15.9356.

58. "Huxian ziyi" 狐仙自縊, in Yuan Mei, *Zi bu yu*, 14.272.

59. Other examples of the more civilized type are "Fangjia yuan hu" 方家園狐, in Zhang Jingyun, *Qiuping xinyu*, *jiuan* 11; and "Gulou hu" 鼓樓狐, in Fang Yuankun, *Liangpeng yehua*, 1.16b. A story of the Guangxu era that was copied into more than one collection and included in the newspaper *Shenbao* is "Jiahu ji"; see note 48 to this chapter.

cluding it in his collection.[60] In the late Qianlong period, the story goes, foxes come to dwell in the spare buildings of the Jiang family. The human father of the house finds the perfect literary companion in the person of the fox patriarch, and his daughter Ying'gu has the run of the fox household. There are other stories in which a child is the only one who can see the foxes and seems to be a kind of medium,[61] and shadows of that tradition remain here, but in this case the daughter's intimacy with the foxes seems to emphasize both the innocence of the connection and its extreme domesticity. The two worlds intersect in the innermost part of the women's quarters, at the very heart of human domesticity. The women of the two families exchange gifts of fruit; the foxes give the most rare and unseasonable delicacies, and the Jiangs repay them with local produce. When the fox mother helps the human child to bind her feet more skillfully, in a way that both makes them smaller and causes no pain, this both recalls foxes' associations with the charm of the female body and involves the foxes in the most intimate domestic affair. The detail that the bandages have been treated with sugar rather than the usual alum again emphasizes innocence. The sympathetic foxes are finally driven out, without the Jiangs' consent, by a friend with a talent for exorcism. Yet the parting is still amicable, and the foxes leave presents for the entire family, a rare book and painting for Jiang and jewels for Ying'gu's dowry. The foxes are a source of small-scale aesthetic pleasures, good calligraphy, clever conversation, and fruit out of season, amiable marvels contained within the home. These figures are a far cry from the rustling heard in an abandoned storage room of the early stories. Foxes as charming companions for a child recall the first-person reminiscences above. However, as Yu Yue's comment suggests, such positive examples of the fox lodger story seem in some ways defensive, a conscious attempt to battle the assumption that such lodgers would mean trouble.

---

60. Xu (?), *Ting yu xuan biji*, 1.10. The preface of the *zaji* section is dated 1791. The tie between this collection and *Youtai xianguan biji* seems to be one of locality, since both authors are from Deqing in Zhejiang. The textual differences between the two versions are relatively slight. See "Hu jin renqing" 狐近人情, in Yu Yue, *Youtai xianguan biji*, 10.6a.

61. "Guanku huxian," in Qian Yong, *Lüyuan conghua*, 16.13a.

Examples of the fox lodger are included in collections of every period discussed here: the late Ming, the Qianlong, and the Guangxu. The plot formula is sturdy and flexible enough to contain all the variations of late imperial foxes. The fascination of such stories no longer lies in the possibility that foxes might come to stay, but rather in how that situation is resolved. Interest in the intersection of a human and an alien household focuses on the successes and oversights of patriarchal management in both. In contrast, when men went to live with foxes, it was a temporary idyll and wish fulfillment experienced by a single individual, an extension of the romance. The incorporation of the fox into the human world was both more common and more mundane in every sense.

From Domestic Chaos to Domestic Order

If the presence of the fox in the home is part of the shared language of the late imperial fox story, what can an individual author or narrator use it to express? As the preceding discussion has revealed, the fox in the home can be either unsettling or settled. One part of the fascination of the domestic fox for literati authors is how a force of chaos becomes a force of order.

The two most famous authors of the Qing classical tale shared this interest, but their understanding of domestic order and the role of the alien in that order diverged. I see Pu Songling and Ji Yun as both creating and transmitting, using elements that existed outside their own stories to create new visions of the fox. As we have seen, Pu Songling recorded relatively uncomplicated tales of haunting by foxes, resident foxes, and fox lodgers, but he also used haunting and residence as stages in accounts of complex relationships with foxes in his long *chuanqi*-style tales.[62] However, I would argue that the influence of the fox at home goes deeper than this. Whether annoyances or entertaining curiosities, foxes had become extremely familiar by the late imperial period. Pu's unparalleled accomplishment lay in combining descriptions of the strange with depictions of domestic relationships as his vixens and ghosts come home to stay as brides and mothers. Although cause and effect are difficult to disentangle

---

62. See, e.g., "Qingfeng," in *LZ*, 1.112–18; and "Jiaona" 嬌娜, in ibid., 1.57–65.

here, the resident fox provided a model of harmonious cohabitation. Pu was interested in domestic order as a familial order centered on the marriage tie.[63] His vixens often have natal family loyalties of their own, even as they strive to assimilate themselves into human families. Pu was passionately concerned with incorporating his vixens into human domesticity by the story's end, but his sense of erotic tension and marvel forbids them from being established there in the beginning.

In contrast, Ji Yun preferred to have foxes as part of a stable domestic order from the outset. The focus of his attention was the dialogue between male heads of households rather than the romance between human and fox. The fox's assigned task in the domestic sphere seems to be to bring order to human families. As we saw above, for Ji and his close friends, foxes in the house could be a reflection of their family's cultural values; but other families required fox intervention. The domestic setting makes it convenient for the fox to play the role of moral judge: a haunted room allowed a fox to judge the morality of passing strangers, but the house fox becomes an arbiter of family morality. Foxes are both intimate members of the household and detached outsiders. A fox could also serve as a repository of a family's moral tradition and reprimand the younger generation for lapsing from parents' standards of behavior.[64] A plot involving a resident fox can only be set into motion by some imbalance in the household's moral order. For example, in one anecdote a maid carouses with the household foxes, who live in the back building where firewood is stored. At first the master of the house blames the foxes and upbraids the fox patriarch: "We have gotten along for many years, and other than getting firewood every day, we don't bother each other. How could you suddenly go beyond the bounds of propriety and take a maid of good family as a prostitute, to pour wine for you? When the sons and younger brothers are debauched, where are their fathers and older brothers? Isn't the head of the household ashamed?" The fox responds that he has already beaten his sons for their transgression

63. See the analysis of "Qingfeng" in Chapter 5 for a thorough discussion of the transition from haunting to domestic harmony and the combination of the domestic fox with the romance.

64. *YWCT*, 16.948, story 97.

but points out that it was the maid who approached them first. Because this maid was loose and had lost her virginity long before, they dared to dally with her but not with any of the other beautiful young maids. In the end the fox lays the blame at the feet of the human patriarch, because the maids are not being married off at the proper times. Human patriarch and fox patriarch split the responsibility for the failure in coexistence, but the fox has the last word.[65]

In *Yuewei caotang biji* foxes avidly point out improper family relationships, in a reversal of their own skill at becoming false duplicates of family members.[66] In one tale a rural man who has lived at peace with a fox for decades suddenly hears it laughing. He asks it what is so funny, and the fox replies, "I am laughing at the man who treasures his sworn brother more than his blood brother, who treasures his present wife's children from an earlier marriage more than his former wife's children. Why are you so angry?" He defends this message further with a quotation from the classics, and the human man is ashamed enough to change his behavior.[67] In later collections foxes take harsher measures to correct the wayward by acting as punishing spirits rather than commentators.[68]

For Pu, foxes' domestic presence means that they have become entangled in human relationships. Ji's foxes are involved in the domestic scene in the role of commentators and judges, the same position that Ji took in his stories. Despite their obvious differences, Ji and Pu shared central assumptions about foxes' presence and familiarity. Both authors also had creatures other than foxes speak in intelligible, human voices, and in Pu's case they, too, have intimate relations with humans. Yet it was the fox that led the way by suggesting the particular blends of ordinariness and strangeness that each man achieved.

The domestication of the fox begins with the fact of their pres-

---

65. *YWCT*, 17.985, story 124.

66. The type of the fox as doppelgänger has its most famous early example in a tale in Gan Bao, *Soushen ji*, *juan* 18, no. 422.

67. *YWCT*, 9.453–54, story 179.

68. E.g., the tale of the unfilial brother in Baiyi jushi, *Hutianlu*, xia 48b. For an almost identical tale, see "Shanyang hu" 山楊狐, in Tang Yongzhong, *Yijiong baibian*, 5.43b.

ence in homes and local space. But as a result of this location, the originally alien fox became familiar and intimate, associated with the home, the family, and the personal. The domestication of the fox directly influenced the settings of fox tales, but it also had more subtle influences on foxes' portrayal. In the Tang Miss Ren, for all her human traits, was exposed as different from a human being in the domestic sphere, because she could not sew her own clothing. The later tradition almost overcompensates for this deficiency.

CONCLUSION

An international perspective helps shed light on the compelling ordinariness of the domestic fox. In Western Europe, accounts of poltergeists became common only after the Reformation, chronologically an interesting parallel to the late imperial rise in fox haunting. In a history of ghosts, *Appearances of the Dead*, R. C. Finucane argues that in Victorian times, ghosts haunting houses are not named individuals known to the living but anonymous, mischievous strangers. One might speculate that in both the Chinese and the British cases anonymity and indoor settings are results of an increasingly urban society. For both societies, the home is an important sphere of physical and spiritual control. Finucane argues that Victorian ghosts are distinguished by their relative dullness and lack of purpose because accounts of these apparitions served only one purpose, to prove the existence of the supernatural in an age of conflict between rationalism and reason.[69] Although his observation of dullness and purposelessness applies to the fox as poltergeist, his explanation for the rise of such a phenomenon are alien to the Chinese setting. However, even for the English case, Finucane's arguments are somewhat oversimplified, since he does not seem to consider the very different range of interactions with personalized spirits made possible by spiritualism.[70] The English in the Victorian era had a whole range of experiences of the strange: scrupulously documented, impersonal knocks; the sentimentalized and personalized voices of the

69. Finucane, *Appearances of the Dead*, pp. 211–12.
70. Alex Owen, *The Darkened Room*.

spiritualism movement; and fairies collected in other people's folklore. As we shall see, foxes can assume all these roles.

As an explanation of the importance of domestic fox-poltergeists in the Chinese context, I would contend that the growth in literacy and publishing, particularly *zhiguai* publishing, had an effect similar to the scrupulous efforts of the British Society for Psychical Research, which collected thousands of middle-class Victorians' accounts of their experiences with the paranormal.[71] The encounter between an ordinary man and a relatively "ordinary" representative of the strange was considered worthy of being recorded. The material of *zhiguai* moved away from cosmographic speculation to ever more personal experiences of the supernatural. Stories of fox haunting are a sign that the disturbing and the strange can visit the hearth of any man.[72] Interest in both the fox as obnoxious poltergeist and the fox as co-resident rely on the paradoxical pettiness and ordinariness of the strange. Not only does the presence of a fox in the home, whether throwing stones or painting lotuses, not foretell the fall of a dynasty, it does not even presage domestic disaster or decline. The fox is a move away from the most deadly confrontation with another world; it offers the possibility that an ordinary man could manage such a confrontation successfully and live to tell the tale. If the Victorian poltergeist, and the record made of it, insists that ghosts exist, a Qing-era fox instead says that this strangeness is right here with me in the ordinary world, and this is how I survived this test of my home.

The democratization of perspectives on the strange has definite limits. The perspective of this chapter is dominated by those who could afford to have neglected storage rooms or lonely garden pavilions, as well as of those who moved from government office to government office and could afford to rent lodgings where they went.

---

71. Finucane, *Appearances of the Dead*, pp. 190–91.

72. Campany (*Strange Writing*, p. 353) argues that a "democratic" approach to the strange, in which ordinary people, and not only kings and rulers, could interact with denizens of other worlds, is already characteristic of *Soushen ji* and other Six Dynasties *zhiguai* works, which he groups under the heading, "The Perspective of Heaven and Humanity." These works were the most influential on the tradition as a whole; perhaps this is a tendency that exists throughout the tradition and is further expanded in the Qing.

One suspects that people in smaller homes, with fewer objects for foxes to fling around, either dealt with their foxes in woodpiles or had the conflict with foxes staged across their own bodies, as foxes possessed their wives, sons, or daughters-in-law. The perspective is also dominated by male heads of households: servants, women, and children cope with the disturbances caused by foxes, but the management of the disturbance or occupation remains the responsibility of the male head of the household. Movement from place to place does not destroy the partriarch's sphere of moral responsibility; it moves with him wherever he goes.

Both the haunting fox and the resident fox are inventions of the late imperial period, and their geographic spread allows one to tell a clearer literary-historical story than many other types of fox story. This suggests a simple metanarrative: the fox moves in, first in northern China and then everywhere. The fox at first makes trouble but gradually grows tame, and humans and foxes adapt to one another. Such a story has explanatory power, but it has limitations. It has interesting parallels to the most popular contemporary theory on the fox, the theory of fox progress in which each individual hairy animal gradually grows more and more human through its efforts. The unsettling strange does seem necessarily to predate the strange settling down, and the Tang accounts suggest that the haunting fox predates the resident fox. Nevertheless, the possibility of humans entirely accustomed to the fox is present as early as the resident fox itself, in southerners' accounts of curious northern habits. For the fox, domestication was neither linear nor permanent. There is never a moment, not in 1795, not in 1895, when civil lodgers have entirely supplanted the hairy figures glimpsed in the corners or the noisemakers on the roof. The tradition provided a convincing explanation of individual progress for this range: for every civilized fox, there was an impish, unevolved animal throwing a household into disorder. If the only fox one ever encountered personally was a rustling in the woodpile, that did nothing to contradict other people's splendid stories of bizarre apparitions or drinking companions. This wide range of variation, confounding all metanarratives save perhaps the one the tradition provides for itself, is not limited to the fox who comes to stay.

The fox probes the human household as both a physical and a moral space, and the stories present a range of results of that test. To use Freud's terms, the fox is a test of how a household can not only become *unheimlich* (uncanny/unhomelike), but how the *unheimlich* can turn *heimlich* again.[73]

73. Freud, "Das Unheimliche," in idem, *Gesammelte Werke, chronologisch geordnet,* 12:231.

{4}
Fox Worship

ZHIGUAI AND POPULAR RELIGION

All the generic problems of the *zhiguai*, including the questions of where it stands along the lines between fiction and history, the elite and the popular, folklore and literature, and belief and fantasy, are at their most acute when we turn to the relationship of *zhiguai* and popular religion. The term "popular religion" itself can be understood in two senses: first, the religious ideas and practices shared by the widest possible range of social classes in a society; and second, the religious ideas and practices of the lower classes as distinguished from those of the elite. As the elite-authored literary form devoted to recording the popular, unofficial, and unorthodox, *zhiguai*, and more broadly *biji*, form a repository of records of popular religion in both senses: it is in them that literati authors recorded both their own unorthodox ideas and practices and those they attributed to others. Yet at the same time, *zhiguai* collections are primarily anthologies of narratives, and they can serve to entertain or to argue, as well as to document.

In recent scholarship, there have been both studies that use religion to understand *zhiguai* and those that use *zhiguai* to understand religion. In studies of very different moments in the history of the genre, Campany, Dudbridge, and Chan conclude that the *zhiguai* is fundamentally a religious genre, in the sense that it both reflects and projects a particular conception of man's place in the universe and his relationship to extra-human forces. Their studies put different amounts of emphasis on "reflection" and "projection": Campany stresses *zhiguai* as a means of persuasion, and Chan emphasizes Ji Yun's didacticism. Dudbridge, on the other hand, sees Tang *zhiguai* as reliable records of the religious experience of ordinary people, rather than examples of proselytizing by their authors. In the following discussion, my emphasis is also on the *zhiguai* as record rather than persuasive tool. I agree that *zhiguai* can be religious, in the sense that they construct a cosmology and that they can teach how and how not to interact with non-human forces, but they are also literary.

Studies that use *zhiguai* to understand religion tend to focus on religion as an organized system of interaction with non-human forces and on *zhiguai* as documents of these interactions. Studies of premodern popular religion often rely heavily on *zhiguai*, and more broadly on *biji* for source material, because the genre describes both encounters with the divine and local customs.[1] These narratives are especially treasured as records of cults outside the official, state-sanctioned pantheon and calendar. Although most scholars acknowledge the potential problem of elite mediation in records of the religious beliefs and practices of other classes, genders, or regions, the material is too valuable to be wholly disregarded. My interests overlap with those scholars of popular religion who assemble accounts of a particular deity, for my focus is on a particular creature rather an individual author or the genre as a whole. But, in contrast to them, my interest is first of all in the stories, rather than the extra-textual practices the stories document. In this regard, Dudbridge, as a literary scholar, remains the most useful model because of his meticulous close readings of narratives.

This chapter is not a history of fox worship as practice in the Ming and Qing. Xiaofei Kang has written a masterful study on that topic, using many of the same sources on which this book depends.[2] Whereas she uses narrative to cast light on popular religion, I use

---

1. E.g., Hansen, *The Changing Gods of Medieval China*; Hymes, "Personal and Bureaucratic Hierarchy in Chinese Religion: Evidence from the Song Dynasty"; von Glahn, "The Enchantment of Wealth."

2. Xiaofei Kang, "Power at the Margins"; see also Li Shouju, *Huxian xinyang yu huli jing gushi*.

popular religion to cast light on narrative. The two are woven together extremely tightly in the character of the fox. My study examines the forms that fox worship took in narrative, and how the fox that was the object of worship in stories related to the rest of the narrative tradition of the fox. Stories of the supernatural and practices of worship are ways of imagining and giving shape to a relationship with non-human forces, and in different ways, both are interested in regulation of that relationship. To return to the terms "lore" and "pattern" employed in the previous chapter, worship involves lore as shared knowledge of the worshipped being ("foxes can bring wealth"). To control relations with that other creature and take advantage of the knowledge of lore, patterns of ritual practice and of expected response from the other are established. Yet there remains a crucial difference between worship and narrative: practices of worship depend on regularity and repetition, and narrative on the exception that violates that repetition, even though that exception itself is partially constructed of familiar patterns.[3]

I argue that the patterns and lore of popular religious practice, however distorted, intertwine with other elements to form the Qing literary fox story. The divergence between the demand for regularity and that for exception complicates the overlap between the lore and patterns of worship and the practices of narrative. Moreover, precisely because of its vivid literary life, the fox is a more challenging object of study than many other cult figures. Worship appears in the *zhiguai* corpus in a variety of forms—ethnographic accounts of the practices of worship; individual stories of worship; and stories that are not overtly about worship but share patterns or lore with accounts of worship. The discrepancy between general descriptions and narrative examples observed in earlier chapters also applies here, and as is the case with foxes as residents of human dwellings, individual narratives outnumber general statements.

Perspective is crucial in accounts of fox worship. Worship is most often viewed from the outside and is usually held at greater distance

---

3. One can exaggerate the link between worship and orderly patterns. Many gods have disorderly origins, and one often turns to the gods in response to disorder, which is sometimes interpreted as their doing; see Shahar and Weller, *Unruly Gods*, pp. 8–12.

from these authors than the presence of a fox in the home. Human practices seem to demand judgment in a way other kinds of interactions with foxes do not. Since judgment is passed more often on the humans linked to foxes by reciprocal ties than on the foxes themselves, differences of class, gender, and region come into play.

As we have seen, the presence of a fox in a home created a point of intersection between the human and the non-human world and could be a source of chaos or of stability and containment. Although worship is a means of controlling an interaction with a non-human force, in these narratives we also see tension between order and chaos: the question is whether worship is portrayed as a stabilizing force or a disruptive one. The answer depends on the triangular relationship linking author, fox-worshipper, and fox.

This chapter is organized according to different patterns of interactions between humans and foxes that fall under the rubric of worship. Fox worship could include different kinds of exchanges across the boundary between worlds and could involve material goods or information. Such exchanges could occur directly between the worshipper and fox or might involve a human intermediary.

EARLY HISTORY

The records of fox worship before late imperial times are too scattered to allow us to reconstruct its history. There is one strongly worded statement from the Tang: "Since the beginning of the Tang, many of the commoners have worshipped fox spirits. They make offerings in their bedchambers to beg for their favor. The foxes share people's food and drink. They [the worshippers] do not serve a single master. At the time there was a figure of speech saying, 'Where there is no fox demon, no village can be established.'"[4] This description suggests important points of continuity with the later tradition: foxes are worshipped in the home with offerings of food, and an elite writer describes the practice from the outside. Different families worship different foxes. The discrepancy between this general state-

4. *TPGJ,* 447. 3658. Cf. the translation in Kang, "Power at the Margins," p.33. See also Li Jianguo's discussion of the early fox worship tradition, *Zhongguo hu wenhua*, pp. 113–15.

ment of popular belief and the individual narratives of relations with foxes is great. Given the paucity of materials on the practices of fox worship in the Tang, we cannot connect, other than speculatively, the fox as local spirit worshipped in the home and the fox as illusionist and seducer found in narratives, although Kang links this description to the sexual tradition on foxes.[5] In contrast to the situation in the Qing, the early narratives are not close enough to fox worship to give an image of it, whereas in the Qing narrative and practice grow closer. This might simply be a by-product of the sheer volume of Qing *zhiguai*. However, if one follows Dudbridge in reading Tang *zhiguai* primarily as records of religious experiences, encounters with foxes were clearly an important part of that experience. Ji Yun linked the prevalence of fox worship and the large quantity of fox stories in *Taiping guangji*, but the stories in *Taiping guangji* themselves do not seem to make that link.[6] Rather, Ji seemed to be projecting backward the direct relationship between fox worship and fox stories he saw in his own time.

In Tang stories about foxes demanding worship, which seem generically quite distinct from the "ethnographic" account quoted above, they tend to take the forms of bodhisattvas to hoodwink people. This is clearly related to Tang anxieties about the powers of Buddhism; in the Qing, fox worship is directly linked not to the fox's skill at transformation and illusion but to a broader range of domestic trickery and other powers.[7]

In the Song there are scattered references to fox worship, most notably the destruction of a "Fox King Temple" in Shanxi by a Confucian official, which is recorded in the official dynastic history.[8]

---

5. Kang, "Power at the Margins," p. 77.

6. *YWCT,* 10.503–4, story 229.

7. There are Ming and Qing works that use the concept of the fox as sham bodhisattva, but this seems to be an earlier trope still available to be played with rather than a central element of the tradition. Examples include Feng Menglong's version of *Ping yao zhuan, Xin ping yao zhuan*, 3.2a; "Xiaomei" 小梅, in *LZ,* 9.1210–16; and "Huxian maochong Guanyin sannian" 狐仙冒充觀音三年, in Yuan Mei, *Zi bu yu,* 7.135. For a translation of Yuan Mei's story, see "A Fox Fairy Plays Guanyin for Three Years," in Louie and Edwards, *Censored by Confucius,* pp. 63–68.

8. "Wang Sizong zhuan" 王嗣宗傳, *Song shi* 287.9650. Li Shouju (*Huxian xinyang yu hulijing gushi*, pp. 55–56) concludes from this that in the Song foxes had

However, there is a relative dearth of foxes in the literary record of the Song. A Jin story describes placatory offerings to foxes, a form of narrative that became more common later.[9] The inherited textual tradition is enough to support the conclusion that Ming and Qing fox worship had roots in earlier periods, but there is not enough evidence to trace a direct lineage.

THE NICHE OF THE HUXIAN

Like the word "haunting," the word "worship" demands a closer examination. The words used in the original stories for a direct relationship with foxes are most often *dao* 禱, *feng* 奉, or *ji* 祭, "to make offerings," or simply *shi* 事, "to serve." When a human intermediary represents the fox, different words are used to describe the relationships both of the medium to the fox and of the medium to clients. I use the word "worship" to describe relationships based on respectful offerings on the human side, in expectation of supernatural benefits granted by the fox.

What niche does the fox fill in the complex ecology of Chinese popular religion? In these stories, who worshipped foxes, where, and to what purpose? "Niche" is indeed the key word. Although there are scattered references to fox temples,[10] smaller-scale sites of worship are more common. The same spaces that house resident foxes serve as shrines, whether they are rooms in houses or outdoor burrows. People of both sexes and many different classes, ranging from peasants to scholar-officials, are depicted as making offerings to foxes, although it is rare for an author to describe himself as making such an offering. Foxes could offer protection, wealth, prophecy, or medical prescriptions.

As always with the fox, its liminal position is key. Worship involves the entire range of the fox, from the animal that scuttles

---

evolved from household spirits to regional tutelary deities housed in temples. Intriguing as these references are, there is insufficient evidence to conclude this was the case on a national scale. See Kang, "Power at the Margins," pp. 78–83, and Li Jianguo, *Zhongguo hu wenhua*, pp. 127–31 for a discussion of other Song sources.

9. "Hugong qu hu" 胡公去狐, in Yuan Haowen, *Xu Yijian zhi*, 2.26.

10. For a reference to a *huxian miao* 狐仙廟, "fox temple," see the story "Hu laoren" 胡老人, in Dongxuan zhuren, *Shuyi ji*, 4a.

among the rafters to a human figure somewhere between a beneficent *xian* and malign *yao*. Foxes are positioned among the pettiest of the supernatural powers. They remain local and unofficial and were never incorporated into an orthodox pantheon.[11] The fox-deity at each small shrine is worshipped as an individual, often with a name, but no individual fox transcends that local sphere of influence. The worship of one particular fox was a way to claim a piece of the larger tradition of transformation, ascendance, and benefit. Worship of foxes was based on a shared concept of what the fox was, but the relationship with each fox was individual. The fox accepted offerings on a small scale, usually in the form of wine and food, and in turn might assist with one's personal problems rather than with great affairs of state. Pettiness made the fox accessible.

Fox worship reveals the interconnected nature of cultural phenomena. As with haunting, there are other divinities and creatures who in other times and places played some of the same roles as the fox. In what follows I make judgments as to what is more central and what more peripheral to the fox, but these boundaries are never absolute. Other creatures (such as the Wutong; discussed below) could also be the most minor and closest representative of the other world. But no other creature can match the fox in the range of different kinds of stories that combined with stories of worship and colored them.

When foxes are worshipped in the Ming and Qing, it is usually under the name *huxian* 狐仙, "fox transcendent." This term first appears in scattered references in the late Ming and becomes increasingly common throughout the Qing, to the point it becomes synonymous with "fox."[12] What is a *xian*, and what does it mean to be

11. The one exception is the association between foxes and Taishan Niangniang, one case in which foxes are affiliated with a cult of a larger goddess. Taishan in Shandong is in the heart of fox territory. See Pomeranz, "Power, Gender, and Pluralism."

12. For a discussion of the meaning of the term in the context of worship, see Kang, "Power at the Margins," pp. 300–303. See also Li Jianguo, *Zhongguo hu wenhua*, pp. 199–207.

As for the history of the term *huxian*, in the late Ming it is used as a title for a reprinted Tang story of foxes who ascended to the status of *xian*, but fox and *xian* were not yet a linked concept; see Mo Chizi, *Humei congtan*, 3.13b. The earliest

both fox and *xian*? Originally, a *xian* was a being, human or otherwise, who achieves immortality through Daoist self-cultivation. In a looser sense, *xian* was sometimes applied to members of the divine hierarchy, particularly beautiful young women, with no particular emphasis on their earlier self-advancement. To call a fox *xian* was to render its transformations morally acceptable, just as to call it a *yao* implied immoral transformations. The term emphasizes the final goal of foxes' self-improvement rather than their origins. It could simply be a polite term, a reflection of the taboo on calling the fox a "fox."[13] In addition, a worshipper would never admit that the figure

---

references to the linked concept are in the approximate contemporaries *Liaozhai* and *Shuyi ji*. The *Shuyi ji* tale tells of a fox that was worshipped in a temple in Dezhou and answered questions as a disembodied voice; see "Hu laoren," in Dongxuan zhuren, *Shuyi ji*, 4a. Pu Songling's use of the term seems inconsistent. He relatively rarely used it for his famous vixen heroines in the body of his stories, but he did so more commonly in his "Historian of the Strange" comments. It seems to be a term he used when making more general comments about what distinguishes his heroines from ordinary mortals. It is, however, hard to determine whether the term is being used as a general term for an ideal woman or in specific reference to the fox. He used the term more commonly in stories related to the context of fox worship, such as "Chou hu" and "Shangxian" (both discussed below.) Other examples include "Yu qian" 雨錢 (*LZ*, 4.505), a story that revolves around the fantasy of foxes being able to grant wealth. The fox in "Wang Cheng" 王成 (*LZ*, 1.105) also introduces herself as *huxian*. She had been the lover of the protagonist's ancestor, but in this context she is a financial rescuer. In "Chu Suiliang" 褚遂良 (*LZ*, 12.1647), the fox also calls herself *huxian*; the emphasis here is also on destined rescue and ends with the vixen's dramatic departure to the heavens.

Authors of the Qianlong period reveal divergent attitudes: Ji Yun delibrately avoided the term, although he would politely address a fox as "*xianjia*" 仙家 (transcendent). Yuan Mei used it generously for a divergent range of fox characters. This seems to reflect Ji's concern with keeping fox worship under control and Yuan's far more casual attitude toward the strange.

In some of the Daoguang and Guangxu collections, however, the term *xian* seems to have become interchangeable with "fox." For example, in a tale of a midwife summoned to deliver the baby of a mysterious family, the figures are introduced as simply *xian*. However, since they live in a mound of firewood and the expectant mother delivers four or five babies at once, all of which have small tails, it is clear what kind of *xian* they are; see "Baita si" 白塔寺 in Li Qingchen, *Zuicha zhiguai*, 3.365.

13. On keeping taboos on uncomplimentary terms for foxes as central to fox worship, see Li Shouju, *Huxian xinyang yu hulijing gushi*, pp. 83–85. Cf. the custom of

to whom he/she made offerings was a *yao* or a *guai*, rather than a *shen* or a *xian*. If *xian* in general offered an alternative to a bureaucratic understanding of the heavens—unconventional figures defiant of authority[14]—foxes were also on a heterodox path to power or respectability.

WORSHIP AND CONFRONTATION

The ties between the subject of the preceding chapter, fox haunting and the resident fox, and fox worship are extremely close. Most simply stated, once human beings, in the hope of receiving benefits, offer the fox food or incense, whether to placate an intruder or to show respect to a resident, the line is crossed. The majority of the stories cited in the previous chapter are, arguably, disguised accounts of worship, which merely omit description of offerings to the fox. This significant detail fundamentally changes humans' complicity in the relationship with the fox. It is easy to construct a pattern of destructive foxes tamed to become house foxes, but that pattern is seldom contained within individual narratives themselves. Similarly, it is tempting to posit worship that begins as bribery of hostile forces and develops into a more decorous relationship. The shift from destructive demon to protective spirit is common in popular religion,[15] but, again, this transition is not generally contained within the narratives themselves. Within individual narratives, haunting tied to offerings is unstable, whereas residence tied to offerings is stable.

As a direct response to destructive haunting, the offering is an alternative to exorcism. The Jin dynasty narrative, set in the Song (1191), alluded to above can serve as a starting point. It takes the very old form, introduced in the previous chapter, of a new

---

calling fairies "the good people" or "the people of peace" in Ireland or England (Kirk, *The Secret Commonwealthes*, p. 1).

14. Shahar and Weller, *Unroly Gods*, p. 10. For foxes to be *xian* is, however, already a form of domestication. In contrast to the carefree carousing of some humans who have become *xian*, foxes who have achieved that goal tend to exhibit self-control.

15. On the continuity between gods and ghosts, see ibid., p. 11; and Katz, *Demon Hordes and Burning Boats*.

officeholder confronting local spirits, the representatives of local beliefs.[16] The official residence in Jimo 即墨, Shandong, in a corner of the old city wall, was infested by foxes, who, in the form of official prostitutes, made trouble by seducing men and women. (On the fox-prostitute link, see the following chapter.) The local population, unable to do anything else, made them offerings. This had been going on for more than fifty years. The new magistrate cannot tolerate this usurping of a public office by monsters and opens up and uses the office. He drives them out first by ignoring their approaches as he reads at night and second by exorcising them from one of his slave girls. One of the departed foxes is discovered possessing a woman in an outlying area, which is taken as proof that the foxes are gone. The local elders put up a stela celebrating the magistrate's accomplishment.[17] Here worship is the last resort when exorcism seems impossible, but it is the opening of a story rather than the conclusion. It is tempting to read the women's possession, too, in terms of confrontation with local popular religion: even one of his own slaves attempts to speak with a defiant local voice and is silenced. The story ends by celebrating the righteous triumph of orthodoxy over monsters and over the local sacrifices that were a capitulation to monsters.

The *Liaozhai* story "Zunhua shu hu" 遵化署狐 (The foxes in the Zunhua county office) covers the same territory but comes to a different conclusion.

Lord Qiu from Zhucheng[18] was in office in Zunhua. In the official office there had long been a lot of foxes. In the rearmost building, a whole clan of the vulpine sort lived, taking it as their home. From time to time they would come out and trick people; if one tried to drive them out, they be-

16. For a Song case regarding such expectations of new officeholders, see Li Shouju, *Huxian xinyang yu hulijing gushi*, p. 55. For an interpretation of Song stories of conflicts between officials and local gods as means of discussing conflicts between officials and local interests, see Boltz, "Not by the Seal of Office Alone." For Tang accounts of the confrontation between officials and local gods, see Dudbridge, *Religious Experience and Lay Society*, p. 136.

17. "Hugong qu hu," in Yuan Haowen, *Xu Yijian zhi*, 2.26.

18. Also in Shandong, not far from Qingdao and Jimo.

came more fierce. Those who took office here could only make offerings of meat to them and dared not be remiss.[19]

Several aspects of this introductory passage are noteworthy. First, the local officials themselves have assumed the responsibility for making these offerings, a description of the officials' compromise with local powers as well as of humans' compromise with foxes. Second, an opening that presents an accustomed pattern is inevitably an introduction to a story in which the pattern is broken. Third, the interaction between officeholder and fox differs from that between a fox resident and its host family in that knowledge of the fox is passed on between the unrelated successive occupants of a particular post rather that within kin groups. Foxes are inherited with the other trappings of office.[20] Finally, foxes are once again intimately tied to a transient society in which people move from place to place.

Qiu is angered by these practices, and the foxes, intimidated, send an emissary in the form of an old woman to plea to be allowed three days to move out. Qiu refuses and immediately carries out a massacre, from which one fox escapes to take revenge. The escaped fox, in the form of an old man, exposes hidden money that Qiu had embezzled to seek a promotion. Here the moral equation of an exorcism by local officials is reversed: although the general logic of "the monstrous cannot defeat the orthodox" is not refuted, it is the official's own moral faults that allow the fox to take revenge. The fox appears in the form of a wronged citizen, whose wife has been slain. In his final commentary, Pu Songling wrote: "Foxes who haunt men are very deserving of execution. But to make them submit and cast them out is also a fulfillment of one's ethical qualities. Qiu could be said to be deeply flawed. If one put a great Confucian in his place, how could a hundred foxes be a match for him?" As in the story, in the course of the comment judgment shifts from the foxes to the official, who was not reasonable enough to allow the foxes three days to depart. Defensive fox worship is an unstable practice, but ending it is not unambiguously virtuous.

---

19. "Zunhua shu hu" 遵化署狐, *LZ*, 2.244. For another account of fox troubles in the same place, see Qing Chengzi, *Zhiyi xubian*, 2.10a.

20. E.g., Xue Fucheng, *Yongan biji*, 2 21b.

Following the text of this story in the 1824 *Liaozhai zhiyi yigao* 聊齋誌異遺稿, the editor Duan Ji (dates unknown) appended a long story about the same situation, that captures the ambivalent attitude of literati toward making offerings to resident foxes, and demonstrates the greater domestication of the fox worship tradition by the high Qing. The opening reveals a double spatial structure of fox residence: foxes have infested an abandoned hall at the official quarters in Linqing,[21] but there is a separate "fox chamber," clearly an established shrine. The story does not clarify who has been making offerings there. Yutang,[22] the son of the local magistrate, presents a text in parallel prose requesting their departure. The request, couched in polite language and addressing the fox as *xian*, reiterates the division between the realms of *xian* and mortal, human and animal. A text like this is a means of self-presentation as well as exorcism: Yutang imagines himself as the "crazy scholar," unintimidated by the supernatural. The close of the passage offers the fox wine and spirit money in exchange for its departure. The offering is, in this context, a face-saving compromise for both sides.[23] Although the foxes depart temporarily, they return, making more trouble. Yutang prepares a second text, a threat with no conciliatory gestures. This second attempt succeeds in driving out the foxes. But this show of strength is followed by a telling line "Burning incense in that room on the fifteenth and thirtieth of each month was an old custom, and so we [I] maintained it."[24] The final concession is to "old custom" and not to the fox as such, but it reveals a potential for compromise with local custom and other species after the human side has exhib-

21. In Shandong, near the Hebei border, southwest of Dezhou. This is also where Lang Ying gathered his stories.

22. Yan Dengjun 言登浚 from Changshou.

23. For a similar use of worship as a negotiation tactic in which the exorcist persuades haunting foxes to agree to leave after receiving three days of offerings, see "Ye Faming" 葉法明, in Fang Yuankun, *Liangpeng yehua*, 2.21b. For another case of defensive offerings in a government office, see "Datong shiyuan" 大同使院, in Xu Kunguo, *Dunzhai oubi*, xia, 26b. For an established place for foxes, with an established schedule of sacrifices, in a military office in Fuzhou, see "Fuxian lou" 福先樓, in Zhang Jingyun, *Qiuping xinyu*, 5.20b. In this story, trouble, in the form of possession, comes when a concubine relieves herself under the altar.

24. *LZ*, 2.246–47.

ited its authority. This is a clear example of the fox making the transition from chaos to order, from unruly disturbance to regularly scheduled ritual, from the heterodox to the accepted customs of a place.

Yutang's confrontation straddles the borders between private and public: he himself is not the official, and he does not directly evoke government authority in his exorcism text. One example of an entirely private account, an anecdote in *Kuai yuan*, explores the theme of fox worship as blackmail. Like the stories of foxes in Beijing homes, this is a southern man's description of his northern travels, and as with the accounts of resident foxes and fox lodgers, *Kuai yuan* provides an important early record of the themes of the late imperial fox tale. In a certain place in the north, people raise (or simply feed) foxes until there is a swarm of them (*min yang hu cheng qun* 民養狐成群), and they often cause trouble. An old man who hates them plans to kill them with a short sword. One day a white fox bites him and he strikes out at it only to discover that he has accidentally slain a neighbor's five-year-old child. Despite his protests that he has been framed by a fox, he is sent to prison and sentenced to death. The fox declares if the man's family prays at the fox shrine (*hushe* 狐社), he will revive the boy and free the convict. The family gathers at the shrine to pray, but the old man refuses to beg the fox for mercy. Finally the fox relents.[25] Although the old man wins in the end, the story seems to regard both sides as equals. Foxes are sufficiently petty deities, close enough in position to humans, that there can be a struggle between the two sides. The power of the fox seems to depend on the complicity of the locals, since it was the local custom of "raising" foxes (an unusual formulation, with suggestions both of "raising" livestock and caring for one's elders or one's children) that precipitated the crisis. Beyond the margins of this story of an individual confrontation, established institutions are revealed: the keeping of foxes and the fox shrine. The ending is ambivalent: the skeptic has not become a fox worshipper, but nor has the fox been harmed or local custom altered. Significantly, it is an older man who resists while his family willingly complies with fox

---

25. *Kuai yuan, juan* 9, story 9.

worship. The unresolved relationship and bloodiness of the fox trickery mark this story as early; Qing stories would try to provide a resolution and would not allow the death of an innocent. Here, also, foxes and the shrine are already present before the story begins; the first compromise with foxes has already happened. But this fox's attempts to extort worship in a campaign of mischief involves the forces of law. Worship is not the worshipper's answer to disturbance but a fox's grab for power.

A Daoguang-era collection contains a comparable anecdote concerning an unsuccessful would-be god.[26] A fox, already established in a corner room of an abandoned house at the opening of the story, conjures up a miniature child, which it then accuses the human family, who has moved into the house, of killing, in a strong echo of the *Kuai yuan* story. Nonetheless, the change from an actual child to an artificial substitute seems a taming of the motif. The fox demands that the family set up an altar to him, allow daily sacrifices, and give him their daughter in marriage. Extortion in this story is much more self-conscious and forthright: the entire scheme is devised to trap the family. This story also offers a contrasting portrait of a kindly female fox who talks to women through the walls, offering advice and providing information about her wicked counterpart. As we shall see in the discussion below, this fox is communicating in the form of a fox séance. The evil spirit is finally suppressed by the gods of the orthodox bureaucracy, and all foxes, kindly and evil, are driven from the area. A Qing collection could not tolerate an ambiguous ending like that of the *Kuai yuan* tale.

Offerings to foxes should be considered in the larger context of gift giving. An appropriate level of gift giving is a friendly gesture in a social relationship, but there is a point when it exceeds proper boundaries and becomes a bribe. When an established relationship with a fox is disturbed, offerings are seen as a reasonable way to smooth things over. Ji Yun made this point in one of his anecdotes. A man moves into a neighborhood in Beijing (where Ji Yun once had a house). He is told that his house is inhabited by foxes, but new residents can avoid problems by making an offering. He is, however,

26. "Zhi hu" 治狐, in Yongna jushi, *Zhi wen lu,* 1.19b.

too stingy. His new concubine is mocked and shamed by disembodied voices in the walls who discuss her appearance and related every move she makes in bed. Exorcism is unsuccessful, and he is told that although monsters can be expelled for doing harm, laughter and mockery do not merit this response. The man sighs, "Only now have I learned that the rituals of social relations (*yingchou* 應酬, "giving and receiving feasts") cannot be abandoned."[27] In a much lighter tale from the Guangxu era, a Beijing family makes an offering of chicken to their family's fox to stop his teasing of their southern-born tutor.[28]

In the Qing, narratives tend to reflect stages of negotiation between humans and foxes that either are relatively under human control or under the control of the larger moral order. Extorted worship can begin a narrative, but only worship in a more decorous guise can end it. It is acknowledged that people make offerings to foxes in the hope of forestalling disturbances, but narratives do not endorse the practice, unless it is presented in a tone other than fear or desperation, for example, the offer of a final meal before an exorcism. I know of no text that gives an ethnographic description of the proposition "foxes torment the people until they make offerings." In any specific context, this opening can only be an introduction to the figure who will resist and correct that situation. This containment can be explained in terms of the limits of both the morally acceptable and the interesting. The link between offerings to foxes and placation and fear is recorded in the stories but not allowed to become too explicit; at the same time, a refusal to accept the status quo opens up the possibility of narrative interest.

FOXES AND PROTECTION

As we have seen, foxes can make the inversion from forces of chaos to forces of order. The stories summarized in the preceding section depict worship as a symptom of an unbalanced relationship with a fox that demands correction. Worship, as an attempt to mediate relations between humans and an inhuman force, is portrayed either as a human lapse in morality or control or as an inhuman attempt to

27. *YWCT*, 13.694–95, story 154.
28. "Shudeng zizou" 書燈自走, in Dai Lianfen, *Libian xuan zhiyan*, 1.17a.

control humans. But as we have seen, tales of fox worship can reverse that valence. Instead of being the embodiment of arbitrary destructive forces, the fox, within the ties of worship, can itself control these forces. This reversal can happen in both the public and the private settings discussed above.

If worship is presented as a stable force, humans relate directly to foxes in their own homes or offices. In addition to a place to live, foxes receive moderate offerings of food, wine, and incense. In one of the *Yuewei caotang* stories about a resident fox who corrects the human family's moral faults discussed in the previous chapter, the fox warns the master of the house of bandits or fires in exchange for annual offerings of wine and chickens. He offers protection but not profit.[29] Notably, these specific tasks are negations of the crimes of mischievous foxes, which are particularly well known for setting fires and stealing. A human family provides the fox with a living space and shelter; the fox in turn preserves the space and livelihood of the human family. This measured relationship stands in contrast to other, unstable ties with foxes (see below).

Because of its stability, this relationship alone does not make a narrative. Nor does the general statement in the form I have phrased it above, "Men feed foxes; foxes protect men," ever appear as a freestanding ethnographic account. Instead, the ties of protection are more likely to be mentioned at the beginning of the narrative as background to some exceptional further development of the relationship. A typical example is another eighteenth-century story in which a man dutifully adds thatch to a fox's dwelling every year to be rewarded in the end by the fox with a lavish feast.[30] Narrative interest happens when man and fox cross established lines into more intimate contact.

The same restraint that might make such relationships uninteresting makes them unobjectionable. Ji Yun, for example, found this relatively restrained relationship between fox and man fairly easy to accept and considered moderate offerings to a fox signs of mutual respect and a stable relationship. If the offerings are unchanging and not motivated by desire for gain, Ji regarded them as part of custom-

---

29. *YWCT*, 9.453–54, story 179.

30. "Tuan hu" 團狐, in Xu Kunguo, *Dunzhai oubi*, xia, 27a.

ary rites that should be maintained, as in the case of the man whose concubine is teased, as opposed to the more self-serving forms of fox worship, which he routinely condemned. It is telling, however, that Ji Yun's account of regular offerings as part of a stable relationship is situated in a rural area, in the home of a tenant farmer; the man whose concubine was teased by the foxes is an unnamed member of Ji's own class. In what may be a revelation of his ambivalence, Ji said nothing about making offerings in descriptions of his own family's dealings with their foxes.

Foxes assume a protective role in official offices as well as in homes. When a new arrival in office is informed that all his predecessors made offerings to foxes, it is possible for him to react to this as tradition, rather than heterodoxy. Acceptance becomes more possible in the late Qing.[31] In *Yongan biji* 庸庵筆記 (Notebook from the Common Studio; first ed. 1897), Xue Fucheng 薛福成 (1838–94) approached the resident creatures of his office with an attitude of curiosity and subjected them to empirical investigation. Before his arrival as an official in Ningbo, he had heard there were three giant snakes known as the "three generals" in various offices there. But when he looked for them, he found only a small backroom set aside for worshipping the spirits of good fortune. It contained an image of three old men, and the locals identified them as foxes. (All the images in fox shrines seem to be human in form.)[32] Xue noted strange noises in the ceiling that are not quite like those made by mice; these sounds served to forewarn him of news in a telegraph. When his servants lost small objects or suffered from minor aches and pains, making offerings in the backroom proved efficacious, but they were of no use in major matters. In the end, he never decided if the noises were made by snakes or foxes.[33] Here, an official copes

31. On the relation between officials and foxes, see Kang, "Power at the Margins," pp. 265–78.

32. Li Wei-tsu, "On the Cult of the Four Sacred Animals," p. 52. In contrast, when the foxes are evil spirits to be expelled, they are displayed in fox form; see the illustrations of protective deities driving out foxes, in Doré, *Researches into Chinese Superstitions*, vol. 5, p. 549.

33. "Ningshao tai dao shunei hushe" 寧紹台倒署內狐蛇, in Xue Fucheng, *Yongan biji*, 2.21b.

with both his inheritance from his predecessors and local culture, but he finds them unthreatening and even fascinating local curiosities.

In an extreme example of a reversal of chaos and order, in two late Qing sources foxes are made guardians of an official's seals and documents.[34] One of the stories occurs in Taiwan, a vivid demonstration of the expanded geographic range of the fox. The fox in that story claims that every yamen has a *xian* (although he does not specify *huxian*); the more accomplished are openly worshipped, and the less developed act in secret.[35] Although Kangxi and Qianlong sources describe officials compromising with the foxes in their quarters, these remained private arrangements, with the man rather than the office. Foxes in offices seem to occupy the interstices between national and local culture. Perhaps, these official foxes were not entirely the product of local culture; officials arriving at their posts after a period in the fox-ridden capital may well have found the fox a comprehensible and familiar explanation for the strange sounds and occurrences in their new residences. In no small part because of publication of *zhiguai*, foxes had, by the nineteenth century, again crossed the line between north and south, the strange and the common, the popular and the elite.

FOXES AND WEALTH

Foxes dispensed wealth long before the late imperial period. In the Tang, Miss Ren informed her lover what goods he should buy to sell at a profit, and Song imitations of her story also depict vixens supporting their lovers.[36] As well as using their precognition to make profitable deals, foxes use their skill at physical mischief to become natural thieves. Gifts from foxes and other animal spirits are often revealed to be stolen goods. In the Qing, this talent for theft becomes codified in worship. The wealth granted by foxes remains morally tainted and is acknowledged to be attained from illicit sources. In contrast to the fox as protective spirit, the relationship be-

34. Han Zhai and Han Dun'an, *Doupeng tanzu*, 23b. The text is undated, but it must be Guangxu at the earliest. See also Kang, "Power at the Margins," pp. 288 96.

35. "Wuzhen sou" 無真叟, in Wu Changchi, *Kechuang xianhua*, 2.57.

36. "Xichi chunyou" 西池春遊, in Liu Fu, *Qingsuo gaoyi*, pp. 203–211.

tween the demonic fox and the benign fox is different for the fox as the spirit of wealth: the chaotic powers of the fox are harnessed rather than reversed.

A group of Ming texts document a link between sexual liaisons with foxes and their power to grant wealth. The earliest example is the account in *Qixiu leigao* 七修類稿 (Categorized manuscript of the seven compositions; 1530) of the stories the author, Lang Ying 郎英 (1487–1566), heard from inhabitants of Shandong in 1530. Adopting the stance of an ethnographer, he asked them to explain the fox spirits, which he had heard were common in the area. According to these local informants, foxes steal things to give to their human lovers. When the favored human dies, they transfer both their carnal and material favors to another. Lang ended his general account with the comment, "People also don't find it very strange," an assertion of normalcy similar to those found in southerners' accounts of northerners' cohabitation with foxes. In one of Lang's examples, a man's grandmother dies, and the fox transfers its attention to his mother, suggesting a tradition maintained within the patriarchal family.[37]

Another Ming text, from *Yanshan conglu*, relates the same lore in the form of specific examples. In the Jiajing period, the wife of a Mr. Zhou from Dezhou (as noted above, this was historically a center of fox activity) is seduced by a fox. At first Zhou is troubled by this, but then the wife tells the fox what they need, and the fox steals other families' things to give to her family. As a result, they become very rich. Behind his house, Zhou gathers sheaves of grain to make a large space for the fox to nest. The housing provided for the fox is a rustic image and resembles a place where a physical fox might actually burrow.[38] Years later, his grandson forgets this and plans to build

37. Lang Ying, *Qiuxiu leigao*, 48.9b. The word used here for male foxes' relations with human women is 染. This idea of a family tradition of improper intimacy with foxes can be compared to the Japanese idea of Kitsune-mochi. There are taboos against marrying into such families. See Kida Teikichi, *Tsukimono*, pp. 465–67. Although there is no mention of a specific taboo in the Chinese stories, one assumes no one would be eager to marry a daughter into a family with such a reputation.

38. On heaps of straw as possible lodgings for the sacred animals, see Li Wei-tsu, "On the Cult of the Four Sacred Animals," p. 10. For a man who worshiped a fox who lived in a heap of straw in his courtyard and added straw to restore the spirit's roof, see Doré, *Researches into Chinese Superstitions*, vol. 5, p. 697.

a room on this spot. As he removes the sheaves of grain, the fox says angrily, "I have made your family rich for a generation, but one day you forget everything I have done for you and drive me out. Do you think I cannot make you poor?" The grandson is terrified and adds more sheaves year after year. From a distance it looks like a mountain, and the family remains the richest in the province some fifty years later when the story is recorded. In a second example, a fox in Shangcai (also in Shandong) seduces the daughter-in-law of a Mr. Yuan. Yuan traps it in a sack, intending to burn it, but the fox begs to be spared, saying, "If you let me go, I can make you rich. At such-and-such a place there is a hidden treasure. Please check first." Yuan digs where he has been told and discovers a cache of gold. He lets the fox go. From then on the fox steals things for him. All the wives of the family go along with the fox's wishes, and the family gets richer and richer. An official wants to prosecute the family, but the fox sends him a warning dream; frightened of the fox's power over good and ill fortune, he dares not interfere.[39]

Financial benefits are also central to the attempted seduction of a virtuous woman by a male fox in the Ming vernacular novel *Dongdu ji*. The fox proposes a long-term arrangement—sexual favors in return for gold, pearls, and other treasures—and remarks, "Even if your husband finds out, it is better than carrying firewood for a living."[40] This different perspective, with its recording of the dialogue between the woman and the fox, instead of an exclusive focus on the human and male point of view, is typical of the polyvocal nature of the vernacular novel.

In both ethnographic descriptions and narratives of specific cases, property violations are linked to sexual violations of household boundaries. Although the ethnographic descriptions refer to lovers of both sexes, it is clear that interest focuses on men who grow rich from male foxes' sexual ties with the women in their family. This seems the most lurid way to imagine the morally tainted wealth resulting from a pact with a demonic creature. In these classical tales, a male fox's relationship with human women is seen as a stable arrangement that can span generations (this contrasts with the fre-

---

39. *Yanshan conglu*, *juan* 8, story 11.
40. Fang Ruhao, *Dongdu ji*, 40.213.

quent presentation of such relations as debilitating illnesses in purely sexual stories; see the following chapter). Even the unsuccessful seducer in *Dongdu ji* suggests this is the way for a fox and a woman to have a long-term relationship. Both *Yanshan conglu* anecdotes share the same basic form: a stable relationship is threatened with interruption, but the threat is resolved and the relationship continues. In the first story, the point of conflict between fox and man is not sexual access to human women but the space in which the fox resides. In the second story, it is not entirely clear whether the source of the Yuan family's wealth is the sexual relationship between the fox and women of the family or Yuan's release of the fox. The far more widespread motif of the captured fox that rewards the man who releases him is blended with the idea of the adulterous fox granting wealth.

Needless to say, Ji and many other Qing authors would have objected to this linking of sexual misconduct, worship of the alien, and material prosperity. The powerlessness of the official in the second *Yanshan conglu* tale would seem particularly galling. Both *Qixiu leigao* and *Yanshan conglu* record this material with a lack of moral judgment that would have been impossible in the Qing, when even a pornographic fox story would not depict a human man enjoying the fruits of cuckoldry. Nor would the long-term stability of these relationships in earlier stories would have been tolerated.

The *Liaozhai* tale "Chou hu" 丑狐 (The ugly fox) makes a frank link between a man's sexual compliance and a fox's financial assistance. A hideous vixen, who is one of the few *Liaozhai* foxes who introduces herself as a *huxian*, financially supports a poor man on the condition that he be her lover. When the man betrays her by hiring an exorcist, she takes away everything she has given him. The same rich furnishings and clothes appear in the house of the next man she chooses, but she deserts that family as well when her lover dies.[41] This absolute reversal of her favors is typical of the fickleness of the fox as a spirit of wealth in later accounts. Pu Songling reserved this kind of explicit relationship between sex and wealth only for a nameless fox who is far from his ideal. For his named fox heroines, this connection is cosmetically disguised—they provide gifts rather than

41. *LZ*, 8.1107–9.

bribes. In a reversal similar to the one that turned exorcism of foxes from an official office into an exposé of bureaucratic corruption, Pu Songling turned a story about vulpine inconsistency into a story about human greed and inconsistency.

A story of gifts and their repossession without the sexual element is found in *Shouyizhai kechuang erbi* 守一齋客窗二筆 (Second notebook from lodging as a guest; 1798). In an unnamed place in Shandong, a mysterious old man generously supports a local innkeeper in expanding his business. After many years of friendship, the innkeeper protests that he has never been to his benefactor's house. He is invited to a splendid feast, but afterwards discovers that he cannot find the mansions where he had feasted. The fox confesses his true identity, and the man schemes to kill him and take the rest of his gold. The fox, knowing of the intended betrayal, rebukes him and, by pointing in each direction, causes all the prosperity he had funded to go up in flames.[42] Vladimir Propp argued that motivation is among the most flexible elements in a folktale: the basic element of miraculous but unstable prosperity remains, although here, as in "Chou hu," it is transformed into a warning against betrayal and greed. In contrast to the Ming tales discussed above, both of these are tales of instability and loss.

The direct link between foxes' sexual attentions and material favors disappears in stories of the fox as a bestower of wealth later in the Qing, remaining only in a repressed form. Tales of profitable adultery and cuckoldry vanish. Texts denigrating spirit mediums assert that they are sleeping with their foxes, but not more sympathetic tales. The question is whether this sexual element in foxes' relationship with human families has been discarded or simply covered over. What is the relationship between the tradition of worship and tales of sexual foxes?

I believe the overlap between the fox as object of worship and the sexual fox is relatively small.[43] In the case of Mr. Zhou from Dezhou, the element of the fox's sexual relations is more easily removable

42. "Huhuo ji" 狐火記, in Jin Pengchang, *Kechuang erbi*, 1.16b. For a stable account of a profitable relationship with a fox friend, see "Jiu you" 酒友, *LZ*, 2.217–19.

43. Kang ("Power at the Margins," pp. 101–6) finds the sexual side of the fox more closely tied to the worship tradition.

from the story than the thatching of the fox's dwelling space. Paul Katz's word "reverberations," used to describe the ways that distinct visions of a single divinity interact, is useful here.[44] To put it another way, the presence of a fox in one's life in any form, whether as an inhabitant of an abandoned room or of a possessed woman, could potentially be translated from loss to profit. Sex is one of the possible aspects of an exchange between the worlds, but it is not the most central. An exclusive, profitable relationship with a fox can be imagined as a same-sex friendship rather than a sexual relationship, as the two Qing examples show. As shall be explored in the following chapter, the main tradition of foxes as sexual partners focuses on deception, seduction, and depletion, on foxes as prostitutes rather than on humans prostituting themselves.

The instability of profitable relationships with foxes outlasts the textual exploration of sexual associations. It is formulated as a general statement in the late Qing, in the context of the worship of five animal spirits, the fox among them. *Jinmen zaji* 津門雜記 (Miscellaneous records from Tianjin; 1885) describes spirits' unreliable favors: "If someone has a predestined tie with a spirit, the spirit will bring that person good fortune. This is called doing a *xian*'s business; all business will be doubly profitable, and harvests bumper crops; but once it is over, the wealth will scatter and one will incur debts, or disaster will strike."[45] The late Qing was, like the late Ming, another moment in the fox tradition when general ethnographic statements were possible. An anthropologist's description of these beliefs in the early decades of this century is almost identical. Spirits can bring financial benefits to a family for a time, but when the particular member of the family with which it is associated dies, the spirit will move on and the family will decline. Spirits can only transfer things from one home to another; they cannot create them. For these reasons, some people avoid them because they are inconstant and destructive if offended.[46] If one looks at this material in chronological order, there is a shift from ethnographic statements and specific narratives of stability to narratives, followed by ethnographic statements, of instability.

---

44. Katz, *Demon Hordes and Burning Boats*, pp. 114–15.
45. Zhang Tao, *Jinmen zaji*, middle *juan*, p. 20.
46. Li Wei-tsu, "On the Cult of the Four Sacred Animals," pp. 9–11.

Foxes can bring success to business enterprises as well as to private households. A story in *Zuicha zhiguai* states that merchants worshipped foxes with particular devotion.[47] According to Li Shouju, the association of fox worship with merchants was more prominent in southern China, particularly Fuzhou, Nanjing, Wuhu, and Hangzhou, where commerce was a more important part of the economy, whereas in the north it was more an affair of personal protection for a household.[48] Although these cities had become important locations for fox stories in the second half of the Qing, this merchant milieu is not reflected in narratives in the same way as are the family-based spirits of wealth or the interactions of government offices.

In "The Enchantment of Wealth: The God Wutong in Social History," Richard von Glahn traces the history of the Wutong 五通 spirit as a god of wealth in Jiangnan, making heavy use of *zhiguai* sources, including books important to this study, such as *Kuai yuan*. "Wutong" are a category of mountain demons or monsters that could appear in the form of children or a range of animals, such as pigs, apes, snakes, and ox-headed demons.[49] The Wutong's similarities to the fox were noted by Chinese authors. According to Hong Mai, both could grant illicit wealth. "In their illusory transformations and demonic deceptions, they [Wutong] are in general like the fox demons of the north. They can sometimes cause men to become suddenly wealthy; therefore petty men like to welcome and worship them."[50] This comparison implies there might have been an association between foxes and illicit wealth in the Southern Song, although there is a lack of other sources confirming this. The Wutong were also known for molesting human women, and in this regard they also overlapped with the fox. At the same time, a comparison with the Wutong reveals what the fox might have been if it had filled fewer ecological niches in the literary environment.

---

47. "Wang Jianbing" 王建屏, in Li Qingchen, *Zuicha zhiguai*, 1.16.

48. Li Shouju, *Huxian xinyang yu hulijing gushi*, pp. 82–83.

49. They sometimes became conflated with five deified brothers known as the Wuxian or with shrines that the Ming founder erected for sacrifices to the war dead; see Zong Li and Liu Qun, *Zhongguo minjian zhushen*, p. 265.

50. Hong Mai, "Jiangnan muke" 江南木客 *Yijian zhi, dingzhi*, 19.695.

Von Glahn argues that in the Ming the spirits of wealth were regarded as unreliable, demonic forces because money itself was regarded as a potentially destructive force. With increased financial stability early in the eighteenth century, the Wutong were replaced as gods of wealth by less ambivalent deities.[51] The first part of his argument fits the fox as a god of wealth well. The late Ming texts cited above are contemporary with the emergence of the Wutong as demonic gods of wealth. In this period the fox seems indeed to have played the role in the north the Wutong did in the south. However, the later part of his historical argument does not seem to apply to the fox tradition. The *Jinmen zaji* account reveals that the fox has not completely lost its demonic nature in the late Qing. Some of the informants of Li Wei-tsu, an early twentieth-century anthropologist who studied the cult of five animal spirits in the suburbs of Beijing, told him that the more orthodox god of wealth was nothing but a piece of paper and that only the animal spirits were efficacious (albeit mercurial). The very respectability of the new gods of wealth made them less approachable for some.[52] Perhaps money became a more stable and respected force for some classes in some regions, but for others it never lost its demonic nature. Or perhaps a period of financial stability in the high Qing, with tame gods of wealth, was followed by a period of instability in which the demonic gods returned. In any case, the comparison with the Wutong reveals the economic meaning of foxes' gifts. The fox is not a spirit of fertility but of sex without fertility. Foxes did not promote increased production but engaged in what was, in the Confucian vision of the economy, the suspect world of profit without production. They grant willful individual favors, beyond the profits from lawful toil.

In literary romances describing affairs with vixens, material benefits are almost as essential a part of the fantasy as sexual fulfillment. Admittedly, the fox as provider could have more than one origin. Courtesans from Li Wa through Du Shiniang also provided nearly miraculous financial assistance, and material opulence was an indispensable part of an encounter with a divine woman. The perfect lover who also bestows wealth seems a simple redoubling of wish

51. Von Glahn, "The Enchantment of Wealth."
52. Li Wei-tsu, "On the Cult of the Four Sacred Animals," p. 8.

fulfillment. However, the specific association of foxes with wealth in the popular tradition colored the romance as well.

There is, however, an opposing tendency to control this fantasy and insist that foxes cannot grant money to those destined to be poor, as in He Bang'e's "The Red Girl."[53] There are two explanations for this: on a general level the control of wish fulfillment seems to be a universal reflex of folklore (consider the tales of three wishes that often go wrong); and in this specific case, it may be a conscious attempt by authors and narrators to prevent foxes' willful favors from upsetting the moral order. Hong Mai considered worship for the sake of profit the action of petty men. Ji Yun's defense against the idea of the fox as the provider of wealth was to relate stories in which foxes use their talents at redistributing wealth to punish misers by handing out their hoarded wealth to the needy.[54] Ji's stories focus on the punishment of the miser rather than the gratification of those who receive the foxes' gifts, which never exceed what the miser himself should have given. This seems to be a conscious argument against what Ji considered self-indulgent aspects of the tradition; his foxes restore economic balance rather than create new imbalances.

When dealing with spirits as petty and volatile as foxes, humans must come to private arrangements with each one. Both in practice and even more in narrative, the participants can conceive of these arrangements in social terms, as ties with friends or lovers. The choice of these particular ties is significant; it is more difficult to incorporate foxes into the family as formal family members through marriage or adoption than is the case with ghosts.[55] The crucial question, as with gift giving, is whether profiting from a fox can be contained within the bounds of friendship and social relations.

---

53. "Hong guniang," *YTSL*, 2.37–39. This appears in one of Lang Ying's stories, in which a fox leaves a laborer, saying he has no good fortune, to take up with the wife of a yamen runner; see *Qixiu leigao*, 48.9b. See also *Yanshan conglu*, *juan* 8, story 3. For a humorous treatment of the topic, in which the issue is a man's moral unworthiness of vulpine benefits, rather that destiny, see "Yu qian," in *LZ*, 4.505.

54. E.g., *YWCT*, 10.210, story 215; 5.86, story 202; and 23.544, story 116. For another tale of a fox who punishes a miser, see "Tie gongji" 鐵公雞, in *YTSL*, 11.308–9.

55. Yu Kuang-hong, "Making a Malefactor a Benefactor."

THE FOX SÉANCE

The fox as a source of wealth was a vision of exchange between two worlds, potentially unstable and threatening and happening at others' expense. It suggested an alternative moral system in which one is rewarded for feeding a fox rather than for doing good deeds. When information travels across the boundary between worlds, the exchange is not as threatening.

The fox séance brings up the problematic presence of a medium, the person through whom the fox speaks. Li Wei-tsu divided the spirits into two kinds, house spirits that interacted directly with a household and altar spirits that relied on an intermediary. This distinction can be phrased in terms of private and public: the fox as a spirit of wealth aids only its chosen household, but the fox as a source of information can use that household, or that individual, as a base from which to answer the questions of outsiders. One could also describe this as a distinction between amateur and professional relationships with the fox, but this distinction is harder to draw. Once a medium is involved, the narrative perspective of "inner" and "outer" stories becomes crucial. If the story is told from the perspective of the household in which the fox resides, the relationship appears amateur and takes the form of a social exchange, with outsiders consulting the fox out of curiosity. If it is told from the perspective of those curious outsiders, the family with the fox connections take on the characteristics of professional mediums.

Here is a *Liaozhai* story that purports to be a matter-of-fact description of a fox séance:

"Shang xian" 上仙 *(The lofty transcendent)*

In the third month of 1683, I went with Gao Jizhang[56] to Jixia,[57] and we lodged together at an inn. Jizhang suddenly fell ill. It happened that Gao Chenmei had also followed Mr. Nian[58] to the commandery; so I discussed finding treatment with him. I heard Lord Yuan Lin say, "The Liang family

56. According to Lu Zhan'en's annotation, this is his *zi*. His name was Zhibo 之駁, and he passed the *gongsheng* exam in 1697. See *LZ*, 5.691.

57. To the north of modern Linzi xian 臨淄, Shandong.

58. His name is Heng 珩; his *zi* is Congpei 蔥佩; and he received the jinshi degree in 1643.

in the south of the city has a fox transcendent who is skilled in the art of Lord Changsang [i.e., healing.]"[59] So we went together to call on them.

Liang was a woman of forty-something, who had an air of the fox about her.[60] We entered her home. In the middle of the inner room a red cloth enclosure was hanging. When we peeked into the enclosure, there was an image of Guanyin in the middle of the wall, and two or three other scrolls besides, one portraying a rider brandishing a halberd, with a throng of followers on horseback. Below the northern wall there was a table, on which there was a small seat, not even a foot high,[61] with a brocade cushion. She said that when the transcendent came, it would stay here. Everyone lit sticks of incense and lined up to bow. The woman rang a chime three times, indistinctly chanting something. Once her prayers had ended, the guests went to a couch outside to wait. The woman sat below the screen arranging her hair and stroking her chin as she spoke to the guests, relating the marvelous manifestations of the transcendent.

After a long while, it was becoming dusk. Since everyone was afraid it would be hard to get back in the middle of the night, they imposed on her to summon the fox spirit again. The woman struck the chime and prayed again. Then she turned back and said, "The Lofty Transcendent likes night conversations best. You can't ever meet him at any other time. Last night there was a group of licentiates waiting for the examinations who brought meat and wine to drink with him, and the High Spirit also brought out a fine vintage to toast the guests in return. They composed poetry and laughed. When they finally dispersed, the night was almost past." Before she was finished speaking, we heard many faint sounds from within the chamber, like the cries of flying bats. Just as we were intently listening, suddenly there was a sound like a huge stone falling on the table, a startling noise. The woman turned and said, "How you frighten people!" Then we heard a sound of sighing from the table, like a healthy old man. The woman concealed the small seat with a banana-leaf fan. On the chair a loud voice said, "Destiny brought us together! Destiny!" In a loud voice he invited us to sit, and he seemed to fold his hands in a polite greeting. When he was done, he asked, "How may I instruct you?"

---

59. Changsang jun 長桑君 was a legendary doctor of the Warring States period.

60. Pu is playing here. She arrives *sui sui* 綏綏, which is an allusion to the poem "You hu" 有狐, from the *Weifeng* 衛風section of the *Shi jing*: 有狐綏綏，在彼淇梁. "There is a fox going slowly, by the dam on the Qi" (Karlgren, *The Book of Odes*, p. 43). *Sui sui* became the most common allusion for evoking a fox.

61. The original measure is a *chi*, around 32 centimeters.

Gao Chenmei followed Master Nian's intentions, asking, "Have you seen the Boddhisattva or not?"

He replied, "The Southern Ocean is one of my old haunts; how could I not have seen her?"

"Does Yama also have replacements or not?"

He answered, "It is the same as in the world of the living."

"What is the current Yama's last name?"

He replied, "Cao."

Then Gao Chenmei sought medicine for Gao Jizhang. The fox said, "After you return tonight make an offering of tea, and I will grant him medicine. What illness could continue?"

Everyone asked questions, and he explained everything thoroughly. We took our leave and went home. After that night, Jizhang was a bit better. Chenmei and I packed and went back first, and so we didn't have time to visit the fox again.[62]

There is no mention of money changing hands, but it is clear that this woman is a professional medium, and the "guests" are her customers. Financial interests become overt only in tales of bad mediums; otherwise payment is masked, both in stories and in social practice, in the form of gifts. This is also the case in contemporary accounts of fox worship.[63] Medical prescriptions are one of the most useful kinds of information the other world foxes or any other creature can provide. The story is inconclusive, neither crediting the fox with the cure nor discrediting it.

Pu's attitude toward this woman is not entirely respectful, and his tone is playful. He describes her as *sui sui*, using the binomial adjective that describes a fox in a *Shi jing* poem and is frequently used as a euphemism for fox. The fox does not appear immediately when summoned, but only when her clientele are threatening to walk out. This might raise doubts about her abilities, or it might be a deliberate tactic on her part to tease her customers and give a bigger buildup to the fox's entrance. Gender and class add tension to this situation: a woman with no visible male relatives plays host to a group of up-

62. *LZ*, 5.691–92. See also the translation and discussion in Kang, "Power at the Margins," pp. 118–19. Interestingly, the story immediately following this one is an account of worship of an ape spirit, with Nian as the informant; see "Hou jing shan" 候靜山, in *LZ*, 5.693–94.

63. Dorfman, "The Spirits of Reform," pp. 265–66.

per-class males, serving as an intermediary for them to communicate with a fox taking on the role of an upper-class male.

The focus of the story is on the performance of the séance. Pu was interested in its staging, with its series of enclosures and screens obscuring vision. The performance makes the transition from animal-like or inanimate noises, of the sort that might disturb the owners of a haunted house, to a polite upper-class social exchange, in a way which would not seem unfamiliar to Victorian-era spiritualists. The woman, in her introductory remarks, is clearly selling a vision of literati social exchanges with the fox. Once the fox appears, the medium herself vanishes from the narrative. Our last glimpse of her is holding the fan that supposedly shields the fox from view, but then conversation with the fox takes over, with the verbal replacing the visual. There are many stories of foxes as drinking and literary companions of elite men (*Liaozhai*'s "Jiu you" 酒友 [Drinking companion], for example). This story makes the link between the séance and tales of friendly conversation with foxes clear. One could communicate with a fox not just to gain practical knowledge of the future or medical cures, but as a means of entertainment. The questions the visitors ask the fox revert to a joking tone. The fox is used as a source of information on the other world, but the questions also imply some skepticism about the fox's knowledge of the upper echelon of divinities. For Pu these punchlines are essential to the interest of this story.

The scene of the interview with a disembodied fox is one of the most important manifestations of fox worship in literature. One fox story recorded in a wide range of collections is the account of young Xu of Yixing's romance with the vixen Shuzhen in 1682. A prominent feature of this story cycle is a conversation between the fox woman as a disembodied voice and the neighbors and, after her departure, the continued encounters of the family and other literati friends with several of her maids under séance-like circumstances. The interest in this story seems to lie in the social nature of the séance experience, even more than in the private experience of the romance. Some versions are told from the family's perspective, and some from the perspective of the visiting friends. The convention that a vixen is visible only to her lover makes the lover seem like a medium. When the vixen Shuzhen holds a mass audience with her new family and neighbors, they apparently anticipate secret revelations. Instead, she lectures them on virtue.[64] The Jiangnan setting of this story is conspicuous, in comparison to the contemporary stories of haunting or protection that remain focused on northern China. (See the discussion of this story cycle from the perspective of the romance in Chapter 6.)

In many stories, once it is known that a household is inhabited by a fox, whether as a lodger or a lover, the locals throng there in order to have their illnesses cured and to ask questions. Examples from *Liaozhai* include "Hu xie" 狐諧 (Fox jokes), in which a vixen jokes with her husband's friends, as she remains unseen.[65] In "Weishui hu" 濰水狐 (The fox from Weishui), all the local gentry flock to socialize with a fox lodger, although in this case he shows his human form, and there is no hint of unusual revelations.[66] The "interview with the fox" plot became very popular in late imperial collections, most markedly in Ji Yun. As we saw in Chapter 2, Ji has many stories consisting entirely of conversation with a fox. However, in the literary vision of the fox séance, the overt role of a medium seems to be eliminated, along with the problematic questions of gender, class, profit, and performance she evokes. The fox's chosen family member in effect plays this role, but these stories are views from the inside.

When the idea of the conversation with an unseen fox is taken up in the literary tradition, the prophetic or medical content of the fox's words is commonly replaced, as in the tale of Shuzhen and young Xu. Some fox characters routinely eschew prophecy, perhaps because it is regarded as too self-serving for humans to want to know their fates or too reminiscent of the practice of professionals. Descriptions of a fox of extreme erudition who knows everything about the past but refuses to discuss the future are common.[67]

---

64. Zhang Chao, *Yuchu xinzhi*, 14.257. See other versions of this story in Wu Qian, *Fufengqiao chuanxin lu*; and Jin Pengzhang, *Shouyizhai kechuang biji*, 4.11a.

65. *LZ*, 4.500–504.

66. *LZ*, 2.273–74. Other examples include the female fox who provides cures in "Hu yi" 狐醫, in Wu Woyao, *Wo foshanren duanpian xiaoshuo ji, fu biji xiaoshuo wuzhong*, p. 250.

67. Yu Yue, *Youtai xianguan biji*, 10.6a.; Qian Yong, *Lüyuan conghua*, 16.20b.

However, in longer literary tales prophecy can also be used as a structural device, providing riddles that are solved at the end of the story or advice that the human hero attempts but fails to heed.[68]

Foxes sometimes communicate by automatic writing using the planchette, *fuji* 扶箕 or *fuluan* 扶鸞, which plays cultural roles ranging from oracles in temples to ouija-board-style games at home. Foxes certainly do not monopolize the planchette: a wide range of other petty, approachable figures, including *xian* and ghosts, can speak by this means. An example of a conversation conducted by planchette in *Youtai xianguan biji* incorporates topics often found in an encounter with a formless fox friend: the morally correct way of seeking immortality, details about historical characters, and the comparison of fox advancement to human advancement.[69] The almost flippant inquiry into the ways of the other world evident in "Shang xian" is common in tales of automatic writing; like the interview with the fox, communication with the other world can be entertainment. The appeal of the planchette seems the exclusion, at least in some cases, of the professional medium. This was one of the most popular means of directly communicating with the alien, and accounts of planchette conversations tend to be among the most personal of *zhiguai* and the closest to the author's self and experience.

The Qing imagination was attracted to the strange embodied in words and to tales in which the alien could literally be interrogated. It was as a voice that the foxes' sphere of influence extended beyond a single household. This most appealing vision of the fox, however, was accompanied by the figure of the medium. That presence forced a choice: the medium could be erased, with focus remaining only on the fox's words, or the medium could be the center of attention.

---

68. An example of the former is "Liu jijiu" 劉祭酒, in Zeng Yindong, *Xiao doupeng*, 9.173–76; of the latter, "Xiaomei," in *LZ*, 9.1210–16.

69. "Ming Wu Xiansheng" 明五先生, in Yu Yue, *Youtai xianguan biji*, 7.11a–b. For a *Yuewei caotang* anecdote that associates foxes with the planchette, see *YWCT*, 9.463, story 188. See also Chen Qiyuan, *Yongxianzhai biji*, 10: 2.3b. An anomalous story in a Guangxu collection is told entirely from the point of view of an old fox; see Duxiang Yuyin, *Kejing ke'e ji*, 3.29a.

DISCREDITING MEDIUMS

Stories about any religious practice can be told from a variety of perspectives: in these tales, we find both the stories mediums and their clients tell about themselves and the stories that others tell about them. All these stories, however, deploy a shared set of images, including erotic or friendly relationships with the fox. However, when authors told stories about mediums who serve other people's needs rather than their own, attitudes toward foxes themselves and other people's practices of fox worship diverged. In the minds of literati authors, foxes could be domesticated, but lower-class, often female, professional practitioners of fox worship could not. This split was typical of attitudes toward much religious and divination practice: for example, Richard Smith describes widespread literati interest in divination coexisting with contempt for lower-class diviners.[70]

Some stories link professional practice as a fortune-teller or healer with a sexual relationship with a fox. A fox has her (his) lover set up shop offering magical services and secretly provides the prophecies or medicines herself.[71] Such a story often closes with exposure of the "trick" or the fox and the end of the practitioner's career. Although the prophecies are accurate and the cures are effective, these tales still have an air of deception. The fox does not transmit knowledge that the human can use in its absence; the human only acts as a mouthpiece. This recalls Doré's remark that people had contempt for

---

70. Smith, *Fortune-tellers and Philosophers*, p. 221.

71. Interestingly, in one Ming example, it is a male fox in an adulterous relationship with a human woman who buys her husband off by establishing her as a healer; see "Hu yi" 狐醫, in Lu Yanzhi, *Shuoting*, shang.6b. This is very similar to the stories linking adulterous relationships with foxes and the acquisition of wealth; indeed, healing is regarded primarily as a source of income. In Qing stories, it is always a vixen in a relationship with a man who provides these benefits. In one case, a vixen helps her lover make his fortune by setting up a shrine and handing out cures and prophecies. However, in the end she is destroyed by the Daoist patriarch; see "Zhu xianren" 朱仙人, in Feng Yuankun, *Liangpeng yehua*, 4.11b. An account of the same figure is found in "Zhu Fangdan" 朱方旦, in Xue Zhuanyuan, *Jianggan congyu*, 3.7a. For another example, without the sexual element, which has a fox helping a man pretend he is a skilled physiognomer, see Wang Jian, *Qiudeng conghua*, 2.2a. See Li Jianguo, *Zhongguo hu wenhua*, pp. 292–94.

mediums because of their sexual relationships with their spirits, but that seems to apply predominantly to female mediums. The gender dynamics of this story type are interesting: although the mediums discredited for fraudulently claiming relationships with foxes are female, in the Qing the figures genuinely provided livelihoods by foxes are male. Perhaps it was considered too dangerous to allow women to use extramarital affairs as a means of private enrichment. Even in the stories of profitable adultery, it was the patrilineal family, rather than the woman herself, who benefited. The difference between these stories and the accounts of oracular foxes who attract the curious is the calculated emphasis on profit. In the stories of oracular foxes, the attention of the "clients" comes unbidden; in these, the fox deliberately sets up a business.

The most vituperative abuse is reserved for mediums who fraudulently claim a relationship with a fox. In one of Pu Songling's stories, a true fox exposes a false one. The real fox, who is a scholar's friend, exposes an old spirit-medium who "claims to represent a fox god, in order to make profits from the sick." The term "fox god" (*hushen* 狐神) is only used in the charlatan's lie. She is exposed by being pelted with stones by the real fox.[72] Here a scholar's supposedly pure intellectual friendship with a true fox is juxtaposed with a lower-class figure's economic exploitation of a fabricated fox. The accusation of deceiving people for financial gains is the most common grounds on which practitioners are attacked.

Ji Yun further developed the use of a true fox to discredit a false fox. Because of his origins in the heart of fox territory, for Ji Yun the improper worship of foxes was a local, and even a personal, issue. Like many of his contemporaries, he was far more sympathetic and credulous toward foxes than the human mediums and magicians who trafficked with them; as always, he created order by making divisions. In his vision such people were either charlatans or sorcerers with genuine power who had enslaved foxes. Ji's most pointed exposé of a false medium is the following story:

The female sorceress Grannie Hao was a cunning village woman. When I was young, I saw her at the house of my Aunt Lu in Cangzhou. Grannie

72. "Hu Si Xianggong" 胡四相公, in *LZ*, 4.559.

Hao claimed a fox spirit possessed her body and foretold people's good and ill fortune. She knew every single trivial event of people's households; therefore a throng of people believed her. In fact her followers spread out, colluded with the maids and old servant women, and had them find out secrets for her, in order to perpetrate her fraud.

Once a pregnant woman asked whether she would have a boy or a girl. Grannie Hao answered that she would have a boy, but she had a girl. When asked why the spirit's words were wrong, Hao glared at the woman and said, "You should originally have had a boy, but on such and such a day of such and such a month, your mother's family sent you twenty cakes. You fed six to your parents-in-law and hid fourteen to eat yourself. The god of fate punished you for being unfilial by changing your son into a daughter. Have you still not realized your mistake?" Since the woman didn't know this event had been spied out in advance, she was terrified and admitted her crime. Grannie Hao was always as clever at fabrication as in this case.

One day just as she was burning incense and summoning the spirit, she suddenly sat up straight and said clearly, "I am a real fox spirit. Although my kind may dwell together with humans, we keep to ourselves to cultivate our *qi* and refine our forms. Why would we be willing to have a pact with an old village woman to predict the trivial details of people's lives? This woman has a hundred sinister schemes and makes a fortune with her deceits, using my kind's name. Therefore today I have really possessed her so that everyone should know her deceit." Then he listed her secret misdeeds and named her helpers. When he was finished, Hao woke as from a dream and left awkwardly. Afterward no one knew what became of her.[73]

Several points in this story are notable. First, this dubious figure is part of Ji's family history, but it is noteworthy that he met her at the home of a female relative. His mention of the family connection raises the question of whether Ji's female relatives were believers in the sort of fox worship he abhorred, an immediate connection that might grant his opposition a particular intensity. A comparison with the erudite foxes in his father's garden suggests he inherited two distinct bodies of fox beliefs and rejected the one from the female side. Second, in *Yuewei caotang biji* only tales of false mediums use the

73. *YWCT,* 4.184–85, story 179. In a parallel case, a woman who had made a great deal of money by claiming to have a fox spirit in her home is then eaten out of house and home by a group of avaracious foxes, who accuse her of profiteering in their name; see *YWCT,* 9.451, story 176.

term *hushen*. The use of *huxian* might have made these stories seem too plausible. Third, Grannie Hao's spy network seems entirely female and lower-class, although her customers include gentry women as well. Instead of a fox violating the boundaries of a household and spying from the rafters, lower-class females provide the same disruption. (Interestingly enough, Ji's account of Hao's *modus operandi* is remarkably close to contemporary PRC exposés of practitioners of "feudal superstition.")[74] Third, Ji portrayed Grannie Hao as manipulating the language of moral retribution in her lie, using filial piety to lend it plausibility. Ji, who invested heavily in the didactic function of the *zhiguai*, acknowledged that ideas of moral retribution could be twisted by the unscrupulous. Fourth, although elsewhere Ji did admit that genuine possession by foxes was possible and even common,[75] and although he made foxes sympathetic by identifying them with his own elite social position, for him dangerous fox worship is lower class and female. Like Ji, the fox in this story clearly places itself above both the medium and the concerns of her customers. Finally, Ji was not alone in depicting the humiliation of female mediums; another example, in a more graphic form, is the humiliation of a female medium by male foxes in one of He Bang'e's stories (see Chapter 2).

A strong contrast to Ji's treatment of foxes possessing mediums can be found in a story from the collection of his contemporary and kinsman by marriage, Zhang Jingyun's *Qiuping xinyu*.[76]

The concubine of the *juren* Zhou from Dongguang was suddenly possessed by a vixen.[77] She laughed and wept in fits, babbling nonsensically. She said, "My home is in the west mountains. I have been practicing self-cultivation for more than a hundred years. Now I am about to achieve immortality and

---

74. Anagnost, "Politics and Magic in Contemporary China."

75. *YWCT*, II. 247, story 45.

76. On this collection, see Maeno, *Chūgoku shōsetsu shikō*, p. 331. According to Maeno, Zhang and Ji did not have a close connection, but Zhang did include two anecdotes about Ji's own family, one of which Ji corrected, which proves he had read Zhang's collection, p. 344. By Zhang's own account he attended the funeral of Ji's son. For a translation of Zhang's anecdotes about Ji, see Keenan, *Shadows in a Chinese Landscape*, pp. 153–57.

77. Dongguang is in Hebei, not far from Ji's hometown and the Shandong border.

have come to find a *xiangtou* 香頭, in order to cure illnesses and bring good fortune for people. If you let me out of here, this illness will be cured on its own." [Zhang notes: *xiangtou* is the colloquial phrase for mediums who are possessed by spirits.[78]] Zhou thought this a great humiliation, and in his rage he would not allow it. Then she leaped around with her hair disheveled, her cries getting worse day by day. Since there was nothing he could do about it, he simply listened to the noise.

One day he happened to say to her in jest, "I've heard *xian* can bring wealth. I'm in dire financial straits just now—can you help me?" Before he finished speaking, there was a booming sound in the sky, and something was thrown down. When he gathered it up, he got more than ten ingots.

One night at the third watch, Zhou wanted to drink wine but thought silently that since it was already late at night, he wouldn't be able to buy any. Before he had formed the words, suddenly he turned his head to see a jug of wine behind the candle. He touched it and almost burned his hand; when he poured and drank it, it was actually a fine brew. From then on they lived at peace. But he locked her in the concubine's chamber and would not hear of letting her go out.

One day Zhou saluted her formally and said, "I have heard that transcendents and mortals walk different paths but are governed by the same principles. Now, it has already been several months. My concubine may die, but she may not go out; this you know as well as I. If her destined time in this world is already over, please take her quickly. If it isn't over yet, what good will it do you to possess her? I will prepare to give you a parting feast without shame. Is that acceptable?"

She looked up and said nothing, as if she was considering something. After a while, she said, "Enough. What you have said is eminently reasonable. We shall do as you say. It is acceptable that you prepare to see me off." Zhou then cooked a chicken, prepared wine, boiled several dozen eggs, and gathered fruit. He bowed, wished her well, and laid out the food. She was happy, pouring the wine and grabbing the chicken, clasping the fruit and grasping the eggs. She took long gulps from a big goblet, and in an instant everything was gone. Then she pulled up the blanket and lay down exposing only her head. The next day when she awoke, her behavior was as usual.

---

78. This story shows that the term *xiangtou,* which was widely used to refer to shamans in the Guangxu era and as late as the first half of this century, was already current in the Qianlong, but it was evidently still sufficiently unfamiliar to compel the author to supply a gloss. *Hanyu dacidian*'s (s.v., vol. 12, p. 439) only reference for the term in this sense dates to the twentieth century.

When she was asked about the former incidents, she said she had been aware of none of them.[79]

Here, the literati protagonist is alarmed and ashamed at its intrusion into his household, and the fox/concubine herself is advocating the practices of popular religion. Note it is not the fox's possession of his concubine that enrages him, but her attempt to become a medium and play a public role in popular religion. The conflict between literati values and popular religion is contained within the narrative and ends with a compromise. In contrast, Ji Yun would have attempted to exclude this conflict from the narrative altogether, allowing no compromise.

This tale combines aspects of different kinds of relationships with foxes. Possessing a medium and curing humans' illnesses are portrayed as part of a vixen's project of self-improvement, the explanation that often attempted to encompass all the diverse strands of the fox tradition. Her gifts allow him to enjoy some of the benefits of fox worship or a relationship with a fox even while they are locked in a struggle. The fox's gift of wine in response to his silent wish is typical of tales of fox romance or friendship, as we saw in He Bang'e's "The Red Girl." His behavior establishes the boundaries of what a man of his class can tolerate: he can accept a monetary gift, typical of the private, household-based relationship with a fox, but he will not accept public establishment of his household as a site for consulting a fox. In the end he gets rid of her by arguing with her rationally, a tactic typical of the Qianlong generation. However, rational argument alone is not enough; he must follow the popular practices of fox worship to a certain extent in order to appease her. We have seen similar examples of a parting gift in exorcism stories. He disposes of her with a rustic sacrifice that seems quite close to the fox's animal nature. Ji would have permitted no such compromise; his foxes act to undermine popular beliefs, rather than grant them legitimacy. The willingness to compromise is not limited to this story; Zhang's collection in general seems to take a more forgiving attitude toward forced worship. In another story the fox blackmails a household into

79. "Zhou Xiaolian" 周孝廉 (listed in the table of contents as 狐祟), in Zhang Jingyun, *Qiuping xinyu, juan* 9.7a–8b.

offering it sacrifices by sending a plague of snakes, but once its demands are met, it has a harmonious relationship with the master of the house.[80]

One could also interpret this anecdote psychologically, using the understanding of spirit possession as a weapon of the weak and marginalized. For a brief time a concubine is able to speak with the voice of a more powerful female and thus alter the dynamic of the relationship with her husband. Although he concedes the changed relationship, giving her face by acknowledging her possession, he rejects an attempt to institutionalize and publicly establish this change in her status by insisting on a return to the status quo. His ultimatum to the fox could easily be read as an ultimatum to the concubine. In return for her capitulation, the concubine is allowed to escape responsibility for the demands of the fox.[81]

The portrayal of possession in this anecdote is rather exceptional. Possession exists at the interstices of haunting, fox worship, and sex with foxes. It is one of the other meanings of *sui* and demands the services of an exorcist; it lurks in the background of accounts of the fox séance, and is more overtly present in the claims of discredited mediums. When it enters narrative in the Ming and Qing, possession is usually read sexually. Sexuality provides an excuse for otherwise unjustified possession. Nevertheless, fox possession as such is not as clear a part of the tradition as it is, for example, in Japan.[82] Diane Dorfman describes possession as both the disease mediums of the four animal spirits are called on to cure and the source of their power, as is the case with spirit-mediums and fox possession in Japan, but this is not the relationship depicted in *zhiguai* texts.[83] In these narratives, it is usually imagined in terms of a relationship with an external, if invisible, being. Authors may have averted their eyes from an economy of possessing spirits both providing business opportunities and swelling the ranks of mediums.

80. "Hu" 狐, in Zhang Jingyun, *Qiuping xinyu*, *juan* 12.

81. See Lewis, *Ecstatic Religion*; and Bargen, *A Woman's Weapon*.

82. See Koizuga, *Kitsune monogatari*, pp. 26–43. For a rich supply of material on fox possession from the perspective of Meiji attempts to eliminate superstition, see Kida, *Tsukimono*. See also Figal, *Civilization and Monsters*, pp. 97–101.

83. Dorfman, "The Spirits of Reform," p. 263.

A non-narrative rejection of the powers of predominantly female mediums is found in a Guangxu collection, Zhang Tao's *Jinmen zaji* in the context of worship of the five animal spirits.

The female mediums of Tianjin claim that they pray to spirits, can act as mediums, and cure people's illnesses. People call them *guniangzi* 姑娘子 [auntie]. Since the locals are foolish and ignorant, if someone falls ill, people often call them. The mediums burn incense, mutter as if talking in their sleep, and suddenly say the spirit they pray to has descended. Sometimes the spirit calls itself Mistress White, sometimes Grandma Yellow, and sometimes Auntie Hu. Of the names the spirits take, most are female. As iron is pulled by a magnet, so many women are easily deceived. The members of humble families believe in this steadfastly. Sometimes the mediums treat illness with pills, and sometimes with holy water. They take credit for their successes, but if they fail, they call it fate.[84]

Zhang next introduced "the five great ones" (*wu da jia* 五大家), the five sacred animals and their surnames: the fox is Hu; the weasel, Huang (yellow); the hedgehog, Bai (white); the snake, Liu (willow); and the rat, Hui (gray). The use of female kinship terms, although common in addressing all sorts of deities, emphasizes the gendered nature of both the practice and this critique. He closed, "Every household worships them very respectfully; when I speak of it, I laugh to split my sides." The financial grounds for criticizing worship have remained the same. In this account, the fox itself is absent, and the mediums are discredited in human terms. This general ethnographic account of the worship of the five animal spirits is in striking contrast to the specific examples from the bulk of the Qing. The tradition has come full circle back to an external perspective on a local practice.

A contempt for professionals who offered the services of fox spirits for a price seems to be the flip side of literati authors' affection for the fox and fascination with the possibility of profit, protection, and otherworldly conversation. These lower-class figures offered compet-

---

84. Zhang Tao, *Jinmen zaji*, zhong, 39a. Virtually the same information is also included in Yu Yue, *Youtai xianguan biji*, 13.12a. A fox-healer makes the same excuse in an anecdote in Chen Qiyuan, *Yongxianzhai biji*, 2.3b: "I can cure illness, but I can't cure fate." In that context this sounds less like a lame excuse than an attempt to subsume the foxes' powers to the larger order of fate.

ing visions of the fox and competing claims to power over them. Mistrust of spirit-mediums seems shared among a wide range of upper-class authors, although attitudes ranged from Zhang Jingyun's willingness to compromise to Ji Yun's absolute disassociation of foxes from these figures.

Money has proven even more central to this discussion of fox worship than discussions of belief and disbelief. Diane Dorfman's discussion of the contemporary worship of the five animal spirits in the suburbs of Beijing focuses on the use of the animal spirits in constructing *nongmin* 農民 (peasant) identity, in which the two axes of morality and immorality and wealth and poverty are crucial. Genuine healers accept gifts but never explicitly demand payment. They offer a model of moral wealth, as other prosperous farmers do, opposed to the immoral wealth of corrupt officials. The poor, however, are seen as those most likely to be tormented by the depredations of spirits, for in the atmosphere of the reform era a stance of moral poverty is no longer possible.[85] These stories, in contrast, show a literati, as opposed to a peasant, perception of the place of money in the construction of acceptable and unacceptable worship as well as the place of worship in perceptions of money. A juxtaposition of foxes as spirits of wealth and the exposés of false mediums reveals that in the Qing, money is the means by which falseness is exposed. For people of other classes, especially women, worship cannot be contained within a comfortable range of social relations between spirit and medium or between medium and clients. Fear is focused not on delusion and dangerous belief as such but on the improper circulation of money outside of households as a consequence of lies and mistaken beliefs. The anxiety about foxes as gods of wealth is that they take things from elsewhere by untraceable routes; the anxiety about mediums is the same—that wealth flows from household to household along obscure paths of female relationships. The figures regarded with suspicion are women operating as mediums outside any clear household structure. Acceptable worship, like acceptable fox residence, is contained in its place and provides prosperity by keeping wealth where it is by averting bandits and fire.

85. Dorfman, "The Spirits of Reform," pp. 265–66.

The case of *wenxiang jiao* 聞香教 (the sect of smelling the scent) in the late Ming provides an illuminating contrast of a belief that was considered dangerous as such, with an emphasis on an organized group rather than individual deception. Records of a popular sect named for the fox, *xuanhu jiao* 玄狐教, include little more than its name. More is known about *wenxiang jiao*, which was linked to *xuanhu jiao* in at least one text.[86] The story of the origins of the sect, which became involved in a series of peasant uprisings in the Ming and Qing, contains elements familiar to readers of the fox tale. Wang Sen 王森 (1542–1619), the founder, found a fox in the talons of a hawk, and the fox begged Wang to rescue it. When he did, the fox broke off his tail to thank him. The tail gave off an enchanted scent, and whoever smelled it became entranced and saw visions. Wang relied on this means to found a sect. In an alternative version, the fox appears in the form of a tiny old man sleeping soundly by the roadside, who rewards Wang for waking him with a gift of enchanted incense. In this case, both the fox and his gift appear in more human guise.[87] The grateful fox is a very familiar theme, and the discarded fox tail as an enchanted treasure is also recorded in other sources.[88] This cult flourished in the heart of traditional fox territory, the area around Tianjin.

Despite this origin myth, the sect seems to have been of mixed ancestry and involved many elements with no connection to fox worship. In its own religious tracts, the origins of the scent that gave the sect its name were more lofty and divine than a grateful fox.[89] This suggests that both the fox and the narcotic deception of the masses were stories that others told about the sect. Since the fox has already departed and left only his tail behind for the use of a human worshipper, the emphasis is on the human who can use the fox's powers rather than the fox itself. This emphasis on the human seems typical for *yao* in cases of popular rebellion. Even in the story told by outsiders, the fox is not depicted as a demonic fomenter of rebellion;

---

86. Tan Qian, *Bei you lu*. 集7, 冊11, no. 67, 紀文 56. See Li Jianguo's discussion, *Zhongguo hu wenhua*, pp. 185–190.

87. Huang Zunsu, *Shuo lüe*, 21a–22a.

88. "Hu wei" 狐尾, in Yu Jiao, *Meng'an zazhu*, 9.2a–3b.

89. Ma Xisha and Han Bingfang, *Zhongguo minjian zongjiao shi*, p. 614.

rather, it innocently follows its own code for repaying favors. Foxes are linked to rebellious *yao* in Feng Menglong's version of *Pingyao zhuan*, and Li Shouju suggests that it was inspired by *wenxiang jiao*. But this vision in a late Ming vernacular novel seems distinct from the treatment of the fox in Qing classical tales.[90]

In the permutations and combinations of elements of strange stories and popular religion, the fox could play the role of rabble-rouser as well. However, *zhiguai* authors contemporary with the *wenxiang jiao* did not seem to consider this organized cult central to the fox tradition, since the records of the relationship are found in historical miscellanies rather than in *zhiguai* collections. In the Qing, the focus had shifted even more to financial and gender-based, rather than political, anxieties about fox worship.

CONCLUSION

Comparison of Chinese fox worship with the Japanese case is enlightening. The Chinese fox was never associated with a major divinity as strongly as the Japanese fox is linked to Inari.[91] According to Karen Smyers, for worshippers in Japan the fox remains the most accessible and attractively flexible representative of the more official cults, even though leaders of those same cults constantly try to distance themselves from the fox.[92] In China the fox has the same flexibility without the symbiotic relationship with a larger, more structured cult. The narrative consequences of decentralization and heterodoxy seem to be a lack of sanctioned stories by the practitioners of fox worship. We have no sectarian literature as such, but only the chance relationships of *zhiguai* authors to foxes and their worshippers.

Zhiguai represent the range of relationships to the alien their authors could conceive—relationships that, in their view, they themselves and their fellow men were actually engaged in, as well as relationships as these authors imagined they should be or wished

90. Li Shouju, *Huxian xinyang yu hulijing gushi*, p. 162. See also Kang, "Power at the Margins," pp. 155–56.

91. The link between foxes and Taishan Niangniang seems much more regional and marginal to the fox tradition.

92. Smyers, *The Fox and the Jewel*, chap. 2.

they would be. The imagined relationships are, however, bound by the conventions of the conceivable established by the first category. The switch from general ethnographic description to particular narrative, and back, marks a shift from a moment when those conventions needed to be introduced to one when they did not.

As the contrast between the recurring patterns of worship and the exceptions of narrative makes clear, there is a difference between amateur and professional relations with the fox. From the perspective of worshippers, one's relationship with guardian foxes is a long-term situation and enters the narrative record only when there is a change: the fox leaves with death of its favorite human or intervenes in disturbances in the human household. One seeks out a medium, however, in exceptional circumstances, when afflicted with illness or eager for novelty. For the person outside the medium's household, even a relatively unremarkable visit to a medium, as in Pu Songling's "Shang xian," is worthy of comment. But for the medium, relations with both the fox and clients who come to consult the fox are matters of routine, conceived in social or familial terms.

The fox illustrates the tensions between the two understandings of popular religion, as everyone's religion and as the religion of everyone save the literati author and his peers. Literati men talk to their own true foxes, who disclose the falseness of lower-class women's foxes; they visit mediums out of curiosity or need but have different kinds of conversations with the fox friends of their peers and the fox gods of mediums; they accept wine and loans from the foxes who possess their concubines but do not allow them, vixens or concubines, to heal strangers. The idea of the fox is shared by a broad cross-section of the population, but not without contention.

5

Foxes and Sex

狐淫獸也，以淫媚人
The fox is a lustful creature, and it seduces people with its lustfulness.[1]

人之淫者爲妓，物之淫者爲狐
The most lustful among people are prostitutes; the most lustful among animals are foxes.[2]

These two comments reiterate the standard judgment: the shape-changing fox is the embodiment of lust. This is the most notorious and familiar aspect of the fox tradition. It survives in the modern vernacular in the derogatory term *huli jing* 狐狸精 (fox spirit) for a seductive, loose, and cunning woman. Yet this very familiarity may prevent close examination of what we glibly assume we know the fox represents. What did it mean to call the fox lustful in the seventeenth or the nineteenth century? What is the precise nature of sexual allure and danger in the fox narrative? How did the concept change in different literary genres and in different historical periods? The first quotation above does not specify the gender of the seductive alien or of the seduced human, but the second, through the comparison with prostitutes, implies that the most lustful among animals are female. This raises the question of how ideas of alien sexuality intersect with gender. What does it signify to equate an animal and a

1. Chen Ding, "Liehu zhuan" 烈狐傳, in Zhang Chao, *Yuchu xinzhi*, 10.193.
2. Baiyi jushi, *Hutianlu*, 3.32b.

particular type of woman? This chapter is an attempt to answer these questions.

EARLY HISTORY

The centrality of sexual, especially feminine, deception to the conception of the fox is clear in the early, influential statement from *Xuanzhong ji* that opened this book: "When a fox is fifty years old, it can transform itself into a woman. When it is one hundred, it becomes a beautiful woman or a shaman; some become men and have sex with women. They can know events from more than a thousand li away and are good at witchcraft, beguiling people and making them lose their senses. When they are a thousand years old, they can commune with the heavens and become heavenly foxes." A variant text has foxes becoming "lustful women" *yinfu* 淫婦.[3]

In Six Dynasties *zhiguai*, foxes who assume human form and seduce humans are described in both theoretical statements and individual narratives. The fox, however, seems to be but one of many creatures capable of this kind of sexual deception. The tales do not attribute any overt motive to these creatures. When the true identity of the lover is revealed, humans appear to be repulsed more by this gross transgression of categories than by any sense of concrete danger.[4]

Beginning in the Tang, the association of the fox with sex is summed up in a single word, *mei* 媚, "to seduce," "to bewitch."[5] For

---

3. "Shuo hu" 說狐, in *TPGJ*, 447.3652.

4. The one great exception is the story of Azi 阿紫, in which a man seems in danger of himself becoming a fox as he experiences unimaginable pleasures; in this story, however, humanity and foxhood are permeable in both directions, since it is explained that a wanton woman named Azi had once been changed into a fox. Gan Bao, *Soushen ji*, *juan* 18, story 425.

5. Alternatively written with the homophonous character 魅, used also in the *Xuanzhong ji* reference. This character affiliates seduction more closely with ghosts and monsters than with women; my impression is that this usage is less common after the Tang. In the *Hanyu da cidian* (s.v., vol. 4, p. 390), the references for this meaning of *mei* date to the Tang at the earliest, and all the examples have to do with foxes. A Wanli-era anthology of fox stories, the only such exclusive collection, is entitled *Humei congtan* 狐媚叢談, although the anthology's contents are not limited to seductions.

both men and women, to be bewitched by a fox could mean either to surrender one's will to a visible, external seducer/seductress or to be possessed by a disembodied spirit. The distinction between these two kinds of *mei*, enchantment and illness, could waver over the course of a single narrative.[6] One brief anecdote illustrates the ambiguity between a medical condition and a relationship particularly clearly: "In the Tang Feng Jie suffered from an illness caused by a fox demon. His father later got an exorcist to cure his illness. The demon suddenly wept and told him, 'I had planned to stay with you forever, but now I am under duress from this exorcist; I cannot come here again.'" To everyone else the fox is simply a disease, but the fox's lover hears an individual voice.[7] *Mei* suggests that the danger of foxes lay primarily in their skills at deluding humans and the subsequent loss of judgment and control. The threat of physical destruction seems to have been secondary in these early stories, but in later stories the emphasis shifts to life-threatening sexual depletion. After the Tang, possession and seduction grow further apart as the two possibilities become more strongly marked by gender: women are still possessed by male foxes, but much more narrative interest is devoted to the vixen as seductress.

What narrative shape does vulpine sexuality take? For men, the Six Dynasties beast lover story is often an undisguised one-night stand and adheres to a basic structure of encounter, consummation, and exposure, quickly followed by expulsion of the beast. In later stories, such brevity becomes rare; the far more common pattern is a relatively detailed description of the first encounter with a fox in woman's shape, followed by the line, "And then she would come every night and vanish at dawn." Sometimes the human lover is the only one who can see her, a detail that underlines the private nature of the experience. These trysts continue until she is exposed, usually

6. For example, "Li Yuangong" 李元恭, in *TPGJ*, 9:449.3671; "Changsun wuji" 長孫無忌, in *TPGJ*, 9:447.3657; "Yang Bocheng" 楊伯成, in *TPGJ*, 9:448.3664.

7. "Feng Jie" 馮玠, in *TPGJ*, 10:451.3684. I am indebted to Dudbridge's distinction between the inner and the outer story, Religious Experience and Lay Society, pp. 12–16.

by a third party[8] or, in later stories, by the appearance of symptoms of sexual parasitism. In the Six Dynasties, the story would end with the knowledge that she is a fox; in later stories, the man, overwhelmed by her beauty, is able to brush that knowledge aside, and the ending of the relationship requires outside interference. The beginning and the end of the relationship, seduction and disillusionment, receive the most narrative attention, but the substance of intimacy, the middle of the story, is elided. The vixen who appears at night and vanishes by day offers a sexual relationship distinct from the rest of a man's life and thus represents a tempting and dangerous lack of responsibility. This basic structure remains powerful throughout the tradition, although as we shall see in the next chapter, vixens also come to assume the nonsexual responsibilities of concubines or even wives. In the case of afflicted women, the minority case, the basic narrative pattern has a different emphasis: illness followed by diagnosis and exorcism. As we shall see, although structurally similar, the male and female patterns differ greatly in perspective and the potential for elaboration.

Rhetorical use of the fox as a symbol for the dangers of sex and narratives about sexual relations with foxes are related but separate traditions. For example, only about half the Tang stories of affairs between men and foxes in *Taiping guangji* imply these affairs are dangerous for the man. Yet in poetry and other genres of the same period, the fox is unambiguously the epitome of a dangerous woman.[9] The crucial difference here is rhetorical purpose: the poems require a powerful image of sensual deception, whereas the anecdotes occupy the more ambiguous space of individual experience and narrative interest. The fox as a rhetorical device is exclusively female, whereas a fox in a particular narrative can be of either sex. I will

8. An early example of this type is "Shangguan yi" 上官翼, in *TPGJ*, 9:447.3659. This resembles the "Demon Story" plot type that Hanan (*The Chinese Vernacular Story*, pp. 44–49) identifies in vernacular stories. An example of the extended one-night stand is "Quzhou shaofu" 衢州少婦, in Hong Mai, *Yijian zhi*, yijuan 2:4.820–21.

9. For examples from the poetry of Bai Juyi and Yuan Zhen and the prose memorial Luo Binwang directed against Empress Wu, see Monschein, *Der Zauber der Fuchsfee*, pt. IV. The most powerful example is probably Bai Juyi's poem "Gu zhong hu" 古冢狐; see *Bai Juyi ji*, 1:4.87–88.

argue that the distinction between "the Fox" and "a fox" apparent in the Tang remains useful in explaining the differences between depictions of foxes in classical and in vernacular fiction in later periods.

THE RISE OF THE VIXEN

In later periods, the sexual plot grew steadily more important. Although based on sheer statistics the proportion of sexual stories is lower in *Liaozhai zhiyi* than in *Taiping guangji*, the sexual stories are the longest and most elaborate of Pu's fox stories. Of the 88 fox tales in *Taiping guangji*, 43 involve a sexual liaison with a fox. In *Liaozhai zhiyi*, the proportion is 34 out of a total of 86 stories.[10] Because these 34 are among the most famous and most influential stories in the collection, the proportion of such stories becomes higher in imitations of *Liaozhai*.

Along with increasing attention to the sexual plot came a shift in gender. Although the sexual experience of men and women with supernatural lovers had always been treated differently, attention to the male experience grew steadily larger. The word *mei* itself has a strong, although not exclusive, association with women. The quotation from *Xuanzhong ji* reveals the primacy of the female form; the fact that foxes could also become men and have sex with women is mentioned as an afterthought. Li Jianguo argues that there was a progressive feminization of the fox in literary history. In the Six Dynasties, male foxes were more common, but in later periods vixens outnumbered them by constantly increasing margins.[11] As we have seen, however, foxes of both sexes inhabited homes and received offerings in the late imperial period; it is the sexual tradition that females came to predominate. This assumption has become absolute in the present: the modern colloquial *huli jing* is reserved for women.

The inclusion of famous fox stories in the great Ming compendia of stories about women, such as *Lüchuang nüshi* 綠窗女史 (The green window history of women) and *Guang yanyi bian* 廣艷異編

10. For an exhaustive list of the fox stories in *Liaozhai*, see Gu Meigao, "Tan hu," pp. 252–53. Some of the stories on this list mention foxes only in passing, however.

11. Li Jianguo, *Zhongguo hu wenhua*. For a similar argument about the Song-Ming period, see Li Shouju, *Huxian xinyang yu huli jing gushi*, pp. 151–52.

(Expanded anthology of the glamorous and strange), indicates that vixens were considered a subcategory of women, at least women as they were conceived in anthologies focusing on the alluring and extraordinary.[12] In contrast, male foxes never appear in anthologies of stories about famous men. This says as much about the narrative roles of men and women as it does about foxes; the narrative territory of women is closer to the bizarre. Men as men were not a topic for a fiction anthology; they had to be further specialized—knight errants, for example—to become noteworthy. Female foxes could easily find a place in fictional representations of women because females of different species fit into the same matrix of passion, chastity, and lust.

THE FOX BODY AND THE FEMALE BODY

What is the nature of the vixen's body? Her human body is a desirable illusion. In Tang and earlier stories the exposure of her original body ends both the narrative and desire. Passion and disenchantment are given two distinct forms; the fox body belongs only to the morning after. In later narratives, it often does not appear even then. The fox body becomes increasingly remote, as in more and more narratives her true identity is exposed with the mere name "fox." In a progression of convergent evolution matching the vagueness of the fox body in tales of haunting and the absence of the fox body in the images in fox shrines, "fox" comes to imply a desirable, long-lived woman with magical skills as much as it does a hairy mammal.

There are a few late Ming references that speculate about the relationship between the fox and physical femininity. Passages in *Kuai yuan* and *Wanli yehuo bian* 萬曆野獲編 (Private gleanings of the Wanli reign; 1605) link foxes' skill at transformation with an appetite for menstrual blood. According to one *Kuai yuan* story, discussed in Chapter 3, shape-changing foxes are common in the north because northern women throw their soiled menstrual rags in the gutter, where foxes eat them and gain the ability to transform.[13] As *Yehuo*

---

12. Qinhuai yuke, *Lüchuang nüshi*. The *yaoyan bu* 妖豔部 (category of the monstrous and glamorous) in *juan* 8 opens with three fox stories under the general title *hufen* 狐粉 (fox powder). See also Wu Dazhen, *Guang yanyi bian*, 6:30.2a.

13. *Kuai yuan*, 14.8a; "Jingshi humei" 京師狐媚, in Shen Defu, *Wanli Yehuo bian*, 28.729.

bian points out, menstrual blood is a significant ingredient in alchemy; esoteric Daoist practices may have suggested the link between its consumption and transformation. Foxes' taking of blood-stained cloths may be zoologically accurate, yet the hint in the anecdote in *Kuai yuan* that foxes have an innate preference for the women's quarters suggests that this is the culturally rather than biologically defined fox. Foxes are linked with the most secret and "dirty" aspect of femininity. Their transgression is linked to pollution, both in the form of menstrual blood itself and its presence in the public gutter. Women whose bodily fluids are not properly contained indoors produce creatures who violate species boundaries.

Foxes are also linked to the most artificial aspect of femininity. In the Ming work *Gujin shiwu kao* 古今事物考 (Investigation of things old and new), the infamous Shang concubine Daji 妲己, identified as a vixen both here and in a series of vernacular novels, is credited with the invention of footbinding. Since she had not yet changed her small fox paws to human feet, she wrapped them in bandages to conceal them. Thereafter all the palace women imitated her.[14] Since the vixen is more attractively female than are human women, foxes are credited with defining femininity. This anecdote acquired a life of its own in speculations about the origins of footbinding but not in the narrative tradition on foxes, and it never seems to be taken entirely seriously when cited. Making the link in the other direction, one eighteenth-century account depicts a hunter who killed a fox, discovering that it had a woman's arched bound feet and red shoes.[15]

These texts from roughly the same period explore the linking of the vixen with femininity as pollution and femininity as artifice, the vixen as a by-product of the female body and as its inventor. Women and vixens are used to explain each other's strangeness.

---

14. "Chanzu" 纏足, in Wang Sanpin, *Gujin shiwu kao*, 4:6.30b; "Chanzu" 纏足, in Chu Renhuo, *Jianhu ji*, 1.6b; Qian Xiyan, *Xixia*, *juan* 1. Chu Renhuo is criticizing the story as recounted in *Gujin shiwu kao*. Qian Xiyan also claimed he saw this story in another (unnamed) book and said it should be respected as the most ancient account of footbinding's origins (a comment that may very well be tongue in cheek.) The only other story I have seen linking foxes and footbinding is *Ting yu xuan biji*, 1.10. In this fox lodger story, discussed in Chapter 3, the fox mother helps a girl to bind her feet even smaller without pain.

15. Wang Qishu, *Shuicao qingxia lu*, 3.12a.

These immediate bodily traces are, however, minor details of the tradition and appear in explanatory asides rather than in the narrative proper. They were forgotten in Qing as part of a general shift of attention away from the fox body.

SEXUAL PARASITISM

The psychological dangers of *mei* are inherent in the fox tradition from the Tang on, but a clear idea of the physical danger of relations with foxes developed more slowly. As discussed above, in the Six Dynasties, to be seduced by a fox was to be confronted by a disturbing confusion of categories; in the Tang, it might bring a loosening of one's grip on human reality, but it was not necessarily fatal. Nor during this early period were foxes' motives for seducing humans spelled out.

In later tales, the fox's role as a sexual vampire became increasingly codified. Foxes were described as practicing *caibu* 採補 (gleaning from another in order to replenish oneself) or *caiyang buyin* 採陽補陰 (to harvest *yang* in order to replenish *yin*). They drained humans of sexual energy to achieve immortality, a process that led to emaciation and eventual death for their victims. Parasitism became a rational, if immoral, path of advancement. These notions fit foxes and other creatures into a more general conception of sex as a battle between two partners, in which the one who brings the other to orgasm first emerges victorious and claims the loser's *jing* 精 as the spoils. This idea is rooted in the understanding of *jing* as both sperm and life essence, which must be conserved for longevity and health. Ideas of conserving sexual energy to preserve life focus on the male, which explains why the female who compels a man to squander his finite store of energy is an object of greater cultural anxiety than male sexual predators on women.[16] As well as preserving their own energy,

16. For a study of Ming medical conceptions of male conservation of life, see chap. 6, "Nourishing Life: Ming Bodies of Generation and Longevity," in Furth, *A Flourishing Yin*, pp. 200–201. Furth argues that the idea of a man nourishing his life with the sexual conquest of many partners fell from favor in the medical literature of the Ming even though it continued to attract interest in erotic fiction. See also Douglas Wile, *Bedchamber Arts: The Chinese Sexual Yoga Classics Including Women's Sex Texts*.

men could accumulate more vigor by harvesting the sexual energy of human females. However, anxiety still focused on the idea of exhaustible men dealing with inexhaustible women. Foxes followed similar practices; along with more acceptable means of pursuing immortality, such as meditation and breathing exercises, a sexual regimen is part of their assimilation into human practices of Daoist advancement.[17] In the late imperial period, parasitism is seen not as an innate physical trait of the fox but as a conscious choice. This motivation makes foxes seem cold and calculating: they fulfill a numerical goal rather than satisfy an appetite.

The idea of sexual parasitism converts foxes' desire to ambition; conversely, human male desire becomes a wasting illness. There is a shift in emphasis from distraction to depletion. Symptoms such as weight loss and enervation often replace revelation of the fox body as the means of exposing the lover's true nature. The problem posed by the fox becomes pathological excess, instead of deception or violation of species divisions.

This idea of parasitism as a means of advancement for foxes appears in the written record in the latter half of the Ming.[18] Xie Zhaozhe put it succinctly, "When they [foxes] enchant humans, they often take human essence and *qi* 氣 in order to complete their *neidan* 內丹."[19] The *neidan* is the inner elixir that is the fruit of Daoist self-cultivation, the equivalent of the external elixirs of alchemy.[20] For the fox, it was a more physical artifact than it was for human adepts; it seems to have been envisioned as a corporeal accumulation of

17. Sex is not the only means by which foxes glean human energy. Ming collections in particular seem to posit a period during which they drain the *qi* in humans' exhaled breath before they can assume human forms and seduce people at all. However, the seduction itself is not described as parasitic. See, e.g., Lang Ying, *Qixiu leigao*, 48.9b; and Xu Changzuo, *Yanshan conglu, juan* 9, story 6.

18. Li Shouju (*Huxian xinyang yu huli jing gushi*, pp. 159–60) attributes this development to the Song and Ming, but all the evidence she cites comes from the Ming. She also notes the gender difference between the concepts of sexual parasitism in Wei-Jin esoteric practice and Ming fiction. For a study of female sexual parasites in another cultural context, see Silver, *Strange and Secret Peoples*, pp. 178–83.

19. Xie Zhaozhe, *Wuza zu*, 9.14.

20. For an introduction to interior alchemy in the Song, see Robinet, *Taoism*, pp. 215–56.

victims' sexual essence, subject to theft and loss.[21] One early narrative example is the story "Hu dan" 狐丹 ("Fox Elixir") in *Humei congtan.* Set in the Chenghua 成化 reign (1465–87), it relates a vixen's relationship with two brothers, which ends when one of her lovers attempts to steal her *dan* and causes its loss. She had already practiced self-refinement for hundreds of years; the *yang* essence of human men was the last ingredient she needed to achieve immortality.[22] This vixen claims that the relationship will also grant the brothers long life. In this and many other Ming classical tales, a vixen's sexual gain does not necessarily result in harm to her human lover.[23]

Ironically, in the Qing, just as many amorous vixens were being vigorously dissociated from parasitism, the idea of parasitic foxes was solidified by this opposition. It was Qing authors who made absolute the link between the fox as femme fatale and sex as a means of advancement. In the Qing, only wicked vixens had sex with men for their own benefit; good foxes did it for love or to repay a moral debt. The idea of two possible paths for advancement is well developed and repeated in many different texts.[24] In the Ming the moral lines were not yet so clear-cut. Although a superficial examination of the fox tradition may give the impression that dangerous, parasitic foxes are an earlier tradition and benign foxes are a later revision, in fact the creation of the virtuous vixen crystallizes the image of the parasitic vixen. They are by-products of one another.

---

21. Li Jianguo, pers. comm., 1996.

22. The idea of a man's *yang* essence as the final ingredient for immortality is very common; examples include "Dabie shanhu" 大別山狐, in Feng Menglong, *Qingshi leilüe* 情史類略, 12.939 (trans. Mowry, *Chinese Love Stories from Ch'ing-shih*, pp. 95–98). This plot was adapted as a vernacular story "Zeng zhima shipo jiaxing, xie caoyao qiaoxie zhen'ou" 贈芝麻識破假形，擷草藥巧諧真偶, in Ling Mengchu, *Erke po'an jingqi*, 2:29.1371–411. See also the vernacular novel *Zhaoyang qushi* 昭陽趣史 and the play *Jiaopa ji* 蕉帕記.

23. Humei congtan, 5.23b–25b. I have not succeeded in locating this story's source, but I doubt very much that it originated in Humei congtan. The idea that a fox can borrow a man's energy to become an immortal is present in *Gengsi bian*. This fox, too, insists that the relationship will not harm her lover; see "Linjiang hu" 臨江狐, in Lu Can, *Gengsi bian* 庚巳編, 1.24a.

24. For one of the clearest explanations, see *YWCT*, 10.503–4, story 229.

In a *Liaozhai* tale of a parasitic fox, "Dong sheng" 董生 (Licentiate Dong), the narrative elaboration and flourishes one expects of Pu Songling embellish a fairly straightforward tale of a deadly lover. Allan Barr cites this story as an example of a relatively simple tale of an encounter with the strange, typical of the earlier sections of *Liaozhai*.[25] The vixen's arrival is foretold by the concern of a skilled doctor who reads Dong's pulse; she is read as a physical illness from the beginning. When Dong returns home after the conversation with the doctor and puts a hand under the blankets to test for warmth, he finds a young woman lying there. At first he is delighted, but when he gropes her lower body, he finds a bristly tail. The sexual symbolism of his discovery (whether we take the tail as suggesting a phallus or pubic hair) is blatant. Only in a portrait of a harmful fox would Pu allow this reminder of a fox's animal nature to survive.[26] Dong is ready to flee, but the woman grabs his shoulder and asks him where he is going. He quakes and asks that the *xianren* forgive him.[27] She laughs and says, "What have you seen to make you think me a *xian*?" "I do not fear your head, but your tail," he replies. She challenges him to find her tail again, and his attempt uncovers only smooth human buttocks. This absence is just as suggestive as the tail's presence; again, Pu would not give such a graphic description for a benevolent fox. Dong is convinced that he was mistaken. The relationship is consummated, and the narrator notes only that he "was exceptionally pleased."

Then the plot leaps ahead: after more than a month, Dong has become emaciated and returns to the doctor. When he is advised that he has the pulse of a man afflicted by a monster, he returns

---

25. Barr, "A Comparative Study of Early and Late Tales in *Liaozhai zhiyi*," p.161.

26. In stories in which foxes' imitation of humanity is less than perfect, it is always the tail that gives them away. This story type can be found as early as Six Dynasties *zhiguai*; see "Sun Yan" 孫巖 from *Luoyang qielan ji* 洛陽伽藍記, in *TPGJ*, 9:447.3655.

27. Note how the term *xian* is used as flattering and defensive language, avoiding the word *fox*; I suspect this is the *xian* of popular worship. In keeping with foxes' elevated status in the tradition of popular worship, Dong's reaction is extremely different from the protagonists of earlier fox stories, who would drive out and conquer the fox at the first sign of her animal identity. Her nonhuman identity is a strength rather than a weakness. See the discussion in the previous chapter.

home and rejects the fox. Yet he dreams of having sex with her and wakes to find the sheets wet and cold even when he sleeps surrounded by his wife and son to ward her off. This further advances the portrait of the fox as illness: she becomes manifest as involuntary ejaculation, a pathology that drains away the last of his life. After many days, he coughs up blood and dies. The fox then appears in the home of one of Dong's friends, who, however, avoids the same fate, thanks to a warning from Dong's spirit.[28] In the end, she is punished for her crimes, but the infernal judge notes that it was Dong's own self-indulgence that brought him to his doom. This final judgment is typical of Qing treatment of parasitic foxes.

The vixen as sexual parasite must be placed in the context of general concepts of the dangers of sexuality. Throughout the tradition, the sexual dangers of the fox differed in degree rather than in kind from the sexual dangers of human women, and in the most sympathetic portrayal of vixens, even the difference in degree is disputed. This lack of sexual distinction leads to the vixen's defensive argument, used by *Liaozhai's* Lianxiang 蓮香 among others, that it is sexual indulgence, not the relationship with a fox, that is dangerous. When Lianxiang asks her lover about the difference between foxes and humans, he replies with what was presumably conventional wisdom: if you consort with foxes, they will drive you to your death. She negates this distinction by claiming that overindulgence with a human partner is equally dangerous: "Someone of your age can restore his energies three days after having had sex; even if you consorted with a fox, what harm could it do? But if you go at it day and night, then people are worse than foxes. How could all the diseased corpses and sickly ghosts of the world have been poisoned by foxes?"[29]

Although vixens and human women pose similar dangers to human men, only vixens stand to profit by it. Female lust is characterized as *yin* 淫, with its implications of flooding and

28. *LZ*, 2.133–36.

29. *LZ*, 2.222. One late Qing tale plays with the conventions of the parasitic fox by making it appear that a vixen is draining her lover but ending by blaming the man's illness on his own sexual desires. The fox offers in turn the medicine to cure this excess, taking Lianxiang's moderation further. See Li Qingchen, *Zuicha zhiguai*, 1.7.

terized as *yin* 淫, with its implications of flooding and dissipation of energy, but only vixens can accumulate sexual energy and reap its benefits.[30] The possibility of the sexually triumphant female is apparently too alarming to contain within the human species.

As well as the straightforward use of parasitic foxes as a cautionary tale about the dangers of sex, such stories can also be stretched to describe all forms of opportunism. Ji Yun uses sexual parasitism as a means of discussing ill-won financial wealth or humans who enter into relationships with ulterior motives.[31]

With sexual parasitism, the dangers of female sexuality are codified and exaggerated, but lust itself is somehow not part of the picture. Profit largely replaces illicit pleasure as foxes' potential for sexual chaos is directed into orderly acquisition. In the evolution of the fox tradition, anxiety about sex with the alien shifts from the violation of boundaries by means of illusion and deception to male depletion and female gain.

FOX STORIES AND PORNOGRAPHY

Given the centrality of sex to the plot, there is a surprising lack of explicit erotic description in the majority of fox stories. In most cases, the erotic attention focuses on the promise of availability and flirtation before consummation. Interest lies in the moment a man is bewitched; seemingly the results go almost without saying. Fox stories share this pattern, as well as the omission of description of the sexual act beyond a few euphemisms and clichés, with most classical romances. However, the omission of erotic description also has a par-

30. I am influenced here by McMahon's interpretation of eighteenth-century erotic fiction in *Misers, Shrews, and Polygamists.* The sexual schematic McMahon draws in his study illuminates the role played by the parasitic vixen. The successful polygamist is opposed on the one side by a female shrew and the other side by the male miser. The vixen is the only female who can equal the successful polygamist; she defeats miser and polygamist alike, far more successfully than the human shrew. For the shrew and the *ars erotica*, see ibid., pp. 61–65. Note also the connection between the fox and shrew in *Xingshi yinyuan zhuan* 醒世姻緣傳. In non-erotic fox tales, foxes sometimes force misers to distribute the wealth they have been hoarding; this is perhaps a parallel to the vixen's triumph over those who would hoard their sexual reserves.

31. *YWCT*, 11.563, story 32; 9.416, story 130.

ticular meaning for the fox story, given the elusive nature of the fox body. Even in their earliest or crudest forms, the bestiality of animal spirit tales is veiled. The man becomes aware of the identity of his lover only after the sexual act. There is never physical contact with the body of the animal.[32] Therefore, no particular positions or sexual behaviors set foxes apart.[33] The attraction of the fox tale was clearly not based on explicit sexual description but on the idea of a sexually available and willing species. The precise details of the vixen's wantonness were left up to the imagination.

Fox stories range from chaste romances to soft-core pornography. Along the entire spectrum, the sexual description is identical to that in similar tales involving human partners, suggesting that the genre of the story, rather than the presence of the fox, determines the nature of erotic description. Erotic description in the classical tale is likely to consist of elegant euphemisms; vernacular fiction allows more graphic description. This principle is demonstrated most clearly by one fox work that can unquestionably be described as pornography, the Qing dynasty vernacular novel *Yaohu yanshi* 妖狐豔史. The hero has sexual adventures first with a pair of parasitic foxes and then with a virtuous fox, his destined bride. The distinction between

---

32. "True" bestiality is another category of the strange altogether. Ji Yun, who regarded tales of affairs with foxes as commonplace, remarked that a tale of a man who had sex with his pigs illustrated the extremes of human depravity; see *YWCT*, 12.612–13, story 82. See also "Quan jian" 犬姦, *LZ*, 1.49–50, which graphically depicts a woman's sexual relation with a dog.

33. I have seen only one exceptional anecdote that identifies foxes' sexual parasitism with a particular act. In a story in *Zuicha zhiguai*, the protagonist is a servant who can see unearthly things with one of his eyes. Having already observed two foxes using human skulls to turn themselves into beautiful women, he then spies on his master having sex with one of them. He is confronted by the grisly spectacle of the fox taking his master's genitals into her mouth and sucking the life out of him, while the skull bobs up and down on her head. This anecdote reveals the frightening possibility of actual bestiality, which is usually so well concealed as to be forgotten. Although in this case fellatio is used as the most shocking illustration of parasitism, it does not reflect a general vision of sex with vixens, nor a cultural attitude toward oral sex. See "Du sheng" 杜生, in Li Qingzhen, *Zuicha zhiguai*, 2.303. In *Zhaoyang qushi*, Hede, the reincarnation of a vixen, can best even the most stalwart of men in sexual combat, an ability attributed to her past as a fox; but this is a matter of sexual power rather than a particular act; see Guhang yanyan sheng, *Zhaoyang qushi*, 1.115.

the two kinds of vixen is made plain in the erotic description; the graphic details of the affairs with the two monstrous foxes and the suggestive euphemisms for the relationship with his virtuous bride illustrate Keith McMahon's distinction between the chaste description of monogamous relationships and erotic description of polygamous ones.[34] The sexual description does not depart from the familiar territory of vernacular pornography with its preoccupation with penis size and endurance.[35]

In comparison, the most risqué classical tales, such as some stories in He Bang'e's *Yetan suilu*, reveal different interests. Although this collection relates more graphic sexual details than most classical fiction, it is still quite restrained in comparison with *Yaohu yanshi*. Confirming the association of polygamy with erotic fiction, these tales provide a wide range of sexual partners for the human protagonists. Interestingly, as we have seen in the case of the recalcitrant *juren* Ding in Chapter 2, some of the most lurid descriptions occur when men attempt to resist foxes' advances. Resistance has the potential for greater dramatic conflict than tales of submission, since in effect it prolongs the process of *mei*. It also serves to emphasize both the man's self-control and the vixen's charms, as it makes their resistance all the more admirable and their eventual succumbing to temptation all the more understandable. For example, a man whose younger friend has an affair with a fox involuntarily ejaculates whenever he overhears them having sex; the narrative dwells on his experience rather than that of the vixen's lover.[36]

Liuhe neiwai suoyan includes relatively extensive erotic descriptions, but it is couched in an obscure style apparently intended for schematic argument rather than titillation. The story "Duan bing" 短兵 (Hand-to-hand combat) is essentially a description of a series of sexual battles between various characters of both sexes. The sexual description is presented entirely in either vague terms of *yin* and *yang* or the imagery of combat. By means of a homosexual seduction, a Daoist initiates the young hero into parasitic sexual practices. He

34. McMahon, *Misers, Shrews, and Polygamists*, p. 104 and Song Zhuxuan, *Yaohu yanshi*.

35. See the Introduction to Hanan, *The Carnal Prayer Mat*.

36. "Zhuang Zhusong" 莊斷松, in He Bang'e, *YTSL*, 8.226–28.

subsequently uses these techniques to slay many prostitutes, including a Miss Hu. Miss Hu's friend, in turn, avenges her death by sexual means. In the end, all the participants in this drama are revealed to be foxes, a conclusion typical of this quirky collection, which, in a way reminiscent of vernacular fiction, immerses the reader in a world of supernatural figures without a human reference point.[37] In particular, it resembles the world of satirical supernatural novels such as *Zhan gui zhuan* 斬鬼傳 (A romance of devil killing; 1688) and *He dian* 何典 (What sort of book is this?; ca. 1830), which are almost entirely peopled by the ills of this world in the form of ghosts.[38] Foxes are used as symbols of deadly sexuality, but the fact that there are no human characters in the story by no means implies that such vicious battles are the exclusive territory of foxes. On the contrary, the absence of human characters clearly places the story in the allegorical mode: the foxes are symbols pointing to the human world rather than interacting with it.

In the vernacular novel, the fox may be called on as "the usual suspect" when a symbol of lust is required. The fox is employed more often in novels ostensibly exposing the dangers of sex than in those unabashedly using sex as entertainment. The eighteenth-century novel *Yesou puyan* combines an espousal of orthodox Confucian values with explicit erotic description.[39] One of the most extended erotic passages in the novel depicts an evil sorcerer's concubines engaged in a competition of sexual displays. The sorcerer has imprisoned the hero of the novel and attempts to use his female underlings to drain the hero's sexual energy; in this case, it is a human being who is the supreme sexual parasite. The most accomplished of the concubines, Ninth Sister, wins the contest with an implausible display of vaginal gymnastics and is awarded the privilege of sleeping with the hero. After overcoming her in this sexual battle, the hero forces her to reveal her true form as a fox and crushes her while she is in a post-orgasmic stupor. Immediately, the air fills with the stench of her flatulence. Her face remains human, but her body is that of a

---

37. Tu Shen, *Liuhe neiwai suoyan*, 6.15a.

38. For a discussion of these works in the context of later exposé novels, see David Wang, *Fin-de-Siècle Splendo*, pp. 205–8.

39. See McMahon, *Misers, Shrews, and Polygamists*, pp. 150–75.

fox, and the description emphasizes the sharpness of her claws.[40] In an absolute reversal, sex is the vixen's moment of defeat rather than mastery. The grotesque image of the fox body with a human face is appropriate for a novel ostensibly using erotic description as a moral warning. The fox is a means of making sex monstrous. It seems, in general, that when the fox is a fantasy, the erotic possibilities are suggested rather than described; when she is a nightmare or warning, the description can be far more graphic. Of course, fantasy and nightmare are never entirely distinct.

Classical and vernacular fiction develop the vixen's association with sex in distinct ways. Vernacular pornography provides a carnival of sexual consummation, whereas a classical work like *Yetan suilu* focuses on titillating frustration. In *Yesou puyan*, vixens' sexuality is a carnival of another sort, a grotesque warning. When a classical tale chooses to focus on a particular fox, it can modify or reverse the species' categorical association with seduction. The vernacular novel draws a larger canvas, and the fox is only one of its many subjects. In that context, the stereotype is often used and expanded rather than twisted or rejected. *Liuhe neiwai suoyan*, with its exceptionally long, convoluted classical tales using foxes as symbols rather than individual marvels, stands between the two types.

FOXES AND PROSTITUTES

The link between foxes and sexuality is further developed in vixens' strong association with two sexually marked categories of women: prostitutes and kingdom-destroying imperial concubines. These associations raise the question of the relationship between species and gender categories: species seems less determinant here than gender, since certain categories of women slip out of the human. The combination of sexual availability and peril led to an early association between foxes and prostitutes. In the Tang, the similarity of roles was plain. In "Renshi zhuan," Miss Ren states that she was an

40. Xia Jingqu, *Yesou puyan*, 68.2b–3b. In the 154-chapter edition these events happen at the end of chap. 69 and beginning of chap. 70. Note that the evil concubine Daji is also exposed as a fox with a woman's head when she is slain in *Wu wang fa Zhou pinghua* (1:2.85–86); this precedent may also have influenced this scene.

entertainer, and all of her contacts in Chang'an seem to be in the entertainment quarters.[41] The story "Xue jiong" 薛迥 in the *Taiping guangji* makes the equation more explicitly: a group of prostitutes is revealed to be foxes.[42] This tendency is so strong that Li Shouju uses the phrase "prostitute-ization" to describe the changes in depiction of foxes in the Song and Ming.[43] The comparison is stated as a general principle in some late imperial collections. In "Yatou" 鴨頭, Pu Songling baldly asserted that all prostitutes are foxes, but did not claim the converse, that all foxes are prostitutes.[44] The essential point of similarity is that both prostitutes and vixens who have become women are sexually aggressive, available women of unknown origins, whom men pursue at their own cost.

The fox-prostitute equation is based on a negative vision of both. Even so, the comparison makes it possible for foxes to take part in the literary theme of "the prostitute with a heart of gold."[45] Both foxes and prostitutes are considered evil as categories, but could be remarkably good as individuals. Both quotations on the generally lustful nature of foxes with which I opened this chapter are followed by praise of an extraordinary individual; interest in both the exception and the rule is dependent on the tension between them. In the one story in which Pu Songling directly explored the fox-prostitute equation, "Yatou," Pu Songling allowed himself to have it both ways. Yatou herself is the prostitute-fox with a heart of gold, but her procuress-mother and her sister are unredeemed villains.

The fox-prostitute equation serves to set foxes apart from other kinds of supernatural lovers. In "Lianxiang" in *Liaozhai*, one of the distinctions between the two unearthly women is that the fox Lianxiang claims to be a prostitute, whereas the ghost Miss Li claims

---

41. Shen Jiji, "Renshi zhuan," in *TPGJ*, 10:452.3692–96.

42. *TPGJ*, 10:450.3682. For a discussion of further development of the fox-prostitute link in the Song, see Li Jianguo, *Zhongguo hu wenhua*, pp. 141–42, and in the Qing, pp. 331–37.

43. Li Shouju, *Huxian xinyang yu huli jing gushi*, pp. 156–59.

44. *LZ*, 5.600–606. For other texts that make the same statement, see, e.g., Baiyi jushi, *Hutianlu*, 3.46a, and Pinghua zhuren, *Jiuwei hu*, 4:1.1 (the main character of this vernacular novel is a prostitute with the nickname Nine-Tailed Fox).

45. See Dudbridge, *The Tale of Li Wa*.

to be a woman of good family.[46] Lianxiang has only a given name, and Li only a family name. This captures the difference between the two species: ghosts have a respectable human ancestry; foxes are outsiders.

Ji Yun made unique use of the fox-prostitute equation as part of his exploration of fox-human comparisons. In Ji's world, foxes are more purely wicked as metaphors than they are in themselves; rather than discarding the disreputable aspects of the fox tradition, Ji transferred them to humans. In Ji's view, the human rather than the fox bore most of the blame for the seduction. However, the negative vision of foxes was still so widely accepted that Ji could call on it easily to demonize prostitutes. Ji's primary basis for comparing prostitutes with foxes was parasitism: money is made the equivalent of a man's vital essence, and prostitutes drain both.[47]

In some cases, Ji explored the analogy with a direct confrontation between foxes and prostitutes. In one tale, two prostitute sisters are possessed by foxes. When a Daoist arrives to exorcise them, one of the foxes appears to him in the form of a student and argues, "These two women have ruined men's careers, fortunes, and families. A human being is defined by her human heart; since these two had the hearts of beasts, why should you care if beasts slay beasts? These two also drained the spirits of men [as foxes do]." The Daoist has no answer to these arguments.[48] The male foxes' possession of the prostitutes suggests a fatal sexual relationship. Male foxes (in the guise of articulate, elite men) themselves deploy the fox-prostitute comparison in argument; the result is that male foxes are made a

---

46. *LZ*, 2.220–32. In another edition, "Yatou" has the title "Huji" 狐妓 (fox prostitute); see Pu Song Ling, *Pu Songling quanji*, 1:470. For another *Liaozhai* story making the fox-prostitute link, see "Xin Shisiniang" (4.540–47); in this story, a fox maid poses as a prostitute in order to attract the attention of the Zhengde emperor and engineer the hero's rescue. This in turn seems based on the story "Huji" 狐妓 in Lu Cai 陸采, *Yecheng kelun* 冶城客論, which links two fox prostitutes in Linqing, Shandong, in a more tangential way; see Xue Hongji's 薛洪勣 entry on *Yecheng kelun* in Liu Shide, *Zhongguo gudai xiaoshuo baike quanshu*, p. 668.

47. Consider the pun on jing 精 (semen) and *jin* 金 (gold), which David Roy ("A Confucian Interpretation of *Jin ping mei*") notes in *Jin ping mei*. Ji himself tended to equate sex and money in karmic equations.

48. *YWCT*, 13.724, story 188. For another example, see *YWCT*, 13.725, story 189.

source of order and female humans a source of destruction bearing all the traditional stigma of foxes.

The result of the confrontation, but not its implications, is reversed in a story in which a man hears his fox friend moaning in the underbrush. The fox reveals that he caught a venereal disease from a prostitute. Since she looked healthy, he decided to drain her essence. When her essence was mixed with the rest he had collected, it contaminated the whole. Since the ravages of the disease are now visible on his face, he is ashamed to see his friend.[49] This gruesome medical detail makes the fox's parasitism seem more physical than it often does. The contrast between this story and others makes it clear that the sexual danger posed by foxes usually lies in exhaustion rather than infection, in sex itself rather than in sexually transmitted diseases. This story overtly relates prostitution and venereal disease, a link that Li Shouju sees as the true reason for the association of foxes and prostitutes.[50] I do not think it is the sole cause, but disease certainly adds another element to the compound of sexual and financial exhaustion and social disorder that formed the fox-prostitute comparison. Although the fox brought his doom on himself, the fact that this story is related from his friend's point of view makes him the (male) object of sympathy and the prostitute the poison. The would-be sexual parasite is instead the victim of his own appetites.

One particularly complex story that turns on the idea of lies becoming true also blurs the boundaries between fox and prostitute.

There was a son of a rich family in Xinjiang,[51] with an obese body and a waddling gait. Since he also did not take care of his appearance, his face was always covered with grime. Nevertheless, he was fond of wandering the pleasure quarters; whenever he met a woman, he was sure to stare at her. One day when he was walking alone, he met a young woman of striking style and beauty. Since at that time the roads were slippery after rain, he

49. *YWCT*, 14.811–12, story 264. This story is related along with two tales of supernatural beings paying prostitutes with fake money or with goods stolen from their own coffers.

50. Li Shouju, *Huxian xinyang yu huli jing gushi*, pp. 157–58.

51. The original has *huibu* 回部, which referred to Xinjiang and the region south of Tianshan.

went forward to proposition her, "It's so slippery; wouldn't you like someone to support you?" She replied with a stern expression, "Don't bother me. I am a vixen. All my life I have only prayed to the moon to refine my form; I've never seduced men to drain their energy. Who do you think you are to dare say this? I will bring misfortune down on you!" With that she threw sand in his face. In his surprise, he lost his footing and suddenly fell into the ditch. By the time he had crawled out with considerable effort, he did not know where she had gone. After this he was uneasy, worrying she would haunt him, but nothing happened after all.

Some days later his friends invited him to drink. A young courtesan who had just made her debut was pouring the wine. When he looked at her closely, he recognized the young woman from before. Suspicious and confused, he knew not what to do. He forced himself to ask her, "On that day after the rain, did you go to the east village?" The courtesan replied, "My elder sister went to the east village that day to see our aunt, but I didn't go. My sister resembles me, and you must have met her." Her words were extremely confusing. Since he was unable to judge whether she was a monster or a human, one woman or two, he made an excuse to flee the party.

After he left, the courtesan told the story: "In truth I loathed his ugliness and feared he would be violent; so I invented lies hoping to avoid him. Fortunately, when he fell over on his own, I hid behind the heaps of firewood in the field. I didn't expect he would think it was real." Everyone at the gathering collapsed with laughter.

One guest said, "Since you've already entered the brothel, how can you choose your customers? He is a man who can buy your smile with a thousand pieces of gold. Why don't I take you to visit him?" He took her along to the fooled man's place. Only when she told him the names of her "parents" and husband in the brothel were his doubts dispelled. (These two prostitute sisters are the ones known as "Big Yang" and "Yang the Second." When the noted literati of the day wrote "willow songs" (*yangliu ci* 楊柳詞), it was an allusion to their surname.) She apologized, "When you favored me with your affections the other day, I had only known you for a short time, and so I answered you in jest. I didn't realize it would be so rude; I am very uneasy at having wronged you. I dared to bring my blanket and pillow to present myself as recompense." Her words were elegant, her seductive poses lavish. He was enchanted by her and kept her there for several nights. He summoned her "husband" and gave him the fees per month for her company. They were intimate for a year, and he finally died of "wasting thirst."[52]

My late brother Qinghu said: "When she appeared to be a fox in human form, he feared her, fearing death. When she was a human acting as a fox, he did not fear her, nor did he fear death. This shows that she could qualify as a member of this category [vixen]. She had already told him, 'I will bring misfortune down on you.' This man died at the hands of a prostitute, but one could also say that he died of a fox."[53]

The beginning of this story is similar to other of Ji's anecdotes about genuine morally righteous vixens who rebuff their suitors. We have seen the opening scene in Chapter 2—a young woman walking alone on slippery, muddy paths—in the tale of the rational man who rejects a fox. This is a story, as Ji's elder brother suggested, about belonging to categories. The young prostitute claims membership in a category of women with the power to reject a man; another man forces her to fulfill the role of the category to which she properly belongs. The category of prostitute proves to be interchangeable with the kind of fox she claimed not to be. Her very helplessness and reluctance serve to identify the true source of the evil: male lust. No reference is made to her profits or her desire as she becomes the unwitting instrument of destined retribution for the man's excesses. His death, of pathological thirst and urination, summons up associations of excessive desire and sexual spending. In the other stories, the prostitutes are unthinking predators or even inanimate poisons; here a spark of resistance is made visible through the reference to powers of the fox, but it vanishes as the young woman fulfills the role of her (relatively new) profession. Species categories here are defined by function. Nevertheless, although fox and prostitute are interchangeable in this respect, it is the prostitute, the human acting as a fox,

52. The original is *xiaoke* 消渴, the Chinese medical term for an illness characterized by excessive thirst, excessive urination, and weight loss. The contemporary diagnosis would be adult-onset diabetes mellitus, which is often associated with obesity (Dipesh Navsaria, pers. comm.).

53. *YWCT*, 20.1146, story 39. For another translation, see Monschein, *Der Zauber der Fuchsfee*, p. 312. I am indebted to an anonymous reviewer for advice on this translation. The final lines in the original contain an ambiguity that is lost in translation: the statement about fearing the fox as human but not the human as fox is both a judgment of this man's predicament and a general statement.

who is the more deadly and the more damnable, according to this rhetoric.

The other grounds for comparison between foxes and prostitutes is deception. The illusory nature of fox romance can by association undermine all romance, as illustrated by the tale of a young man who was fond of whoring. He has an affair with a fox, but despite their frequent encounters, he continues to visit the pleasure quarters as well. She upbraids him for this, telling him she can take the shape of any woman he desires—she only needs to see the woman once to imitate her—and save him the money. They try it, and she instantly became indistinguishable from the woman of his choice.[54] He never goes out again, but one day he tells her that he regrets that it has all been an illusion, still inferior to the real thing in his mind. In reply, she points out those she imitated were just as much illusions as she was, and so were all the famous beauties of history. (There are echoes here of the tradition, discussed below, in which the fox can pass judgment on the entire roster of historical beauties.) Whether it comes after hours or years, the final day of parting renders all romances equally illusory. He is enlightened by this and, even when the fox leaves years later, never goes whoring again.[55] This story equates fox illusion with the general illusion of romance; it is neither better nor worse but simply more transparent. The fox finally dispels the allure of the courtesan; who is better qualified than the illusionist herself to see through illusion and expose it?

As early as the Tang, the association between foxes and prostitutes was double-edged: it presumed them to be sexually amoral, but it also gave foxes, as it did exemplary prostitutes, the opportunity to rise above that assumption. Although in the Qing the equation of foxes and prostitutes is stated far more baldly, it is only a part, albeit a powerful one, of the fox tradition. Authors may elect to explore it

---

54. The fact that a supernatural woman could take on many faces is a possibility that Pu Songling also exploited in some of his plots, e.g., "Chang'e" 嫦娥, in *LZ*, 8.1069–79. Although the games of pretense do prove dangerous in that story, in general Pu took joy in the theatrical possibilities of the illusion rather than using it to undermine the romance. For a story that explores this theme thoroughly, see Zhou sheng, *Yangzhou meng*; and the discussion of this story in the following chapter.

55. *YWCT*, 1.14, story 13.

exclusively in individual stories, as Pu Songling did in "Yatou" or Ji Yun did in his anecdotes, but it did not necessarily color every depiction of a relationship with a vixen. The equation is even more marginal in the literature describing prostitutes. The literature describing foxes and that describing prostitutes were much further apart in the Qing than they had been in the Tang; for example, the nineteenth-century novels of the demimonde depict new urban realities rather than draw on the tropes of the traditional fox stories. When the author of the late Qing courtesan novel *Jiuwei hu* 九尾狐 (The nine-tailed fox) gave his main character the nickname of the fox, he made it clear in his first chapter that this is artifice. There is no suggestion that she really is a fox.[56]

FOXES AND THE INFAMOUS BEAUTIES OF HISTORY

The linkage of foxes and kingdom-toppling concubines develops different aspects of foxes' sexual danger and reveals a different way of connecting women with the alien. When foxes are associated with prostitutes as a group, the emphasis is on analogy rather than literal identity. In contrast, a series of fatal imperial concubines are identified as actual vixens. The analogy between foxes and prostitutes worked both ways, explaining each side in terms of the other. The fox identity is used to explain the destructiveness of certain historical women, but historical women are not used to explain foxes. This asymmetry seems related to the weight of dynastic history: whereas most foxes and prostitutes are private ills, confronted time after time by countless private men, the clash of destructive sexuality with imperial power must always be public and specifically situated in time. The association of foxes with the infamous beauties of history adds a demonic dimension to human stories and projects vixens' potential for beauty and danger onto a larger screen.

---

56. Pinghua zhuren, *Jiuwei hu*, 1.1. David Wang (*Fin-de-Siècle Splendor*, p. 200) does, however, discuss a lesser known late Qing novel in which the four great Shanghai courtesans are exposed as animal spirits. He links this to the "carnival of the grotesque," which is rather different in spirit from the fox-prostitute links discussed here. For example, Wang Tao's works include numerous stories of courtesans and a smaller number of fox stories, but the two worlds seldom cross. See also Zamperini, "Lost Bodies."

This topic was developed largely in vernacular fiction and was of less interest to authors of the classical tale. This follows from the private/public distinction that reflects the two genres' differing relationships to historical narrative: the classical tale tells the stories of individuals, and vernacular fiction relates historical spectacles with large casts. In this section, I explore the development of the vulpine concubine as a figure of violence in a series of Ming novels, as compared to a figure of glamour and historical entertainment in the later classical tale and other works.

Monschein has made a thorough study of this theme, both in the Tang, when it was first established, and in the vernacular novels of the Ming. In the Tang, the correspondence between deadly foxes and deadly women was established in many genres: Luo Binwang 駱賓王 (before 640–84) compared the Empress Wu to a fox spirit in an essay, and in the classical tale Miss Ren dies at the same place as Yang Guifei.[57] A poem by Bai Juyi concludes that if a fox's illusory beauty could be deadly, real beauty was even more dangerous.[58] Foxes take part in the demonization of these women; less often, they can, as in Miss Ren's case, also assume their air of tragedy.

The historical woman most strongly identified with a vixen is Daji, the wicked favorite who was the downfall of the last Shang emperor. The idea that she was a vixen seems to date at least to the Tang; in the Yuan and Ming, her story is developed in *Wu wang fa Zhou pinghua*, *Lieguo zhizhuan*, and *Fengshen yanyi*. These three novels develop a shared body of material, with likely ties to the oral storytelling tradition, relating the fall of the Shang and the rise of the Zhou. Daji plays a central role in the Shang's destruction.[59] Her story reveals that kingdom-destroying concubines are not interchangeable. Since there is no literary tradition of nostalgia for the glamour of the lost Shang, Daji is a subject of narrative rather than poetic

---

57. There does not seem to be much specific identification in the late imperial period between Yang Guifei and the fox; for a story in which a fox plays her role, see "Xun chashi ma gong" 巡茶使馬公, in Wang Tonggui, *Ertan leizeng*, 47.5a.

58. Monschein, *Der Zauber der Fuchsfee*, pp. 149–59 and pt. VI.

59. In addition, *Humei congtan* contains a version of her tale in classical Chinese that seems to have been adapted from *Lieguo zhi*. The *Fengshen yanyi* plot was also developed in the puppet theater.

1. Daji's possession, *Wu wang fa Zhou pinghua*

elaboration; this clearly sets her apart from Xishi or Yang Guifei. As a result, her portrayal is far less ambivalent, her destruction unmitigated by sympathy.

In a scene that establishes an atmosphere of horror, the fox inserts herself into historical narrative with a nighttime assault on the girl Daji. The vixen consumes the girl's soul and takes her place, occupying her body in a hybrid of parasitism and possession. In the classical tale, when a fox assumes another's guise or possesses her, the real person is usually not destroyed, but in this case the original Daji disappears without a trace. This replacement allows the fox to be a pure predator. At the same time, the connection between the fox story and the historical narrative seems contrived.[60]

In all these sources, Daji is far more cruel and much more bloodthirsty than her sisters in the classical tale. Even the most voracious of vixens in the classical tale only destroy men through sexually inflicted illness; they have no appetite for blood or violence. Daji, in contrast, has a literal as well as a metaphorical appetite for human flesh.[61] Her inventive tortures build upon legends of evil concubines and empresses rather than the fox tradition.[62] The combination of fox and fatal concubine creates a different sort of evil than that

60. The more common means of artificially adding fox material would be through reincarnation, as in *Zhaoyang qushi*, *Xingshi yinyuan zhuan*, *Pingyao zhuan*, and *Jiaopa ji*. See Wang Tonggui, *Wu wang fa zhou pinghua*, 1.4a; Xu Zhonglin, *Fengshen yanyi*, 1:4.34; Yu Shaoyu, *Chunqiu lieguo zhi*, *juan* 1; and Mo Chizi, *Humei congtan*, 1.

61. Mo Chizi, *Humei congtan*, 1.2a.

62. Monschein (*Der Zauber der Fuchsfee*, pp. 201–2) also notes how "tagged-on" the fox plot seems.

wrought by a fox on her own, as to a certain extent violence replaces lust. Even her excesses have a problematic relationship to the destined order: the vixen had originally been summoned by the goddess Nü Wa and charged to destroy the dynasty, but in the end Nü Wa rebukes her for having been too cruel.[63] The vixen/concubine occupies the awkward boundary between divine revenge and chaotic evilThe structure of vixens' relationship to the destined order is another difference between the vernacular and classical tale genres. In the vernacular novel, destiny is often a principal structural device, and the vixen's assigned karmic duty of destruction of a particular ruler is spelled out in the initial chapters. This, too, is part of the reader's superior knowledge relative to the characters. In the classical tale, the vixen herself explains the workings of destiny, usually after rewards and punishments have been meted out.

A vital difference between the ruler and the commoner plagued by a vixen lover is power: the vixen as imperial concubine exploits her lord's power, whereas in the latter case, most of the power, be it sex, knowledge, magic, or money, rests with the vixen herself. Daji's sexual powers do not destroy Zhou physically; rather, they destroy his sovereignty.

The fox material is concentrated at a few points in Daji's story: the introduction of the fox, repeated threats of exposure, and her final unmasking and death. The dynamic of exposure is very different from the earlier classical tale's focus on exposing the demon lover in order to expel her or the later classical tale's description of the man's indifference to his lover's real identity. In the classical tale interest focuses mostly on the initial instance of *mei*, rather than on its results; in contrast, these vernacular novels can be read as an elaboration on the disastrous consequences of Zhou's beguilement as he inexorably loses his kingdom. The reader knows from the beginning that this dangerous woman is a fox. Although readers of the classical tale might suspect that a dangerous woman was a fox, the author

63. Ouyang Jian (*Zhongguo shenguai xiaoshuo tongshi*, pp. 413–14) points out this inconsistency.

usually would not tell them outright.[64] Repeated risks of exposure lead to an escalation of violence as Daji destroys those who would reveal her secret, until in the end the deceived king is the only one who does not know that she is a fox. The central theme of his delusion is thereby underlined. The concern here is with deception rather than depletion. The final exposure of the fox is also dramatized: no man is capable of beheading Daji in her human form, since her beauty is too bewitching. The reader alone remains immune. In *Wu wang fa Zhou pinghua*, only when she is exposed by a magic mirror is she destroyed; in *Fengshen yanyi* it requires a magic weapon. The illustration of her destruction in *Wu wang fa Zhou pinghu* shows the figure of a nine-tailed fox still retaining a woman's face.[65] For the omniscient reader, the pleasure in the drama of exposure lies in wondering when the characters will realize the truth rather than in the surprise of the strange.

The Ming dynasty novel *Zhaoyang qushi* continues where the story of Daji left off, but takes a very different tone. The fox spirit who had become Daji is not content in the heavens after her taste of life on earth, and she sets off to a secluded cave to establish her own fox kingdom, an undertaking reminiscent of Sun Wukong's kingdom in *Xiyou ji* 西遊記 (Journey to the west), which provides a model for using a supernatural animal as a protagonist. Her defeat of a swallow spirit in sexual battle leads to a war between their minions. Finally, a divinity banishes them both to the moral world.[66] The swallow is reborn Zhao Feiyan 趙飛燕 and the vixen as Zhao Hede 合德, both of whom become concubines of the emperor Han Chengdi. Some of the distinctions between the sisters reflect ideas about their species. Whereas Feiyan is slender, Hede is plump; and although both are enthusiastic about sex, Hede is more shameless. Unlike Feiyan, she

---

64. This appears to be one of the many ways in which "Renshi zhuan," with its opening, 任氏，女妖也 "Miss Ren was a female monster," is an extraordinary text; see *TPGJ*, 10:452.3692.

65. Wang Tonggui, *Wu wang fa Zhou ping hua*, 1:2.85–86.

66. Guhang yanyan sheng, *Zhaoyang qushi*, 1.67–84. For another example of a "second-generation" reflection of the Daji story, see Feng Menglong, *Xin pingyao zhuan*, 15.6a–11b; in this story, Hu Yong'er hears Daji's story sung and aspires to be like her fellow vixen. For a translation and discussion, see Monschein, *Der Zauber der Fuchsfee*, pp. 241–42.

makes no fuss about losing her virginity. Moreover, both Hede's nature as a former vixen and techniques she has learned from books make her so sexually indomitable, that she can compel men who pride themselves on their sexual endurance to ejaculate quickly.[67] The vixen as the emblem of female sexual insatiability is a diverting variation in the novel's sex scenes. True to her nature as a reincarnation of Daji, Hede is the more violent of the two, she brings about the death of her emperor as well as her rivals. In contrast, all of Feiyan's excesses are sexual. Hede kills Chengdi with an overdose of an aphrodisiac.[68] His death by hemorrhaging ejaculation evokes death by a parasitic vixen, but the artificial means makes this scene closer to Pan Jinlian's killing of Ximen Qing in *Jin ping mei* 金瓶梅 than to the fox tradition. When the two concubines die and their souls return to the heavens, they are berated for their misdeeds in human form, but in the end, thanks to the intercession of Chengdi in his immortal form, they are allowed to practice ascetic self-cultivation.[69] Such a mild conclusion would never have been permitted the Daji of the other novels; *Zhaoyang qushi* moves the fatal concubine theme out of the realm of historical drama and into the territory of pornographic entertainment enlivened by supernatural and historical costumes.

An appearance by a vixen in another of the vernacular genres, drama, also relies on the persona/character of one of the great historical beauties, Xishi 西施. Unlike Daji, however, Xishi has been regarded as a figure of doomed glamour rather than scheming violence. In the Ming play *Jiaopa ji* 蕉帕記 (The plantain kerchief), she has been punished by being reborn in fox form; as the play opens, she has undergone hundreds of years of self-cultivation and requires only a man's *yang* energy to achieve immortality.[70] In contrast with

67. Guhang yanyan sheng, *Zhaoyang qushi*, 1.113.

68. Ibid., 2.206.

69. Ibid., 2.209–11.

70. Shan Ben, *Jiaopa ji*, 9: 5243–370. Selected scenes are translated in Birch, *Scenes for Mandarins*, pp. 107–39. I owe the idea of "Xishi as experience" to Birch. This play was also rewritten as a novel, *Jiao ye pa* 蕉葉帕, in the Qing (in Fu Xuancong, ed., *Zhongguo gudai xiaoshuo zhenmi ben wenku*, 6:1–67). The love triangle plot here is substantially similar to one already developed in both classical and vernacular fiction; see note 22.

the Daji novels, in this play the historical person seems tacked onto the fox plot and a comedy of mistaken identity, rather than the other way around. Like many other vixens, Xishi has become a figure of erotic knowledge who both seduces a young man and arranges a human match for him.

In the classical tale's interpretation of the theme of foxes and historical beauties, the beauties of history become a series of roles that foxes can take on playfully, as Xiaocui 小翠 does in the story bearing her name.[71] These vixens assume the appearance of historical beauties to amuse their lovers and themselves or in the service of elaborate schemes. Such stories are consciously aware of history becoming drama and fiction and seem to distance themselves rather self-consciously from the theme of the fatal beauty.

The theme of the vixen as an actress playing historical roles reaches its height in the late nineteenth-century story "Laohu tan lidai liren" 老狐談歷代麗人 (The old fox discusses the beauties of history).[72] The various versions of this text, appearing in a magazine, an individual collection, and a *congshu* on the topic of women, also illustrate the range of genres through which such a piece could move in the late Qing publishing world. The material of the classical tale

---

71. *LZ*, 7.1000–1008. For another example, see Zhou sheng, *Yangzhou meng*.

72. It appeared first in Wang Tao's magazine *Yinghuan suoji* in the fifth month of 1873; see "Laohu tan lidai meiren ji" 老狐談歷代美人記, *Yinghuan suoji*, 8 4a–6a, with the marginal note: "This text was written by Xue Fucheng." The final authorial comment in "Huxian tan lidai liren" 狐仙談歷代麗人 (The fox immortal discusses the beauties of history) in Xue Fucheng's *Yongan biji* version (5.120–24) claims primacy for his version; a friend had seen his story and submitted it to the *Shenbao guan*, whose editors revised it. He published it in his own collection in order to restore it to its original form. In Xue Fucheng's version, the fox is not imitating Xishi. Her first model had been the Lady Wei, the wife of King Wu of Qin, and she is presently guiding a group of students in studying Empress Zhang, of the Han. Xue Fucheng's interest seems to lie in using the fox story to rehabilitate relatively obscure historical beauties. On Xue Fucheng, see Hummel, *Eminent Chinese of the Ch'ing Period*, p. 331. The version in *Xiangyan congshu* (first collection published 1911) is substantially similar to that in *Yinghuan suoji*, with some details and final commentary omitted; see "Laohu tan lidai meiren ji," *Xiangyan congshu*, vol. 2, collection 3, 4.267–74. This version is also translated and discussed by Monschein. The similarity of this story to other historical romances in *Yongan biji* makes me inclined to believe Xue Fucheng's claim of authorship.

had always been shared among collections, but the speed and frequency with which this occurs were transformed by changes in publishing during the Guangxu era. Newspapers, other periodicals, and large Western-style publishing houses all abetted the process.

This story combines foxes' ties to historical beauties with the theme of advancement to immortality, two aspects of the tradition that usually remain distinct. The story opens with a device more frequently associated with ghosts, the encounter with a historical beauty in the ruins of her palace.[73] A scholar studying in the shadow of the ruins of the ancient palace of Wu happens to read a passage in the *Wuyue chunqiu* 吳樾春秋 (Spring and autumn annals of Wu and Yue; ca. 40 CE) that describes Xishi. Just as he sighs that he will never be able to see this woman, a figure who is the very image of Xishi appears outside the window.[74] The woman quickly explains that she is not Xishi herself but her *huashen* 化身 (incarnation), a term usually used to describe a Buddhist avatar. She is a fox, and imitation of a beauty such as Xishi is crucial to her species's development:

> Those of my kind who are seeking to become transcendents (*xian*) must first choose a beauty of the world and imitate her. After five hundred years, our forms will resemble hers; after another five hundred, our spirits will. For extraordinary beauties, each stage takes a thousand years. If there is an extraordinary beauty the like of whom the world has not seen, then it takes even longer to achieve resemblance in form and spirit. Once we resemble that person in spirit, then we can become transcendents by way of humanity. This takes even longer than rising from the state of beasts to humanity, but the accomplishment is even higher.[75]

In the previous century, Ji Yun had argued that foxes must attain immortality by way of humanity, although this emphasis on physical beauty is directly opposed to his moral definition of "the human way." For both Ji and the author of "The Old Fox Discusses the Beauties of History," foxes in human guise had long since ceased to

---

73. Zeitlin, "Return of the Palace Lady."

74. This is the *Yinghuan suoji / Xiangyan* congshu version.

75. This idea of fox advancement, with the periods of study set at only 100 years each, also appears in the Daoguang era collection *Yijiong baibian*; see "Su'e" 素娥, in Tang Yongzhong, *Yijiong baibian* 7.4a.

be a strictly physical imitation; they must transform their interiors as well. When the protagonist asks why her kind imitates human beauties, she explains that the finest exemplars of humanity take distinctive forms for the two sexes: female foxes mimic the guise of great beauties; male foxes imitate scholars. This is a pat way of explaining the sexual division in the fox tradition. She then takes the clichéd equation of human beauties and transcendents literally and concludes that great beauties and transcendents are essentially the same.[76] Here, to be a fox is to be an imitator; there is no "real" fox nature to be concealed.

The Xishi avatar's continuous close study puts her in a unique position to judge the beauties of history, and the bulk of the story is taken up by her appraisals. She takes some pleasure in overturning historical convention: some beauties are overrated because they were the concubines of powerful men or literati, and some remain unknown precisely because they were so virtuous. She denies all morally questionable tales about the beauties she ranks. For example, Xishi never left in a boat with Fan Li. On the other hand, she does not consider infamous, immoral women beauties.[77] This conversation about beauties takes the place of sexual consummation, whether with the fox or with Xishi. Although th0e story is obsessed with historical beauties, the sexual element is kept firmly under control, which creates an atmosphere of restrained if intense historical voyeurism. It is the fox herself who divorces beauty from kingdom-toppling sensuality, the elements that had been conjoined in her person. In

76. Although so entirely different in content, this story is in the same form as the stories in *Yuewei caotang biji* and *Zi bu yu* in which foxes lecture human interlocutors about foxes' means of advancement; see *YWCT*, 10.503–4, story 229; and Yuan Mei, *Zi bu yu*, 1.9.

77. There is a related type of story in which male foxes are granted the authority to judge the beauties of history. The judgment of beauties is the particular expertise of foxes. They are seldom called on to narrate other kinds of historical stories; other aspects of human affairs are instead left to ghosts. For an anecdote in the form of an interview with a fox, see "Huxian" 狐仙, in Wang Jian, *Qiudeng conghua*, 10.18a. Alongside the topics of fox and human self-advancement, the conversation includes discussion of the great beauties of history and dismisses many of the legends about such beauties as fictitious. In this story as well as the examples discussed below, the foxes' judgments are not simply based on beauty but have a moral component as well.

Jiaopa ji, the combination of the fox and Xishi in a single figure adds both magic and historical glamour to a love story; Xishi is almost the third figure in a triangle. In this story, the vixen as Xishi is a commentator on the literary traditions of both foxes and beauties.

Although the idea of a gallery or roster of the beauties of history was not a new one, I am tempted to relate this particularly self-conscious use of the theme to the late Qing publishing context. Texts that related the stories of the earlier beauties were being republished and repackaged at an unprecedented rate. The fox personifies perfect access to the history, images, and even the spirits of past women. Nevertheless, meeting the fox rather than Xishi's ghost makes this a historical simulation with a narrator rather than a direct encounter with traces of the past.[78]

When mortal women like Pan Jinlian in *Jin ping mei* or Qingwen in *Honglou meng* 紅樓夢 are compared to vixens, it is in this generalized sense as the embodiment of harmful sexuality.[79] From the point of view of other women, these are women who have an untoward and unhealthy power over men. Because of this interest in power and beguilement, these portrayals are closer to the vernacular fiction tradition of the deadly concubine than to the vixens of the classical tale. This usage also seems to betray traces of the social use of the fox tradition as an insult.

The classical tale looks back on the narrative of history and amends it from the point of view of an individual commentator. Vernacular fiction attempts to tell the whole story. The two genres cross-fertilize extensively yet maintain their distinct identities as this theme evolves over time. The association of foxes with historical beauties thus ranges from the fox as an emblem of woman as a destructive historical force to the fox as a detached judge. The

78. Another sequence of stories in *Yongan biji* makes further use of the fox to explicate stories of historical beauties. A fox who had been the confidante of an empress of the Northern Qi tells her story. The form of these stories is the same: a man who desired foxes is rewarded with conversation rather than sexual intimacy. See "Beiqi shougong laohu" 北齊守宮老狐 (The old fox guardian of the palace of the Northern Qi) and "Beiqi Lihou wei dixian" 北齊李后爲地仙 (Empress Li of the Northern Qi is an earthly transcendent), in Xue Fucheng, *Yongan biji*, 5.114–17.

79. Lanling xiaoxiao Sheng, *Jin ping mei cihua*, 5 75.2231; Cao Xueqin, *Honglou meng*, 2:77.1109.

man-eating beast with a woman's face of *Wu wang fa Zhou pinghua* and the prim commentator of "The Old Fox Discusses the Beauties of History" represent two extremes of the tradition.

MALE FOXES AND WOMEN

The association of the fox with female sexuality should not cause us to forget that male foxes played sexual roles as well. In this and the following section, I examine gender roles first in male fox/woman and then in same-sex fox relationships in order to throw the assumptions of the most common case into sharper relief.

The vast difference in depictions of a vixen's affair with a man and a male fox's affair with a woman is as old as the beast lover story itself and increased with literary development. Stories of male foxes possessing or molesting women are more common in the Tang than later. There are seventeen such stories in *Taiping guangji* (as compared to 26 stories of relations between vixens and male humans). In contrast, in the Ming-Qing material, relationships with vixens outnumber sexual relationships with male foxes by at least twenty to one. Male fox lovers did not undergo a process of humanization or romanticization; if anything, the relatively human-seeming fox suitor of the Tang almost vanishes.[80] Of course, a story of a woman with a male fox lover could not become a male fantasy, but it does not even seem to have become a major focus of anxiety. Male foxes who molest women are not well developed even as villains.[81] The contrast with medieval and early modern Europe, where human women's congress with male devils is the object of intense scrutiny, is striking. Even Pu Songling, with his wide range of variations on traditional themes, did not deviate from conventional depictions of male foxes.

A male fox in a sexual role is seen less as a character than as a medical affliction. In the Tang, for both sexes the experience of fox

---

80. On the sharp decline in tales of fox bridegrooms after the Tang, see Li Shouju, *Huxian xinyang yu huli jing gushi*, pp. 151–52.

81. Sexual anxiety seems to be focused to a greater extent on lustful monks and Daoists. In the legal literature, sexual anxiety is directed against the "rootless rascal," the poor, unmarried man outside of the family system; see Sommer, *Sex, Law, and Society in Late Imperial China*, pp. 101–3. Male foxes take on that role relatively rarely, just as fox lodgers are not beggars.

seduction was often seen by outsiders as a set of symptoms and by the affected person as an encounter with an individual creature; in the later tradition, human males' subjective experience of a sexual encounter becomes the predominant theme, but women's experience remains an affliction viewed from the perspectives of outsiders. Although this reflects primarily male authorship, it had a far-reaching influence on the shape of the fox tradition. The line between spirit possession and sexual molestation remained ambiguous for women.[82] In contrast, in late imperial tales a vixen is not imagined as a spirit occupying her lover's body, even though in some stories she is only visible to her lover. A vixen may be attracted by a man's desires, but her presence is not considered a psychosis. As a result of the man's autonomy, his rejection of his parasitic lover often plays a vital role in driving her out. The fox possessing a woman must be driven out by others, since her loss of will is assumed.[83] With her loss of control comes exemption from moral responsibility.[84]

Pu Songling's "Gu'er" 賈兒 (A merchant's son) gives a fascinating description of a woman's gradual loss of will in an affair with a fox. This woman's depiction does not differ in kind from earlier and contemporary accounts of possessed women, but the descriptions of the process and of her behavior are more vivid and detailed. Her affliction begins while her husband is away; the lonely, susceptible wife of a traveling merchant is a standard literary figure.[85]

---

82. Spirit-mediums were assumed to have sex with the spirits they served and were held in contempt by the rest of the community as a result; see. Doré, *Researches into Chinese Superstitions*, 5:599.

83. Even in stories in which a woman is depicted as conscious and conversing with an external lover, the impetus to drive the fox away comes from outside. See, e.g., the woman instructed by her father to poison her fox lover; *YWCT*, 13.700, story 162.

84. See Furth, *A Flourishing Yin*, p. 90, on this gender difference in the medical tradition of "dreaming of having sex with ghosts." A man having such experiences is blamed for indulging his lusts; a woman is considered a victim, a view that avoids directly addressing the issue of female desires. For another discussion of pathological female desire, see Furth, "Concepts of Pregnancy, Childbirth, and Infancy in Qing China."

85. Compare the female protagonist of "Jiang Xingge chonghui zhenzhushan" 蔣興哥重會珍珠衫 (The pearl-sewn shirt), in Feng Menglong, *Yushi mingyan*, pp. 1–39.

His wife slept alone and dreamt she was having sex with someone. She woke and felt him and found it was a young man. Observing that his manner was different from a human's, she knew he was a fox.[86] Before long, he got down from the bed and left. He had already vanished before the door opened.

That evening she invited the old cook to keep her company. She had a ten-year-old son who usually slept in a separate bed, and she also summoned him to sleep with her. Late at night, when the cook and her son were both asleep, the fox came again. She babbled as if talking in her sleep. When the old cook awoke and called her, the fox left.

From then on, she was confused, as if she had lost something. At night, she dared not extinguish the candle and told her son not to sleep soundly. In the middle of the night, her son and the old cook nodded off leaning against the wall. When they woke, they did not see her and thought she had gone out to go to the bathroom. After waiting for a long time, they started to get suspicious. The old servant was scared and dared not go to look, but the boy took a torch and cast its light in every corner. When he went to another room, he found his mother lying naked there. When he approached to help her up, she did not shrink away in shame.

From then on she was mad, singing, weeping, yelling, and cursing in a thousand different variations each day. At night she refused to sleep with anyone, sending her son to another bed, and dismissing the old cook. Whenever he heard his mother laughing and speaking, he would get up and shine a light on her. She instead cursed her son, but he paid no heed.

Here the erotic dreams of a sexually deprived woman are the perilous gateway to demonic possession and madness. Her resistance seems to be inevitably worn away. Only in the initial stages of her encounter with the fox is the experience narrated from her perspective. After the night when her son finds her naked, her perspective is lost in madness. Her certainty that this is a fox has no effect on her decline. The ambiguity between dream and reality, her psychological state and the fox's alien presence, might be romantic in a man's story, but here it is pathological. The clever boy of the title destroys the fox

86. This passage bears a striking resemblance to a Qianlong rape victim's testimony. A sleeping woman felt someone on top of her, and at first thought it was her husband, until she realized that the body felt different from her husband's. Unlike a woman accosted by a fox, however, she put up violent resistance. See Sommer, *Sex, Law, and Society in Late Imperial China*, p. 107.

lover through a series of tricks, finally killing him with poisoned wine. The oedipal interpretation of this tale is obvious: the son destroys his mother's monstrous lover, rooting out the disturbing sexuality that makes her a stranger, while her husband remains curiously uninvolved. The possibility of a fox molesting a woman is placed clearly in the repertoire of the "lower" fox tradition, the realm of tricks, tell-tale tails, and violence. After the fox has been defeated, the woman "was extremely emaciated; her mind gradually became more clear. But her coughing grew worse, as she spit up several *sheng* of phlegm." Her affliction is still manifested as physical illness. In the most widely transmitted textual version of the story, she dies soon afterwards. Although this may be a textual error, the fact that such an error survived in the tradition implies that the death of such a woman was conceivable and palatable.[87] With her loss of will, she herself seems lost. The mention at the end of the story of another woman whose fox ailment is cured after the defeat of this fox suggests that this affliction is not rare. The basic principle that "monsters arise from people," cited commonly to explain the psychological and moral causes of supernatural affliction, seems to apply imperfectly to women.[88] There is no indication that she had any predisposition to this illness, other than the simple fact of being a woman sleeping alone; similarly, her affliction is described in clinical terms rather than the moral terms that would be applied to a man.

Pu's other story of an amorous male fox, "Hu shi" 胡氏 (Madame Hu), resurrects a type that was relatively common in *Taiping guangji*, the gentlemanly fox who comes courting the protagonist's daughter. Many aspects of this tale recall older story types, particularly its emphasis on physical illusion, as the foxes' weapons and tools are revealed to be leaves or other natural objects. At first the vulpine suitor makes his requests within the bounds of human propriety, but once refused, he resorts to an attack by a small fox army. The human father's resolution of the situation demonstrates the difference between

87. *LZ*, 1.125–29. I am indebted to an anonymous reader for pointing out the different versions in manuscript versions of *Liaozhai*. The 24-*juan* manuscript has 愈 (cured) instead of 卒 (died); see Pu Songling, *Pu Songling quanji*, 1:125.

88. 妖由人興, a reference to the *Zuo zhuan*, 14th year of Duke Zhuang; trans. Watson, *The Tso Chuan: Selections from China's Oldest Narrative History*, pp. 207–8.

fox brides and fox grooms. He reasons with the rejected suitor that his daughter could not live in the fox world, for their carriages, horses, houses, and chambers differ from those in the human world, a contention not supported by the narrative tradition. However, he is perfectly willing to wed the fox's daughter to his son. Domestic bliss in the extended family is achieved by this means.[89] Vixens can effortlessly cross the borderline between animal and human worlds, but human women are not allowed this liberty. The analogy to lower-class women who could enter higher-status households as concubines, whereas elite daughters should marry only into households of comparable social status, is suggestive. Females, whatever their species, are sexually upwardly rather than downwardly mobile.

Since Ji Yun attempted to incorporate foxes into a conservative moral order, he would have been disturbed by the triumph of the forces of sexual chaos over a woman with no proven sins. Because he placed all the will and power in sexual relationships on the male side, he had to use heavenly revenge rather than the women's own will to protect virtuous women harassed by foxes and other beasts. In one case, a fox who accosts a chaste widow is struck by lightning; in another, a gibbon spirit who assumes the form of a chaste woman's husband is revealed in a flash of lightning and later found outside afterward with its head split open. Ji reaffirmed that most of the time humans harassed by monsters bring it on themselves with lust, but monsters who take advantage of human ignorance are punished by heaven.[90] The virtuous must have nothing to fear.

The novel *Yaohua zhuan* contains a rare description in vernacular fiction of a male fox's molestation of a woman. It provides an interesting contrast across generic boundaries with the works of closely contemporary classical tale authors, such as Ji Yun. According to one of the prefaces, the novel was written as a response to *Honglou meng*.

---

89. *LZ*, 3.302–5.

90. *YWCT*, 14.804 and 14.806–7, stories 259 and 261. Ji did include one anomalous case of a woman who was driven to her death by fox molestation through no apparent fault of her own, but this story is exceptional in other ways as well (the fox always appears in a different shape, sometimes male, sometimes female). Ji himself admits he cannot explain this story; perhaps the moral inconsistency is one of the aspects he cannot explain. See *YWCT*, 14.801–2, story 256.

Because the author found that novel lacking as a warning against the dangers of desire, he decided to undertake the project himself.[91] The protagonist is originally a male fox who attempts to deflower one hundred virgins in order to achieve immortality. He is slain by a sword-bearing female transcendent and is reborn as a woman to repay for his sins and rescues the same number of virgins he had ruined before. Although vernacular fiction allows narration from the fox's point of view, his last rape is depicted from the young woman's, and her family's, perspective. It is very plain that this is a rape: she physically resists her unseen attacker and ultimately fails, lapsing into unconsciousness. When she is found, the physical wounds on her genitalia are described, something I have never seen in other descriptions of women molested by foxes. There is no implication that she went mad or that she experienced any pleasure.[92] In contrast, the male fox is assumed to have savored pleasure as well as success. The inclusion of these graphic physical details may be related to the novel's goal of exposing the evils of lust.

The choice of a male fox rather than a vixen as the representative of lust is interesting. The male fox's female colleague elects to pursue immortality by moral means. Perhaps the moral clarity of rape as opposed to a human male's problematic consent to a vixen's advances made the male fox the more appropriate symbol. This male fox appears to be a hybrid between the image of the lustful fox and the conviction, most famously stated in *Honglou meng*, of the debased nature of men as opposed to female purity. Redemption comes by means of gender reversal: the male fox atones for his sexual crimes in female form.[93] As is common in vernacular fiction, the fox material is used as a supernatural frame with little direct relationship to the bulk of the novel's plot.

---

91. Ding Bingren, *Yaohua zhuan*. The author's own preface states that the goal of the novel is a warning against the dangers of *se*, but it is the preface (*bianyan* 弁言) by another author that focuses on the contrast between the two novels. See also Ouyang Jian, *Zhongguo shenguai xiaoshuo tongshi*, pp. 576–81.

92. Ding Bingren, *Yaohua zhuan*, 1.8–9.

93. Cf. Ji Yun's account of a man who is raped by a male fox to make up for his sexual misdeeds in a previous life; see below.

Ji Yun recorded one positive case of a fox's affair with a human woman and commented on its strangeness. Despite Ji's conservative reputation, this is the only such example I have discovered in the entire tradition.[94] Ji heard that in his village a thirteen- or fourteen-year-old girl had been seduced by a fox. Every night they would laugh and be intimate. The words used are ambiguous; until the end of the story one assumes this implies intercourse, based on the conventions of fox possession stories, but the word *xia* 狎 itself is not exclusively sexual. Contrary to expectations, the girl is not mad and behaves normally during the day; the fox also gives her generous presents and provides for her family. After more than a year, he tells her father he is returning to the mountains and will not come again. He provides for her dowry and instructs the father to find her a good match, saying she is still a virgin. According to Ji Yun, this had happened in his hometown recently, and all the maids and old women were talking about it. He wrote that he had never heard of this kind of fox seduction story and speculated that it must have been the result of some karmic debt.[95] It is significant that it is the women of the village who are particularly excited by this story; it is a female version of the male fantasy vixens represent, an affair with financial benefits and no strings attached. Ji often used karmic retribution to explain away apparently morally troubling incidents. Here he seemed to be straining his imagination to conceive of a nondisruptive relationship between a woman and a fox, a thought-experiment that seems more feasible in the classical tale than in the vernacular novel.

The stories of profitable adultery discussed in the previous chapter also do not depict women's experience with male foxes as afflictions; nor do they focus on the sex as such. The attention of the stories re-

---

94. For an exceptional story in which a man in effect plays the role of the male fox lover, see "Fu duan huwei" 斧斷狐尾 (Cutting off the fox tail with an axe), in Yuan Mei, *Zi bu yu*, 5.89.

95. *YWCT*, 16.926–27, story 79. Ji drew a parallel between this fox and a man who had preserved the virginity of his maid and married her off; the fox is in the position of an upper-class man relative to a peasant girl, herself of a similar social class to the maids. This is rather similar to a tale of a wealthy old man who kept taking young concubines and then marrying them off with dowries, still virgins; it turns out he had been having anal sex with them, not wanting either the trouble of children or the shame of keeping a catamite. See *YWCT*, 22.1229–30, story 96.

mains on the male heads of households who profit from the arrangement.[96] This is tantalizing evidence of an alternative vision of women's relation with foxes, but it does not seem widely shared.

A woman's sexual ailments are seen as madness, whereas a man's are considered a failure of self-control. Even the man who dies of a vixen is perceived as deluded but not insane. Male desire creates an external embodiment of female sexuality, with both character and narrative. Female desire is not granted the same creative force; rather, it remains a set of opaque symptoms. The person of the male fox as a sexual being remains obscure.

FOXES AND HOMOSEXUALITY

Given the drastic differences in the depiction of male foxes' affairs with women and the reverse situation, same-sex affairs with foxes provide an interesting opportunity to explore gender roles. Concepts of male homosexual relationships in traditional China made a stark distinction between the active and the passive sexual roles.[97] Accordingly, stories in which a fox boy replaces a fox woman as an object of desire, although not common, exist in more than one collection. However, only Ji Yun, and in a single instance his kinsman Zhang Jingyun, considered the possibility of the fox as the active sexual partner, with the human man thus in effect taking the passive role of the possessed human woman.

In his most prominent example of a homosexual relationship between a man and a fox youth, "Huang Jiulang" 黃九郎, Pu Songling emphasized the deadliness of the sexual encounter.[98] The boy Jiulang resists the protagonist He's sexual advances more vigorously than almost any of *Liaozhai's* vixens and claims to be doing so for He's own safety. When he acquiesces under duress, He eventually dies, although his soul claims another body. This danger seems to be the intersection of Jiulang's species and his sex. Foxes are not necessarily

96. Lang Ying, *Qixiu leigao*, 48.9b; Xu Changzuo, *Yanshan conglu* 8, story 11.

97. Sommer, *Sex, Law, and Society in Late Imperial China*, pp. 116–18.

98. There is another fox as catamite in "Xianü" 俠女 (*LZ*, 2.210–16), but this is a minor character quickly eliminated by the woman warrior of the title. He is sexually loose and sharp-tongued, mocking the main characters for consummating their desires while assuming poses of propriety.

sexually dangerous in *Liaozhai*, and even within this story Jiulang offers his female cousin as a harmless substitute for himself. This motif of substitution is common in *Liaozhai*'s fox stories; in this case, the difference between the more dangerous and the safer object of desire is gender rather than species. Apparently Jiulang has no control over his deadliness in his role as a catamite, although in general *Liaozhai* vixens can elect not to be parasites. At the end of the story, this deadly sexuality is used as a tool of revenge, as Jiulang drives the human hero's enemy to his death through debauchery. Jiulang flaunts the wealth he gained by absconding with the late villain's goods, with no one aware that he is a fox.[99] I doubt the moral ambiguity of his triumph would be possible for a vixen, because a vixen who used her destructive sexuality as a tool in such a way, even if for a good purpose, could not be allowed to enjoy her triumph. It should be remembered that unlike Ji Yun, Pu Songling did not attempt to make a rational analysis of the intersection of homosexuality with the fox romance in this story. He played with the juxtaposition of the various patterns, and were there another story on the same topic, it might well have come to different conclusions. However, that potential inconsistency does not make his fictional conclusions any less revealing.

Although He Bang'e's *Yetan suilu* can safely be considered an imitation of *Liaozhai*, its example of a homosexual fox story is not an imitation of "Huang Jiulang." In "Bibi" 碧碧, the human hero has a long-standing predilection for homosexuality. He accosts a beautiful young boy he meets along the road, but the boy strikes him, causing him to fall down a cliff. He hangs caught on a branch, only to be rescued by a beautiful young woman who, in a sexually suggestive gesture, throws her footbinding bandages down to him. She demands that he marry her; his mother refuses until the entire fox clan forces them to comply. The couple lives together happily until the vixen's nephew, who turns out to be the boy from long ago, comes to visit. Once again, the hero tries to kiss him and is rebuffed. The boy

99. *LZ*, 3.316–23. The story also provides an interesting interpretation of homosexual desire. The human hero is cured of his taste for boys when his soul is housed in another body; this event seems to establish sexual orientation as determined by the body rather than the mind.

flees, and the man's fox wife also rebukes him and vanishes. The commentary remarks on the virtue of the fox youth, noting that many women could not equal it.[100] This seems a forced variation on the usual comparison between a virtuous vixen and women. Like "Huang Jiulang," this story makes marriage with a vixen relatively safe and displaces both danger and virtue to the side of homosexuality. Homosexuality is used for the most part as a way of adding objects of sexual desire to the story. In other stories in this collection, the source of additional tension would probably be a young niece or sister rather than a nephew.

Ji Yun treated a human male's pursuit of a fox boy in exactly the same way that he would the romance with a vixen, since the human maintains the active sexual role. In the one such example in *Yuewei caotang biji*, the man who pursues a fox youth ends up stripped naked, his clothes thrown in a cesspool, and his horses' tails cut short. Ji thwarted the ardent lover's expectations just as he would have in a heterosexual affair.[101]

Perhaps because Ji Yun's motives in describing such a relationship are exactly the opposite of He Bang'e's desire to titillate, he focused to an unparalleled extent on the reverse situation, the male fox's sexual domination of a human male. This is a nightmare rather than a fantasy and upsets what Sommer calls the hierarchy of penetration.[102] An anecdote about a herd boy's molestation by a male fox provides a vivid illustration of the narrative consequences of gender variation:

> Near the coast in Cangzhou 滄州[103] there lived a fourteen- or fifteen-year-old herd boy. Although he was the son of a peasant family, his countenance was fair and flawless. One day when he woke up from a midday nap on the riverbank, he felt as if he was carrying something on his back, but when he looked it had no form; when he touched it had no substance; and when he listened, it had no sound. In his terror he went home to tell his parents, but they could do nothing about it. After several days it gradually felt as if he was being embraced, then caressed, and then it felt as if he was being smothered in a nightmare. Finally he was raped. From then on, the thing

100. "Bibi" 碧碧, *YTSL*, 1.7–10.
101. *YWCT*, 20.1140, story 34.
102. Sommer, *Sex, Law, and Society in Late Imperial China*, pp. 116–18.
103. In Hebei, near the Hebei-Shandong border.

had intercourse with him constantly, but it still had neither form, nor sound, nor substance. Occasionally the boy received money, presents, fruit, or treats, but not too much.

A neighboring schoolmaster told his father, "I fear this is a fox. You should conceal a hunting dog. Wait until you hear the sounds of seduction, then break down the door and sic the dog on it to catch it." The boy's father did as he was told, and the fox leaped howling through the window and perched on the roof, jumping up and down and throwing things, cursing the boy for betraying him.

The schoolmaster called to the fox and said to him, "Since you can transform yourself and are sentient, you must know the way of the world. When men and women take joy in one another, they are moved by passion, but still I don't know how many vow in the morning that they will be buried together, but by the evening are on different boats. As for catamites, they are originally not of female substance; when they carry their blankets to follow a lover, they are simply marketing their sex."

The schoolmaster's argument continues with an eloquent and allusive lecture on the faithlessness of male favorites once money or power is gone. Moreover, he adds, since the fox's gifts to the boy had been paltry compared to those other betrayed lovers, he could expect loyalty least of all. The story closes, "After he spoke the fox was silent for a time, and then he heard it stomp its foot and say, 'Stop. Only now do I realize I am a fool.' It sighed many times and left."[104]

The story opens as a tale of medical possession in which the victim is seized by an impersonal (if physically graphic) madness rather than being seduced by an anthropomorphic character. The formlessness of the creature emphasizes this difference; this fox exists only in the boy's sensation of physical violation. The boy's sexual experience with a dominant male fox is portrayed as possession, just as it would be for a woman. As often in descriptions of possession, such as "Gu'er," there seems to be a transition here that implies loss of the boy's perspective. The precise, disturbing phenomena of the initial experience turn into generalized, constant harassment, viewed by his parents.

104. *YWCT*, 7.331–32, story 42. For a story about fox lodgers who molest their host's handsome young son, see "Hu bu ru yu" 狐不入獄, in Zhang Jingyun, *Qiuping xinyu* 5.26a.

Once the voice of the schoolmaster takes over the story with the authority of the exorcist, the nature of the fox changes fundamentally. It is elevated from a medical phenomenon to an equal with whom an educated man can reason, unlike the boy, who remains silent and passive. When this happens, the roles of romance with a vixen are reversed: the fox is the fool deceived by illusion, and the herd boy is cast as the fickle seducer, profiteer, and object of desire. The argument that it is homosexuality, rather than rape or spirit possession, that makes the relationship fundamentally false is intriguing.[105] This is the only case in which a reversal of roles allows the fox to be the one who desires and the one who is deceived. Some sympathy is transferred to the fox's side as the male desiring subject, and its feelings are genuine if not pure. In all other cases, Ji insisted that it is humans, not foxes, who feel lust. Class is also an issue, and the schoolmaster seems to identify more with the fox than with the afflicted peasant. The closing argument is similar to the vixen's argument to her male lover on the illusory nature of all romance, especially romance with prostitutes. The same references to the romance, even if discredited, would be unthinkable when describing an affair between a fox and a woman, because female virtue would be compromised.

The negative associations of sexual molestation by a fox make it possible to understand it as punishment for misdeeds in a former life, a darker version of the destined tie that vixens often claim when commencing an affair with men. The karmic punishment explanation is equally possible for women and men who take the passive sexual role. The use of destiny as an explanation helps Ji to deal with the problem of involuntary fox possession. He can tolerate a suspension of human will only if it is justified by a moral lapse in another life, over which the individual once had control. As we saw in one of the stories from the night of storytelling discussed in Chapter 2, a fox taking revenge on a man who had earlier had an affair with his wife seduces the man's second wife and not his first one, since the first

---

105. Ji did seem to believe in general that homosexual affairs are more artificial than heterosexual ones; he argued elsewhere that lustful women are naturally so, but catamites become as they are by training; see *YWCT*, 12.643, story 109.

had been virtuous and the second wanton.[106] In another anecdote, a boy is seduced by a fox who sleeps with him every night and shows no signs of departing as the boy enters his twenties. Someone advises the victim to grow a beard. When his whiskers get a bit long, the fox shaves them in the middle of the night and applies makeup to his face. When an exorcist finally confronts this fox, he tells his story: in their past lives, he had been a woman and the boy had been a monk who imprisoned and sexually abused her for seventeen years. In despair, she died and complained to the infernal courts, which decided the debt would be repaid in a future life. But it happened that on account of other crimes, the woman was reborn as a male fox and crept about in the woods for a hundred years without being able to meet his enemy. Now that he had refined his shape, he happened to meet the former monk and took revenge. When seventeen years pass, he will leave on his own. The exorcist is powerless.[107]

Being forced to play the female role is essential to the punishment. Here sexual violation is repaid in kind, making the reversal of roles very literal. The gendered role-playing of cosmetics and beardlessness reprises a situation in another life. In general, in late imperial fox stories, sex with a vixen, even if fatal, is not a punishment for misdeeds in a former life but an immediate punishment for excessive lust. Sexual rewards for favors of other kinds done for foxes are more common. In Ji's own system of karmic equations, however, sex can repay sex as a punishment but never as a reward. This use of destiny, in which humans are punished by being reborn as foxes,[108] serves to link foxes more closely to the human world, fitting them in the same matrix of good deeds and misdeeds.

There is a similar story of an old gardener who goes mad when molested by a male fox as revenge for noncarnal wrongs in another life. Originally, the old man should have been the fox's wife, but the

---

106. *YWCT*, 1.630, story 96.

107. *YWCT*, 9.430, story 148.

108. Note that in vernacular fiction it is usually the other way around, with foxes reborn as people, as seen in *Zhaoyang qushi*, *Xingshi yinyuan zhuan*, and *Yaohua zhuan*. This is the difference between the supernatural as the frame of a narrative or the heart of a narrative. In the classical case, a human life is a gloss or explanation on a fox's actions; in the case of vernacular fiction, the fox life provides some explanation for a human's character.

gender of their incarnations was mismatched, and the fox was unwilling to wait. Homosexuality is an unnatural solution prompted by inconvenient karmic circumstances. In Ji's anecdotes this fate is usually suffered by men of relatively low social status, presumably because of the humiliation involved. Here age is an additional humiliation, as an old man is used in a way usually reserved for young boys. Some argued the fox only told this story of revenge to seduce the old man, but Ji rejected this on the grounds that a fox would pursue a man only for beauty or vital essence, neither of which this victim could offer.[109] Ji seems willing to admit the pursuit of beauty as a motive far more readily in the case of a same-sex fox affair than in heterosexual relationships.

Although *Liaozhai*'s "Feng Sanniang" 封三娘, the single example of a lesbian fox romance, belongs more properly with the romances since it is not explicitly sexual, it seems appropriate to discuss it here.[110] A woman, Miss Fan, forms an intense friendship with the mysterious Feng Sanniang, who later is revealed to be a fox. Although there is never any overt sexual description, their longing for one another is described in precisely the same terms as a heterosexual romance. One of the Qing commentators remarked that since Liaozhai had already written about everything else, he felt compelled to deal with this theme as well.[111] There is indeed a sense of experimentation with every possible permutation of the fox romance; foxes' sexual expertise makes them the appropriate figures to explore sexual variation.

Despite its novel twist, the story follows the same pattern as a romance in which the fox, after an affair with a man, replaces herself with a more suitable woman. Despite her special relationship with Miss Fan, when the vixen Feng arranges her friend's marriage, she plays the familiar role of the fox as matchmaker. This manipulation does not seem entirely benign. Without Fan's consent, Feng gives a

---

109. *YWCT*, 16.911–12, story 63.

110. *LZ*, 6.610–17. Another story of a woman with a mysterious supernatural companion seems a platonic version of a man with an invisible lover, but it is not expressed as a romance; see "Wang Dajie" 王大姐, in Jin Pengchang, *Shouyizhai kechuang biji* 4.30b.

111. *LZ*, 6. 611.

love token once received from Fan to the man she has chosen for her. This affectionately motivated coercion is repaid in kind when Fan decides that the only way to keep her friend with her is for both of them to marry the same man. She plots to get Feng drunk and have her (Fan's) husband molest her.[112] When the deed is done, Feng declares that Fan has ruined her chances of immortality and departs. The mechanics of substitution in the story are very intricate. First, the fox, desired by both the woman and man, succeeds in replacing herself by bringing them together, but when the woman tries to substitute her husband for herself and have him consummate her desires, it ends the relationship.

This story makes the fox's self-improvement and sexuality absolutely irreconcilable. On parting she says, "I saw your lovely visage and was suddenly seized with love and admiration, like the silkworm that entangles itself. This brought us to the situation today! This is the destined destruction brought on by the sorcery of passion; human power has no effect on it.[113] If I stay longer, the enchantment will begin again and have no end." In this case the fox is the one who feels desire and eventually loses control, in spite of the fact that she has engineered her own substitution so well. This confession of overwhelming passion is unparalleled by heterosexual vixens. Desire between the two women is a potentially destructive force, but it is heterosexual consummation that ultimately severs their tie, in strong contrast to many *Liaozhai* stories in which polygamy is the harmonious solution to narrative entanglements. Is that solution impossible because of Feng's active desire? Is it impossible for a woman to be the central figure of a polygamous triangle? Although the patterns of heterosexual fox romances are used, the switch in gender is not a superficial detail. It seems that like a male fox who desires a human boy, a vixen enamored of a woman is moved by passion rather than being its object.

---

112. There is a similar quality of two female characters each trying to force the other into intimacy with the male protagonist in "Chang'e," in *LZ*, 8.1069.

113. There is irony in a fox speaking these words. Passion, not she herself, is the monster who will meet a destined *jie* 劫, "fated destruction." To say that human power has no influence on passion is to forget she is not human.

TRANSSEXUAL FOXES

Since foxes transgress every other boundary, perhaps one should be surprised how rarely they switch sex. Xie Zhaozhe argued that all male animals take female shapes to seduce men, since it is *yang* that they covet, but this seems to be a minority opinion.[114] (Although this theory attempts to explain the overwhelming number of female fox spirits, it does seem to ignore a body of evidence to the contrary.) One clever twist on the theme is presented in the story "Hu Haohao" 胡好好 in *Ershi lu*. A fox seduces both a husband and wife, coming to him as a beautiful woman and to her as a handsome youth. When the truth is finally revealed, each of the humans is forced to watch while the fox has sex with the other. The fox manages to be the center of desire but to declare itself innocent: it had merely given the wife the sperm it had drained from the husband.[115] Although this is a particularly graphic example, to be the focus of lust while remaining unmoved is a common role for the fox. The story escapes by the same route as the fox; it indulges the sexual fantasy of a ménage à trois while claiming in the end to be a story of retribution. Some vernacular short stories and erotic novels, for example, *Rouputuan* 肉蒲團 (The carnal prayer mat; late seventeenth century) use the same logic of retribution, that a husband's adultery will be punished by a wife's, but as one of the commentators to *Ershi lu* remarked, in no other case was the revenge be so neat and immediate.

Another story in *Ershi lu* takes the playful switching of "Hu Haohao" even further. "Axi Alian" 阿惜阿憐 is unique in that the fox heroine states straightforwardly, "My brother and I are foxes; he can

---

114. Xie Zhaozhe, *Wu zazu*, 9.14.

115. Yue Jun, *Ershi lu*, 2.6b. For another story that seems a variant of this one, see "Jianzhong shuangti" 繭中雙體, in Loudong yuyi ke, *Jinghua shuiyue*, 7.6a.

Western lore about succubi and incubi makes similar claims that demons use the sperm they receive from men as succubi to have sex with women as incubi. Children conceived by demonic couplings are of this biological origin rather than literally being offspring of the devil. In the West, this theory is based on the conviction that it should be impossible for the Devil to create life; the motivation in the Chinese case is rather different. See Kramer and Sprenger, *Malleus Maleficarum*, pp. 21–28.

also be female, and I can also be male."[116] The ability of a fox to switch sexes is never ruled out, but this is the only case I have seen in which it is treated as a matter of course. This seems to have been a particular fascination of this author, as it is a possibility no one else explored. The story has an inconsistent attitude toward the sexual possibilities of transsexualism. When Axi becomes male, he/she is a beautiful boy. Lavish description is devoted to his/her dress, and he/she is referred to by a term used to describe catamites, *luantong* 孿童. When her lover tries to embrace him/her comparing him/her to the famous male favorites of history, he/she objects, saying that those men confused *yin* and *yang*, an odd claim for someone in his/her position to make. Her brother, on the other hand, agrees to become female and to be the protagonist's second wife, with no apparent sense of shame. In this story transsexualism is no violation, but homosexuality is. A sexually outrageous situation returns to an apparently conservative arrangement, heterosexual polygyny.[117]

Tales of same-sex fox liaisons and transsexual foxes are far outnumbered by their heterosexual counterparts, but these relatively rare variations serve to expose assumptions about sex roles. On the other hand, these exceptional narratives on homosexual ties with foxes can cast light on attitudes toward same-sex relationships in general. The

---

116. There are a few other examples. For a fox spirit that takes both male and female form to seduce victims of both sexes, see Fang Ruhao, *Dongdu ji*, 40.317. Similarly, in *Sanjiao Kaimi*, another fox demon takes the forms of both sexes to seduce lovers of both sexes. Apparently, this fox was originally male. It had assumed female form to seduce a young man, but since it had not yet transformed its genitalia, the would-be lover was shocked to discover a penis; see Pan Jingruo, *Sanjiao kaimi yanyi*, 1:5.65. Often, however, the foxes switch sexes just as a convenient disguise, not for sexual purposes; see, e.g., *Kuai yuan*, 14.no. 11; and "Ganyu yao" 贛榆妖, Tan Rumu, *Zaolin zazu*, 16b. There are also examples of cross-dressing rather than transformation; e.g., "Liu jijiu" 劉祭酒, in Zeng Yandong, *Xiao doupeng*, 9.173–76. Those stories in which a man imagines he is embracing a beautiful vixen lover who then turns into a fearsome man are a different category; they belong to the tradition of Lu Zhishen pretending to be the bride. The change in gender thwarts sexual expectations rather than exciting them further. Examples include "Huxian qinzui" 狐仙親嘴, in Yuan Mei, *Zi bu yu*, 23.475; and "Biyun" 碧雲, Xuan Ding, *Yeyu qiudeng lu, xulu* 1.477.

117. *Ershi lu*, 7.7a–13a. Both of these stories were copied into the Guangxu collection *Kejing ke'e ji*, compiled by Duxiang Yuyin.

fox as *luantong* is considered somewhat more dangerous than the vixen as the object of a man's affection, but it is a difference of degree rather than kind. The use of sex as punishment or reward serves to remove lust and passion from the equation altogether. When the fox is granted the active sexual role, he or she might become the one who is overwhelmed by passion. This exceptional case thus raises the question of the relation of vixen lovers to lust and passion.

ARE VIXENS LUSTFUL?

The linking of the "male" sexual role to desire in the homosexual fox story raises the question: What is the precise nature of the vixen's ties to sex? To what extent is *mei* a deliberate act, and to what extent is it in the eye of the beholder? Foxes are clearly objects of desire, but do they themselves feel desire? Again vernacular fiction and the classical tale give different answers to the question.

I have already noted the crucial difference between the two genres: vernacular fiction often describes the thoughts and feelings of supernatural beings, even villains, whereas the most sympathetic vixen in the classical tale is seen from the outside. Of course, the amount and sophistication of psychological introspection varies considerably among vernacular novels. In the various versions of the Daji cycle, Daji seems almost more a destructive force than a character. The focus lies more on her bloodthirsty cruelty and destructiveness than on her sexual appetites; she uses King Zhou's lust to manipulate him rather than feeling lust herself. *Zhaoyang qushi*'s vixen sets out to find a man for the twin purposes of parasitism and lust, which fits the far lighter tone of this novel's depiction of a fatal concubine and its prurient interest in nymphomania. When she gets drunk, her desires are aroused, but once she has made a sexual conquest, she gloats about it entirely in terms of the *yang* energy she has plundered from her partner.[118]

The vixen in the vernacular novel *Huli quanyuan* provides a more complex case study for the question of a vixen's motivations. This novel is exceptional because it is an extended vernacular version of the same kind of story common in the classical tale, an account of a

118. Guhang yanyan sheng, *Zhaoyang qushi*, 1.87.

private citizen's entanglement with a fox and her eventual exorcism. Most other vernacular novels tell different kinds of fox stories. The opening of the novel, when the fox descends from her mountain to seek a lover, is close enough to the opening of *Zhaoyang qushi* to suggest influence.[119] She is a bloodthirsty fox on the model of Daji: although foxes are very rarely portrayed as literal man-eaters, in a fit of rage she eats a small boy.[120] Her motivations for pursuing the hero are always mixed: she has sex with him in order to drain his *yang*, but she is smitten by his beauty.[121] Even when her attentions cause him to waste away, she still claims to herself that she loves him. When she is vanquished at the end of the novel, her love of the hero is given some affirmation by the promise that she will meet him again in her next existence.[122] This novel was adapted from a *tanci*; one wonders whether the mixed demonic and sympathetic portrait of the vixen is influenced by this generic origin.[123] It is a confused and unsubtle portrayal, as the basic frame of a demon story is expanded in two contradictory directions allowed by vernacular fiction, subjectivity and crude violence.

In the classical tale, Ji Yun once again answered the question of a vixen's desire more definitely than any of his fellows, but his extreme position serves to reveal the basic fact that vixens in the Ming and Qing are almost never described as consorting with men for the sake of sexual pleasure or love alone. Ji's contention that foxes themselves are not lustful but seduce people only to drain their energy distinguishes self-destructive from self-serving appetites. For him parasitism negates lust rather than being its extreme form. Lust is, for him, an exclusively human trait of which foxes are only the ob-

---

119. *Huli quanyuan*. Also included under the title *Xianhu qie bao lu* 仙狐竊寶錄 in *Zhongguo gudai zhenxi xiaoshuo*, vol. 5, chap. 2.

120. Ibid., chap. 4.

121. For example, at the end of Chapter 3, she regrets that the illness she has caused diminished his good looks.

122. *Huli quanyuan*, chap. 22. For an argument that the novel takes a sympathetic attitude toward the possibility of love between men and foxes, see Ouyang Jian, *Zhongguo shenguai xiaoshuo tongshi*, pp. 618–19.

123. The tone of this novel also reminds me of some of the portrayals of the snake Miss Bai in late vernacular versions of *Baishe zhuan*; perhaps there was cross-species influence in addition to the shared conventions of vernacular fiction.

jects. The only exceptions are the stories of homosexual relationships with foxes, mentioned above. Another apparent exception is a story in which the vixen admits she loves the man for his beauty and takes meticulous care not to sicken him through overindulgence. This image is undercut, however, by the story's comic conclusion: the fox leaves the man once he grows whiskers and loses his beauty. This ending reveals that the main point of the anecdote was to mock a hirsute friend rather than to make a statement about the fox.[124] Fox desire overall is placed in the margins.

CONCLUSION

The earliest role of the fox in Chinese narrative was a means of imagining the intrusion of the alien into the most intimate human sphere; it later developed into a means to describe those aspects of human sexuality that seemed most alien. The fox fills in a void in the map of sexual possibilities. The vixen offers sex without a social price but comes to embody sex as a psychological and physical danger in itself. The vixen's territory overlaps with that of other sexually extraordinary categories of women, prostitutes and the destroyers of kingdoms, merely lying a step further away from the realm of "normal" women. The male fox as a sexual being remains a pathology demanding exorcism or cure rather than narrative development.

There is a split between foxes as objects of desire and foxes as lustful creatures themselves. In the stories there is a fascination with men's surrender of will to desire, rather than with the vixen's own desire. When attempting to depict vixens as actively lustful, it seems necessary to link sexual desire to other appetites, whether bloodthirstiness or the parasitic pursuit of self-improvement. Lust is depicted largely through these associations rather than in its own right. Even in the depiction of a creature that is supposed to be the embodiment of lust, the direct desire for sex is often veiled. Although the supernatural creature was designed as an image of sexuality, a void remains at its center.

---

124. *YWCT*, 21.1176–77, story 60.

{6}

The Fox Romance

Another definition of the fox bridges the gap between the wanton and destructive foxes of the previous chapter and the foxes who are the subject of this one:

> They [foxes] are also extremely lustful, and if a person is contaminated by their spittle, he will certainly be enchanted; therefore one calls them "seductive foxes." In the Tang there was a memorial "Fox seduction can deceive the ruler" written to compare them to the lustful women of the human world.[1] Although they are monsters, there are good and wicked ones among them, like Miss Ren who was willing to die for Zheng; they can even be capable of chastity. . . . Don't say that monsters do not have good hearts; one must be destined to meet them.[2]

In the preceding chapter, I examined the damning generalizations of the opening lines; this chapter discusses the exceptional individuals of the last two sentences. As in this quotation, however, the fox paragon is always silhouetted against the backdrop of wanton and seductive foxes.

The division between this chapter and the previous one depends on distinguishing sex from romance, and harmful relationships with foxes from beneficial ones, but these divisions should not obscure the interdependence of the two poles. The distinction between the se-

---

1. The reference is to Luo Binwang's memorial denouncing Empress Wu.

2. "Zeng zhima shipo jiaxing, xie caoyao qiaoxie zhen'ou" 贈芝麻識破假形，擷草藥巧諧真偶, in Ling Mengchu, *Erke pai'an jingqi*, 2:29.1371.

ductress and the good-hearted vixen is not imposed from without but is articulated in the romances themselves. I begin with a word of caution. "Romance" is perhaps a misleading title for this chapter, for I discuss a range of conjugal ties between men and vixens, which include duty as much as passion.

MISS REN AND THE ORIGINS OF THE FOX ROMANCE

As we have seen in several cases, there is a link between subject matter and generic form. The fox romance, like other forms of the romance, is narrated most frequently in elaborate *chuanqi* tales rather than the relatively simple narratives of *zhiguai*. A romance depends on the character development *chuanqi* makes possible, and the sympathetic fox heroine is a marvel of *chuanqi* rather than the anomaly of *zhiguai*. One difference is immediately apparent. The foxes discussed in the preceding chapter were largely nameless, distinguished only by age and sex, but this will be a history of a series of named individuals.

Because of this generic difference, textual history is more important to this subject matter than the shared body of lore discussed in other chapters. Although *chuanqi* also have ties to casual oral storytelling, in the late imperial period relations of individual texts to other texts overshadow relations to the vast matrix of oral narrative and experience. Because of this, this chapter, unlike the others, focuses around a textual lineage. A single text, "Renshi zhuan," invented the idealized fox romance, and a single collection, *Liaozhai zhiyi*, brought it to maturity. "Renshi zhuan" was a textual presence in the Ming and Qing; it was included in the very popular Ming collection of early stories, *Yu Chu zhi* 虞初志, anthologies of extraordinary women like *Guang Yanyi bian* and *Lüchuang nüshi*, and Feng Menglong's *Taiping guangji chao* 太平廣記抄.

Among all the vixens of *Taiping guangji*, only Miss Ren appears in a story that bears her name, rather than the name of her human lover. The story begins by marking its own and its heroine's difference. Its opening, "Miss Ren was a female monster," upends the conventions of fox illusion and exposure by revealing her identity at the outset and places her at the center.[3]

A poor man named Zheng follows a lovely woman through the streets of Chang'an and spends a night with her in her home on the outskirts of the city. On his way back the following morning, he asks a barbarian bread-seller about her and is told this must be the fox who seduces local men. This pathbreaking story contains the entirety of the older *zhiguai* plot: the story begins with the conventional frame of a supernatural one-night stand followed by exposure of the fox, but it goes beyond that at their next meeting. Zheng cannot forget her beauty despite her identity and declares that her species does not matter to him. She argues, "The reason that people despise us is that we harm people, but I am not like that." Her denial overturns a tradition that claims an animal in human form is harmful in and of itself, regardless of its actual deeds. She declares she has a choice, and it is choice that makes the romance possible.[4]

After the two lovers set up housekeeping together, the plot is further complicated by the additional element of a love triangle. Wei, Zheng's nephew and financial benefactor, attempts to rape her. Ren dissuades him, arguing that as he is rich and has his choice of women; it would be ignoble to take the only thing a poor man has. Wei is so impressed by her loyalty that he lets her go and becomes her platonic admirer and friend. The juxtaposition of the two men's different views of her gives Ren a depth beyond her species identity. One man recognizes her species; the other recognizes her virtue. One goes beyond how one was expected to treat foxes, and the other treats her in a way he treats no other woman.

A variety of elements in the story are picked up in the later tradition. First, as mentioned in the previous chapter, Ren establishes foxes' identification with prostitutes. She tells Zheng that there

---

3. It could be argued that the opening line is a later interpolation, but even so, by the Ming it had become an accepted part of the story. Other Tang tales in *Taiping guangji* share some aspects of *Renshi zhuan*'s plot, but none is nearly as sophisticated or complete. For bibliographical background, see Li Jianguo, *Tang Wudai zhiguai chuanqi xulu*, pp. 265–69. *TPGJ*, 452.3692–97; trans. by Nienhauser, "Miss Jen" in Y. W. Ma and Joseph S. M. Lau, *Traditional Chinese Stories*, pp. 339–45; and Owen, *An Anthology of Chinese Literature*, pp. 518–26.

4. Owen, *An Anthology of Chinese Literature*, pp. 369–70.

are more of her kind in the human world than he suspects, and indeed two other women who catch Wei's eye turn out to be her relatives. Second, Ren's intimate but sexually restrained relationship with Wei, described in the line *bu ji luan* 不及亂, "not reaching the point of disorder" creates a model for platonic friendship in future stories, such as we have seen in He Bang'e's story of young Chu's encounter discussed in Chapter 2. Third, love triangles of two men and one woman are rare in the Chinese narrative tradition in general, and a fox provided one of the few means of imagining such a situation. Fourth, Ren also attempts to provide substitutes for herself by devious means and tricks another woman into becoming Wei's bedfellow. She makes the woman ill and bribes a shaman to tell the woman's relatives that the woman must move to Ren's house in order to recover. The means of her deception alludes to foxes' links to both medicine and shamanism, even though the unpleasant implications of these actions are completely ignored in the final moral assessment of Ren; her loyalty to men outweighs her use of another woman. Fifth, her advice to Wei to buy a horse that he later sells at great profit offers an early example of foxes' link to money. Finally, the one way in which she does not resemble a human being is her inability to make her own clothes; this flaw in her domesticity does not recur frequently in fox stories, but it may reinforce her link to concubines and entertainers, women who lack practical, domestic skills.[5]

When Zheng receives employment elsewhere, he takes Ren along despite her protests that the journey is ill-omened for her. At Mawei, the site of Yang Guifei's death some fifty years before, they encounter a party of hunters, and the dogs attack her, chasing her down once she reverts to her original form. The end of the story, in which Miss Ren dies both as a beast and as Yang Guifei, is one the tradition will later struggle to overcome. At the same instant, she both returns to the older fox story that she left behind when her lover decided to maintain relations with her even though he knows she is a fox and is raised to a different level of historical reference. As a creature both bewitching and doomed, she takes on both Yang's glamour and of pity for her fate. The author Shen's closing sigh, "I am struck

5. On the other hand, that a creature who has conjured her own human guise cannot herself complete the disguise is intriguing.

that such humanity could be found in the feelings of a creature so alien,"[6] elevates her on the grounds of both passion and morality.

Returning to "Renshi zhuan" after studying Qing fox romances reveals how much has changed. She, no less than her lover Zheng, is materially dependent on Wei for the basic necessities of their household, whereas in the later tradition the fox is the source of material support. In the Ming or Qing a vixen would also never be at serious risk of rape by a human man. Any attempted rapist would suffer immediate supernatural revenge, and no vixen would have to rely on moral remonstrance. The virtue of vixens in the later tradition is not exposed in weakness. The moral ambiguity of the love triangle is most often discarded in favor of monogamy or polygyny. When Ren repays Wei for his favors, it is on an immediately practical level, in contrast to the more extravagant rewards for more karmically remote good deeds in the later tradition. In her limitations Ren is more human, not less, than her Qing successors.

THE DOMESTICATION OF THE DEMON LOVER: QINGFENG

Centuries later, another revolutionary vixen appeared, her story in many ways an answer to Ren's. "Qingfeng" 青鳳 in *Liaozhai zhiyi* opens:

> The Geng family of Taiyuan had been a great family in the past, with a vast residence. Afterwards the family declined, but their residence remained, half of it left empty. Therefore strange events began to occur. The doors opened and closed by themselves, and the family were often frightened in the middle of the night. The elder Geng was worried by this and moved to another residence with his family, leaving an old man behind to guard the door. From then on the place fell to ruins even faster. Sometimes the old gatekeeper would hear laughter and speech, and the sounds of flutes and singing. The Geng family had a nephew, Geng Qubing, who was wild and unrestrained. He told the old man to tell him when he saw anything. That night, the old man saw lamps upstairs being lit and

6. Following Owen, *An Anthology of Chinese Literature*, p. 525.

put out and ran to tell him. Geng wanted to go in and see the marvel. The old man tried to stop him, but he didn't listen.[7]

This opening plays on all the conventions of the haunted house. Contemporary readers would have expected foxes; the intrigue would lie in discovering exactly what mischief the foxes will cause or what illusions they will generate. The man who dares to spend a night in a haunted house had appeared in Six Dynasties tales, but then the haunted place was a pavilion in the wilderness, and now it is his own family's urban residence. It is typical of the Qing that the hero's first encounter with the strange should be on his family's own property. After walking along the half-remembered corridors, he finds the Hu family sitting together drinking: an old man, his wife, their son Xiao'er (filial son), and their young niece Qingfeng. The patriarch rebukes him for intruding into another man's household, but Geng protests that since this is his family's property, he should instead be honored as their host. The old man then turns polite and questions Geng about a book written by a relative concerning the Hus' ancestress Lady Tushan, and Geng relates anecdotes about her achievements.

At this point the author has made the identity of the family playfully obvious—the surname Hu is a homophone for "fox," and an ambiguous text in the *Wuyue chunqiu* implies that Lady Tushan, the wife of the sage-king Yu, is a fox.[8] She is presented here as the most respectable, canonical model of a fox wife. Exposing this family as foxes obviously is not the main point of the plot.

As Geng grows drunk, he boldly propositions Qingfeng, and the family retreats. The next night he returns to the abandoned building hoping to see her again, but a wild-haired, black-faced demon appears to frighten him. Undeterred, he paints his own face with ink and grimaces in imitation, and the demon leaves in embarrassment. This is later revealed to be the fox family's attempt to drive him away. This confrontation is a parody of the initial expectations of horrific encounters in haunted houses. The man undaunted by the

---

7. *LZ*, 1.112. For a different translation, see "Fox-girl Qingfeng," in Mair and Mair, *Strange Tales from a Make-do Studio*, pp. 43–53.

8. *Wuyue chunqiu*, 6.4a. On the Lady Tushan tradition, see Li Jianguo, *Zhongguo hu wenhua*, pp. 21–28.

strange is a stock type. Here one must ask who is the real monster: both are disguised, and it is the human man who drives the fox away. Indeed, Geng Qubing's name, "driving out illness," has connotations of exorcism.

Geng stubbornly continues to stay in the house, and the next night succeeds in meeting Qingfeng. She admits that she shares his feelings but tells him that her uncle is strict and is moving the family away the following day to avoid him. They embrace, but just then her uncle returns and rebukes her for dishonoring the family. He drags her into the next room; Geng hears her uncle's yells and her weeping. Then they all vanish. The vixen lover had initially been a fantasy of the woman completely unattached to society, but here we have a vixen with all those entanglements. He meets her in the context of her family and discusses her genealogy. She has a name to dishonor, and male relatives guarding her chastity.

Now the house no longer appears to be haunted, and the Geng family moves back in. More than a year later, when Geng Qubing is sweeping the tombs at Qingming (a common date for supernatural encounters), he sees two small foxes pursued by a dog. One of them looks at him and whimpers as if begging to be rescued, and he covers it with his clothes and takes it home. He places it on his bed, and it becomes Qingfeng. She tells him, "I hope you will not despise me as a member of another species." He replies, "I have longed for you by day and dreamed of you by night. Seeing you is like getting a rare treasure; how could I despise you?" The two are overjoyed and settle down as husband and wife, unimpeded since her uncle assumes that she is dead.

The revelation of the fox body used to be the end of the fox romance, but here it has become the means by which domestic bliss is achieved. That the marriage bed is the site of her restoration to humanity underlines this; Geng's acceptance of the body of the fox is more direct than Zheng's. In the international fairy-tale type involving a transformed wife or husband, the human lover often must overcome this transformation to win the supernatural lover back (as in Beauty and the Beast, the frog prince).[9] In the early fox story, the

9. Leavy, *In Pursuit of the Swan Maiden*, pp. 101–55, 245–76.

human lover could never overcome his own revulsion, but in this tale the fox tradition plays out the second half of this narrative pattern. This seems to be a deliberate rewriting of the tale of Miss Ren: Geng is allowed to save his lover from the dogs. The dialogue about not despising her for her species is very close to a conversation between Ren and her lover, but Ren's lover had not seen her in the shape of a fox when he swore her species did not matter. Qingfeng has to die in order to become free of family obligations. Death, or the near-death of unconsciousness, is often used as a narrative transition in *Liaozhai*, for supernatural figures and humans alike.

Even then their happy ending is not complete. One day Qingfeng's cousin Xiao'er arrives and insists that Geng must save Qingfeng's uncle, who is in the grasp of a hunter. Qingfeng persuades Geng to help, and he buys a wounded fox from the hunter. This fox, too, is restored to his human form and is amazed and delighted to discover that Qingfeng is alive. Qingfeng begs that her family be allowed to move back into its old lodgings, so that she may be both filial niece and faithful wife. The Hu clan moves in, and all live harmoniously as one family. Geng studies with Xiao'er, who in turn becomes a model for the son of Geng's first wife as he grows older. So the story ends.

Again, exposure of the fox body becomes a means of establishing domestic bliss, as the old patriarch is reclaimed into the human order. The simulated deaths, and the two lives saved, have eliminated any shame attached to consummating their relationship against her uncle's wishes and tied up the loose ends. Qingfeng is allowed to resolve the conflict between her relatives by blood and her relatives by marriage. The Qing commentators even admire the old fox for having such a well-ordered family;[10] foxes are made to embody domestic virtues. Geng's human wife is never reconciled with the fox family and is barely mentioned, but her son's incorporation into this familial exchange is the final completion of domestic happiness, an assurance that these ties will last for generations. Foxes still live in the Gengs' house, but they are part of the family, not an intrusion. This vision of

10. He's final commentary, *LZ*, 1.118.

2. "Qingfeng" from *Liaozhai zhiyi tuyong*

cohabitation seems founded on all the late imperial families who lived for generations with the small fox shrine in the next room. This tale weds the confrontation of haunting with the tensions of marriage.

Barbara Fuss Leavy suggests in *In Search of the Swan Maiden* that the beast bride story expresses male fears about a bride's conflicting loyalties between the life that she had before marriage and her new-found domesticity.[11] Pu Songling used the fox story to explore women's divided loyalties between their natal and married families. Pu's ideal is not a woman who abandons her own family without looking back; rather, human and fox families accept each other in an ideal of domestic harmony. Another story, "Changting" 長亭, exam-

11. Leavy, chap. 6, pp.196–244.

ines the same questions as "Qingfeng," but its resolution is less idealistic: the man and his fox father-in-law never come to terms.[12] In both stories the male relative is humbled by being reduced to fox form, and the human male is placed in a position to rescue the fox. "Yatou" presents an interesting vision of this conflict. Although the fox patriarchs are won over in the end, Yatou's procuress mother and prostitute sister are unredeemed. The fox patriarchs represent conservative family values, whereas Yatou's "mother" and "sister" are a false family organized around financial exploitation of men. They die beasts' deaths, butchered and skinned by Yatou's half-human son, even though Yatou had wanted to protect them. Their cruel demise is included but not entirely approved; the half-breed son is in turn cured of his cruelty.[13] A family is made whole by violent expulsion of some elements.

Qingfeng makes up for Ren's domestic deficiencies and in doing so avoids her tragedy. Domesticity is, however, not the only possible resolution for the late imperial vixen.

BEYOND THE BEAST AND BEYOND DOMESTICITY

Although Qingfeng achieves domesticity, there was also interest in vixens who went beyond it. Even as the happy ending with the vixen became possible, there was fascination with particular forms of loss. Two of the most potent paths out of domesticity for the vixen are recorded in the anthology *Yu Chu xinzhi*, and they remain a model for the rest of the tradition, duplicated as late as *Hutianlu*.[14] These two stories should be considered products of approximately the same generation as Pu Songling, if not slightly earlier.[15] The first is the

---

12. *LZ*, 10.1333. The return to similar subject matter in a portion of the book thought to be written much later might suggest a disillusionment with the domestic ideals achieved so easily in "Qingfeng." For a translation, see "Fox Girl Changting," in Mair and Mair, *Strange Tales from a Make-do Studio*, pp. 331–42.

13. *LZ*, 5.600–606.

14. Baiyi jushi, *Hutianlu*, xia, 46b–47a.

15. For a discussion of *Yu Chu xinzhi*, see Hou Zhongyi and Liu Shilin, *Zhongguo wenyan xiaoshuo shigao*, vol. 2, pp. 188–96. *Yu Chu xinzhi* is an anthology of a large range of tales by early Qing authors. As the title indicates, it was composed on the model of the collection of Tang and earlier stories (especially the more elaborate

vixen as *lienü* 烈女 (exemplary woman), the second the vixen as the literary companion and lover destined to depart. Both paths exit human domesticity, but the first is a choice available to human women, and the second is not.

The more straightforward and, in terms of the events described, chronologically earlier of the two stories is "Lie hu zhuan" 烈狐傳 (Biography of a fox paragon). It begins as a fox lodger story—exceptionally from the point of view of the fox: "At the end of the Ming there was a fox who assumed the form of a 60- or 70-year-old man and went to call on the Ge family of Kunshan."[16] Since the fox justifies the relationship of lodging as a destined tie, the possibility of domestic infestation is controlled and granted sanction. While the foxes were in residence, the Ge's son caught sight of one of their daughters and fell ill with longing for her. His father attempted to arrange the marriage. The fox patriarch at first protested that as a member of an alien species she was no worthy match but finally acquiesced. She was an exemplary bride and daughter-in-law. The narrative as a whole is very simple, and the description of her martyrdom particularly so: "Before long came the change of dynasties, and looting troops entered their house. When they saw how beautiful she was, they wanted to rape her. She cursed them, took a knife, and slit her own throat. She was revealed to be a nine-tailed fox." After the story the editor Zhang Chao commented that he had read an entire book of fox stories (one suspects this may have been *Humei congtan*), and although there was no lack of passionate foxes, he had never before heard of such a paragon. "This text can bring glory to a lecherous species of beasts. It is also unusual that Ge sought a marriage with her, and so she repaid him with her martyrdom."[17] Zhang Chao was correct that the human father-in-law's insistence on marriage is unusual; more commonly, the initiative lies with the couple them-

---

chuanqi), *Yu Chu zhi*, but using the works of contemporary writers. It was initially assembled in 1686 and not published until 1700, but later editions included some additional material. Chen Ding was about ten years older than Pu Songling. As for the authors of the two stories discussed here, Xu Jiefeng was probably at least a decade older.

16. The most significant precedent is the beginning of the famous anecdote about the fox who called on Zhang Hua, in Gan Bao, *Soushen ji*, 421.

17. Zhang Chao, *Yu Chu xinzhi*, 10.193.

selves or the vixen's father. Parental sanction and her own passivity eliminate the illicit quality of the fox romance even before the ultimate justification of her virtue. Like most fox lodger stories, this is an account of a relation between families rather than individuals.

This story also has an interesting place in the context of its author Chen Ding's 陳鼎 (1650–after 1711) work. His *Liuxi waizhuan* 留溪外傳 (Outer chronicles of Liuxi) claims to fill in the gaps in official history by preserving the stories of ordinary people who were models of virtue. His collection is particularly rich in stories of Ming loyalists and female chastity; the vixen is placed in the context of her fellows in virtue and historical situation rather than species.[18] Vixens are allowed to prove their virtue by the same means as human women. The only difference the vixen's species makes to such a story is that such virtues seem even more unlikely, and hence more admirable, in one of her status. Katherine Carlitz notes the blurring between stories of exemplary women and fiction and drama in the late Ming as the same illustrations were used for each; a story like this is a particularly vivid example of the blending of exemplary tales with entertainment genres.[19] If the body of a Chinese woman becomes a symbol for the vulnerable, but fiercely defended, Chinese nation, to replace that body with that of a fox demonstrates foxes' transition from being "them" to "us" in comparison with the foreign invaders. The exposure of the fox body has the opposite effect of that of Ren's: the fox dies not in an echo of the dynasty-destroying beauty, but as a female corpse loyal to a fallen dynasty. As a collection of early Qing tales, *Yu Chu xinzhi* sets out to preserve memories of the late Ming and the fall, and even the fox story can serve as a means of remembering the conquest. The fox here goes through a stage of ordinariness to reclaim the extraordinary, but it is the same kind of extraordinary status accessible to a human woman.

---

18. Although the source of "Liexian zhuan" is listed as *Liuxi waizhuan*, I have not found this story in the editions I have consulted.

19. Katherine Carlitz, "The Social Uses of Feminine Virtue in Late Ming Editions of *Lienu zhuan*."

IN KANGXI 21, A MAN FROM YIXING NAMED XU . . .

Although *Liaozhai*'s foxes are the most popular representatives of their species for readers from the high Qing on, they were not the most well-known vixens of Pu's own generation. That claim goes to Hu Shuzhen 胡淑貞, the vixen encountered by a man named Xu 許 in 1682. *Liaozhai*'s foxes are indisputably *Liaozhai*'s, but this vixen belongs to shared experience. Accounts of this story appear in Xu Jiefeng's 徐喈鳳 (*jinshi* 1659) "Huixian ji" 會仙記 (Record of meeting a transcendent; originally in his own collection, then included in *Yu Chu xinzhi*); Wang Shizhen's 王士禛 (1634–1711) *Juyi lu* 居易錄 (Record of living at ease); Niu Xiu's 鈕琇 (?–1704) *Gu sheng* 觚賸 (Excess from the tablet; 1702); Wang Qishu's *Shuicao qingxia lu* 水曹清暇錄 (Record of idleness from the Water Bureau; preface dated 1797); Wu Qian's 吳騫 (1733–1813) *Fufeng qiao chuanxin lu* 扶風橋傳信錄 (The true record of Fufeng Bridge; preface dated 1807); a late seventeenth-century gazetteer of Yixing; and Jin Pengchang's *Shouyizhai kechuang biji*. It seems to have been a celebrated event for the Kangxi generation, which was still remembered and discussed by their descendants in the Qianlong.[20] In contrast with the textual emphasis of much of this chapter, I believe that this is an example of multiple, semi-independent accounts of the same central events, rather than a line of imitations of a single text. In this way the cycle provides a useful contrast with the reception of *Liaozhai*'s vixens.

Of the various versions of the story, the most distinctive and complete are "Huixian ji" and *Fufeng qiao chuanxin lu*. I discuss each of these in turn, referring to the other, shorter versions as sources of comparison. "Huixian ji" is a strong example of *chuanqi* style,[21] whereas *Fufeng qiao* breaks up the marvels into the daily commonplaces of a diary.

---

20. For an argument that Shuzhen influenced the development of the *Baishe zhuan* cycle, see Jiang Ruizao, *Xiaoshuo kaozheng*, 1:317. Xu's surname is an obvious similarity, as is the original encounter by the bridge, but Bai Niangzi leaves and keeps coming back, rather than lingering, halfway gone.

21. See Hou Zhongyi and Liu Shilin, *Zhongguo wenyan xiaoshuo shigao*, pp. 322–24.

One of most conspicuous features of these two texts, in comparison to other romances, is their first-person narration. The vixen lover is more usually kept at a safe "friend of a friend" distance. Xu Jiefeng claims young Xu as a nephew on his wife's side, a kinsman but not a member of the same household; *Fufeng qiao* is related from the perspective of the household of young Xu's grandfather. Yet in both cases, the romance is regarded from the perspective of the older generation, rather than that of the young lover himself. At all of the first encounters with the vixen Shuzhen, young Xu is accompanied by either his father or his grandfather, in sharp contrast with most romances in which the hero is away from home or even conveniently orphaned, to minimize parental interference.

The basic elements of an initial encounter by a bridge, justification of the affair based on a destined tie, the vixen's departure, the lover's visit and otherworldly idyll, and the continued visits by her maids after her departure seem to remain constant in the various versions. Constants and variations reveal both which elements were essential and which secondary as well as the subjects of contention. The protagonist Xu Dan, of Fufeng Qiao village, is the twenty-one-year-old grandson of a late Ming *xiucai* Xu Kejin, but he and his father are simple farmers. He first glimpses Shuzhen and her maid by a bridge along the road when going into the city with his father (or grandfather) to make New Year's calls on the eleventh day of the first month, 1682.[22] They smile at him. In the "Huixian ji" account, Xu, being simple and honest by nature, does not respond, but in other versions glances are exchanged. This is the familiar opening of encountering a beautiful stranger on the road. That night, when lodging at a friend's house, father and son (or grandfather and son) hear inexplicable sounds, either knocking or footsteps on the stairs. They raise the alarm, but neither they nor their host finds anything. After they go back to bed, a female voice announces that she has a destined

22. The exact dates are from Wu Qian, *Fufeng qiao chuanxin lu*, 1.1a. The version of "Huixian ji" copied into *Fufeng qiao* has textual differences with the text that survives in *Yu Chu xinzhi*, suggesting perhaps that the *Fufeng qiao* source was Xu Jiefeng's own collection. In "Huixian ji" he is with his father; in *Fufeng qiao* he is with his grandfather, who is a more central character than his father in both accounts.

tie with young Xu. Frightened, he dares not respond, but she stays until dawn, singing popular songs. This entrance takes the form of a story of haunting. That she sings for them is unusual and suggests the entertainment value of this encounter with the supernatural.

More than ten days later, Xu returns to his room to find Shuzhen sitting on his bed with a maid at her side. Now she introduces herself thoroughly. Her surname is the telltale Hu, but she has not only a name but a *zi*, an indication of a level of individual identity very different from the nameless vixen who died as a Ming loyalist. Even her maid has a name. Shuzhen explains the exact nature of the karmic attachment she claims. As well as being a convention of the romance, claims of predestination serve to dilute the element of willful individual desire in a fox romance and distance a vixen from the parasite who will take any victim. In this case, karmic necessity is founded not on a human's rescue of a fox, but on an unfulfilled love in another life, when they were both human palace attendants in the Song, an explanation that preserves more romance than a karmic obligation of gratitude.[23] It makes the tie of human and fox part of a larger, primarily human story, with the added glamour of the palace in a distant historical period. In Kangxi 21, remembering the Ming was still a politically charged act; it was less problematic for the grandson of a Ming *xiucai*, who had slipped to the status of farmer, to be linked to the Song.

Typical for this story, Xu's first reaction to her appearance and confession is to call his grandfather. The story goes to great lengths to keep the romance morally restrained. In "Huixian ji," their relationship is not consummated until she has won the approval of the head of the household and the community at large. Xu's grandfather concludes that she is *yao er bu xie* 妖而不邪, "a monster but not wicked," a fascinating construction made of two terms often used interchangeably. Therefore he "leaves so that they can realize their destined tie as husband and wife."[24] Here the grandfather's decision, rather than the erotic experience, is emphasized. Literary expression takes the place of description, and the couple's poems plighting their troth are recorded in *Fufeng qiao* and mentioned in "Huixian ji."

---

23. Wu Qian, *Fufeng qiao chuanxin lu*, 1.1b.
24. Zhang Chao, *Yu Chu xinzhi*, 14.257.

The degree of direct parental approval of the sexual consummation of the relationship is one of the more variable elements in different versions of the story. The avoidance of sexuality in *Fufeng qiao* is particularly overt. After two nights of singing and conversation, the grandfather, Kejin, goes elsewhere; when he returns, he finds the bed-curtains open, and it is obvious to him that the destined tie had already been fulfilled.[25] He never explicitly gives his consent but seems to accept it as a fait accompli. In *Juyi lu*, Xu's mother accepts her as a bride, but his father does not and reports her to the local city god.[26] In *Shouyizhai kechuang biji*, several sexual encounters happen before the grandfather becomes aware of the situation. He is opposed but can do nothing to prevent it.[27] This variability suggests a difference of interpretation and interest. Those texts that situate themselves closest to the household have the strongest interest in making Shuzhen acceptable to the older generation; by keeping the relationship private and illicit, views from the outside more resemble other accounts of trysts with foxes. In these versions, the fact of a sexual liaison is essential to the story but is not described in any detail.

As discussed in the section on the fox séance in Chapter 4, Shuzhen presents herself to the community as a disembodied voice and impresses them with her knowledge of the classics. They come to her to ask questions as they would a fox oracle, but in "Huixian ji" she replies by prescribing the virtue appropriate to each person's station—filiality for children, obedience for wives. The content of her revelations is another of the variable elements in different versions. In *Fufeng qiao*, she also reveals odd arcane knowledge about the reproductive processes of lions (in the process of proving that she has actually been to the temples in Hangzhou that she describes), a tidbit later repeated in *Shou yizhai kechuang biji*.[28] In *Fufeng qiao* she also sings more songs from plays.

The emotional center of all versions of the story is the vixen's departure and continued involvement, from a distance, with Xu and his family. There are many possible explanations for the appeal of the

25. Wu Qian, *Fufeng qiao chuanxin lu*, 1.3a.
26. In ibid., 1.26b.
27. "Hunu" 狐女, in Jin Pengchang, *Shouyizhai kechuang biji*, 4.19a.
28. Wu Qian, *Fufeng qiao chuanxin lu*, 1.3a.

departing vixen. It is a way to prevent the marvel from becoming ordinary and to replace the potential boredom of narrated consummation with prolonged desire. The continued tie is an attempt to balance attachment and loss, domesticity and transcendence.

Although her departure is included in all versions, the reasons for it vary. These explanations fall into two categories: either the human world is too flawed to be worthy of the divine lover, or she is ordained by destiny to be a woman who cannot stay. In "Huixian ji," Shuzhen's impeccable behavior does not ensure domestic harmony. Some of Xu's relatives are so worried about him that they verbally attack her and even try to stab her unseen form and hide her husband from her. In response, Shuzhen said that she had come on account of *qing*, "passion" or "true feeling," but since others do not treat her with feeling, she will leave. As the fox becomes benign, the tradition of the harmful fox, in the form of humans' lingering aversion to foxes, provides narrative tension. In *Juyi lu* she leaves in response to Xu's father's attempted exorcism; in the *Gusheng* version she simply grows annoyed at the demands of all the neighbors. In *Shouyizhai* she comes less frequently after Xu marries. In *Fufeng qiao*, rather than anyone attacking her with violence, she makes the identical declaration about not being treated with feeling after some of the neighbors curse her in resentment when she outshines them in a discussion of the classics. In his annoyance at the clamor, Xu goes to sleep elsewhere.[29] This, like the *Gusheng* version, suggests a conflict between the private relationship with the fox and the public role as fox oracle.

But beyond all of these explanations is another overriding reason for Shuzhen's departure; their destined tie has been fulfilled. In *Fufeng qiao*, she begins to sing songs that hint at parting even before the disagreements with the neighbors. Her departure is overdetermined. She still clings to Xu and seems to protest against destiny, even as she explicates it. Claims of destiny serve to negate lust at her entry; at her parting, they counteract charges of fickleness and abandonment. *Qing*, "passion," and *yuan* 緣, "destined ties," have a complicated relationship for a being who is both the voice of destiny and its pawn. *Yuan* from another life are foundations for *qing*, but

29. In ibid., 1.27a–28b.

its pawn. *Yuan* from another life are foundations for *qing*, but *yuan* are exhausted before *qing*.

Shuzhen's exit differs from exits by other foxes because of her lingering ties to Xu and his world. After she has departed, she still sends her maids to her husband with sewing and poems expressing her longing for him. In every version, he is granted at least one idyllic visit with her in a mountain paradise. This story offers both the vixen in the human world and the human man in another world. The nature of this reunion varies. In "Huixian ji," when she invites him to see her one last time, he finds her single-mindedly devoted to burning incense and chanting sutras; she even refuses to sleep with him. The romance was initially controlled by subservience to conventional family morality, and in the end it is denied for the sake of transcendence. In some of the other versions, however, they do have sex again, and Shuzhen has clearly not overcome human passion.[30] Departure is certain, but whether it means transcendence or mutual longing is up for debate.

The tie of man and fox is maintained by the continuing appearances in this world of Shuzhen's maids. They allow the experience of the encounter with the fox to expand beyond the private or even the family level. The moral restraint with which Xu Jiefeng, the author of "Huixian ji," described his nephew's experience contrasts dramatically with the unabashed pleasure he derived from his own encounter with a transcendent. "Huixian ji" strays into autobiography at the typical point: Xu's kinship to the author is introduced at the end, where it is conventional for an author to explain how he came to write this story down. He asked his nephew for an interview with Shuzhen's maid, Su'e, who still carries messages for the couple. A group of friends gather, and Su'e, as a disembodied voice, announces her presence in the middle of the night. She recites a message from Shuzhen in the form of a *ci*, explains the lines and phrases they do not understand, and answers questions about all their past lives and destinies. The other maid, Qiuhong, also invisible, pours them marvelous tea and sings a song. This scene is even more clearly influenced by the fox oracle or the planchette than the scene in which

---

30. For example, in ibid., and "Jiaoqiao huanyu" 蛟橋幻遇, in Niu Xiu, *Gusheng*, 2.33.

Shuzhen answers the group's questions with moral platitudes. Like the planchette, it is a literary and social experience. The friends write *ci* matching Shuzhen's rhymes and make a collection of them.[31] The romance is placed under moral restraints, but those very restraints, like the lovers' separation, heighten the pleasure in communicating with supernatural women from a distance and in creating a fantastic entertainment. The title "Huixian ji" evokes the Tang tale "Yingying zhuan," which is also known as "Huizhen ji," another story in which a private romance becomes a shared literary experience.

The most detailed account of Xu and Shuzhen's story, and the one making the most elaborate claims to authenticity, is found in *Fufeng qiao chuanxin lu*. Wu Qian's preface claims that this is an edited version of the account of these events by Xu's grandfather. Its diary form is unprecedented in a fox story: in form as well as content, these marvelous encounters are rendered quotidian, but precisely that appears to add to their savor. Some Six Dynasties Daoist revelatory texts about encounters with transcendents appear in a diary format, but it is uncommon in mainstream *zhiguai*. The precedent suggests a tie with religious experience.[32] Kejin, as the *xiucai* grandfather of a peasant grandson, has a position of cultural and literary authority to judge these events. At the same time, he bears moral responsibility for supernatural intrusions in his household and views the alien women as daughters-in-law.

The editor Wu Qian's viewpoint adds an additional layer of historical mediation; writing more than a century later, he is looking back at the early Qing from the perspective of the high Qing. He approaches the topic with *kaozheng* fervor, praising the accuracy of the diary version in comparison to the distortions of oral and written transmission, and appends all the alternative versions. Although he applauds the diary's accuracy, he deplores its style:

---

31. This encounter is also recorded in *Fufeng qiao*, on the third of the first month, 1684; Wu Qian, *Fufeng qiao chuanxin lu*, 1.16a. Given this story's focus on *ci* and poetry, it is strange that none of the verse is included. Perhaps it was in an earlier version of the text.

32. See the revelations gathered by Tao Hongjing 陶弘景 in *Zhen'gao* 真誥 or *Zhoushi mingtong ji* 周氏冥通記.

Unfortunately although Kejin was an old *xiucai* who knew the meaning of literature, he was not up to assuming the duties of a historian, and did not ask her about the matters of the imperial harem of those [Song] days, just as in Ling Xuan's encounter with Tongde.[33] . . . He also could not exhaustively research the secrets of the transcendents or the arts of attaining immortality through inner alchemy; what he records are simply the ordinary miscellaneous tasks of this world. And there are also some places where his words fail to express his meaning.[34]

Although Kejin was in a superior intellectual position relative to his family, he is the inferior of his editor. There are echoes here of Shen Jiji's lament, in the closing comments to "Renshi zhuan," that Zheng was unable to do more than appreciate Ren's beauty and did not take advantage of his liaison with her to explore the boundaries between human and inhuman. The ordinariness of the proceedings are both the diary's claim to accuracy and its philosophical and artistic flaw. Wu Qian claims to have excised unnecessary detail, a claim that is hard to imagine given the wealth of domestic detail in his version.

The diary form makes the disproportionate allocation of time, four days of union as opposed to four years of separation, more obvious.[35] After Shuzhen's departure, the tie between worlds is distilled down to poetic exchanges and the most mundane household tasks, the sewing of shoes and clothing.[36] The maids also deliver prophecies and warnings against theft, performing the function of the protective fox spirit.[37] The precise dates of the warnings, reinforced by the diary

---

33. This is a reference to Ling Xuan, the alleged author of "Zhao Feiyan waizhuan," who heard the tales of Zhao Feiyan and her sister from his concubine Fan Tongde.

34. Wu Qian, *Fufeng qiao chuanxin lu*, preface.

35. A comparable earlier case is the Ming tale of a man's long-term relationship with a ghost. After scandal, they agree to meet only once a year for thirty years and leave extensive poetic records of these annual reunions. She also serves the function of a public oracle. See "Wang Qiuying"王秋英, in Mei Dingzuo, *Cai gui ji*, 13.225.

36. E.g., the shoe-bottoms Su'e fetches on the twenty-eighth of the second month, 1682, and the tops she brings to match them on the third of the third month; Wu Qian, *Fufeng qiao chuanxin lu*, 1.5b, 1.6b. Another exchange of shoes occurs in the first and second month of 1683; ibid., 1.9b–10.a.

37. E.g., on the twenty-eighth of the fifth month, Su'e passes on Shuzhen's message foretelling a misfortune in the eighth month that can be avoided by fasting, ritual, and Shuzhen's help at a distance. She also foretells the death of Kejin's wife. On

form, make it seem that Shuzhen and the maids are acting as an almanac. At the same time Shuzhen's protective acts take the form of ordinary religious practice, as she visits temples to offer incense.[38]

At the same time as this glorification of the mundane, the maids' reports give a sense of events unfolding in another world, as Shuzhen faces divine inspections, goes on longer pilgrimages, and moves her residence. Her movements allow glimpses of different levels of the divine world, such as the palaces on the moon, with a double degree of mediation, as the maids relate their mistress's experiences.[39] These acts are both remote and near at hand, anchored by the precise dates and the increasingly familiar figures of the various maids.

That this fusion of the ordinary and extraordinary should take the physical form of young maids is highly suggestive. In life, as in literature, they could pass between the separate realms of different sexes and classes, and by extension different levels of reality, more easily than their mistress could, for this story cycle works hard to give her upper-class respectability. When Xu makes clumsy advances to Su'e, both "Huixian ji" and *Fufeng qiao* stress that these maids are not sexually available;[40] nevertheless, their youth and beauty are not inconsequential for the primarily male audience. The multiplication of the maids allows every man to have his own Shuzhen, as is made plain in Xu Jiefeng's encounter, and even more so in the story "Hou Huixian ji," in which a friend of Xu's has a private exchange with one of the maids. She, too, rejects erotic advances in favor of another form of intimacy when she reveals that they had been brother and sister in another life.[41]

How seriously should we take Wu Qian's claims to have edited a genuine diary? This topic awaits thorough research. I find both possibilities plausible: either there was a diary of roughly the same date

---

the twenty-fifth of the tenth month, she warns of fire; and on the fifth and the seventh of the twelfth month, of thieves. Ibid., 1.7a–b, 8b. All these events date to 1682.

38. E.g., a pilgrimage to Wutai shan announced on the first day of the twelfth month, 1682 (ibid., 1.8a); she makes another offering, when Xu is sick, on the twenty-second of the second month, 1683 (1.10b).

39. The glimpse of the moon palace is related on the seventeenth of the eleventh month (ibid., 1.7b).

40. Ibid., 1.5b.

41. Copied in ibid., 1.23a–26a.

of "Huixian ji" (although how closely it resembles Wu Qian's edited version has yet to be determined), or the diary was a later composition, carefully incorporating all the incidents recorded in "Huixian ji." Wu Qian was a book collector and an energetic editor and preserver of old manuscripts, and this text is preserved in his personal *congshu* alongside his other projects.[42] *Shouyizhai kechuang biji* mentions the existence of a work that sounds very much like Kejin's diary; of the two items of lore learned from the fox it includes, one appears in *Fufeng qiao* and the other does not. In either case, as actual diary or fabrication, it is an extraordinary formal innovation. At the core of this story cycle's appeal is its quotidian quality, of which the diary is the perfect realization. I am convinced that an actual extraordinary experience of a family in Yixing was at the root of these texts. Comparison with Victorian spiritualism is compelling. In spiritualist terms, we could read the story as young Xu's experience as a medium for multiple personas, and his elders' attempts to deal with that situation. The emotional involvement of the grandfather in this experience recalls the experience of the Theobald family, who enjoyed decades of communion with their departed children.[43] The age dynamics of elders managing the experiences of their juniors is similar, but the crucial difference with the Victorian case is gender: unlike the Victorian case, which had mediums and spirits of both sexes, in the Xu family it is men who converse with supernatural women.

In accounts of this relationship, there is an emphasis on the tangible that which the fox leaves in this world. She bears Xu a daughter, who in *Fufeng qiao* seems to remain in that other world, but Xu Jiefeng notes that he has seen her, describing her as a mortal, not a fox. A Qianlong-era author describes seeing one of Shuzhen's poems in her own calligraphy.[44] Poetry, like calligraphy, makes marks in the historical world and becomes shared public memory. According to *Shouyizhai*, an account that makes narrative use of the historical gap between the Kangxi and Jiaqing reigns, Xu's descendants still treasured a portrait of Shuzhen and made offerings to it.[45] She seems

42. See his biography in *Qingshi liezhuan* 72.7b.
43. Alex Owen, *The Darkened Room*, pp. 75–106.
44. Wang Bishu, *Shuicao qingxia lu*, 12.6b.
45. Jin Pengcheng, *Shouyizhai kechuang biji*, 4.19a.

truly to have become an ancestress of a clan, like the fairy/snake Melusine in the European tradition, who becomes the respected ancestress of a noble house despite the fact she could not stay with her lover after he saw her in her reptile form. Shuzhen's story was both respectable enough, and closely enough linked to place, to be included in the local gazetteer.[46]

Shuzhen's identity as fox is stated at the beginning of each version of her story, but there is never any risk of exposure of the body of the fox. Rather, the story focuses more on her identity as *xian*. Xu Jiefeng opened his account with a meditation on what it means to be *xian* or to meet one.

As for my encounter with a *xian*, she was not a true *xian*, but since she resembled a *xian*, I regard her as one. I did not meet her face to face. But she spoke like a *xian*, knowing the affairs inside men's hearts, knowing men's future fortunes or misfortunes—could anyone other than a *xian* do this? When she spoke, it was as if I could see her face; I didn't see her form, but I could hear her voice. I asked and she answered, and all her words were accurate—isn't this like seeing her face?[47]

This is how a fox woman claims her place in the firmament, and this is how the man who has a partial encounter compensates.

Xu Jiefeng's concluding comments focus on the boundary between the strange and the ordinary:

The story of Shuzhen is both strange and not. Only Xu could see her form; no one else ever saw her. She came and went without a trace; the doors and windows did not open, and suddenly she was sitting on someone's bed. If one takes this as strange, this is truly strange. But she started with passion and continued with righteousness. She spoke of the doctrine of the mean, and what she practiced was the norm of human affairs. She often communicated through poems and songs, matching rhymes. If one considers this not to be strange, this is really not strange. *Hu* means "fox"; her beauty and faith to destined ties is "fair," *shu*; that she concealed her face and did not let others see it is "chaste" *zhen*; her name also shows her character. She was a fox but close to being a *xian*. The men of old would sail the seas to seek *xian*, but *xian* are not easy to meet. I got

---

46. *Yixing xian jiu zhi, juan mo* 87a–88b. Xu Jiefeng wrote the abbreviated account of the event in the gazetteer, which may explain its presence here.

47. Zhang Chao, *Yu Chu xinzhi*, 14.256.

to approach one at close range and talk with her and drink fragrant water and hear divine songs. This can be considered meeting a *xian*.[48]

Poetry and virtue are the means by which she makes herself normal; the virtues in her personal name, and the identity declared in her *zi*, Zhongxian 仲仙 (Second Transcendent), counteract the species revealed in her surname. The significance of this story, and I think the secret of its attraction, lies both in the combination of the private experience of the romance with the public experience of the séance, and in the combination of an affirmation of domesticity with its negation. The fairy bride cannot be contained by the bounds of domesticity, but at the same time she affirms its value by making shoes and manages the household from afar. The household goes through the annual cycle of festivals, funerals, and marriages, its daily life touched by the marvelous but undisturbed.

The two possibilities for idealization and redemption of the vixen offered by "Liehu zhuan" and Shuzhen's story are related to two possible kinds of death and deification for human women. The vixen as self-sacrificing paragon takes her place beside her human counterparts. The vixen who becomes a remote figure communicating through spectral poems resembles the deceased women who become transcendents communicating with men by means of the planchette.[49] The gap between fox and woman is larger in the latter case. Human women must die to achieve this state, but foxes can depart voluntarily. The fox is not simply a fantasy of availability and fulfillment; it is also a fantasy of a particular kind of loss.

THE VIXENS OF "LIAOZHAI"

The issues raised by both of *Yu Chu xinzhi*'s fox stories, the relationship between romance and virtue, domesticity and its limitations, and the exit of the fox, were also of keen importance to Pu Songling. Rather than offering a single solution to these dilemmas, he worked through them again and again, creating a unique vixen with each

48. Zhang Chao, *Yu Chu xinzhi*, 14.258.

49. See all the work that has been done on the cult of Xiaoqing, Ye Xiaoluan, esp. Ko, *Teachers of the Inner Chambers*, pp. 91–106; and Widmer, "Xiaoqing's Literary Legacy and the Place of the Woman Writer in Late Imperial China," pp. 111–55.

unique solution. He transformed the entire genre of the classical tale, but his influence on the theme of romance with supernatural women has been even more overwhelming. Even later authors who vehemently rejected him found it impossible to ignore him.[50]

The fame of the longer romances obscures the fact that *Liaozhai* contains a full range of stories from simple *zhiguai* to the longer *chuanqi*. Fox stories, and even fox romances, are no exception. At their simplest, stories of relationships with nameless vixens are dedicated to purposes other than exploring character. In "Huxie" the romance is simply the frame for jokes, and "Hu qie" 狐妾 (Fox concubine) seems to present a series of incidents rather than an individual.[51]

Pu Songling's inventiveness makes it impossible to choose a single representative fox romance among the many included in *Liaozhai* (seventeen, according to Wolfram Eberhard's count, out of a total of 86 stories that at least mention foxes).[52] The fox romances in *Liaozhai* do not provide a list of rules of fox behavior. Unlike Ji Yun, Pu did not demand consistency from his foxes. Sometimes the fox body is shameful and must be discarded; sometimes it can be accepted as human and safely ignored. Sometimes the plot goes through great convolutions so that the children will be purebred humans, but sometimes the half-breed children are the means of taming their fox mothers. Pu twisted the received material of the fox tradition in his own way.

Rather than a single definition of fox nature, analysis of *Liaozhai*'s fox romances reveals recurring roles and patterns in relationships between vixens and their lovers. These recurring features are not unique to fox stories. Pu's foxes have a great deal in common with his other

---

50. *Liaozhai* is also the most studied collection of the classical tale. In English, see Judith Zeitlin's *Historian of the Strange*, a study of a series of themes in the work, such as transference in gender, obsession, and dream; and Allan Barr's Ph.D. dissertation, which discusses issues of dating and editions, Pu Songling's life, and literary antecedents. The chapter in Li Wai-yee's *Enchantment and Disenchantment* devoted to *Liaozhai* discusses the central theme of desire and order. See Zeitlin's and Barr's works for extensive bibliographies.

51. *Liaozhai*, 4. 500–503, and 3.409–13, respectively.

52. Eberhard, *Die chinesische Novelle*, p. 36. The count of 86 comes from Gu Meigo, "Tan hu," pp. 252–53.

supernatural heroines, often more than they would with foxes in another collection, but I do not think that implies that their species is a superficial detail. Pu used foxes to explore a particular range of questions about sexuality, domesticity, and illusion.

Li Wai-yee argues that the principal dynamic of *Liaozhai* is "taming the strange," creating realms of fantasy and then reincorporating them into this world. Romances with supernatural women are a particularly dramatic example of this tension: they must both fulfill desires and rein them in.[53] The taming of the strange is a challenge facing all Qing authors. Pu Songling balanced the urge toward extravagant fantasy and moral constraints with a dexterity that was not duplicated; later writers often lost the joy of fantasy. Foxes are a special case of this general tendency toward domestication of anomaly and fantasy, as they are both the closest to us and the most ambivalent. Vixens' traditional identification with sex made them most obvious objects of wish fulfillment, but their new identity as protective spirits also granted them a role as forces of order.

SERIOUS FOX GAMES

Vixens in *Liaozhai* can loosely be divided into two groups: those in whom the vulpine force of chaos is rendered charming and attractive, transformed into theater and entertainment; and those who are protective providers. Monschein describes these two types as "mischievous imps" and maternal figures; I refer to them as the "younger" and "elder sister" types, respectively.[54] Every vixen can move from one pole to the other, and foxes' talents for chaos are often used in the service of a larger order. The ambiguity in the popular tradition between the fox as poltergeist and the fox as protective spirit is combined with ideas about women to take this form in Pu's work.

"Yingning" 嬰寧 is the purest example of the transformation of foxes' talent for mischief into charming childish silliness.[55] Yingning's *chi* 癡 (folly) is interesting since folly is usually the

---

53. Li Wai-yee, *Enchantment and Disenchantment*, p. 94. See also Barr, "Disarming Intruders: Alien Women in *Liaozhai zhiyi*," pp. 501–17.

54. Monschein, *Der Zauber der Fuchsfee*, part 7.1.1 and 7.1.3.

55. Ibid., pp. 267–71.

exclusive property of *Liaozhai*'s human heroes; its heroines are, in contrast, level-headed. Yingning's species is not enough to make her exceptional; she is given two eccentricities of her own, constant laughter and a fondness for flowers. The hero Wang's conventional lover's folly (*qingchi* 情癡) is answered by her failure to recognize the conventions of the romance. At each stage, from his first smitten stares to his treasuring of a token to his flirtatious advances, she responds with apparently uncomprehending laughter, revealing the silliness of those conventions. Her extreme naïveté is as far as possible from the traditional conniving seductions of the fox, and a particular show is made of her sexual innocence. When he declares his feelings, he has to explain to her the difference between conjugal and familial love. He replies, "They sleep together in one bed," to which she answers, "I'm not used to sleeping with strangers." After this conversation, she blurts out, "Cousin Wang wants to sleep with me," but fortunately her aunt does not hear. However, her innocence never reaches the point of indecent exposure of sexual matters. After they are wed, he is afraid she will openly discuss matters of the marriage bed, but she does not. Her "folly" does not interfere with an initial interlude of domestic bliss; "her craziness did not diminish her charm," and she proves adept at women's handiwork. Even such an apparently silly fox makes up for Ren's failings.

The pursuit of one of her other obsessions, flowers, shatters this bliss. When a neighbor sees her climbing a tree to admire flowers, he takes her laughter as flirtation and directions for a rendezvous. That night, he embraces and penetrates her, only to feel excruciating pain. It turns out that he has embraced a hollow tree with a scorpion in its crevasse, a particularly brutal image of the dangers of sex. Contained within this charming tale is a more conventional and sinister cautionary fox tale. At this moment, her folly suddenly loses its innocence, both laughter and flowers revealing a darker side.[56] The interference of a second man is one of the common plot devices that interrupts the happiness of a human/alien couple.

This crisis causes the transformation of Yingning's character. Rebuked by her mother-in-law, she never laughs again. Once her mad-

56. Li Waiyi, *Enchantment and Disenchantment*, pp. 109–10.

ness is proved to have a method, her kinship with the other foxes who use mischief for their own calculated purposes becomes clear. The Historian of the Strange himself suggests in his final comment that Yingning may indeed have been aware and in control the entire time: "To see how she giggles and titters foolishly, it would seem as though she is totally mindless; yet the ruse beneath the wall is very clever indeed. . . . Indeed, my Yingning conceals herself behind her laughter."[57] Even the most childish fox remains in active control of the plot.

As well as being a story about apparent and true folly, this is a tale examining the interactions of families and generations when a young couple is married. The youth of both Yingning and Wang is essential to the plot. They are children, fatherless, and still under the protection of strong maternal figures. Yingning is Wang's first love and first wife, a standing that gives their affair a different quality from that of the married man whose human wife stands at the margins of the fox story, like Qingfeng's Geng Qubing, Miss Ren's lover Zheng, or Hu Shuzhen's young Xu. Yingning is plainly a virgin, an exceptional situation for a fox. If "Qingfeng" is a story of a woman torn between her husband and her natal family, both "Yingning" and the next story I discuss, "Xiaocui," are stories about daughters-in-law attempting to adapt to their new families. Yingning's heritage is complicated. The hero Wang's maternal aunt had married a man named Qin but died soon afterward. The widower Qin was seduced by a fox, who bore a daughter, Yingning. Qin's story is a miniature of the old story of fox seduction, illness, and exorcism. Yingning's fox mother left, driven away by amulets, leaving her daughter in the care of the ghost of Wang's aunt, who acts the maternal role proper for a first wife's relationship to a concubine's child. This contrived lineage has several functions: it makes supernatural occurrences part of family history, so that Yingning is both an alien woman and Wang's maternal cousin, the perennial focus of romantic fantasies of lovers who meet in childhood. Yingning is a fox's child rather than a fox herself. I am not

---

57. *LZ*, 2.159. Translation from Li Wai-yee, *Enchantment and Disenchantment*, p. 110. For a translation of the complete story, see Mair and Mair, *Strange Stories from a Make-do Studio*, pp. 73–89. An alternative text reads, "When was my Yingning ever foolish?" 我嬰寧何嘗憨耶 (Pu Songling, *Pu Songling quanji*, p. 61).

suggesting that Pu had some rational construction of "half-fox" identity, but that the focus is on Yingning as child, an innocent between the realms of fox, ghost, and man.[58] Yingning's story is completed when she begs that Wang help her rebury her ghost stepmother. Filial piety transforms her twice: she stops laughing for her mother-in-law, and she weeps for her foster mother. Incorporation of the kin from the wife's side, no matter how weird, is essential to true domestic happiness. One could read this story as a fantasy about the transcendent power of kinship ties as much as a fantasy about ghosts and foxes.

Although Xiaocui's 小翠 actions also seem inexplicable, she differs from Yingning in that she always seems to be firmly in control. The story's opening is a good example of how Pu Songling incorporated older *zhiguai* material in a longer story. A fox hides under the body of the youth Wang Taichang to avoid being struck by lightning.[59] His brother says this must be an omen of his future greatness, and he indeed passes the *jinshi* examination at a young age. This anecdote could stand entirely on its own as a brief *zhiguai*. Years later, a mysterious old woman appears and agrees to marry her daughter to Wang's idiot son. Rather than explaining the karmic motivation for the romance at the story's close, Pu included it in the story. The unclear, furry creature of the opening incident is as far from Xiaocui as the mildly frightening tone of the opening is from the playful content of the whole.[60]

---

58. In another story, the vixen mother of a half-fox, Qingmei, leaves the child with her father when he marries ("Qingmei" 青梅, in *LZ*, 4.444). The offspring of mixed marriages are less prominent in Chinese fox romances than in Japanese tales. The exceptions include a speculative and joking anecdote by Ji Yun, speculating on the identity of a half-fox child in his vixen mother's custody (*YWCT*, 9.434, story 154). A story of a man who claimed his mother was a vixen appears in more than one Guangxu collection; see "Daji zhi mu wei hu" 達基之母爲狐, Xu Ke, *Qingbai leichao*, *ce* 34, p. 163.

59. The idea that foxes are especially prone to being struck by lightning as heavenly punishment for their illicit status is fairly common in Ming/Qing *zhiguai*. Human men rescuing vixens from lightning is another sort of favor that foxes repay in sexual currency. The motif is also used in "Jiaona" 嬌娜, in *LZ*, 1.57–65.

60. *LZ*, 7.1000; for a translation, see Owen, *An Anthology of Chinese Literature*, pp. 1113–20.

This story takes the general tendency for supernatural women to have passive husbands to an extreme. Xiaocui's idiot husband is a toy in her hands. In a reversal of "Yingning," he is the one who fails to understand the sexual implications of marriage. She dresses him up as the hegemon Xiang Yu or a desert nomad and herself as an appropriate counterpart, Lady Yu or Wang Zhaojun, all roles that prefigure their eventual separation. Her games link fox illusion to drama, and the beauties of history are subjects of play rather than serious association. All of her magic is translated into the human techniques of the stage; she makes herself up as Wang Zhaojun rather than "really" transforming herself. Her time in the Wang household is structured by a pattern of increasingly outrageous games met with escalating anger from her parents-in-law. She is inscrutable and apparently indifferent in the face of their accusations, silently playing with her belt or the bed. The same fantasy and whimsy that makes foxes an entertaining subject for literature does not necessarily make them endearing housemates.

Each one of her playful spectacles turns out to have a serious purpose in fooling her father-in-law's enemies. She dresses up as a high official and convinces a scheming neighbor that her father-in-law has powerful friends. When later that same enemy catches her idiot husband dressed up as an emperor, he seizes the imperial costume and uses it as grounds to accuse Xiaocui's father-in-law of rebellion. When the emperor is shown the imperial robes, they prove to be ridiculous and shabby toys, so he not only pardons her father-in-law but has his enemy banished for slander. This scene is a reversal of the *zhiguai* commonplace in which a fox's gifts prove to be leaves and weeds; here the exposure of illusion is just as useful as illusion itself.

The next problem that presents itself is the lack of a grandchild. The couple is forced to sleep in one bed, but the idiot complains that Xiaocui kicks and squashes him. It is at the moment when Xiaocui seems most purely a force of chaos that she crosses the line and becomes the protective and healing kind of fox. There are hints of a sexual awakening in this scene: the idiot wants to join her in the bath, and after the bath she smothers him. When he wakes from his unconsciousness, he is no longer an idiot. At the moment when her parents-in-law believe their son is dead, their rage against her reaches its extreme, and the specter of the mischievous fox who throws a household into disorder and destroys young men is raised. Yet instead of causing men's sexual destruction, foxes are given the task of making inadequate men whole.[61]

Xiaocui maintains perfect control over her exit as well. Their wedded bliss after the cure of his idiocy is allowed to endure for only about a sentence. She breaks a precious vase (which also has political importance, since her parents-in-law were considering using it as a bribe), is scolded for it, and uses this as an excuse to depart. The exposure of her species to some extent maintains its traditional position in the narrative. It is on the brink of her departure that she reveals that she is a fox and the daughter of the creature whom his father had saved from lightning. Xiaocui's payment is to the family line, rather than her husband himself. This occasion for departure seems very arbitrary, as the Qing commentators also point out. It seems unlikely that someone of her skill should have broken anything by accident, and her reaction to this scolding is out of proportion. Perhaps after enduring the insults that were necessary to fulfill her karmic debt, she was unwilling to endure more for any other reason.

According to Barr's argument on the relative dating of parts of *Liaozhai*, "Xiaocui" was composed later than "Yingning." It seems to be a later, less idealistic return to the problem of assimilating a strange daughter-in-law into a human family.[62] The emphasis on Xiaocui's relationship with her parents-in-law is even stronger since her husband is such a nonentity for the first half of the story. Yingning and Xiaocui take opposite paths: Yingning succeeds in adapting, and Xiaocui returns to her own world.

THE FOX AS SAVIOR

Examples of the "elder sister" kind of fox, the fox as a source of order, are more numerous than playful vixens in *Liaozhai* and its imitators. It is, however, relatively rare for a fox to assume this role from the outset; it is, rather, the transformation of a sexual or comic diversion into deliverance that fascinates. Both Yingning and Xiaocui's

---

61. A fox cures the hero's stunted manhood in "Qiaoniang" 巧娘, *LZ*, 2.256.

62. Barr ("Pu Songling and *Liaozhai zhiyi*," p. 103) dates "Yingning" to the early period and "Xiaocui" to the middle.

services to their families are disguised. Hongyu 紅玉 enters the story in an undisguised supernatural one-night stand but then finds an acceptable human woman as a substitute. When the man's human wife dies, she rescues his infant son and returns to help the man to re-establish his family. The story closes with approving comments about how hard she works.[63]

Two tales of fox rescuers, "Jiaona" 嬌娜 and "Fengxian" 鳳仙, are also accounts of men coming to terms with entire clans of foxes. Whereas the emphasis in "Qingfeng" was on the ties between generations, here the focus is on ties between siblings and siblings-in-law. The protagonist of "Jiaona," Kong Xueli, is introduced into the fox family through a male-to-male friendship, as he becomes the unofficial tutor of a young man almost his age. The situation of a penniless tutor in the service of a wealthier family was familiar to Pu Songling from his own experience.[64] In this tale the economic relationship is softened by friendship and then familial ties. It is the young male fox (with the approval of the more distant fox patriarch) who acts as Kong's financial support and arranges for him to marry a vixen cousin. Kong's relationship is clearly with the clan as a whole; at the pivotal moment he is asked to rescue the entire family from being struck by lightning. As in "Qingfeng," the happy ending has the fox relatives settle down next door, but the emphasis is on the diversions of drinking, chess, and conversation with his fox peers.[65]

Jiaona appears after this familial intimacy has been established. She is the only one who can heal a sudden illness afflicting Kong, and this situation facilitates an intimacy that would otherwise be impossible. Jiaona is both competent healer and flirtatious child (at thirteen, she is even younger than Yingning), mixing the elder and younger sister types. Although the convention of a fox woman as a

63. *LZ*, 2.276. "Hongyu" seems to be a blend of a fox story with a much harsher story about the crimes committed by unjust ministers and their eventual revenge.

64. Barr, "Pu Songling and *Liaozhai zhiyi*," pp. 177–84.

65. *LZ*, 1. 57–65. For a translation, see "Jiaonuo," in Mair and Mair, *Strange Tales from a Make-do Studio*, pp. 25–37.

healer predates *Liaozhai*, going back at least to the Song,[66] Pu provided graphic descriptions of her medical practices rather than simply having her supply a miraculous pill. When Kong is afflicted with a large, painful growth on his chest, Jiaona encircles the growth with a bracelet, presses down, and excises it. Then she coughs up a red pill and presses it into the wound. This is her *dan*, the inner elixir that is the physical essence of her self-cultivation. The relatively realistic surgical procedure (although the use of her bracelet as a prop again emphasizes her femininity) is combined with the lore of foxes' *neidan*, which in the form of a pill is the standard means by which foxes heal humans, whether in romantic tales or popular worship.[67] The *dan* is a physical manifestation of foxes' difference from humans, but it suggests power and progress, unlike the physical traces of the beast. The gruesome physical details of the treatment only serve to emphasize the hero's enchantment with Jiaona; seeing her beauty, he forgets his pain and hopes the treatment will be prolonged. Since the hero and Jiaona are denied sexual consummation, all attention is focused on their physical contact as she treats him. In the climatic scene when Kong is attempting to save the fox clan from lightning, he rescues Jiaona from a demon but is stricken by lightning and falls dead. She revives him in turn. Her *dan* is the center of an even more intimate scene of healing, as she pushes it from her throat into his, effectively bringing him back to life with a kiss.[68] With this gesture she entirely reverses the tradition of the fox as sexual parasite. Their consummation is saving each other's lives.

Although Jiaona is clearly the focus of the tale, she is not the one Kong marries, because she is too young. Instead he weds her voiceless cousin Songniang, who bears him a son and acts as helpmate as he attains high office. Pu Songling diverts the potential boredom of acquisition, tameness, and domesticity into another character, while Jiaona remains both close and unattainable. Before he meets Jiaona a second time, she is married off to someone else, a realistic conclusion

66. For example, in "Xiaolian ji" 小蓮記, in Liu Fu, *Qingsuo gaoyi, hou ji*, 3.128–29.

67. Li Wei-tsu, "On the Cult of the Four Sacred Animals," p. 59.

68. On the love triangle and the sexual quality of the healing scenes, see Li Wai-yee, *Enchantment and Disenchantment*, pp. 126–27.

thwarting unrequited passion for a younger in-law. Yet her husband and his entire family (elsewhere at the time) are destroyed by the fatal lightning strike, so at the end she remains with her brother's family, conveniently situated for platonic pleasures. In his comment, Pu Songling lauds Jiaona as an ideal of platonic friendship, superior to a romantic relationship. This ideal seems even more difficult to achieve in human circles than romantic bliss, and vixens again fill in a void in humans' social worlds.

"Fengxian" contains the whole range of the fox story, from the playful lover to the exemplary wife who fulfills the desires for both erotic indulgence and orthodox achievement. The relationship begins with Fengxian traded ignominiously for her sister Baxian's pants, which were left behind in an interrupted tryst. The interest in this story lies in the tensions between married sisters in an extended family, rather than between a man and his relatives by marriage, or between human and fox. When the man, Liu, meets all his new fox relatives, it seems an excuse to stage elaborate banquet scenes, with the sisters competing against each other using clever lines and artistic skills.

The story is not allowed to maintain that tone, however; Fengxian abruptly departs, leaving only a mirror in which her image urges her lover to study. The end of the story reverts to a playful tone, but this is only allowed once he has dutifully passed the exam.[69] Fengxian's earlier anger when she thought her father favored another sister's husband above her own because of his wealth also raises the suspicion that she may be improving her husband in order to show up her sisters, rather than for purely selfless reasons. Nevertheless, once again a man is tamed by a relationship every bit as much as the fox is.

Foxes can be rescuers from many different ills: Hongyu provides deliverance from economic and political despair, Jiaona saves a man from physical illness, and Fengxian saves a man from himself. In some later stories, the conjugal relationship is eliminated altogether while the vixen remains a maternal deliverer: we have seen a version of this in the tie between an old man and his vulpine foster-daughter in "The Red Girl" (see Chapter 2). The relative ages of man and

---

69. *LZ*, 9.1177–84.

vixen are reversed in the story "Fox Mother," which appears in more than one collection. An older vixen provides material needs, and even a wife, for a young orphan.[70]

THE FOX REPLACES HERSELF

Substitution of one woman for another is a major structural principle in *Liaozhai*, as it had been in earlier tales. Doubling and mistaken identity are staples of both the uncanny and the romance. In "Axiu" 阿繡, the fox takes the form of the human woman the hero cannot have and in the end brings the human couple together. First she is the substitute, and then she replaces herself. This is a more complex variation on the old theme of the fox as doppelgänger. "Axiu" is one of the few *Liaozhai* fox stories with a trail of fairly clear textual antecedents.[71] This basic plot appears in a Ming story in *Guang yanyi bian* in the animal category under the title "Jiang sheng" 蔣生, and in *Qingshi* in the "fox matchmaker" category under the title "Dabie shanhu" 大別山狐.[72] It is retold as a vernacular story in *Erke pai'an jingqi* and as the play *Jiaopa ji*. A very elaborate classical tale version that includes a considerable amount of poetry appears in *Youguai shitan* 幽怪詩談 (Poetry talks of the spectral and strange; 1629).[73] In outline, a man catches a glimpse of a neighbor girl and falls in love with her. She soon offers herself to him. After they commence an illicit affair, she joins him nightly, but eventually his friends convince him that it is unlikely that a girl of good family could sneak out like this. One night he gives her a leaking bag of sesame seeds and follows her trail after she leaves, only to find a sleeping fox. When she

---

70. "Hu mu" 狐母, in Yu Rukang, *Kuaixin xingshui lu*, 1.11a; in Zhu Yuqing, *Zhucun tanguai*, 10.1a; and in Pan Lun'en, *Daoting tushuo*, 2.25–28.

71. The "sources" cited in such works as *Liaozhai ziliao huibian* are often only the loosest parallels. See Barr, "Pu Songling and *Liaozhai zhiyi*," pp. 195–96.

72. Wu Dazhen, *Guang yanyi bian*, 6:30.2a; Feng Menglong, *Qingshi leilüe*, 12.939. For a translation of the *Qingshi* version and comparisons to the *Guang yanyi bian* version, see Mowry, *Chinese Love Stories from Ch'ing-shih*, pp. 95–98. Since *Guang yanyi bian* is a compendium drawing on earlier material, with particularly liberal use of *Taiping guangji*, it is also quite likely not the original source of this story.

73. See "Zeng zhima shipo jiaxing, xie caoyao qiaoxie zhenou," in Ling Mengchu, *Erke pai'an jingqi*, 2:29.1371 and Bishan woqiao, *Youguai shitan*, *juan* 5.

wakes, she promises to help him to attain the real girl. In a move reminiscent of Ren's tactics for acquiring a substitute lover for Wei, she gives him the means to make the girl sick and then to cure her.[74] The fox fulfills a man's sexual desires in two ways: she provides false and immediate gratification and then helps to make the fantasy entirely real. This plot is closely related to the *Li hun ji* 離魂記 (The disembodied soul; eighth century), plot in which the woman's soul follows her lover while her body stays behind. Both stories fulfill the fantasy of illicit love while allowing the true bride to remain pure.[75]

This story illustrates Pu Songling's talent at embroidering on a received plot, both by adding realistic details to the description of unrequited love and by elaborating the alternation of the real and the false Axiu. The hero, Liu Zigu, falls in love with Axiu, the daughter of a shopowner, calling on her frequently and buying many things he does not need. Her family moves away, and when he sends a matchmaker, he is told she is already engaged. In despair he wishes that there might be one who resembled her, a wish fulfilled by the fox. Once again, illusion appears to be a product of the human mind. Lodging away from home, he unexpectedly meets Axiu. Claiming to be the relative of a neighbor, she comes to him nightly until they are found out by a perceptive servant, who asks why she is wearing the same clothes as she did so long ago and points out that the woman does not entirely resemble Axiu: her face is too pale and thin, and she has no dimples. The fox's imitation is less than perfect. When confronted with the truth, the fox, unlike her predecessor in the Ming story, is unrepentant and unashamed: "Although I am not Axiu, I think I am not inferior to her. When you look at me, do you feel as you did before or not?" She leaves and promises Liu she will

---

74. The ending of the *Guang yanyi bian* version is more ambivalent than the happy ending of the *Qingshi* version. The girl's ailment is described in more revolting detail—her sores reek so much that even her family will not stay near her. She is essentially kidnapped by the hero, who cures her ailment. She resents her family for selling her to this rapacious man and doing nothing to rescue her. Mowry characterizes the *Qingshi* version as the better story. It is certainly a smoother love story, but the rough edges of the *Guang yanyi bian* version are interesting in their own right.

75. There is one crucial difference: the variant in which the double is a fox is more male-centered, and that in which the double is the woman's own soul is a more suitable vehicle for expression of female desire.

return after she has compared her beauty with that of the new bride. Rather than simply playing the deceiver, the fox herself is obsessed with the comparison of true and false.

Liu has less agency in winning his lady love than did his predecessor in the Ming tale, since the fox manages everything. The fox rescues the real Axiu when the area is ravaged by bandits and sends her to meet Liu, who has difficulty acknowledging her as the true Axiu. They ride home together to marry, yet the story does not end there.

In the older story, the division between the part of the story with the false lover and the resolution with the true bride would be absolute. Pu, however, mixes the two; deception recurs after the happy ending, but it is safely contained within domestic space. When Liu and Axiu are reunited, he goes to look at the box of the goods he had bought from her so long ago. He discovers that a container of rouge is merely red dirt. Axiu explains that since she realized he was paying no attention to his purchases, she had tricked him. Just as they are laughing at the exposure of this deception, the fox appears and demands that the matchmaker should be thanked. This story links the deceptions of the human romance—he did not really come to her shop to buy, and she gave him false goods in return—to supernatural deceptions. In another echo of earlier confusion, one night when the hero comes home drunk, Axiu asks him who is more beautiful, she or the fox. He replies that she is the superior, although a shallow man could not detect the difference. Hearing this reply, the vixen reveals she has come back to test him. The second time around the deception is a joke, but it raises the question of how well he knows his wife. Adding another layer to the story, the fox reveals that the relationship between herself and the human bride is not entirely contrivance. The real Axiu herself is the fox's sister reborn. When the fox sisters had seen the Queen Mother of the West they both vied to imitate her beauty. Axiu succeeded brilliantly in a month, but the elder fox sister was not her match even after three. This imitation provides a possible precedent for the later expansion of "Laohu tan lidai meiren." This background complicates the issue of truth and illusion: Axiu's own beauty was originally an imitation, but it is still to be prized as the more successful imitation. In the conclusion of the story, the two women imitate each other in a petty domestic context:

when the real Axiu is away visiting her family, the fox sometimes takes her place supervising her household, and if there is anything missing, she threatens the servants with headaches and fox persecution until they return it. They are appropriately cowed. Yet even when the fox stops coming, the real Axiu imitates her methods in order to keep the household in order,[76] a tactic that begs the question of who the real fox is after all.

In Pu's hands the received plot material retains its basic elements as a fantasy that allows a man to bifurcate his desires, to have both premarital sex and a virginal bride, but it has also become a playful exploration of the nature of illusion and identity. Uncertainty about identity has none of the horror of the earliest doppelgänger tales, in which monsters replaced relatives. Rather, it becomes a game played by women within the house. The popularity of the substitution plot both before and in *Liaozhai* seems based on an awareness of the tension in romantic love between recognition and appreciation of a unique individual and pursuit of an illusory ideal. It is the vixen who raises the question of whether love is based on recognition or illusion, and in Pu's story she keeps raising it after marriage.

FOXES IN TRIANGLES

Pu Songling's interest in the love triangle has been noted in earlier studies.[77] In "Lianxiang" 蓮香, "Chang'e" 嫦娥, and to a lesser extent "Qiaoniang" 巧娘, he uses the triangle to explore the difference between two species as well as two female characters. The elder sister/younger sister roles are revealed more clearly when two women act as foils for each other. In a pair of women the fox does not have a predetermined role; rather, the elder and younger sister roles explore different aspects of fox nature. These love triangles never expand to become quadrangles or more. In this sense the *Liaozhai* romances fit the special case of two-women polygamy, which McMahon, in his analysis of vernacular fiction, considers a variation of the chaste

76. *LZ*, 7.991–98.

77. Barr, "Pu Songling and *Liaozhai zhiyi*," pp. 71–93; Li Wai-yee, *Enchantment and Disenchantment*, pp. 122–136.

romance rather than erotic fiction.[78] Pu Songling's interest lies in the tensions of the triangle, rather than in a long and varied series of erotic partners. In these tales of triangles, it is the incorporation of two women into a single household, not the ties of men and women to their kin by marriage, that is the focus of interest.

"Lianxiang" plays with the structure of the love triangle by nesting two conventional demon stories within each other. The story uses these recurrences to question the relationship among words, expectations, and truth. A young scholar named Sang, who lives alone, is asked in jest whether he fears foxes or ghosts. When he replies bravely, "If a male comes, I have a sharp sword; if a female, I would open the door and take her in," his friends hire a prostitute to call on him pretending to be a ghost. After his terror and subsequent embarrassment when the joke is found out, he accepts the appearance of the two supernatural heroines with inappropriate calm. Mistaken impressions link the heroines: when the vixen Lianxiang introduces herself as a prostitute, this seems entirely plausible; and when the ghost Li first appears, he fears she is a fox.

Under the elaborate recurrences of the plot, the basic outlines of the demon story dominate the first half of the story: a web of mistaken impressions is first established and then unraveled in a pivotal scene of recognition. As in a tale of sexual parasitism, the hero's illness from sexual overindulgence precipitates the scene of recognition. However, it is the two women who expose each other's identity. The second half of the story essentially undoes the demon story by erasing the two women's supernatural identities and turning them into the real human women the hero had assumed they were. Once again, deception turns true.[79]

As mentioned in the previous chapter, the difference between the fox Lianxiang and the ghost Li is that between a prostitute and a girl of good family. In contrast to the sexually experienced but restrained Lianxiang, Li was a virgin before she met Sang. It is Li who makes extravagant oaths of eternal devotion, even though she "comes every night without fail," the mark of a sexual parasite. Lianxiang makes

---

78. McMahon, *Misers, Shrews, and Polygamists*, pp. 115–22.

79. *LZ*, 2.220–32; for a translation, see Owen, *Anthology of Chinese Literature*, pp. 1103–13.

no declarations but prudently rations sex. Since Li reappears every time Sang touches a shoe she left behind, she is the one who is marked with both enchantment and sexuality. Lianxiang is in general the more worldly and knowledgeable; she is the maternal healer, Li the petulant, childish charmer. Li Wai-yee describes Lianxiang as being used to control the ghost Li's desires,[80] as Lianxiang cures the hero of the illness brought on by his overindulgence with Li. Lianxiang is in control of the plot, whereas Li is the focus of erotic interest.

This story is one of the few cases in *Liaozhai* in which a fox openly discusses being a fox. The two heroines exchange facts about their respective species with frank curiosity. Lianxiang argues that she has chosen not to be dangerous to men, but that Miss Li as a ghost has no control over her sexual deadliness. The conclusion that there are harmless foxes whereas a ghost cannot help being deadly is certainly not supported by other stories. Although "Lianxiang" does expose the difference between the species, the tale is primarily interested in exploring the two as parallel conditions.[81] In this case both ghosthood and foxhood are conditions that must be overcome by rebirth in a human body, but this seems imposed by the parallel construction of the story rather than a general principle.

Once Sang's illness is cured, the next problem is to create a happy polygamous family by converting the two into human women. Li's soul takes over the body of a local notable's daughter who had recently died.[82] There is a brief period of unity, but then Lianxiang dies in childbirth, only to be reborn as a human being and rejoin them fourteen years later. Again, confusion in identity is resolved by recognition of the two in their new human bodies. The order in which the two figures appeared is neatly reversed: since Li is the first to attain a human body, when Lianxiang is restored to the polygamous family she is younger by far. Yet Li is still the rightful wife and

---

80. Li Wai-yee, *Enchantment and Disenchantment*, p. 127.

81. The Qing commentator Dan Minglun sensitively pointed out these parallels; see *LZ*, 2.230.

82. A soul claiming the body of another person who had recently died is a relatively common occurrence in *Liaozhai* tales and other *zhiguai*; see, e.g., "Huang Jiulang" 黃九郎 and "Lu Pan" 陸判, 3.316, and 2.139, respectively.

Lianxiang a concubine. Their final unity is sealed when Li's bones are buried together with Lianxiang's fox corpse, and the signs of their earlier selves are united. This odd burial becomes something of a tourist attraction. The story itself contains the marvel's transformation into narrative and spectacle. The interplay of mistaken identities and recognitions seems, like "Axiu," to be making a statement on the nature of love as equal parts of recognition and delusion. Sang is passive, but he is the one who recognizes and misrecognizes, and it is the women who transform their identities around him.

In "Chang'e," the contrast is between a fox and an exiled transcendent. This story is more cloudy and more ambiguous than "Lianxiang." If one accepts Barr's arguments regarding the relative dates of composition of parts of *Liaozhai*, it may represent a more sophisticated return to similar material later in Pu's life.[83] Pu had already played with the structure of recurrences of two supernatural women; now he was interested in a more complex relationship between the two. Whereas the plot of "Lianxiang" is focused on incorporating the two supernatural women into a polygamous family, much of the plot of "Chang'e" focuses on the tensions between the two in the polygamous situation. The predominant vector is escape from the family, not entrance into it. The first half of the story consists of alternation between the heroines, the second the resolution within the household. The transcendent Chang'e and the fox Diandang do not compete for the hero Zong's attentions; on the contrary, they contrive to yield to one another. As Li Wai-yee notes, "Both heroines seem ambivalent about total commitment and thus try to seek each other out as a surrogate mate for the hero."[84] Human domesticity has changed from the ultimate goal of the supernatural women to a trap of the passions.

In the first half of the story, the two women alternate in their liaisons with the hero, but the fox Diandang clearly plays the secondary role; she is Zong's second choice when he cannot attain Chang'e and backs off to allow him to marry his first choice. In the first part of the story, she is united with the hero only for brief periods of time, which receive relatively little narrative attention, whereas Chang'e

83. Barr ("Pu Songling and *Liaozhai zhiyi*," chap. 2) places "Lianxiang" in the second of his eight divisions and "Chang'e" in the sixth.

84. Li Wai-yee, *Enchantment and Disenchantment*, p. 128.

and Zong live as a monogamous couple for some time.[85] When her destined span of exile in the mortal world is over, Chang'e pretends to have been abducted by robbers. Like many *Liaozhai* tales, "Chang'e" contains an older story, in this case the tale of the exiled transcendent who inevitably escapes human domesticity, and works on reversing its conclusion. After Chang'e attempts to exit monogamy, Diandang helps Zong to win her back, and Chang'e in turn makes sure that Diandang is also captured within the polygamous family. Just as Chang'e is thwarted in her exit, Diandang is frustrated in her attempt to substitute another for herself.

During her first union with the hero, Chang'e plays a fox-like role and impersonates historical beauties for her lover's amusement. During the second, polygamous union, Chang'e takes on a more solemn and asexual role, and Diandang is sexual and silly, clearly the younger sister. They seem to embody two aspects of Pu's supernatural women, the one who entangles people in desire and the one who is beyond desire. Diandang not only takes up the historical theatrics that Chang'e had abandoned but also imitates Chang'e, underlining the constant exchange between the two. When a maid participating in Diandang's games dies in the role of Yang Guifei, the reference is also to Miss Ren, who died at Mawei too, but the danger is deflected from the fox herself. The historical theatrics over which Xiaocui had complete control turn dangerous in this story. Domesticity is attained through restraint of these games, rather than, as in Lianxiang, rejection of the physical substance of the fox. Li Wai-yee sees Chang'e as the controller of passion,[86] but it seems to me that Diandang's folly is an equally crucial element in their domestic harmony: without her interference, Chang'e would never have remained in this world. The balance of the two heroines is what allows a paradise on earth—Chang'e's control restrains Diandang, and Diandang's passions keep Chang'e in this world.

The moment when Diandang playfully bites Chang'e's foot, sending a current of desire through Chang'e, provides a fascinating examination of the inherent seductiveness of the fox. This erotic play between the two women takes place with their husband watching.

---

85. *LZ*, 8.1069–79.
86. Li Wai-yee, *Enchantment and Disenchantment*, pp. 129–30.

Biting the foot is a more explicit act than Pu usually describes between men and women. Chang'e curses this seductiveness as an amoral force: "So you don't even choose a proper target before deploying your seductive wiles?"[87] Diandang in reply argues that this seductiveness arose involuntarily from her great affection for Chang'e. This exploration of desire and sentiment seems to be possible only between two women (compare Feng Sanniang's confession of passion). A vixen, or any female, would have difficulty arguing that she accidentally seduced a man because of her affection. To link *mei* to genuine affection goes a long way toward redeeming this trait of the fox. Diandang's love is entangling but, like human affections, not black magic; Chang'e's love would cure her and set them all free.

The contrast between these two stories reveals the range of the fox from beneficent healer to playful force of lust. The contrasts with a ghost on the one hand and a transcendent on the other delineate the fox's territory. The fox stands on the borderline between controlled and uncontrolled desire, acting both as controller and controlled. The love triangle plot uses two women as symbols of different aspects of desire, but the symbolic conflict between the pairs of women is worked out through mundane affection and rivalry. The love triangle working on these two levels seems to be one of the central themes of the Qing romance, embodied most powerfully and famously in *Honglou meng*.

THE DEPARTURE OF THE VIXEN

In "Chang'e," the two women end up remaining with their husband despite Chang'e's strong desire to return to heaven, but not every fox romance in *Liaozhai* ends with the fox secure in domestic unity. It would be tempting to construct a master narrative of the fox romance as long centuries of vixens striving to approach the hearth and home, with *Liaozhai* as the perfect moment of fulfillment. After that moment, the happy ending is debased by repetition and decadence. There is some truth to the master narrative, but its weakness lies in the facts that interest in the departure of the vixen may predate the happy ending and that the two appear simultaneously in Pu

87. Translation from ibid., p. 129.

Songling's own work. The question of how a vixen might stay is accompanied by the question of how she might leave.

As we have seen, the story of Hu Shuzhen raises the question of the vixen who leaves. The imperative that a man who wins a supernatural bride will lose her is suggested by folklore studies, especially by the story of the Swan Maiden, who flies away once she regains her feathered cloak. Overt versions of this story, in which a fox is trapped in domesticity by a man who steals the token of her alien identity, can be found in Ming and Qing collections, but it is not the mainstream of the fox tradition.[88] Comparison with such stories reveals a lingering doubt, shared in many cultures, whether an alien can be entirely claimed by the human, or a woman entirely tamed by a man. The shared structural necessity of a woman leaving the home takes a culturally specific form as transcendence.

This transcendence was essential to the story of human liaisons with superior beings from the earliest times, and foxes claim it as they ascend to the status of *xian*. Pu Songling's definition of a *xian* is a complicated balance of passion and detachment. For a *xian*, to love is to fall to a lower plane, but not irreversibly. This concept of *xian* is gender based; for a male transcendent to surrender to passion for a mortal is a rarer violation, and viewed less sympathetically.[89] A vixen as *xian* is both the perfect object of a human man's desire and a creature who is in the process of overcoming her own desires. The foxes prove that they have achieved humanity by being perfect embodiments of domesticity, but then they must transcend both humanity and domesticity.

Xiaocui is a good example of this tension. Her departure is not simple. After she has angrily departed because of the disagreement over the broken vase, her husband succeeds in finding her again, but she is too proud to return to his parents' house and stays instead in a garden some distance away. She refuses to come back even when her

88. See Leavy, *In Pursuit of the Swan Maiden*. For Ming-Qing examples, see "Huzi gui'er guai'er" 狐子鬼兒怪兒, in Wang Tonggui, *Ertan leizeng, waiji*: *hu*, 1a; and "Chu san nie" 除三孽, in Xuan Ding, *Yeyu qiudeng lu*, 8 344.

89. One exception would be Lu Dongbin's adventures with the courtesan Bai Mudan; see Katz, "Enlightened Alchemist or Immoral Immortal?" in Shahar and Weller, *Unruly Gods*, p. 96.

mother-in-law begs. This intermediate situation, which recalls the continuation of some domestic involvement after Shuzhen's departure in "Huixian ji," ends when Xiaocui replaces herself with a human woman and causes her own beauty to fade while the new bride takes on Xiaocui's former appearance. In the first part of the story, when her husband is an idiot, her primary relationship is with her parents-in-law. Once she has awoken him to sentience and passion, she leaves. Pu Songling comments in closing:

> A fox received an unintended favor, and still thought of repaying it. How base her parents-in-law were to think of a broken vase after she had returned their son to life! The waning moon becomes full again, and she serenely takes her leave; thus do we know that the capacity for deep feelings is greater with fairy transcendents than among the common run of humanity![90]

Pu asks us to accept her serene determination to depart and her attempt to make the loss as painless as possible for her husband as evidence of a passion beyond human capacities.

Deciphering the emotional motives for a vixen's departure brings us back to the question posed at the end of the previous chapter: Does a vixen feel passion? A Propp-inspired structuralist reading would argue that the fact of departure is the deep structure, and the motivation for it a superficial variable. Yet these variations themselves raise questions. When Xiaocui provides for everything her husband could desire, save herself, is this the height of selfless passion, as Pu reads it, or cool selfishness? Different stories depict the emotions of departure differently. Hu Shuzhen clings to her husband. In other stories, the fox longs for her own exit. In "Xin Shisiniang" 辛十四娘, the heroine admits she has grown weary of rescuing her husband, and hence of the mortal world.[91] Perhaps foxes inevitably seem cold because they understand the karmic mechanics that motivate their actions, whereas for humans the sources of our passions remain opaque. Vixens' passion is of a kind

---

90. *LZ*, 7.1008; translation from Li Wai-yee, *Enchantment and Disenchantment*, p. 130.

91. *LZ*, 4.545. Admittedly, Xin Shishiniang's husband is particularly in need of rescue from his own faults, and it is a particularly arduous and thankless job.

not possible for human women: a human woman of childbearing age has no blameless exits from domesticity, save death.[92]

The difference between Hu Shuzhen's story and Pu's is that despite separation, the former never really has a clear ending. The maids continue to pass back and forth between the two worlds; the diary simply ends, and Xu Jiefeng's experience with the séance provides closure. Pu on the other hand always provided artful endings; the relationship between the worlds never simply trails off. In providing a human duplicate of herself, Xiaocui seals the gap she left behind in the world.

VIXENS AND WOMEN

For Pu Songling, romances with alien women were a means of exploring desire and illusion, and their part in human relations between lovers, rivals in polygamous families, or newlyweds and their relatives by marriage. He tried to imagine all the consequences when the demon lover enters the home. Pu shared concepts and lore with his predecessors and contemporaries but transformed them with unprecedented complexity of structure and psychological detail. Illusion and desire become much more finely grained as they are translated into individual characters. In turn, his stories themselves became a compelling object of desire and his heroines the imaginary beloveds of generations.

What does Pu's fascination with the patterns of human and inhuman relations have to do with ideas about real human women? The relationship of romance to lived reality in a society in which the arranged marriage was the norm is likely to be distant rather than close. Nevertheless, we can ask: How does the vixen relate to trends in marriage patterns such as the rise of the market economy and the parallel growth in a market in women and larger numbers of men taking concubines or the rise of female literacy and companionate marriage between intellectual equals? Barr surveys the possible links between the women in Pu's life and his literary heroines, although he cautions

92. An older woman, who has labored through the years of "rice and salt," and raised and married off her children, can withdraw into religious devotion while her daughters-in-law take over practical matters; see Ebrey, *The Inner Quarters*, pp. 126–27; and Mann, *Precious Records: Women in China's Long Eighteenth Century*, pp. 69–75.

against one-to-one identifications.[93] One might think of Pu's foxes and ghosts as a vision of the ideal concubine from a man who was not of the concubine-taking class. In general, the parallel between vixens and concubines is as clear as their relationship to prostitutes: these women are often a man's own choice rather than his parents', of disreputable origins, and attractive largely as individuals rather than as nodes in a network of family relationships. Yet the fantasy of the ideal concubine quickly blends with ideas of the ideal wife, as against the odds the supernatural women manage to win the respect of their parents-in-law and fulfill their duties to their parents. Pu seldom emphasized vixen's "entertainment" value (singing, dancing, or even composing poetry) and focused instead on their uncanny practical cleverness, whether in matters economic, political, or social. As for companionate marriage, foxes are presumed to be their lovers' intellectual equals, if not superiors, but Pu did not include the scholarly exchanges that many imitators did.

In the tale bearing her name, the vixen Hengniang 恒娘 advises a neglected wife how to play the role of a concubine and regain her husband's affection.[94] The *Liaozhai* vixen attempts herself, in contrast, to combine the charm and origins of a concubine with the practical responsibilities of a wife.

The vixen who comes every night and vanishes at dawn promises sexual availability unfettered by domestic ties, but once she stays into the daylight hours, she must be contained in human domesticity. She has powers no human woman does, but those powers are employed in the service of husband and family. Yet in the end she often cannot be contained; or, rather, her exit is the ultimate way of keeping the fox separate.

THE ROMANCE AFTER "LIAOZHAI"

The bulk of the classical fiction of the high and late Qing has been dismissed as imitations of *Liaozhai*.[95] This is unjust, because the inspiration of *Liaozhai*'s model did not preclude invention and individ-

93. Barr, "Pu Songling and *Liaozhai zhiyi*," pp. 184–92.

94. *LZ*, 10.1431.

95. For example, Lu Xun listed *Xie duo*, *Ershi lu*, *Yetan suilu*, *Yingchang yicao*, *Xiliu zhitan*, *Wenjian yici*, *Xijiong baibian*, *Yingtan*, *Yeyu qiudeng lu*, *Dunku lanyan*, *Songying manlu*, and *Songbin suohua*. Hou Zhongyi and Liu Shilin (*Zhongguo wenyan xiaoshuo shigao*, p. 224) add *Kezhong yiwen lu* and *Kechuang xianhua*.

ual interests. Nevertheless, the one topic for which *Liaozhai*'s impact is undeniable is the supernatural romance.

The wide circulation of *Liaozhai*'s romances and the publication of other tales of vixens as ideal lovers created the phenomenon, within stories, of the besotted *Liaozhai* reader dreaming of an amorous vixen or affectionate ghost.[96] This self-conscious textual reference begins within *Liaozhai* itself, in the story "Hu meng" 狐夢 (A fox dream). One of Pu's friends longs for a meeting with a fox, and the vixen who fulfills his desires compares herself to Qingfeng.[97] For a vixen to be an ideal lover is no longer a surprise but an expectation, and there are even men who prefer vixens to human women.

The later romances do not raise new questions other than "How can the vixen stay?" and "How can she leave?" They do, however, sometimes attempt to be novel in their answers. As we saw in He Bang'e's story of young Chu's encounter with the fox in the garden, there can be interest in scenes of flirtatious banter over luxurious meals, with enjoyment of the idea of female companionship and sensual pleasure without pressure on the development of the rest of the plot. Some stories increase the numbers of supernatural sex partners by expanding the love triangle to a quadrangle or more.[98]

In general, the problem balancing desire and order confounds the *Liaozhai* imitations. The imitations never seem to capture the *Liaozhai*'s combination of schoolmistress and playful fox; the two are split, usually at the expense of the playful fox. Their foxes are Yingning after

96. For an argument that this kind of "metafiction" is typical of the eighteenth and nineteenth century, see Margaret Baptist Wan, "Living What You Read: Meta-Fiction in the 19th-Century Popular Novel" (paper presented at the Meeting of the Association of Asian Studies, Spring 2000).

97. *LZ*, 5.618–22. The lover who deliberately seeks out a fox had become a type by the late Qing; see the discussion below of the tale from *Yangzhou meng*. Another example is "Fansheng huanyu" 范生幻遇, Yu Zongjun 俞宗駿, in *Yanyi xinbian* 艷異新編, 1.24a. For an inflated version of this story, in which a man is granted multiple fox lovers of both sexes, see "Wuxiang mou taishi" 吾鄉某太史, in Xu Feng'en, *Lantiaoguan waishi*, 6.12b. Although he is not seeking a lover, the obsessed *Liaozhai* reader Ji Dongfu continually buys injured foxes from hunters, until one proves to be his son's benefactor ("Ji Dongfu" 計東甫, in Lin Shu, *Lin Shu xuan ji, xiaoshuo, shang*, p. 173).

98. "Gu Wuling" 顧武陵, in Xu Kun, *Liuya waibian*, 6.17a–21b, 1793 ed.

she has forsworn laughter or Fengxian only as she appears in the mirror. Later collections succeed in maintaining the moral ambiguity of the fox tradition at the level of the entire book but lose it at the level of the individual character. They tend to err on the side of order rather than desire; their foxes seem too unaffected by *qing*.[99]

An extreme of the arbitrary, stylized form of the fox romance can be found in Wang Tao's *Songyin manlu*, first printed as an appendix to the pictorial *Dianshizhai huabao*. Two splendid idylls of perfect fulfillment with a vixen end abruptly with a return of the atavistic plot device of hunters or hunting dogs.[100] Publishing circumstances suggest a reason for Wang's need to cut romances off: all his stories are limited to three pages of text and one page of illustration.[101] The new medium exposed the enduring appeal of the formula of desire, satiety, and disillusionment and made it inevitable: the vixens had to vanish at the end of the page.

NEGATION OF THE ROMANCE

The repetition of the romance in the Qianlong, and later, aroused a strong response. The *Liaozhai* romances were such a prominent force that even an author who despised them was compelled to respond to them. The word "negation" does not do justice to the humor with which Ji Yun frustrated the expectations of readers and would-be lovers of vixens alike. The old story of a beauty who turns out to be a fox also depends on thwarted expectations, but by late imperial times that very surprise has become expected. Some frustrations of the fox romance are simple physical comedy, dependent on fox trickery, as when a man expecting a fox liaison ends up embracing his teacher

---

99. E.g., "Wusheng yanyu" 鄔生豔遇 in Xuan Ding, *Yeyu qiudeng lu*, 3.116. The vixen in this story manufactures an illusion of an angry father to justify her departure and provides a pill that cures her lover of his longing for her. A chaste fox forswears sexual love for the sake of pure conversation in the pages of the newspaper *Shen bao*; see "Huxian shouzheng" 狐仙守正, *Shenbao* 2/23/1876, 15.9262.

100. "Zheng Zhixian" 鄭芷仙 and "Xiao Buyan" 蕭捕煙 in Wang Tao, *Hou Liaozhai zhiyi quanyi xiangzhu*, pp. 171–76, 259–64. *Songyin manlu*'s alternative title is *Hou Liaozhai zhiyi*.

101. These additional pages are not included in the reprint version; see the original copies of *Dianshizhai huabao* at the Shanghai Library.

instead.[102] Others may disappoint expectations in more subtle ways, but all these stories make fools of characters, and readers, who know the story of the fox romance too well.

One of Ji Yun's more comic reversals makes direct reference to *Liaozhai* foxes. A young man traveling through the outskirts of the city sees a resplendent household that should not be there, and thinking of *Liaozhai*'s Qingfeng and Shuixian, he hopes for a romantic encounter.[103] Just as he dreamed, he meets a woman and her lovely daughter and is invited to a sumptuous feast. While he is listening to the wedding music and waiting to be united with the girl, a man tells him the groom has just arrived and asks if he is willing to be the *binxiang* 儐相, the person who guides the groom in the wedding ceremony. Disappointed, he sullenly drinks their wine. When he returns home and tells his family what has happened, they point out that it was not the fox who tricked him but he himself.[104] Ji mocks the vanity of the *Liaozhai* reader who assumes that every supernatural woman is eager to offer herself to him and places the ultimate source of all trickery in the human mind.

Another man named Luo who dreams of a fox romance goes so far as to write a letter begging for a fox wife and leaves it at an old tomb known to be inhabited by foxes. The vixen who responds to his summons is a beauty who can make herself invisible so that she can satisfy his every desire at every moment. Unfortunately she is also a glutton, and when Luo's household runs out of food, she steals clothing and household utensils to sell for cash. He suspects she is feeding her friends. She is equally sexually insatiable and drives him to the brink of exhaustion. After they become estranged, she and her friends haunt him mercilessly. When a Daoist is summoned to exorcise her, she defends herself and points out not only that she was expressly invited, but also that she has acted according to foxes' widely recognized inherent nature. Since Luo preferred a fox to a woman, he has no grounds to judge her by human standards. Even if she is

102. *YWCT*, 16.951–52, story 99.

103. It is strange that Shuixian, the most obscure of the three sisters in "Fengxian," is alluded to here; perhaps she has become confused with her more famous sisters.

104. *YWCT*, 13.709, story 171.

judged by human standards, her misdeeds are justifiable: men who desire the pleasure of beautiful companions have to be ready to support them, and if they do not, the women are justified in helping themselves. It is common for relatives of disgruntled daughters-in-law to come in mobs to make demands of their sons-in-law. All these personal domestic matters are outside the purview of imperial law. The Daoist agrees that it is inappropriate to use exorcism to deal with domestic disputes. In the end, the impoverished Luo dies of an illness.[105]

Luo's idealistic vision of fox romance leads to a particularly venal and banal form of parasitism that strips away the glamour of the femme fatale. A vixen, rather than providing an alternative to the financial transactions of ties with concubines or prostitutes, proves to be different in degree, not kind. A story in which a human wife and her in-laws act as parasites in precisely the same manner as this fox until they are driven out by another fox demonstrates the reversibility of the comparison.[106] This displacement of fox mischief into the human world is one of Ji Yun's standard tactics. The ending of Luo's story is unexpectedly grim; Ji seemed to feel this extreme retribution is justified by the extreme lengths to which this man went to win a fox wife. Luo's story, and later stories with the same punishment of the man who deliberately seeks out the fox, attacks both the conceit of the man who feels he deserves a divine love and the cheapening of the fox romance through repetition.

As we saw in the discussion of the runaway maid in Chapter 2, the conventions of fox stories are sufficiently well known that deceitful women could play on these expectations, and the role of the fox proves useful as an excuse for illicit female behavior. In one case, a young woman, afraid that word of her affair with a young man will spread, claims to be a fox. This story also suggests a cynical interpretation of the story type in which a fox is the doppelgänger of a human lover: "That wasn't me before our wedding night; it was a fox who looked like me." Her lover is too overcome with passion to care, but later shingles fly down from the roof and a fox scolds her, "I've lived in the garden for a long time. It sometimes happens that the

105. *YWCT*, 17.992–93, story 131.
106. *YWCT*, 18.1060, story 180.

children playfully toss stones to frighten the neighbors, but we certainly don't engage in debauched and deceitful affairs. How dare you insult me?"[107] It is clear which forms of fox mischief Ji considers forgivable. A man's illicit desires are answered by a vixen who demonstrates the baseness of those desires, and a woman is rebuked by a moral male fox. In both cases, the moral focus is on the human.

Lying women also imitate the more respectable versions of the fox romance. In a reversal of the fox replacing the runaway maid in the story discussed in Chapter 2, a man who has a lovely and bright concubine returns one night to find her gone and a letter saying that she was a fox, their destined time together had elapsed, and she did not wish to harm him. He is deeply moved and shows the letter to his friends, who believe it and sigh over it. Later it is discovered she had run off with another man; probably her mother had sold her to two people. In the end one of Ji's commentators remarks that she was a real vixen and that he fears many of the stories of temporary liaisons with supernatural women are of this sort.[108] Deceptive use of fox stories discredits them in general. Ji apparently felt compelled to undermine this vision of a group vicariously enjoying the romance by reading the vixen's letter in a manner reminiscent of the readers of Yingying's letter in *Yingying zhuan*. Reading her letter made them feel closer to a *Liaozhai* romance, and Ji Yun was particularly offended by this combination of literary and erotic pleasure. Ji was also evidently uncomfortable with the idea of domestic bliss on a limited contract. Highlighting the inconsistency other authors ignore, he alone pointed out that the behavior the conventional story accepts as noble and selfless for a fox would be considered betrayal in a human woman.

An extreme example of disillusionment through the fox romance is found in the late collection *Yangzhou meng* 揚州夢. The author, born in 1824, is now known only by his surname Zhou. This story, an example of the fox romance at a very late and self-conscious stage, seems to be a deliberate exploration of the extremes of desire and revulsion. Since this collection contains no other fox stories and relatively few other tales of the strange, it seems likely that this story

107. *YWCT*, 2.61, story 59.
108. *YWCT*, 13.726, story 190.

appealed to the author as a philosophical exploration rather than a fox story for its own sake. It is included in the third of the collection's four categories, *mengzhong qing* 夢中情, "passion in dreams."[109] The frame of the story is itself unusual: a man, Zhao Jingshi, tells the author an account of his relationship with a vixen in a previous life, when his name was Sun Lu. As a youth Sun read the Ming compendium of stories about women, *Yanyi bian*, and fantasized about gathering all the beauties of history together in one room. He resolved to find a vixen to fulfill this fantasy, since only vixens were both passionate and capable of transformation.[110] The linking of the reading of fiction and delusion also suggests a direct link between anthologies and vixens' performance of the roles of historical beauties. One night a woman appeared in his room. She first warned him his plea could easily have summoned a demon to devour him (as happened to some of the suitors of vixens Ji Yun described). Nevertheless, she became his lover, or rather his bevy of lovers, and adroitly anticipated his needs, becoming Yang Guifei when he desired a fat woman and Zhao Feiyan when he wanted a thin one.[111]

After a month of these transformations, he grew thin and weak. Evidently attempting to enlighten him through excess, she assumed that his appetite would be dulled. (The man from the *Yuewei caotang* anecdote also met a fox who could take the form of any woman he desired and thereby eventually came to understand the illusory nature of romance.)[112] The vixen told Sun, "When you are starving, you must fill your belly; so you look at the most precious delicacies and salivate. . . . But if you eat them after you are sated, they are tasteless, the same as the coarsest greens." Using the same analogy, however, he still cannot imagine how one could grow weary of the endless variation of flavors she offers. She tried another tactic and worked in the fields until she grew black and coarse. Nonetheless, thwarting her

109. The other categories are 夢中人 ("people in dreams"), 夢中語 ("speech in dreams"), and 夢中事 ("events in dreams").

110. Evidently this man had also read "Chang'e" or Ji's tale of the fox who assumed the form of all the beauties of history in order to enlighten her lover.

111. This is the typical pair chosen to represent the range and variation of female beauty; Chang'e imitated the same two.

112. *YWCT*, 1.14, story 13; see the discussion in the previous chapter.

attempt to duplicate Xiaocui's means of departure, he continued to perceive her as lovely.[113] She then fell ill, both her health and temper worsening precipitously. Still he doted on her and cared for her, even washing her filthy laundry (underwear, especially soiled menstrual cloth, seems to be implied). The story lists several examples of his clouded perceptions: her curses sounded melodious to him, the stink of her feet was fragrant. When at last she died, he could not bear to bury her still-human corpse, but clung to it as he slept. Then he reflected that as a *xian* she was immortal and her death must be an illusion. Overwhelmed by the memory of her, he had sex with her corpse in the hope she would be revived. This necrophilia is shocking and, despite the erotic interest in ghosts, as rare in *zhiguai* as "true" bestiality; it is included to heighten the portrait of delusion. She was revived, sighing that there was no medicine that could cure him. Next she attempted to destroy his love by seducing young men before his eyes. Although at first enraged, he forgave her even this. At last she was won over by his unconditional love, and their relationship became as harmonious as it was at the very beginning. In the end he died, but his ghost still lingered with her. He saw her dragged off to an infernal court, revealed in the clutch of her captors in her true fox form. The judge decided to punish her for killing Sun when she was only supposed to be fulfilling a debt from another life. Although she had not intended to kill him, she still must spend a term of bitter exile in the human world as his wife. Sun went to seek out her corpse and found a skeleton; only the heart remains, but it is covered with flies. Terrified, he ran away.

In his next life, as Zhao, just as he fears, his betrothed turns out to be the vixen. Although others find her beautiful, when he looks at her, he can only see the beast or the skeleton. This renders him incapable of having marital relations with her. The narrator/author tells Zhao that although he was excessive in his last life, in this one his desire is inadequate. The fox turned woman is worthy of pity, and besides, Zhao risks committing the sin of leaving his family without heirs. Despite these admonitions, he never succeeds in having normal

113. Her decline into dramatic ugliness, followed by illness, is perhaps inspired more by Xin Shisiniang than by Xiaocui; see *LZ*, 4.547.

relations with his wife.[114] In an inversion of the usual story of destined ties between men and vixens, the vixen is trapped with the one man in whom she cannot inspire desire.

Here the fox romance is embroidered with baroque excesses of obsession and disgust. The essential pattern of enchantment and awakening is used as a vehicle for a more extreme statement. Since the fox body alone is not enough to repulse the deluded lover, the grotesque description of the corpse must be added. (The latter also has its precedents, particularly Buddhist reminders that the most beautiful woman will soon be a skeleton.) The undecayed heart teeming with flies is as vivid an image of passion and revulsion as could be imagined. In the first part of the story, the fox herself attempts both to fulfill and to control his desires, but his final awakening is beyond her control. This story is very much a product of the late Qing, when both the fox romance and its negations had become familiar; it employs elements of both while going to almost desperate extremes to make its point. The conclusion effectively negates the idea of *qing wu qing* 情無情, "overcoming passion through the extremes of passion." Far from reaching enlightenment, the protagonist of this tale veers from one form of insanity to another.

Overall, in the path from the sexually dangerous vixen to the negation of the fox romance, one could sketch a dialectic of desire and aversion: a figure of sexual availability and danger first becomes a figure of romantic possibility, with the danger averted; then in turn the romance is foiled. Each subsequent vixen does not replace her opposite; rather, they are in constant dialogue: the paragon is always haloed against a surrounding horde of parasites, and the vixen who extinguishes desire is shadowed against those who fulfill desire.

THE ASEXUAL FOX PARAGON

As "Liehu zhuan" revealed, another method of resolving the fox romance is to elevate the vixen into another realm of virtue. Ji offered one thoroughly exceptional story of a virtuous fox wife, exceptional enough to require thorough justification.

---

114. Zhou sheng, *Yangzhou meng*, pp. 65–66.

Zhou Taiyu related that there was a man named Liu Zhe who became intimate with a fox and then took her as his second wife. Her behavior was like that of an ordinary person: she was filial to her parents-in-law, affectionate with her sisters-in-law, and treated the first wife's children like her own, things that would be hard for an outstanding human to achieve. She grew old and died, but her corpse did not revert to fox shape.

Some said, "She was originally a runaway woman who concealed her story and claimed she was a fox."

Others said, "She really was a fox, but she cultivated herself and attained the human way. However, she had not yet attained immortality, so she grew old and died. Since she had already discarded her fox body, she could die and her corpse was like that of a person."

I said, "All of this is false; her heart was enough to maintain her. Any creature's form can be transformed following its heart. When Empress Xi became a python and Feng Shizhun became a tiger,[115] their hearts first became a python's heart and a tiger's heart, and therefore their forms turned to python's form and tiger's form. Old stories claim the fox was originally a transformation of the wanton woman Azi. Since she was a person with a fox heart, a person could become a fox. This fox had a human heart, and so a fox could become human. The Buddhists and Daoists can sometimes die leaving their bodies in meditation without collapsing, and loyal officials and exemplary women can sometimes leave their bones to endure unrotting. This is all because their spirit is adequate to preserve their shape. The unchanged corpse of this fox is the same sort of phenomenon!"

Taiyu said, "It is truly so. It is said that when Liu first wed the fox, he couldn't help feeling some fear and hesitation. The fox said, 'A wife should be good for the family; as long as she is good for the family, what difference is there between a fox and a person? Moreover people only know to fear foxes, but they don't know they are always consorting with foxes. When a woman's behavior is uncontrolled, so that she brings her husband illness and shortens his life span, how is that different from a fox's parasitism? When a woman leaps over walls and crawls through holes for secret meetings and clandestine pleasures, how is that different from a fox's lustfulness? When a woman's loose lips incite quarrels and cause strife in the family, how is this different from a fox's bewitchment? If a woman secretly steals property and gives it to her own relatives and loved ones, how is that different from a fox's theft? When a woman insults and slanders others so that all the family

115. Empress Xi was the wife of Liang Wudi; Feng was an official who turned into a tiger and ate the people of his district; see "Feng Shao" 封邵, *TPGJ*, 426.3466.

are not at peace, how is that different from a fox's haunting and disturbance? Why don't you fear such a woman but instead fear me?'"

Since this fox's resolve is superior to a person's, it is only fitting that she began as a human and ended as a human. As for all the different kinds of foxlike people she describes, each one's reincarnation into one of the six orders of life[116] is determined by her own heart. One must only fear that when one dies, one will fall into their midst.[117]

Ji was not interested in courtship or flirtation with the fox; rather, his matter-of-fact statements reveal that a man's having a vixen lover needed no further explanation. Once married, she exhibits her virtue in every relationship except that with her husband; to put any stress on that would introduce associations of romance and desire. The only marvel left in this fox is her "being like an ordinary person," yet her virtue in turn belies her ordinariness. In another case of conspicuous ordinariness, the corpse of a fox is crucial to the story in its absence, just as its presence was vital in older fox stories. Death remains the moment of truth when identity, with all of its moral dimensions, is revealed.

The interpretations offered by various commentators resemble those made elsewhere in *Yuewei caotang biji*. As we have seen, Ji was eager to dismiss some sorts of fox stories as the fabrications of lying women, but he would not have this paragon so devalued. Although in other tales he agreed that foxes can achieve the human way without achieving immortality, here he spoke for the absolute domination of the moral over the physical sphere. Interpretations of the lines between the human and the fox vary in different rhetorical contexts.

In general, in the Chinese tradition tales of people turning into animals are far less common than animals becoming people, but here Ji cited the most famous cases. The most relevant here is the wanton woman Azi, who became a fox and is described as an ancestress of foxes in *Soushen ji*.[118] Once a woman fell from humanity; now Ji's fox reverses the process. The original source of lustfulness was human, but the form of the fox is still identified with wantonness. The com-

---

116. The six paths are the paths of heaven, humans, asuras, animals, hungry ghosts, and hell.

117. *YWCT*, 14.823–24, story 276.

118. *Soushen ji*, 18, story 425.

parison of beasts with the hearts of humans to humans with the hearts of beasts is one of the conventional means of defending foxes' virtue and admonishing humans. But Ji took it one step further—this vixen's human heart has transformed her body. Species is defined, on the one hand, by the inner heart and, on the other, by function, but not by origin or any inherent physical quality.

The anecdote is constructed to prove Ji right. After he makes the abstract, historical argument, Zhou Taiyu confirms it with this fox's own words, violating linear narrative order. Once the malignant fox has been erased, the vixen re-creates it in her own words. Ji created his fox paragon not only by maintaining the other, lustful and destructive fox but by displacing all the vulpine vices onto human women. Her monologue provides a catalogue of fox misdeeds, denied in her individual case but established as metaphors for all mischief.

The difference between this vixen and Pu's domesticated demon lovers is dependent both on philosophical and on stylistic differences. This vixen's relations with her human kin by category are flawless, but there is no sense of a tie between individuals, let alone individual incidents that establish those relationships. In contrast, Pu Songling was interested more in narrative particularities than in summaries of exemplary conduct. Even when Pu's heroines are filial or loyal, as in the case of Yingning or Xiaocui, they exhibit those virtues in extraordinary ways. He mixed ordinary female virtues with marvel, rather than having virtue supplant marvel. Ji created his paragon by using arguments based on the fox-human comparison, by appealing to general analogy rather than to her individual character.

Despite the obvious opposition between Ji and Pu, Ji's methods of restoring desire to order are only a more drastic version of those Pu himself used even for his most celebrated fox heroines. Although Pu gave freer rein to wish fulfillment, he never allowed fantasy to disturb the moral order. Pu, however, often restrained erotic desire for the sake of other forms of wish fulfillment, as foxes become proper wives and maternal healers. Although Ji found the erotic aspects of the fantasy particularly objectionable, he resisted the vision of a vixen lover as the deliverer of men unbalancing moral order with their excessive favors to an individual. He instead promised that the perfect vixen lover would do exactly what the perfect wife should do, but no more.

YINGNING, QINGFENG, UNDINE: BECOMING HUMAN THROUGH MARRIAGE

The idea that alien women might attain humanity through marriage to human men is not an exclusively Chinese conception. In Europe, fairy women, once bound by a Christian wedding ceremony to a human man, are thought to attain a soul.[119] This is the only means by which an alien can become human; no alien male ever claims humanity by taking a human bride. This parallel gender construction in the two different cultural realms depends on similar systems of virilocal marriage and patrilineal descent and shared conceptions of the female as more marginally human than the male.

Friedrich Heinrich Karl de la Motte Fouqué's (1777–1843) water spirit Undine, one of the most best-known embodiments of the idea of the alien bride on the cusp of humanity, provides a particularly vivid comparison with the vixen brides of this chapter. Like Yingning, Undine's alien nature is marked at the beginning of the story by her childish laughter and her ignorance of social conventions between the sexes.[120] Neither of them is allowed to continue this indiscretion after losing her virginity. However, for Undine the evening immediately following her wedding is the moment of transformation, when she feels the heaviness of her incipient soul and cries instead of laughs.[121] In contrast, Yingning's hysterical laughter prevents the ceremony from being completed. In the European case, humanity is an absolute state, defined by the presence or absence of the soul, and it is thus attained in a single moment. For Yingning, what is important is not the ritual moment but the change in her relations with her mother-in-law. The transition from laughter to seriousness is not the acquisition of humanity; rather, as for Ji Yun's fox

---

119. Paracelsus, *Liber de nymphis, sylphis, pygmaeis et salamandries, et de caeteris spiritibus*, p. 24. The same is said of the Scandinavian Huldermaidens, who when they marry a human man both gain a soul and shed their tail.

120. Originally published in 1811. Fouqué, *Undine*, pp. 7–9. See Fassbind-Eigenheer, *Undine*, pp. 79–80.

121. Fouqué, *Undine*, pp. 35–36. Fassbind-Eigenherr, *Undine*, p. 82.

paragon, humanity is a matter not of an internal change but of the external actions of being a good daughter-in-law, wife, and mother.

Undine's natal family, in the person of her uncle Kühleborn, remains a potentially destructive force, with whom no rapprochement is possible; in contrast many *Liaozhai* heroes are finally reconciled with their uncanny in-laws.[122] Kühleborn cannot be invited into one's home, and his destructive presence helps estrange Undine and Huldbrand. Both Undine and Yingning prove their emotional transformation by their feelings for the foster parents who raised them, but for Undine, those foster parents are human, whereas for Yingning it is another supernatural being. Undine has deliberately been sent to climb into the human world, but she does this by abandoning her origins, rather than by binding the worlds together. Unlike Pu Songling, Fouqué was not interested in the dynamics of real families after marriage, since he is writing in a fairy-tale world that focuses on young people's quests beyond the family. Parents are present in the story to prove Undine's virtue and Bertelda's vice, but not because the young triangle really has to live with them.

Fouqué's narrative interests are more like Pu Songling's than Ji Yun's; were it translated into Chinese, the *Kunstmärchen* Undine would be a *chuanqi* rather than a *zhiguai.* Thus, ending with Undine's ascent to domestic virtue is not enough. As with Xiaocui, once the alien woman has attained humanity, she surpasses it, with her husband admitting her soul is better than his own. The human man reveals he is unworthy of his divine bride, as Xiaocui's parents did when they scolded her for a broken vase or young Xu's relatives did when they drove away Hu Shuzhen. The difference between individual failure and familial failure is revealing. The conclusion of Undine's story—Huldbrand dies for betraying her and marrying a human bride—is alien to a polygamous society. The loss of Undine is partially folkloric necessity: humans inevitably violate any limitations placed on them by supernatural beings. But unlike Miss Ren, begging Zheng not to make her ride with him past Mawei, Qing foxes stopped placing prohibitions on their husbands. Detachment, rather than human failure, became the more central motive for departure.

122. Fassbind-Eigenherr, *Undine*, pp. 83–84.

The closing figure, with Undine as a stream encircling her husband's grave, is a celebration of both her difference from the human and her human emotional ties, not unlike the fox corpse, which is the final sign of loyalty in "Liehu zhuan." Many of the differences are related to Undine as an embodiment of nature, which a fox is not, an issue to which I will return in the conclusion to this book. Despite coincidences in ideals of women as fey child and steady housewife, differences in family structure and concepts of the human and inhuman conspire to give Yingning and Undine their different endings.

ROMANCE AND FICTION

I opened this chapter by pointing out the generic difference between the fox romance and the subject matter covered by previous chapters. That the romance is described in *chuanqi* is not coincidental but essential to the nature of the romance. When brief *zhiguai* describe intimate relations with supernatural beings, it is usually from the perspective of an outsider relating a few wonderful traces of another man's encounter.[123] But if the pleasures of reading are to lie in the particularities of a relationship, from first glance to parting words, the *chuanqi* form is necessary. With the Hu Shuzhen cycle as the great exception, such tales are usually held at a great distance from the authors and narrators. As a result of this entwining of *chuanqi* and the supernatural romance, the critical response to the content and literary form of the romance are inextricably entwined.

From the perspective of literary conservatives like Ji Yun, invention in the classical tale was dangerous not simply because it was fiction but because it was fiction with pernicious content. The two subjects that cause narratives to be excluded from orthodox histories are the strange and the sexual. The strange became *zhiguai*; the sexual became *yeshi* 野史 and *chuanqi*. The fabrications of the *zhiguai* were thought to feed an unhealthy appetite for the bizarre, alarm people, and promote superstition; *chuanqi*, on the other hand, were seen as promoting emotional self-indulgence and immorality. Romance with an inhuman woman was one of the mainstays of the *chuanqi* genre

123. Examples include the soldier's experience in Xu Changzuo, *Yanshan conglu*; and "Hu qi" 狐妻 and "Hu nü" 狐女, in *Suoshi xian xu lu* xia, 13b.

from its inception, and such a story involved both kinds of dangerous imagination. Ji's criticism of *Liaozhai* reveals the blending of these two kinds of critique. In the colophon by Sheng Shiyan, which lays out Ji's beliefs about *zhiguai*, *zhu anji* 傳記 (what we would call *chuanqi*) is represented by *Feiyan waizhuan* 飛燕外傳 ("Unofficial Biography of Zhao Feiyan"; attributed to the Hun but probably Six Dynasties) and "Yingying zhuan" 鶯鶯傳 ("Yingying's Story"; early ninth century), a story of an imperial concubine and of a private romance, respectively. His objection to the excessive details that Pu Songling records was ostensibly based on plausibility, but it was also inspired by the nature of those details: intimate conversations between men and women.[124]

At the close of one of Ji Yun's accounts of the exorcism of an amorous vixen, the exorcising monk is asked about stories of romantic encounters with transcendents (*xian*). He replies:

> "Some of the tales recorded since ancient times in *chuanqi* are parables, and some are analogies. There are authors who use them to express their gratitude and resentment, there are those who love telling entertaining tales to amaze their listeners, and there are those who embroider glamorous details to compose a romance. There are those who without any basis in reality entrust their feelings to ornate words like poets imitating erotic verse. Out of ten such stories, probably eight or nine are false and only one or two are true; and those that are true are likely all talented ghosts and sentient foxes, without a single transcendent among them."[125]

Ji's approval of this analysis is clear in his regret that the failure to record the monk's name makes it impossible for Ji to seek him out. The monk's speech sums up all the reasons for fictional invention Ji could imagine. Both internal and external motivations for creation, creation for the sake of self-expression and for the entertainment of an audience, are included. The romance with a divine woman is an ancient means of allegorizing a man's anguished relation with the

124. Colophon at the end of *Guwang tingzhi*. In the Shanghai guji edition of *YWCT*, 4, pp. 471–73.

125. *YWCT*, 9.442–43, story 164. It is notable that Shen Zhaoding, mentioned in the next chapter as going mad in pursuit of immortals, was also extremely fond of writing imitations of Li Shangyin's verse to vent his feelings. Fictional invention, eroticism, and danger are again linked; see *YWCT*, 22.1214–215, story 84.

sovereign who fails to appreciate his talents and dates to the model of Qu Yuan and the *Chu ci* (in the third century BCE). More loosely, the divine romance is a fantasy about being recognized and appreciated. Rather than simply being an allegory, however, it mixes erotic longing and ambition. At the same time as diagnosing the fictional nature of such encounters, the critic appreciates the different aspects of pleasure for listeners and readers: humor, glamour, and ornate language. Ji would not deny that Pu Songling was writing, as many of his admirers would claim, to express his pent-up feelings of frustration,[126] but he would argue that *zhiguai* was not the place for such self-indulgence.

Once again, foxes (and ghosts) take a distinctive place in this critique. Transcendents, Ji argued, were above illicit sexual liaisons. Ji devoted the most attention to discrediting the most glamorous variant of the supernatural romance and did so on moral grounds. An ordinary man might well encounter a ghost or fox, but to claim to have encountered a transcendent is hubris. Foxes can safely encompass anything fictional or morally dubious without casting doubt on the moral order of the universe. By the same token, inventing stories about foxes suits the deceptive nature of the species.

CONCLUSION

What kind of fantasy is the romance with a vixen? The encounters discussed in the previous chapter were both fantasies and nightmares of sexual availability. Only females completely outside a human family could offer sex entirely unconstrained by issues of propriety or economics. This flouting of the system that distributed female attention in late imperial society was perhaps even more enticing when sex was only one kind of attention among many. Not only are the vixens of the romance available without the rituals or exchange of gifts necessary to win access to women of good family (even though *Liaozhai*'s romances reconcile the supernatural romance with the constraints of human families, each betrothal remains unconventional) and without the financial price demanded for concubines or courte-

126. Zeitlin (*Historian of the Strange*, pp. 25–34) calls this interpretive strategy the "second wave" of critical response to *Liaozhai*.

sans, they do not even require their lovers to be particularly deserving. The men of the romances are not necessarily talented or virtuous. In some cases, all that is asked is the bravery not to forsake an alien lover, or simply intensity and persistence of desire. The causes of this apparently unmerited female attention are often placed in another life, a displacement that makes a man deserving beyond his own knowledge or the perception of any observers in his surroundings. To dream of the love of a *xian* was to dream of all the attention one deserves but does not receive in this world. But as is apparent in the comment that most romances said to be with transcendents really were with foxes and ghosts, the fox the poor man's *xian*. In loving a human man, not only does she not fall from heaven, but she ascends to humanity. Her inferior status makes her more approachable. She is never entirely an equal of her lover, but the direction of the difference in status is ambiguous.

Longing is directed at the full range of female attention. In some of the imitations of *Liaozhai*, lavish meals, with fruit out of season and the vixen pouring the wine, receive more attention than anything that happens within the curtains of the bed. This is not only because of the delicious flirtation and sexual tension of eating a meal, unchaperoned, with a nubile woman who is neither wife nor kinswoman. Such a meal almost invariably precedes seduction, for to go directly to the sex without sharing food and wine would be to abandon all hint of a social relationship. There is pleasure simply in the attention and in savoring a meal for which one need not pay with money or repay with a return invitation. As we saw in "Jiaona," a platonic friendship with a young woman might be prized even more highly than an affair, because this is a social niche that would be even more difficult for a human woman to fill.

At the same time as vixens become romantic ideals, under the joint influence of the expansion of the fantasies into non-erotic wish fulfillment and the beneficent fox from popular fox worship, the fox becomes the figure who fixes everything, the healer, the teacher, and the provider of wealth. These abilities differ in degree rather than kind from what might be wished from a human wife: the ideal eighteenth-century housewife ministered to family members, was her son's first tutor, and, as well as providing an important influx of capital in her dowry, increased the household's prosperity through prudent management.[127] To a greater extent than Hengniang might admit, it is a challenging balancing act to do all of that *and* be the charming concubine.

As the fox becomes the cure for every one of a man's ills, erotic desire is overshadowed by total satisfaction. Sometimes the erotic element is consciously denied as the vixen acts as the perfect teacher and the perfect friend, but erotic tension is better maintained by vehement denials than by perfunctory descriptions. This veering away from the marriage bed to the hearth or the coffers of the household is parallel to the absence of female desire at the heart of the image of the wanton vixen. Perhaps this suggests a structural limitation of the imagination: we cannot concentrate exclusively on a single object, be it unredeemed lust or perfect love.

The other role of a vixen that no human woman can play is the perfect wife, departing. She renews desire beyond satiety and suggests the limits of domesticity, even as she perfects it. In this, she is quite different from the other great figure of loss, the maiden who dies in virginity or youth and withdraws from domesticity before she enters it. She is a figure of loss endeavoring not to be a figure of loss by filling in her own space.

The supernatural romance in the classical tale is distinguished from other genres of romance by unity in point of view, a characteristic that has profound consequences for the romance. Both the post-*zaju* drama and the vernacular novel, and even the early to mid-Ming *chuanqi* romance with its heavy use of poetry, are dialogic forms that interweave the perspective of the longing man with that of the longing woman. In the classical tale, species and genre reinforce each other so that the romance is viewed only from the male and human side. The *zhiguai* is from its very origin a human encounter with the weird, recorded by the human. As a result the supernatural romance in the classical tale remained primarily a pleasure for male readers. Vixens lacked the cult of sympathy among female readers that grew up around Du Liniang in *Mudan ting* or the heroines of *Honglou meng*, because the genre dictated that they primarily be seen from the

127. See Mann, *Precious Records*, p. 65.

outside, rather than as emotional creatures in their own right with whom one could identify.[128] Just as the extreme of female desire seemed difficult to imagine, foxes' *qing* remained somehow impersonal, if extraordinary. Male readers could not so much identify with the male characters of these romances, since these men were barely characterized and often very passive, as put themselves in the blank spaces they created and join the male protagonists of these tales in appreciating incredible women.

128. Bai Niangzi is the exception who proves the rule. Unlike most animal lovers, her story was developed primarily in vernacular genres, and she was a figure of sympathy. In one anecdote, a woman beat the actor playing the heartless Xu Xian, Bai Niangzi's lover, as a means of threatening her husband; see "Da Xu Xian" 打許仙, in Yu Guolin, *Jiaoxuan zhilu*, 11.8a. Du Liniang as a ghost is sympathetic because she was originally human.

{7} *Becoming* Xian, *Arousing* Yao: *Foxes and Meaning*

It is a commonplace to assert that Chinese authors wrote about ghosts and foxes not to comment on ghosts and foxes but to express opinions about the human world. Although imagining the alien inevitably reveals concepts of humanity, this chapter deals with the overt use of the alien to discuss the human and examines some of the precise ways in which depiction of an alien species produces meaning about the human world.

When Ji Yun laid out all the different "betwixts" and "betweens" of the fox, the last categories mentioned in his list of states transgressed by the fox were *xian* 仙 and *yao* 妖. These two conditions are defined by transformation and ascent, but with opposite moral valences, and their different relations to humanity are expressed in distinct ways in anecdotes. In this chapter, I first discuss the central idea of foxes' self-improvement and its use as a comparison for the human condition. In the second part of the chapter, I discuss the common assertion "monsters are aroused by humanity," which treats *yao* as a by-product of the human. For foxes to be between *xian* and *yao* is to be between a trajectory parallel to humans and one dependent on them. In the former case, an articulate voice makes moral comments by comparing foxes and men; in the latter, the mere presence of the fox is a moral comment.

BECOMING XIAN: THE SELF-ADVANCEMENT COMPARISON

In one of the earliest theoretical statements on shape-changing foxes as a species, from *Xuan zhong ji*, foxes are depicted as beings in transition, advancing step by step from beasts to creatures that can assume human form and make mischief to virtual divinities communing with the heavens. That progression could still be subsumed under the heading of *yao*. In some Tang stories, foxes who are already transgressive *yao* seek to attain sanctioned transcendence by becoming *xian*. By the Qing, fox advancement had become an even more central theme as the attempt was made to fit all the variations of the fox story into a single master narrative. We saw the centrality of this theme to Ji Yun's definition of the fox in Chapter 2. Daniel Hsieh explains this tendency by arguing, citing Jung, that a struggle for progress is essential to trickster figures, who are eternally eager to learn.[1]

Self-advancement is, alongside karmic rewards and consequences, one of the two great structuring principles of the Chinese supernatural. As we have already seen, foxes are involved in both, with karma and advancement often entwined in a single narrative, because a fox can only take revenge or fulfill a passion after years of effort to assume human form. Both karma and self-cultivation are based on an accountant's view of morality, but in karma there are both credits and debits, whereas in self-cultivation there is only accumulation, with occasional risks of a disastrous loss of one's entire fortune. In fox tales, karmic entanglements are always relational, while self-advancement can be a solitary pursuit. Humans might be the fuel for advancement, or they might ruin it by stealing a fox's *dan*, but they are not essential. Karma explains an individual fox's relations with a particular human; self-advancement explains the behavior of the species as a whole. Most relevant to the present context, foxes' karmic entanglements with men have moral meanings for humans in that they demonstrate how humans and foxes are cogs in the same great moral machineries of the cosmos. In accounts of self-advancement, however, foxes follow paths separate from but parallel to the human.

1. Hsieh, "Man and Animal in Chinese Fox Stories," p. 12.

Ji's presentation of a grand unified fox theory, in Liu Shitui's interview with a fox discussed in Chapter 2, is not the only exploration of foxes' means of advancement in *Yuewei caotang biji*. Another example, related by Ji's teacher He Xiu, illustrates several ways of using fox stories to talk about the human world and shows how meaning is produced in the relations between species. It reveals the fox story as a way of talking about learning and as a pedagogical tool itself. In the late Ming, a student traveling alone in the wilderness overhears what was a common sound in settled areas but unexpected in the wilds: a group of students reading aloud. Upon locating the source of the sounds, he finds an old man acting as a teacher to a group of foxes in the original form.

The student thought that since they could read, they would not harm him; so he greeted them politely and sat down with them. He asked, "Why do you study?"

The old man said, "We are refining ourselves to become immortals. A fox who seeks to become an immortal can take one of two paths: the first is to gather life-essence and pray to the Big Dipper,[2] so that one gradually becomes powerful and can transform oneself. Afterwards one can continue refining oneself and achieve true success. This is to seek immortality as a monster. But some fall into evil ways and violate heaven's laws; so this path is quick and dangerous. The other method is first to refine oneself to assume human form, and once one is human, to refine one's inner cinnabar. This is to seek immortality as a human. This cannot be achieved overnight, but if one perseveres for a long time, one will naturally succeed. This path is slow and peaceful. But the form does not change itself; instead it follows the transformations of the heart. Therefore we first read the books of the sages to understand the principles of the three bonds and five moral norms.[3] When our hearts are transformed, our forms will also be transformed."

---

2. To pray to the Big Dipper is a relatively common and early variant of the motif of praying to the moon; see Chapter 2.

3. The *san'gang* 三綱, "three bonds," refers to the relationships between lord and servant, father and son, and husband and wife. The *wuchang* 五常, "five moral norms," are benevolence, righteousness, propriety, wisdom, and trustworthiness (although there are differing accounts).

The scene of the fox classroom had appeared as early as the Tang.[4] For the fox students to appear in animal form, relatively rare for this collection and the Qing in general, seems a concession to the earlier story type. This story also draws on the expectation created by these predecessors that foxes have magic books and are the masters of secret wisdom.[5]

The explication of the two paths of fox advancement is quite close to that found in the fox's conversation with Liu Guoshi and is shared by virtually all of Ji's contemporaries in both vernacular and classical fiction.[6] However, here foxes are not simply compared to Confucian scholars; they are Confucian scholars themselves.[7] The most crucial step toward humanity, and thus immortality, is reading the classics. All other means, whether they harm men or not, are dismissed as dangerous. The primacy of transforming the heart before the body, which we have seen in the discussion of the fox paragon at the end of the previous chapter, seems to be an expansion of the Great Learning: one must first rectify one's heart in order to cultivate one's self, and this is in turn the basis of the entire moral project of regulating family and state. For a fox, *xiu shen* 修身, "self-cultivation," is literal: the physical body is changed. The application of this reasoning to the human world is obvious: if the classics can make even beasts into divinities, what great progress could humans make once books have transformed their hearts and thus their entire selves? The contrast between the students in animal form and their instructor in human form makes the promise of advance tangible.

The student looked at their books. All were the Five Classics, the *Analects*, the *Classic of Filial Piety*, *Mencius*, and the like, but they only had the texts and no annotations. He asked how, since the text was not explicated, they discussed it. The old man replied, "When we read, we simply seek to illuminate principle. The words of the sages are in their essence not difficult. If

4. This scene also had some currency in Ming vernacular fiction. For an adaptation of this material as a vernacular story, see "Xiaoshuiwan tianhu yi shu" 小水灣天狐貽書, in Feng Menglong, *Xingshi hengyan*, no. 6.

5. As in the Tang tale "He Rangzhi" 何讓之, *TPGJ*, 448.3661.

6. See, e.g., the Jiajing-era vernacular novel *Yaohua zhuan*.

7. In other anecdotes Ji reasserted that foxes must read the classics; see, e.g., *YWCT*, 7.304, story 13.

one passes on and receives [meaning] orally and reconciles interpretations of the text, one can know their meaning. Why would we need annotation?" The student was amazed at his perverse argument and had no reply.

He asked the fox master's age. The old man replied, "I don't remember, but I remember in the days I received the classics, there were not yet printed books." The student asked, "In the many dynasties you have experienced, what changes and constants have there been in the world?" He said, "For the most part there aren't great differences. Only before the Tang, there were only Confucians; after the Northern Song, I often heard that so and so was a sage. That's the only small difference." The student didn't understand him and departed with a bow. Later he met this old man on the road and wanted to speak with him, but the old man shook his head and passed by.[8]

When the question turns from why foxes study to how, attention shifts from foxes to the classics and approaches to them. When the fox argues that commentary on the classics is unnecessary, he shifts from explanation of his world, with veiled application to why humans should study, to arguments directly addressing how they should. The vulpine reputation for otherworldly wisdom grants his comments authority. The narrative pattern of the interview with a fox, based on the fox séance, assumes a fox in a position of superior knowledge to the human interlocutor, but this exchange goes further by making the human being play the role of the unenlightened man dependent on commentary, more amazed by the idea of doing without commentary than by having a conversation with a fox. The man's intellectual inferiority is driven home when the scholarly fox snubs him.

Contempt for commentary, as opposed to the "pure" words of the classics, is relevant to important scholarly issues of the day, but here it is not a carefully argued position. This reflects the impulse to return to the texts, discarding the Song commentaries in particular, of the *Hanxue* movement of the Qing.[9] However, this argument cannot be entirely taken to indicate agreement with the *kaozheng* scholars. In their desire to return to the texts, these scholar's intense philological

---

8. *YWCT,* 3.125, story 124.

9. On Ji Yun's relationship to the eighteenth-century intellectual climate, *Songxue,* and *Hanxue,* see Chan, *The Discourse of Foxes and Ghosts,* pp. 113–19, 199; esp. the quote from Dai Zhen on the powers of human reason, p. 117.

labors showed that the classics were anything but easily accessible to the uninitiated reader; they ended up writing their own commentaries.[10] The claim that with enough diligence the classics can be understood without commentary seems instead conservative and wishful thinking, a return to an idealized traditional method of education. It reveals an idealistic belief in the ancient texts, rather than the doubts caused by philological inquiry. The story's setting in the late Ming may add two different nuances to the criticism—it could be particularly directed against the philosophical schools of the late Ming, or it might be intended to reduce the sting of criticism of contemporary scholars by setting it in an earlier period.

Most ancient foxes encountered in Qing texts claim to have been born in the Tang or Northern Song, which would make them the proverbial "thousand-year-old foxes"; in this case this commonplace seems to have particular historical significance, with the introduction of printing as the crucial turning point.[11] The fact that the old fox received the classics before the advent of printing seems to argue that his is a purer knowledge than that of the contemporary world and undiluted by the editing of the Song Confucians. The Northern Song is the point of irretrievable decline, with printing linked to textual distortion. A fox's extraordinary age lends credibility to conventional laments about the decline of the present era. At the same time the fox's claim of historical constancy frustrates the interlocutor's curiosity, as a direct link with the past provides a rebuke rather than any exotic historical insights.[12]

---

10. For an introduction to the philosophical world of the *Kaozheng* scholars, see Benjamin Elman, *From Philosophy to Philology*.

11. For example, the Jiangs' friendly fox lodger from *Tingyu xuan biji*, discussed in Chapter 3, is the same age. For another example of a fox claiming to have been born in the Northern Song, see *YWCT*, 4.74, story 175. It seems possible that making the foxes' memories stretch back to the Northern Song or Tang but no further is not simply counting back the magical sum of a thousand years but represents the literatis' own self-image. They can trace their intellectual pedigree back this far, and after that it gets blurry. Printing is also crucial to humans' grasp on their intellectual territory.

12. In another anecdote, a fox tells a human friend that it seems to him Neo-Confucianism, *Daoxue* 道學, and becoming a sage are two different things since a sage should strive to achieve harmony, but *Daoxue* leads only to contention. The

The fox tale was apparently not a medium for presenting complex or controversial scholarly issues, but it was an appropriate place for simple statements of current intellectual values, conventional wisdom, and sweeping generalizations.[13] The strange frame and perspective, different both because of the historical scope of the fox's experience, and because for the fox learning is literally a transformative experience, renders these opinions more interesting than they would be from a human's lips. The frame does provide some distance between the men telling these stories and the opinions expressed in them, but I believe that distance is intended to create interest by defamiliarizing the familiar rather than to provide a protective cover for dangerous opinions.

He Xiu's story also captures a key transformation of the Qing interest in the supernatural. In Tang stories foxes often possess books of secret knowledge in strange characters not known to humans. Here the foxes' books are the best-known works of the human world, and the fox teacher argues that the classics are easy to understand. The replacement of the older tradition of arcane fox knowledge with Confucian scholarship is made even clearer in a story in which a man overhears a fox reciting at night an examination-style essay. Ji mentioned, for the sake of comparison, a fox poem "Yingtian hu chaoyi kece badao" 應天狐超異科策八道 (The heavenly fox's eight stratagems of surpassing strangeness) included in a story about a stolen fox book in *Taiping guangji*.[14] That poem was phrased in obscure terms of Daoist achievement. Ji speculated that the overheard fox might be trying to pass the examinations. The esoteric fox language has been

---

man who relates this story thought the fox's comment probably reflected the disputes at the end of the Ming. See *YWCT*, 16.918–19, story 70.

13. A variant of the fox-scholar as a mouthpiece for human opinions more common in *Liaozhai* imitations is the fox schoolmistress, in which the vixen instructs her lover, usually until he can pass his exams. See, e.g., "Baishu," in Zeng Yindong, *Xiaodou peng*, pp. 171–73. Even more than in the male fox scholar plot, I think the opinions the vixens endorse are conventional wisdom. However, each man and each time's conventional wisdom varies. For example, two similar stories take opposite positions on the value of eight-legged essays, the conventional literary form of the civil service exam; see "Hu shi" 狐師, in Li Qingchen, *Zuichai zhiguai*, 4.392–400; and "Wu sheng" 吳生, in Lin Shu 林紓, *Lin Shu xuanji, xiaoshuo, shang*, 38–41.

14. "He Rangzhi," *TPGJ*, 448.3661.

replaced by the terms of the human world.[15] Foxes are no longer a separate, alien mystery but reflect the overall domestication of the strange.

Outspoken fox scholars like the one in He Xiu's story display the evolution of the value of foxes' own words; we have already seen this illustrated in the changing relationship of exorcism and explanation. In a famous *Soushen ji* story, an old fox changed himself into a young scholar and went to debate with Zhang Hua. That fox, too, had extensive knowledge of human learning, but to Zhang Hua that only proved he must be a monster. The fox argued that he should be respected on account of his learning, but to no avail: he was exposed and destroyed.[16] None of the fox's scholarly opinions are recorded, since they matter only as part of the illusion Zhang Hua dispelled. In the Tang, there was an emphasis on foxes' secret and esoteric knowledge; its content was desired but inaccessible. In the Qing, the fox becomes a mouthpiece for scholarly opinions or other kinds of knowledge. Its secret knowledge becomes real and accessible enough to be recorded.

Ji's comments on He Xiu's story are also revealing:

> This is probably a parable of the master's. He often said, "When one pursues success in the examinations by discussing the classics, one's words become far-fetched and unreliable; the more beautiful the phrases, the falser the interpretation of the classics. If one founds one's reputation on discussing the classics, disputes will proliferate, and the more detailed the explanation, the falser the interpretation of the classics." This seems to fit perfectly with the meaning of the story. He also often said, "Whenever there is a dazzling technique, there must be something unstable in it. If every step is slow and steady, even if there is a slight misstep, it will not reach the point of serious injury." This also has the same meaning as the two paths of pursuing immortality he mentioned.[17]

Despite the fact that this story shares several themes with other of his fox stories, Ji labeled it as a *yuyan* 寓言 (lit, "lodged words"; i.e., a parable) invented by the narrator He. Ji's grounds for deciding if

---

15. *YWCT* 6.281–82, story 285.

16. *Soushen ji* 421; Dewoskin and Crump, *In Search of the Supernatural*, pp. 216–18.

17. *YWCT* 3.125, story 124.

a story is *yuyan* are not absolute. He used the label most often for stories that seem to fit the narrator's points too neatly or to be plainly self-serving.[18] His decision as to whether a story is plausible or not seems based as much on the character of the man who related it as on the story's content. For example, he defended a tale of an implausibly perfect vixen on the grounds the narrator was an honest man; on the other hand, a braggart is likely to invent a story of his triumph over a fox.[19] In Ji's world men used both true fox stories and inventions to prove their points in conversation, and the two kinds of stories could resemble each other closely in plot and be used for similar rhetorical purposes. One suspects in He Xiu's case it is the discussion of the use of commentary that gets too close to the human world for even Ji to find it plausible. For Ji, *yuyan* are not to be regarded as highly as true stories that illustrate the same points: "If one happens occasionally to write this kind of ornate and clever prose as material for moral edification, there's nothing wrong with that. But if [such stories] are heaped up page after page and turn into chapters and whole books, this is not the proper generic form for writing books."[20] Only true stories can demonstrate that these moral principles are not authorial interpretation but inherent in the universe.[21]

Ji recognized the similarity between the ideas of this story and statements his former teacher frequently made in other contexts. Because he read this story as *yuyan* rather than experience, he interpreted it as revealing more about the raconteur's character and beliefs than it does about foxes. In his first comment, He Xiu uses the fox's criticisms of the modern approach to reading the classics to introduce his own criticisms. He objects to the whole industry of commentary on and expansions of the classics, whether by examination candidates or independent scholars making a name for themselves. Just as the fox implies printing is a force of corruption, this profusion of inter-

---

18. E.g. *YWCT* 8.358–59, story 67; and 11.579–80, story 49. See Chan, *The Discourse of Foxes and Ghosts*, pp. 198–200.

19. *YWCT* 12.610–11, story 80.

20. *YWCT* 22.1228, story 95. "Author of books" here means the faithful recorder of true narratives, as opposed to the "talented man" 才子 who fabricates. This was the contrast established in Sheng Shiyan's colophon.

21. Chan (*The Discourse of Foxes and Ghosts*, p. 199) argues this is why true allegory as such is not very well developed.

pretations and arguments is related to publishing and the market in examination aids and other scholarly work. In this case foxes represent an ideal of creatures morally transformed by the texts and thus superior to the humans whose impure motives for study lead them into misreadings. The second comment about the superiority of slow, reliable methods to quick risky ones is a more general interpretation. Foxes, who were originally representatives of mischief and chaos, are made advocates of stolid perseverance and prudence. This shift in tone is typical of emphasis on the self-improving fox in general.

This story serves to introduce two kinds of rhetorical intersection between foxes and the human world: in the first, the fox directly introduces human issues within the story; in the second, the human narrator interprets the story in commentary. The context in which He Xiu related this tale sheds light on the attention given the theme of fox advancement. Like many of Ji's informants, He Xiu was a teacher and used these anecdotes in conversations with his students. Couching his messages in the palatable terms of fox stories obviously worked as a pedagogical technique, since one of his students remembered both tale and moral well enough to record them years later. The values of diligence and the slow, sure path to success are as closely linked to the pedagogical context as the points about proper motives and methods for studying the classics.

The central comparison of human and fox advancement was common in Ji's generation, and Ji's use of the analogy can be illuminated by comparison with one of his contemporaries. In one of Yuan Mei's stories in *Zi bu yu*, a man encounters a fox claiming to hold the *shengyuan* 生員 degree. The fox explains that the goddess Taishan Niangniang holds an annual examination for foxes; those who pass are allowed to refine themselves to become immortals, and those who fail are condemned to remain wild foxes. He goes on to elaborate how much easier it is for humans than foxes to achieve immortality, since foxes must first attain human form and study human speech. Even among humans, a noble or educated man can achieve immortality far more quickly than an ordinary man could. The anecdote closes by expressing regret that the informant never asked the fox the topics of Taishan Niangniang's examination.[22] Although Yuan used the same comparison as Ji, he emphasized the institution of an examination of unknown and possibly distinctly foxish content, rather than the tranformative power of study of the human classics. Comparison with Ji's vision, which concentrated on slow progress rather than a single test, reveals in turn the arbitrary nature of the examination system in the human world. Although the final expression of curiosity about the examination's content seems superficially similar to Ji's investigations, the tone makes it a joke. Yuan's comparisons give foxes and humanity not a shared moral universe but only shared institutions.[23] The final question also admits the possibility that foxes might be judged by a standard other than the human classics and human morality, a possibility that Ji rejects. However, the basic form of the interview with the fox who explains fox advancement and the final assertion of human advantages are shared. The difference in tone is typical of the contrast between the two collections.

Even among Ji's informants, there are differences of emphasis and tone in the interpretation of foxes' self-improvement. He Xiu stressed general moral self-improvement, but other comparisons are more closely tied to the mechanics of the examination system. Compare the schoolmaster's exhortations of steady diligence in He Xiu's story to the laughing self-deprecation of another of Ji's informants, Gao Guanying 高冠瀛. Depressed by his lack of success, he relates a tale of a captured fox who confesses that there are three paths of fox advancement (rather than the usual two). He is not capable of taking the high road of self-cultivation and Daoist austerities; on the other hand, he does not dare to take the low road of seduction and parasitism. His middle road is gleaning the leftover *qi* shed in people's breath as they sleep, much as a bee gathers pollen.[24] Gao sighs that he is much like this fox; there are paths to success of which he is not

22. Yuan Mei, *Zi bu yu*, 1.9.

23. It is more common to construct entire systems parallel to the human world among ghosts in the underworld and immortals in the heavens; foxes usually remain outsiders. Here we see foxes losing that outsider status.

24. This relatively benign form of parasitism is also described in Lang Ying, *Qixiu leigao*, 48.9b.

capable, as well as paths he does not dare attempt. He closes by asking Ji and another friend for advice, since they have already passed the examinations.[25] In this case, the fact that it is the human and not the fox who makes the comparison reveals that this reasoning is transferable from one voice to another. This rather pathetic fox suits the entire anecdote's plaintive tone. He Xiu's fox was one of the superior and successful ones of his kind, as the high degree holder He may well have regarded himself. Gao in turn creates in his fox an equivalent of his hapless self. This story illustrates how the fox-human comparison could appeal to figures at all strata of literati society, both those successful in the highest circles and the desperate local graduates. However, it also reveals a lacuna in the foxes' accounts of self-improvement: we never hear the voice of the fox who chose the quick and lawless way to success.

Tales of fox advancement often share a common ending. Both Yuan Mei's tale of the fox licentiate and Ji's introduction to fox society (as related to Liu Guoshi, see Chapter 2) close with a final assertion of human superiority. *Qiudeng conghua*, which belongs to roughly the same generation, contains a similar assertion by a figure described in the anecdote's title as *huxian*. When his human interlocutor praises foxes' abilities, he replies that of all the world's creatures humans are the most superior, but they are destroyed by their desires.[26] In earlier periods human superiority would have gone without saying, but in the Qing the humanization of foxes has proceeded far enough that there seems to be a need for humans to defend their own status. The definition of the fox's identity has raised questions about human identity, and foxes now have a voice to comment on humanity. The statement of human superiority is inevitably accompanied by an injunction for humans not to waste their natural gifts. This reprimand, contrasting vulpine diligence overcoming natural disadvantages with human squandering of their natural gifts, is in

25. *YWCT* 18.1083, story 199. In another anecdote with a very similar tone, a man mocks a fox for his drastic shifts of moods when he discovers years of self-refinement have been in vain. The fox replies that the man's mood swings in response to his successes and reverses in the examination system are much the same. See "Zhe sheng" 浙生, in Li Qingchen, *Zuicha zhiguai*, 4.475–79.

26. Wu Jian, *Qiudeng conghua*, 10.18a.

some ways a further refinement of the use of the animal paragon to shame flawed humans. The repeated refrain reveals an image of humans as the spoiled favorite children of the universe.

As the fox approaches perfection of its imitation of humanity and almost effaces its animal origins, stories move from making parallels between species to reasserting differences. Another anecdote from *Yuewei caotang* makes this move in a different way.

Guo Shizhou said, "Zhu Jingyuan was friends with a fox. One day he was drinking at Jingyuan's house, got very drunk, and fell asleep under the flowers. When he woke, Jingyuan asked him, 'I have heard that your kind often change your shape after you get drunk; therefore I covered you with a blanket and guarded you myself. But you did not change. Why?'[27]

"The fox said, 'This depends on the degree of our strength in the Way. Since those whose accomplishments are slight can create only illusory forms, when they are drunk, asleep, or startled, they change. Those whose accomplishments are considerable can shed their forms, as immortals shed their corpse. Since they have already converted to the human way, the human form is their original form; how could it change?'

"Jingyuan wanted to study the Dao with him. He replied, 'You cannot. As for studying the Way, it is easy for humans and hard for creatures. Human *qi* is pure, and the *qi* of creatures is impure. Achieving the Way is easy for creatures and hard for humans, since the hearts of creatures are unified and the human heart is complicated. Those who would refine their forms first refine their *qi*; those who would refine their *qi* first refine their hearts. This is called the leadership of one's intent. When the heart is settled, then *qi* gathers and the form is fixed. When the heart wavers, then *qi* disperses and the form withers. What Guang Chengzi told the Yellow Emperor was a secret formula of the Daoists, not an invention of old Zhuang. To dwell in deep mountains and dark valleys, hearing nothing and seeing nothing, only concentrating one's spirit and associating with heaven and earth, passing a hundred years like one day—could human beings do it?' Zhu then gave up."

This tale is a complicated play of similarity and difference between foxes and men. Ji first insists on foxes that have become absolutely human but still allows for a difference in aptitudes; he resists making foxes secret masters of enlightenment. The tale makes familiar

27. A human friend of a fox does the same thing in "Jiuyou" 酒友, in *LZ*, 2.217–19.

moves: Daoist immortality is moved firmly out of human reach, but humans' unique gifts are reiterated. It is a fox who seems on the verge of effacing all external difference who must insist on internal differences, but for both species improvement of the heart is key to all other progress.[28] This story is unique in describing psychological differences between humanity and others, but the distinctions are interestingly ambiguous. The purity of human *qi* might relate to Mencian beliefs about the innate goodness of human nature. Foxes have no fundamentally good nature; instead their moral substance is initially compromised. On the other hand, humans are credited with more complexity, in contrast to foxes, who in Ji Yun's world are entirely focused on their single task of self-improvement. Both of these points allude to Zhu Xi's explanation of the difference between humans and other creatures as a contrast between *chun* 純 "pure" and *bo* 駁 "impure" *qi*.[29] According to Zhu, the *qi* of animals is blocked and they cannot become enlightened. However, sometimes they are capable of a single outstanding virtue. They can exceed humans in that virtue because it is all they have; since humans are capable of so much more, they become confused more easily.[30] This paraphrase of Zhu Xi is placed in the mouth of a fox who contradicts Zhu's statements on the limits of animals' achievements. A concept of the fox as formed of corrupt stuff but single-mindedly bent on improvement has as its mirror image an innately superior but easily distracted humanity.

Ji appended an apparently unrelated story that casts fascinating shadows on this one. He introduced this second story with the line "Because of this I recalled. . . ." This is one of the few cases in which Ji recorded a stream-of-consciousness association between his various anecdotes. A certain classmate of Ji's asked an actor why of all those who played women's roles he alone dominated the stages of the time. The actor replied:

"As well as making our bodies those of women, we must also make our hearts female, and afterward our gentle passions and seductive postures drive the audience to distraction. If I have one speck of a male heart, then

28. *YWCT* 12. 625–26, story 111.
29. "Xingli" 性理, in Zhu Xi, *Zhuzi yulei*, 4.90.
30. Ibid., 4.95.

there will be one spot that does not resemble a woman, and I will not be able to contend for the favor granted to those of moth eyebrows and blue-black hair. If I am going to go on stage as a virgin, then I order my heart; although I laugh and joke, I do not lose my innocence. When I am a wanton woman, I cast my heart loose, and although I sit quietly, I cannot conceal my lustfulness. If I am a noblewoman, I make my heart respectful, so that even when I am in poor clothes, my noble air remains. If I am a base woman, I constrict my heart, so that even clad in rich adornment, I have a base attitude. When I am a saintly woman, I soften my heart, so that even when angry, I have no rash expression. When I am a wicked woman, I make my heart rebellious, so that although I argue reasonably, I speak no mild words. I put myself in the position of every single one, whether in joy or rage, grief or pleasure, gratitude or resentment, love or hate. I take it not as a play but as real, so that others also see me as real. When others perform as a woman, they cannot maintain the heart of a woman, and when they play every kind of woman, they cannot have every kind of female heart; this is why I alone dominate the stage."

Li Yudian said that this story was lascivious and not worth talking about, but its principle gets at the essential. Although this is a small matter, by analogy it can be applied to great affairs. In the world there has never been anyone who was able to succeed at anything without his heart being in it. Nor has there been anyone who failed when his whole heart was devoted to a pursuit. If your heart is devoted to an art, you will be skillful. If it is devoted to a career, you will succeed. Liao, good with a slingshot, or Pian, good at making wheels, are small examples; the four ministers of Yu and Shun's governing the world are great examples, but the principle is the same. This story and the theory about refining *qi* and the form can reinforce each other.[31]

Although the link between the two stories is made on a philosophical and moral level, the second story brings up many portions of the fox tradition that the earlier anecdote had effaced and rejected. This happens continuously throughout the collection: discarded elements still lurk around the edges and are often, as here, displaced into the human world. Li Yudian reads the same final message of single-minded effort in both stories. However, the actor brings up associations of illusion, seduction, and illicit sexuality that Ji had

---

31. *YWCT* 12.645–46, story 111.

tried to leave behind with the red fox corpse. Although the heart is essential to the ability to assume human shape, the actor can change his heart for the purpose of pleasing and seducing an audience and a patron, just as foxes use transformations to seduce. A female impersonator does anything but distract from the body. The "truth" of his heart will show no matter what he is doing, but both that internal nature and his actions are artifice. Essential human characters must seem fixed and recognizable so that he can emulate them, but the fact they can be so effectively imitated devalues them. Any reality he attains is framed in the context of the theater. This in turn begs the question of whether an accomplished fox in human form is really human only in the same way as the most skilled female impersonator is really female. Is inner conviction and a convinced audience enough to change identity? The story raises these unsettling questions between the lines, but association with the outlandish perfection of fox and transvestite seems to make exhortations to perseverance attractive.

Part of the popular conception of fox advancement that is not included in these visions of steadiness is the idea of a destined *jie* 劫, "a foreordained disaster," usually a lightning strike, which most do not survive. Only those who survive can continue their ascent to the status of *xian*. On the level of individual narrative, we have already seen, in the case of Jiaona and Xiaocui, how fleeing a lightning strike binds foxes to the human world with ties of gratitude, since cowering behind a man of virtue or destiny can save them.[32] On a more general level, this idea puts a check on non-human creatures' ascent. In some parts of the tradition, this vulnerability was attractive both in individual narrative and as a general realignment of the balance between human and inhuman power. However, precisely the arbitrariness of the bolt from the blue that makes a destined calamity dramatic causes it to be excluded from these systematic explications of fox advancement. Ji Yun, for example, criticized He Bang'e's accounts of foxes avoiding karmic disaster on logical grounds, arguing that if the fox were innocent, heaven would not strike it by lightning; and if

32. Another example of this kind of tie is the vixen saved by the future Judge Bao. She rescues him three times in turn. See Yu Yue, *Qixia wuyi*, *hui* 2–4.

guilty, heaven would not limit itself to one attempt at punishment or allow it to escape so easily.[33]

Why is the idea of foxes' advancement to immortality and transcendence so central to how they generate meaning in comparisons with humanity? In this era, benign methods of pursuing immortality seem to have undergone a transformation not unlike that undergone by sexual parasitism: as they declined in frequency in actual practice, they became more important as literary tropes, particularly in depictions of other creatures. The vocabulary of Daoist cultivation, particularly *xiuxing* 修形, "to refine one's form," and *neidan*, "inner elixir," proved a rich source of metaphors for all sorts of efforts. The link with *xiushen*, "self-cultivation," a central concept in the *Great Learning* and the first step toward an ordered family and nation, is particularly direct. Thus the idea of foxes' transcendence, far from subverting mundane morality or worldly success, became conflated with both.[34] An extreme example of Confucian content in a Daoist guise is found in an early Republican collection. When asked how one can achieve immortality, the vixen tells her would-be lover that immortality can be pursued only by following the Doctrine of the Mean.[35]

He Xiu's fox and his diligent fellows may provide an interesting mirror of contemporary philosophical debates. Dai Zhen 戴震 (1723–77), a contemporary of Ji's who even contributed a few anecdotes to *Yuewei caotang biji*, rejected Zhu Xi's idea of "returning to the original mind," and instead emphasized the importance of continuous education. He compared the immature mind to the immature body: far from being a perfection from which man lapses, the original mind is simply weak and underdeveloped.[36] Foxes are the extreme example of this principle: their original state is most certainly not desirable, and education can raise them to unimaginable heights. The parallel can be

33. *YWCT* 7.296, story 4; "Afeng" 阿鳳, in *YTSL*, 2.44–48.

34. Another story with a fox lecturer who seems to take a more world-renouncing view ends with the comment, "The fox's words were only a vulgar version of *Laozi*, but they were probably good enough for self-improvement" (*YWCT*, 4.178–79, story 175).

35. "Huli gu" 胡麗姑, in Yang Fenghui, *Nan'gao biji*, 3.13a. In *BJXSDG*, vol. 14.

36. Yu Yingshi, *Lun Dai Zhen yu Zhang Xuecheng*.

pushed too far, but the concept of fox nature was influenced by changes in the conception of human nature.

The concept of self-advancement as a distinguishing trait of the fox is almost universally accepted in both the popular and the literary tradition. The fox heroines of the *Liaozhai* imitations and the more humble foxes of five animal spirits worship all share this ambition.[37] In vernacular fiction, an animal spirit embarking on an ambitious project of self-improvement is often the opening of a narrative.[38] When an overweening demon is defeated, the victorious exorcist sometimes expresses sympathy for all the centuries of effort now gone to waste.[39] Some defeated monsters are allowed to return to a curriculum of self-improvement; self-improvement provides closure as well as opening.[40] This trajectory thus served, in vernacular *shenmo xiaoshuo* 神魔小說 (novels of gods and demons), to make a monster a sympathetic protagonist. The centrality of self-advancement is one of the unique traits of China's imaginary cosmos. Although the fox may share its roles as trickster, femme fatale, and petty deity with supernatural creatures in other cultures, particularly European fairies, the role of earnest student seems unique to the Chinese tradition. Mobility between categories of creatures is fundamental to the vision of the cosmos since the first appearance of the fox, but the Qing brought an increased emphasis on the creatures' own efforts. What does the importance of this concept say about the culture?

The self-improving fox was related not only to ideals and fears of social mobility but also to ideas of moral self-determination. Fox accomplishment was part of an entire world in which virtue could be quantified in monetary terms, as is evidenced by the popularity of "moral ledgers" in the late Ming and Qing period, which balanced moral accounts in terms of the merits and demerits of human deeds.[41] It was also an age that emphasized an individual's control over his or her moral balance sheet.[42] Although the overall

37. On the later, see Dorfman, "The Spirits of Reform," p. 262.

38. As in *Xi you ji*, *Zhaoyang qushi*, *Leifengta chuanqi*, and *Huli quanyuan*.

39. As in *Leifengta* and *Huli quanyuan*.

40. As in *Zhaoyang qushi*.

41. Brokaw, *The Ledgers of Merit and Demerit*.

42. Johnson et al., *Popular Culture in Late Imperial China*, pp. 15–16.

fascination with self-improvement was shared throughout the culture, the direct equation of foxes' pursuit with Confucian study was a literati invention and of interest primarily to that audience. Good foxes' advancement was linked to education, and evil foxes' advancement to ill-gotten money.[43] Like ill-gotten money, it was inconstant: the elixir of a wicked fox was a treasure that could be stolen, whereas the fruits of diligence could be thrown away only by the fox's own errors.

Zongqi Cai argues that a crucial difference between Chinese and Western philosophy is a focus on process as opposed to a focus on truth.[44] The focus on self-advancement and the very concepts of *xian* and *yao* suggest that Chinese concepts of species were based on ideas of transformation rather than fixed identity. But the process is not open-ended: a fox may always be in the process of becoming human, but it never reaches that point.

What is the relationship of the fox progress theme to the fox tradition as a whole? Part of its appeal lies in its attempt at a master narrative. It is a single explanation for the wild variety of the fox tradition, for the malicious bogeyman to the benign divinity, from the sexual vampire to the paragon of virtue. All these are different stages of progress or different choices among the possible roads. Establishing a curriculum for foxes' advancement is reassuring as well as explanatory. The orderly progression seems less disturbing than the uncontrolled crossing of the borders between species. The fox's trajectory can be envisioned in its different relations to us, as we have seen in the stories discussed in earlier chapters: they can be perfectly parallel to us, but always at a distance; or they can intersect with us as they are passing elsewhere. It is the male foxes who often appear as parallels; the vixens who intersect with us and then depart.

Thus the self-improving fox could personify many different vectors of advancement—moral self-cultivation, education, financial gain, and social mobility—with varying appeals for audiences of dif-

---

43. *YWCT*, 9.416, story 130. In another story, foxes who seduce and drain humans to develop their own *neidan* are compared to bandits, and foxes who take the slow, steady route to immortality are likened to peasants tilling their fields; see *YWCT*, 4.178–79, story 175.

44. Cai, "Configurations of Comparative Poetics," p. 107.

ferent classes. For the literati, all these elements remained focused on preparations for the examinations. The crucial elements of the comparison, for all classes, are moral choice and steady effort. The comparison is flexible enough to provide both models and warnings. The emphasis on diligence in the end delivers the hopeful message that extraordinary transformations are possible through individual effort.

AROUSING DEMONS: FOXES AND THE MIND

From a shared concept of the ascending fox, I turn to four shared words. A single formula, *yao you ren xing* 妖由人興, "Anomalies arise from men," provides the last word in many Ming and Qing *zhiguai*. Comparison with the original context in *Zuo zhuan* puts the evolution of tales of the strange in sharp relief: a battle of two snakes, one from within and one from outside the city, had been interpreted as an omen of the city's conquest. When asked whether there are really portents, Shen Xu responds, "When people have something they are deeply distressed about, their vital energy flames up and takes such shapes. Portents (*yao*) arise because of people. If people have no dissension, they will not arise of themselves. When men abandon their constant ways, then portents arise."[45] Portents are real, but they are not independent phenomena; the human world remains central. The snakes could foretell the city's downfall because they reflected the human disturbances of which the invasion was a consequence. Strangeness occurs in nature only when humans abandon their own norms. Here *yao* are external, mindless omens. In later tales, in additional to the broader sense of *yao* as any violation of the normal, the word takes on the more specific meaning of non-human creatures assuming human shape. Omens are replaced by sentient beings who will take advantage of humans' emotional upheavals by assuming the forms of desires or fears in order to dally with men. Like the earlier portents, they are real, but still dependent on the human world. *Yao* have traced a trajectory from the monstrous results of public in-

---

45. *Zuo zhuan*, 14th year of Duke Zhuang; translation from Burton Watson, *The Tso Chuan: Selections from China's Oldest Narrative History* (New York: Columbia University Press, 1989), pp. 207–8.

stability, which have national significance, to private outbreaks of monstrosity.

As meanings of *yao* change, so too does the concept of the human from which the monstrous arises. There is often a shift from the group to the individual. But what is the nature of the human interior involved, and what is the precise nature of the relationship? By following this phrase through various contexts, we can discover different visions of the link between monsters and the human mind. It can be used to explain the apparently inexplicable, to condemn human moral weakness, to marvel at the inventions of human desire, or to deplore a descent into madness, whether private or communal. At a direct level, human substance and attention can turn inanimate objects into monsters, as compared with plants and animals who attain the ability through their own, independent aspirations.[46] In the late Qing it was used to describe the sorcery-fearing hysteria of the masses from the perspective of a skeptical upper class.[47]

One of the most common uses of the phrase is to condemn the immorality of the man who is tormented by a monster. In this meaning, "monsters arise from people" is simply an inversion of *yao bu sheng de* 妖不勝德, "monsters cannot defeat the virtuous,"[48] a phrase used in *Shi ji* to describe an incident that occurred during the Shang. The emperor is terrified of an inauspicious plant; a minister tells him if he reforms his virtue, he will have nothing to fear. He does, and the plant withers. In the Han, the statement meant that the virtuous ruler has nothing to fear from anomalies; in the Ming and Qing, the message was applied to everyone. One relatively early example of the simple reassurance that strange creatures do not violate the larger moral order appears in a Kangxi collection, in a fairly typical tale of a

---

46. One example of many is a tale of a man who gets a nosebleed and idly makes clay figures of blood-moistened mud. They become monsters, which he eventually returns to crush. See "Mai suan weng" 賣蒜翁, in Dai Lianfen, *Libian xuan zhiyan*, 2.6a.

47. For example, the *Shenbao* used the phrase frequently to describe the 1876 outbreak incident of the queue-cutting hysteria that Kuhn describes in *Soulstealers*; see "Yaozhuan die qi" 謠傳迭起, *Shenbao*, 7/24/1876, 17.10634

48. *Shi ji*, "The Biographies of Yin," vol.1, 3:100.The earliest source for *yao bu sheng de* 妖不勝德 seems to be the Han work *Qianfu lun* 潛夫論; see *Hanyu da cidian*, vol.10, p.588.

demon lover. A man meets a beautiful woman while out riding one night; he tries to follow her but cannot catch her. He cannot forget her, and later she appears at his door, claiming to have been summoned by his thoughts. As their relationship continues, he begins to waste away; she eventually drives him to his death. The narrator concludes with the comment "monsters arise from people." The man invited his doom with his lust; a morally upright man would never suffer such a fate.[49]

"Monsters arise from people" in the sense of moral censure for the victims of monsters was a cliché in weird tales throughout the Qing. It comes to resemble the commonplace often seen in vernacular fiction (notably in *Shuihu zhuan* and *Jin ping mei*) *se bu mi ren, ren zi mi* 色不迷人，人自迷 "Beauty does not bewitch people; people bewitch themselves."[50] At its simplest, it is a statement that sin is the sinner's own fault and reiterates a message of moral responsibility. This moralizing simplification did not, however, exhaust the possibilities of "monsters arise from people."

Another important range of interpretations of the human origins of monsters/demons is medical. Chinese traditional medicine has its own version of "monsters cannot defeat the virtuous," with "evil" meaning pathology and "the correct," healthy practices. Already in the Han, Wang Chong had explained ghosts as a by-product of human illness.[51] Paul Unschuld argues it was in the Ming dynasty that demonology was incorporated into the rest of the medical tradition and included in the same correspondences as the human mind and body. Some medical authorities believed demons to be real, and that people drew their attacks with physical or emotional weaknesses.[52] Whether ghosts or demons are a (possibly illusory) by-product of illness, the cause of illness, or "opportunistic infections," medical concepts weave these creatures intimately to individual humans. These ideas are an important reminder of the interdependence of the physical and psychological in the Chinese medical system. Monsters can

49. Dong Han, *Zhuanxiang zhuibi*, *shang*, 25b.

50. This line is found in a variety of sources in Ming vernacular fiction and drama; see Roy, trans. *Plum in the Golden Vase*, 1:479, note one.

51. "Ding gui pian" 訂鬼篇, in Wang Chong, *Lunheng xiaoshi*, 22.931.

52. Unschuld, *Chinese Medicine*, p. 215–23.

have an important role to play in that relationship: for example, the fox demon is the means by which a man's deviant desire becomes a physical syndrome.

The Ming novel *Dongdu ji* interprets *yao* as the direct result of human failings, with a broad cast of animal spirit characters. "If you do good deeds, then auspicious spirits will help you; if you do evil, strange creatures will become monsters."[53] An avenging shrimp demon arises as a consequence of the violent deaths of many of its kind at the hands of a fisherman; a mouse demon fat from an official granary emerges to take revenge on a corrupt underling who does more harm than he/she does; a dog becomes a demon as a consequence of a jealous, shrewish wife cursing in front of him.[54] In comparison with the more common classical tale vision of existing monsters responding to human failings, here human failings prolifically manufacture *yao*. Domestic conflicts within households are seen from the perspective of the demons, such as the Quarreling Demon King 反目魔王, who try to find a lodging in various human hosts, often only to find other demons already there.[55] Individuals, because of their faults, allow these demons entry into their breasts, but once the demon lodges there the faults are exacerbated. In this cosmology, *yao* are external creatures, and *mo* 魔 are internal. As a consequence of vernacular fiction's ability to view the narrative from the perspective of the supernatural creatures, in addition to the narrator's general statements about how human actions result in *yao*, the individual creatures comment on the particular human failures that gave them birth. This sprawling set of subplots is not simply several classical tales stitched together: both the perspective and the nature of the moral relationship to humanity differ. This crowded, demon-infested landscape is a mode of vernacular fiction similar to satirical ghost novels like *He dian* 何典 (What sort of book is this?; ca. 1830), with the additional complexity of having both *yao* and *mo* as criticisms of human failings.

One guide to this crowded world is a male fox, who begins as a seducer but becomes a moral force. The fox serves as a familiar refer-

53. Fang Ruhao, *Dongdu ji*, p. 293.
54. Ibid., pp. 252, 296, 293.
55. Ibid., pp. 216–18.

ence point. He is more flexible in meaning than the other creatures he encounters, which are linked to specific origins, whereas he wanders far from his original forests of lust. This capacity for transition is again typical of the fox, who is appealing as a protagonist because he can perceive both the supernatural and the mundane worlds. In this chapter I make the distinction between foxes as moral by-products of humanity and as moral actors parallel to humanity. All the animal spirits *Dongdu ji* have the potential to be both, but the fox makes one of the clearest transitions between the two.

Pu Songling had his own interpretation of the powers of the human imagination to summon alien beings. He never quoted the statement *yao you ren xing*, although he made the similar remark "Illusion is born from human beings" in the comment on "Huabi" 畫壁 (The painted wall), a story in which a man's desire apparently animates an entire world within a mural.[56] In his stories, human desire variously animates paintings, summons flower-spirits, and brings a paper figure to life. In one of the clearest examples, an obsessive bookworm has a relationship with a paper cutting of a woman who falls out of one of his books. Pu's comment to this story reads, "If things are accumulated, they can arouse jealousy; if you love them, they can give birth to demons *mo*; this woman's bewitching beauty (*yao*) is the demonic power of books."[57] There is more overt emphasis on the power of man's desires for creatures that are less likely to take on human form than foxes, partially because foxes have a longer independent history of transformation, and, unlike paintings or flowers, they are not objects of human admiration in their original forms.

In *Liaozhai*, human words have the same effect as human desires in conjuring and animating the supernatural. They, too, are human fabrications granted reality only by our minds. Lies and jokes as well as wishes always come true in some twisted way. Within the stories it is a very daring argument for the power of fiction: once words have been uttered, they exist with the same reality as anything else in the tale.[58] We have already seen this in "Lianxiang." The joking question, "Aren't you afraid of ghosts and foxes?" prompts first the

56. *LZ*, 1.17.
57. *LZ*, 11.1457.
58. Zeitlin, *Historian of the Strange*, p. 166

appearance of a false ghost, a prostitute playing the part as a joke, and then the real thing, which the protagonist assumes to be false. After the first joke, he is unable to recognize the truth when he hears it and does not believe that his two lovers are a fox and a ghost.[59] In "Yingning" the hero's friend lies, saying Yingning is the hero's cousin; but the lie turns true, since it turns out she is the offspring of a kinsman's affair with a fox.[60]

This mixture of jest with the serious goes beyond the literal fulfillment of jokes: in *Liaozhai* supernatural creatures are summoned by humans' intense desires, but they respond by mocking the very obsessions that made them real.[61] In an ironic twist, the creatures aroused by the human imagination are not contained by it but take on a life of their own. Rather than being an extension of the obsession, they balance it, and this very balance means that they are not in the end seen as destabilizing *yao*. For Pu the power and danger of the human imagination are above all fascinating and beautiful, an outlook that seems related to his own liberal attitude towards fictional invention.

Pu's interest in the psychological underpinnings of relations with alien creatures was shared by his successors throughout the Qing. Ji used the principle of the human origins of monsters in a variety of fox stories; foxes could be summoned by a chance remark or joke as much as by intense passions.[62] Only harmful foxes are explained in this way, however; the well-behaved and well-educated foxes had more control of their comings and goings. If the fox quietly making his way forward provides a mirror for a human literatus, the fox as dependent *yao* is a funhouse mirror that distorts and enlarges human flaws by making them monstrous or a magic mirror that reveals the monstrosity hidden under the surface. By making harmful foxes dependent on human vices, Ji eliminated any fear of lurking external monsters only to direct the dread of monstrosity inward.

---

59. *LZ*, 2.220–32.

60. *LZ*, 2.147–59.

61. Notably in "Huangying" 黃英, in *LZ*, 11.1446–52; and "Shu chi" 書癡, in *LZ*, 11.1153–58.

62. For Ji's use of the formula, see Chan, *The Discourse of Foxes and Ghosts*, p. 145.

Ji lacked Pu's interest in the surface of the illusions humans can create. Pu found invention a potentially delightful prospect, whereas Ji saw mainly its dangers. This issue lies at the heart of the literary and philosophical divide between the two men. As we saw in the previous chapter, there is a moral tone to Ji's critical disapproval of Pu's generic mixing and fictional invention. There is a personal basis for his concern: Ji's son was an avid reader of *Liaozhai*, and Ji hinted that he blamed this obsession, along with his son's enthusiasm for emulating late Ming schools of poetry, for his untimely death. "He saw a manuscript copy of *Liaozhai zhiyi* and fell into that pattern. He fell and could not turn back, to the point that he died."[63] In the Qianlong era, the obsessed man of the *Liaozhai* tales has become real, with *Liaozhai* itself as the object of obsession. Ji's diagnosis of his son's condition conflates fiction with obsession and pathology.

Yet Ji, whose assessment of the human capacity for invention was so utterly different from Pu's, shared an interest in lies and jokes coming true. Ji often appended the comment "monsters arise from people" to these anecdotes; clearly he believed that human words do just as much to arouse the strange as do inner psychological states. In one anecdote that uses this conclusion, a family trying to prevent children from playing in empty storerooms put up a sign warning that a fox spirit dwelt there and should not be disturbed. Evidently, the domestic fox could be used as a childhood bogeyman. After several days they heard a voice from outside the window saying, "I have arrived, having received your kind summons. I will guard this compound for you." After this, people who went into the rooms were pelted with tiles, and even servants moving the stored junk dared not enter.[64] Ji delighted in making a real fox expose a false fox. In another anecdote a fervent skeptic who rejected the existence of ghosts is terrified by a local wit disguised as one. He is convinced the ghost is real until the joke is revealed by others. In a twist reminiscent of "Lianxiang," when the haunting continues, he is convinced it is still a trick, but now it is real. Ji Yun concludes that a

63. Appended to final *juan* of *YWCT*, p. 1300.
64. *YWCT*, 11.565, story 34.

fox took advantage of his fear.[65] There are similar anecdotes in which a real ghost responds to skepticism about ghosts.[66] Nevertheless in Ji's world a fox was more likely to play the role of a ghost or another being than vice versa, a further demonstration of foxes' flexibility and role as jokers. The serious implications of the consequences of human emotion and belief do not dampen the humor of the joke turned true.

More commonly, Ji used human weakness to explain the parasitism of vixens or depredations of tile-throwing foxes. To make all actions of foxes dependent on human faults deprives them of any power besides moral response. Although Ji eliminated the horror of arbitrary monsters preying on innocents, he created the new specter of ever-vigilant and omniscient moral judges. Nor are they granted this power of judgment because of a superior moral understanding; rather, it is a visceral, involuntary response. Wicked foxes are terrified of virtues and take advantage of our weaknesses. An imperial emissary could be attacked by a fox once he thinks of taking the wife of one of his inferiors as a concubine;[67] on the other hand, a parasitic vixen leaves a man alone after he has a generous thought to save a neighbor boy from a life as a singing boy. The thought stabs her with physical pain.[68] In both cases the thought that affects the fox is sexually tinged. Ji made foxes creatures for whom our shortcomings and virtues are achingly palpable. By moving the responsibility for fox depredations from foxes and placing it in the human mind, Ji made the same move as he did when using the human-fox comparison to displace foxes' faults onto people. In Ji Yun's universe, human desire grants foxes the only ability they have for harm; in contrast, their ability to do good, or offer commentary, is based in the external moral order.

This idea of the relation between the human will and foxes applies differently to men and to women. As I noted in Chapter 5, in Ji Yun's vision women had to be protected by the laws of heaven rather than their own will. Women's unsatisfied carnal desires can cause foxes to

---

65. *YWCT*, 1.16, story 15. For a translation, see, Chan, The *Discourse of Foxes and Ghosts*, p. 273.The confrontation of skeptic with real ghost is a type established much earlier; see, e.g., Gan Bao, *Soushen ji*, no.378.

66. *YWCT*, 6.265–66, story 267

67. *YWCT*, 1.19–20, story 19.

68. *YWCT*, 10.496, story 222.

prey on them just as happens to men, but these desires are to some extent beyond their control. This point is brought home in an example from *Yingchuang yicao.* When an exorcist fails to drive out a fox who has possessed a woman, the *yao you ren xing* explanation is phrased in terms of his lack of virtue rather than hers. She seems an entirely passive participant in the drama.[69] Women are credited neither with the creative power of invention nor with the resolution to drive foxes away.

In *Yuewei caotang biji*, the visibility of our inner conflicts to foxes is dramatized in the story of a man named Wang Banxian. Wang calls on a fox friend, who laughs and says, "Last night you dreamed you went to Fan Zhu [a famous local courtesan] and enjoyed yourself greatly." Wang remembers that he had indeed dreamed this and asks how his friend knows this. The fox replies,

> "Humans live from *yangqi*, and when the *yang* rises, the *qi* is released through the top of their heads. When they sleep, the spirit gathers in the heart, and the spirit light and *yang* energy reflect each other like a mirror. When dreams are born in the heart, their reflections appear in the *yangqi*, coming and going, appearing and vanishing. Little human figures a few inches high appear there, like a picture or a play, or like squirming insects. All the things that you would not tell anyone appear in all their hundred forms. Gods and ghosts can see them. Enlightened foxes can also see them, but cannot hear what is said. Last night I passed by your house and happened to see your dream."

The fox goes on to relate the different appearances of the auras of good and evil men, in which a single good or evil thought is visible as a discoloring thread.[70]

Here the fox friend again plays the role of the accessible guide to the supernatural. Foxes, whether in their own possession of human beings or in shedding or disguising of their bodies, or in their perceptions of us, offer a possibility for dramatic visualizations of the body and spirit. Here Ji Yun projected morality into the visual spectrum, so that the human psyche becomes a performance that foxes observe and review. It is significant that the dream the fox spies on is

---

69. "Shenyang nuzi"沈陽女子, in Changbai haogezi, *Yingchuang yicao,* pt. 3, 1.324–25.

70. *YWCT*, 3.140–41, story 137.

erotic and thus a moment of particular vulnerability to foxes. At this vulnerable moment, Ji replaced possession or predation with observation. The idea, that gods and ghosts know all human thoughts is here translated from a moral commonplace to a spectacle. There seems to be a suppressed link between foxes and the theater; in fact human dreams present exactly the same kind of spectacle as a play put on by foxes in the forms of diminutive actors, directed by a mysterious monk, in another *Yuewei caotang* anecdote.[71] The fox friend responds to the dream by laughing rather than by taking advantage of his human friend's weakness, and so the dream does have the nature of harmless entertainment.

Although Ji used this idea of the pre-existing alien observer responding to human psychological motions most often, he also considered the possibility of internal monstrosity. Another story that uses the *yao you ren xing* line appears to be a clear case of a mental breakdown. Ji notes that the last communication from Shen Zhaoding 申兆定, a man who had lodged in his home for an extended period, had been highly incoherent.[72] Apparently when Shen first fell ill, he saw two round objects before his eyes, whether they were open or closed. Two maids emerged from them and led him to a grand mansion, where he met an immortal beauty who proposed marriage. He refused, using the excuse that he could never become accustomed to living in such a place. She sent him away angrily, and he woke from his dream. A month later, the circles appeared in his eyes again, and the maids emerged and led him to another house, secluded and lovely. He was charmed by the place and succumbed to the beauty's demands this time. From then on Shen wandered in dreams. The woman forbade him to communicate with his friends, and his illness worsened until he died. Ji does not explain how he came to know of Shen's hallucinations, but he observes that Shen had in his middle years become enthralled with gods and immortals, an obsession that prompted this madness. *Yao yi ren xing, xiang you xin qi* 妖以人興，象由心起, "Monsters arise from men, and images are created in the heart." Ji closes the anecdote with a sigh of regret: Shen was a tal-

71. *YWCT*, 15.842, story 2.
72. His *zi* was Tiechan 鐵蟾 and he came from Yangqu 陽曲; *juren* 1760.

ented and broad-minded man but his passion for the strange finally harmed his life.[73]

Shen's symptoms show a loose resemblance to hallucinations caused by a brain tumor. From our perspective, a man's medical condition cloaks itself in the forms he has learned from reading fiction. The elaboration of the *Zuo zhuan* reference makes it clear that literary images are also a danger. In this case, the fatal beauty really is inside Shen's mind. Although this is not a fox story, the combination of literary creativity, sexual desire, and delusion links it closely to the portion of the fox tradition that most alarmed Ji Yun. Shen Zhaoding was also known for writing imitations of Li Shangyin's erotic poetry.[74] For Ji, indulgence in fantasies that mixed literary creativity with eroticism, as exemplified by *Liaozhai*, could be fatal.

The beauty who lured Shen Zhaoding to his death is given no identity more concrete than *mozhang* 魔障, *mara*, an illusion that is an obstacle to enlightenment. Foxes are in general less likely to be read as pure products of the psyche than are ghosts. As early as Wang Chong, the psychological explanation of ghosts had held an important position in the debate about their existence. There was no comparable debate about the existence of shape-changing fox spirits. Wang Chong even offered "the spirits of ancient animals" as one of his many plausible explanations for ghosts.[75] In the eighteenth century, too, ghosts were the more subjective experience. A relatively obscure contemporary of Ji Yun's answered the question of whether ghosts exist by saying:

> A ghost is myself. Since I exist in the world, there are ghosts; how could such a thing as ghosts exist independently? When doubts arise, they arise from the human heart, and ghosts arise relying on the human heart. It is my wicked heart that creates ghosts. My heart is able to create ghosts, but ghosts are truly not able to disturb me. All affairs in this world begin with doubts; after a long time, they begin to be believed; when belief is deep, the false becomes the true, the fictional the real; this is a natural force.[76]

73. *YWCT*, 8.397–98, story 111. Cf. Pu Songling's story about an optical disorder that allows travel to another world; see "Gu sheng" 顧生, in *LZ*, 8.1154–55.

74. *YWCT*, 22.1214–15, story 84.

75. Wang Chong, *Lunheng xiaoshi*, 22.934.

76. *Qi you ci li*, 1799.

This passage postdates *Liaozhai* and was doubtless influenced by its depiction of the reality of desires and fictions. In the eighteenth-century debate about the existence of ghosts, this bifurcation continued: ghosts were the most contested and the most internal phenomenon; foxes and other anomalous spirits were more readily accepted as external realities.[77] Since ghosts are former humans and they bring into question man's fate in the afterlife, they raise more sensitive issues than a separate species on an independent trajectory. For all of their delight in illusion, foxes have a more independent, solid substance.

Skeptics could use the *yao you ren xing* reasoning to question accounts of the supernatural, but to grant anomaly human origins does not necessarily make it spurious. The *yao you ren xing* cosmology reasserts both human primacy and the moral order, since no man whose heart is without monstrosity need face external monsters, and it draws attention to the perilous instability of the human heart. When narrative attention shifts from dynastic history, as in *Zuo zhuan*, to the experience of individuals in *zhiguai*, the source of chaos shifts from dynastic decline to the single individual.[78]

In formal terms, *yao you ren xing* is an argument made by the human commentator outside the story, in contrast to the idea of fox progress, which is articulated largely by the fox. It is neither the person whose mind created the monster nor the monster itself but a third party who diagnoses the relationship. Moral meaning is already created in foxes' response to human incitement, but it is articulated by the *zhiguai* collector who can read *yao*. This is in contrast with the long conversations, suggesting parallels, of the fox progress story.

This focus on the human heart/mind as the breeding ground for monsters resonates with Terry Castle's argument that in eighteenth-century European literature and culture, just as ghosts were rationalized as products of the mind rather than real, external beings, the mind itself became the new lair of the uncanny. Ghosts were not

---

77. Chan (*The Discourse of Foxes and Ghosts*, p. 85) explores the eighteenth-century debate at some length. Hong Liangji 洪亮吉 (1746–1809) made a similar distinction between "anomalous spirits" and ghosts and deities.

78. *Yao* in the sense of rebellion, however, still refers to the masses as well as the individual.

abolished but transferred, a process she terms the "supernaturalization of everyday life."[79] The intellectual contexts for this shift and the thriving *yao you ren xing* cosmology in late imperial tales, particularly the eighteenth century, are dramatically different. In high Qing China, absolute skepticism about the supernatural was a somewhat eccentric minority position.[80] The similar conclusions based on different cultural premises raises the question: perhaps the societal repression of beliefs in the supernatural was not necessary for the transition from external to internal monsters to take place; perhaps it only required any form of taming of the strange. The parallel between Castle's "supernaturalization of everyday life" and the Qing domestication of the strange is compelling. The human mind would seem to be the most domestic of all domestic space, but perhaps it was also the last remaining wilderness.

The examples of Wang Banxian and Shen Zhaoding discussed above resound particularly strongly with Castle's arguments. Wang Banxian's dream as an external spectacle bears a strong resemblance to her discussion of "phantasmagoria," which at first meant the illusions created by magic lanterns and only later, by metaphorical extension, hallucinations. Although magic lanterns as such, a great vogue in contemporary Europe, were probably not known in China in Ji's lifetime, shadow puppet plays most certainly were.[81] The comparison of the dream's external projection of the heart's inner reality to mirror reflections and shadows makes it seem likely that this was the model for this vision of the human interior. The crucial difference between Ji's and his contemporaries in Western Europe's use of the same imagery was this: for the Europeans supernatural creatures were the creations of the mind, whereas for Ji both the phantoms of the mind and external phantoms existed, and only to these external phantoms were the phantoms of the mind entirely visible.

According to Castle's argument, when the mind became a ghostly place, the difference between ordinary thinking and spectral visions

---

79. Castle, *The Female Thermometer*, p. 123.

80. See Chan, *The Discourse of Foxes and Ghosts*, pp. 79–86.

81. Castle, in *The Female Thermometer*, pp. 140–67. As a matter of fact, one of the early magic lantern shows in France was called "Ombres chinoises," (ibid., p. 146).

became blurred. The dangers of unhealthy overindulgence in reverie were linked to the dangers of masturbation.[82] The mixture of poetic imagination, erotic self-indulgence, specters, and madness precisely matches Shen Zhaoding's situation. Again, the crucial difference between the European and the Chinese beliefs was that in the Chinese tradition there was no contradiction between a belief in the existence of the supernatural and a belief in its psychological origins. It was the very reality of what man could create and summon that made thinking and desire potentially wonderful, or perilous.

Foxes have a fascinating relationship to the human interior. They are separate from us in a way ghosts are not. Since they themselves use a human form to conceal an alien body, they raise the question of the relationship between the mind and body. Yet the issue is further complicated by their association with possession: that alien presence could occupy us or, by beguiling us with surface, could cause us to forget our innermost selves. Yet as the *yao you ren xing* argument shows us, they can be both the embodiment of our innermost desires or, by a neat reversal, the judges of those desires. They are the other to whom we are permeable; they easily become the other within.

CONCLUSION

Both the discourse of fox progress and the discourse of monsters aroused by humanity are used by the same authors, and Ji Yun deployed both most articulately. Foxes share both of these discourses, particularly the latter, with other creatures, but they are unique in being able to play both *xian* and *yao* with such ease. As closely as they may approach humanity, they must remain alien enough to allow the projection of not only human ambition but also human desire and foibles into another space. The visions of *xian* and *yao* produce contrasting visions of humanity: we are the spoiled children of the universe, who squander our gifts when we should instead be diligent students; at the same time, we are plagued by fancies, desires, and fears that can give birth to strange phenomena.

82. Castle, in *The Female Thermometer*, p. 184.

Conclusion

My title, "Alien Kind," alludes to foxes as both an alien species and a peculiar category. As Ji Yun so memorably affirmed, that peculiarity lies in their liminal position. Other cultures feel the same need for a "middle" category of alien, but the exact parameters of liminality differ. The important axes of middleness are morality, power, and proximity. The "middle people" are neither inherently benign nor innately malign; rather, they are morally ambivalent. They have powers that humans do not, but these powers are finite and are balanced by weaknesses. Since their habitat intersects at least partially with our own, they brush against humans much more often than creatures ensconced in entirely separate worlds. In this Conclusion, I compare foxes to some of these other "middle people" in order to throw Chinese concepts of the alien and the human into sharper relief and to return to the question of the relationship between species of supernatural beings and the genres in which they are depicted.

Because of the wealth of material and the parallel complications of folklore collection and literary adaptation, I will compare foxes primarily to Western European (mostly German, English, and Irish) fairies and elemental spirits. The following discussion is guilty of oversimplification, since it conflates different periods of European fairylore and Chinese foxlore, although the range in time, from the fifteenth through the nineteenth century, remains roughly parallel. Fairies share a great many roles with late imperial foxes: the household protective spirit, often providing favors in exchange for a humble offering of food, like the English brownie or Scandinavian *tomte*; the mischievous kobold, who torments households; the fatal lover; and the grateful supernatural creature. Some plots, such as the tale of a midwife summoned to an unearthly household in the middle of the night to deliver a child, are virtually identical in the two traditions.[1] I do not think these tales are directly related; rather, these parallel niches suggest that distinct societies have similar chinks in the familiar, where the alien can approach. Not only are there parallels in the narrative niches these species fill, but there are parallels in the explanations of their place in the universe.

EXPLAINING THE MIDDLE SPECIES: PARACELSUS AND JI YUN

Particularly striking parallels with Ji Yun's attempts to rationalize the difficult in-between position of foxes are found in *Liber de nymphis, sylphis, pygmalis, et salamandris* by the fifteenth-century German philosopher Paracelsus. His "in-between" figures are the spirits of the four elements: nymphs for water, sylphs for air, pygmies for earth, and salamanders for fire. To a certain extent, he was a defender of these creatures and endeavored to delineate their differences from both demons and human beings. Because he derived his concept of these creatures by applying logical principles to received folk material, from the outset his task, as well as his sympathetic stance, was very similar to Ji Yun's.

Like Ji Yun, Paracelsus also felt that he had to justify writing about marvels; he argued that marvels are more worthy of description than the court, for they are the works of God as opposed to the works of men. The pretext that one can use the bizarre to observe the wonders of God's creation is not unlike Ji's claim that one can examine universal principle through the strange just as well as through the

1. Examples for foxes include "Hu taitai" 胡太太, in Xu Kun, *Liuya waibian* (1793 ed.) *juan* 12; and "Baita si" 白塔寺, in Li Qingchen, *Zuicha zhiguai*, 3.365. The parallels suggest that for both cultures, midwifes were liminal creatures themselves, summoned to serve in households of varying social status; and childbirth was a charmed moment, when the worlds could mix.

ordinary. For both men, an apparently peripheral topic of dubious morality is central to a universal moral project.

According to Paracelsus, the elemental spirits fall between men and ghosts. Their flesh is different from man's, in that it is not solid and can pass through matter; but they are like human beings in that they eat, drink, and bear children, as ghosts do not. They are a mix of ghost and human, like two colors mixed together or a sweet and sour flavor.[2] They are, however, neither ghost nor human. Since they have no soul, when they die, they are like animals, extinguished forever. Paracelsus compared them to apes, the closest animals to humans, but in general they are above the animals. "Thus they are people, but die with the animals, change with the ghosts, and eat and drink with men. . . . Their customs and gestures are human, as are their speaking and appearance, and all their virtues, the better and the cruder, the subtler and the grosser." They cross two of the same borderlines, between man and ghost and man and beast, that Ji sketched in his introduction to the fox. Like foxes, they resemble human beings as closely as possible. Paracelsus also emphasized their internal variety just as Ji Yun's various fox spokesmen did. "They are smart and rich, understanding, poor, or foolish, like we descendants of Adam: they are made in our image just as we are made in the image of God."[3]

Paracelsus explained the stories of romances between humans and elves or nymphs using the same logic: they (apparently exclusively the females) strive to unite with men just as men strive to unite with God. This justification seems to share the desperate quality of a vixen's pursuit of a human lover and a human self. As we have seen in the discussion of Yingning and Undine, in both cultures alien females can become almost human through matrimony. As is true for

---

2. Paracelsus. *Liber de nymphis, sylphis, pygmaeis et salamandris,* p. 13–14. All translations from the German are my own. Cf. Kirk, *The Secret Commonwealthes of Elves, Fauns, and Fairies,* p. 1; Kirk places the fairies between men and angels.

3. Paracelsus, *Liber de nymphis, sylphis, pygmaeis et salamandris,* p. 15. Note how the Western comparison has three levels, the other, man, and God, whereas the Chinese has only two, man and the other. This fits well with distinctions made between Chinese and Western allegory; in the Chinese case there is not an essential comparison between the human world and the divine. See Plaks, *Archetype and Allegory in Dream of the Red Chamber.*

foxes in most cases, the children they bear men are human, with human souls; sometimes even the mothers win souls through their ties to men.[4] Paracelsus defended the integrity of these relationships: a man married to a spirit should remain loyal to her.[5] But unlike Ji, who refused to focus on the romance with an alien woman exclusively, Paracelsus enshrined it at the heart of his explanation of the species.

The most obvious difference between the two traditions is the absolute division in the West between the possession and the lack of a soul. On that question there can be no in-between for Paracelsus, although these creatures are as close as conceivable to a borderline case. Although they have human understanding, they need not follow God because they have no soul. Ji could not admit such a moral exemption. The soul allows Paracelsus to put a final limitation on the elemental spirits' imitation of humanity, since all of their other attainments are rendered meaningless by this one missing quality. It is this limitation that gives them their meaning: they prove to humans how we have been favored with the gift of a soul. The fact they cannot become human reminds us that we in turn cannot become gods.[6] This general case, which highlights both our privilege and our limitation, sets off the special case of the fairy bride, who is like us in her passionate aspiration to transcend her origins.

The Chinese tradition has no such absolute answer to the question of what makes men unique. Buddhist ideas of reincarnation serve to blur the boundaries between species; the afterlife becomes the point at which men and beast can be confused, not distinguished. In Daoist visions, humans themselves can effectively change species to become transcendents. Yet although the boundaries of humanity seem on the surface less clearly drawn in the Chinese case, they are not entirely permeable. Foxes reincarnated as humans are used, primarily in vernacular fiction, as a device to explain exceptional sexual appetites, as is the case for Hede in *Zhaoyang qushi*, or extraordinary desire for revenge, as in *Xingshi yinyuan zhuan*, and not as a means of considering the boundaries of humanity. The human fallen to fox

4. Paracelsus, *Liber de nymphis, sylphis, pygmaeis et salamandris*, p. 24.
5. Ibid., p. 31.
6. Ibid., p. 16.

form, regaining human form again after centuries of work, is more common: but in this case, the human story, narrated by the fox, gives an elevated justification to typical fox actions, be it an attempt to pass oneself off as human in a community of monks or a sexual liaison.[7] Species identity in former lives provides motivation, but it does not reshape identity in this life. As for Daoist advancement, allowing foxes to skip over humanity altogether and become *xian* sidesteps the issue of whether foxes can become truly human.

The question of whether the boundary between humanity and the other can dissolve is the fundamental tension in Qing *zhiguai*: the marvelous has become so common, so close, and so familiar, with the demon lover becoming the good housewife, that the distinction is on the verge of dissolving even though it cannot be allowed to dissolve. The fox, ever the confounding in-between, is the embodiment of this problem. Despite what appears to be a dramatic difference between species defined by the presence or the absence of a soul, with death as the moment of truth, as opposed to species defined by the wheel of rebirth and the ladder of cultivation, the rhetorical uses of the self-improving fox are similar to the double meaning of the elemental spirits: the diligent fox, starting in a burrow and aspiring to the heavens, reminds us of human striving, human superiority, and human limitation.

Paracelsus' analysis brings us back to the questions of theory and practice discussed in Chapter 2. Cultural differences dictate a different relationship between theory and practice for Paracelsus, or for Robert Kirk (ca. 1651–92), the author of *The Secret Commonwealthes of Elves, Fauns, and Fairies*, than for Chinese authors. The first systematic theories on the middle people in the European context are to a greater or lesser extent responding to the theorizing of demonology and explanations of witchcraft. Both Paracelsus and Kirk are setting fairies or elementals apart from demons, already an object of organized attention, and the men who have commerce of various sorts with them apart from witches. There are two reasons for this focused attention. First, weird and sinister species reflect more critically on a single omnipotent creator than they do on a system of natural

7. On the link between the transformed fox and repentance, see Heine, *Shifting Shape, Shaping Text*, pp. 166–75.

principle, a factor that compelled the Europeans to provide more systematic explanations. Second, ties between humans and inhuman beings were more threatening to the European social order, which created important judicial genres for perceiving the supernatural, such as confessions of witchcraft, and theorizing on the nature and limitations of the crime; these were much less common in China.[8]

Just as Paracelsus systematized received lore, so his theorizing, centuries later, inspired authors of the literary fairy tale. From the Chinese perspective, this would be as if Ji Yun's unified fox theories came first and Pu Songling's romances later. Additionally, there is a crucial difference in the publishing climate and perceptions of historical change. When Fouqué, about fifty years Ji Yun's junior, read Paracelsus, he perceived a far greater cultural gap in the four hundred years that had elapsed than Ji Yun did when he read Hong Mai, who predated him by six centuries. Fouqué was inspired to reinterpret Paracelsus' ideas to fit his own times; Ji believed he was working in Hong Mai's tradition, albeit after an interruption of generic deviance. In Chinese terms, most European histories of the literary fairy tale begin in the last century of the Ming, without the sense of a generic history stretching back a millennium.

HUMAN AND ANIMAL, NATURE AND CULTURE

One obvious difference between foxes and European fairies is that between an ambitious quadruped and a (or several) humanoid species. Many subspecies of fairies can take animal shape or have some physical attributes of animals, but they are not seen as animals themselves. This is related to another glaring difference: in Europe people can descend to animal form through illness or curse, whereas in East Asia animals more often assume human form.[9] This seems related to the lower status of animals in Europe based on the insurmountable boundary of the soul. In the European context, human shape is something humans can lose (although the demonologists argue that

---

8. In the Chinese case, it is sorcery with human perpetrators, especially in organized groups, that is more threatening than any interference of ghosts or demons itself; see Kuhn, *Soulstealers*, pp. 94–118.

9. The exception would seem to be the selkies or swan maidens, but still their animal shape is viewed as clothing, concealing a human shape within.

this is a demonic illusion, and that shapes never really change) but not something animals can gain, even as an illusion. The beings closest to humanity are primarily given hominid forms. Other than the exceptional case of the fairy bride, descent is of more interest than ascent. In East Asia, the vector of ascent is crucial, whether it is genuine ascent or trickery honed with advancing age. With animals available as the closest aliens to the human, the parallel hominid races (like the sometimes hominid Wutong, who at least are not clearly identified with a single animal species) fill fewer supernatural niches.[10]

Paradoxically, however, it is the European fairies, not the Chinese foxes, who are seen as representatives of wild nature as opposed to human culture. This difference is founded on different understandings of nature and culture, which, to overgeneralize crudely, were separate and opposed spheres to a greater degree in Europe than they were in China. The difference is determined by a romantic attitude toward nature that gives accounts of fairies from the nineteenth century on elegiac perspective, as signs of a natural world that was becoming lost to contemporary urban man.[11] In some of the Victorian interpretations of fairies, the gap between fairies as the embodiment of nature, as opposed to man, is made even clearer by emphasizing their connections to plants and even inanimate elements rather than to animals.

A concept of "elemental beings" requires a concept of fixed elements, which both form the substance of the sylphs and like and provide their habitat. Humans alone are mixed beings. The Chinese conception of elements as phases does not provide a similar, stable bestiary. Foxes are clearly identified with *yin*, but even that is relative; this identification is not nearly as strong for them as it is for ghosts. Foxes are not entirely different from us either in habitat or in substance.

The stronger tie between fairies and wild nature is determined by their habitat: only the domestic spirits, like brownies, are primarily imagined indoors. The others are creatures of woods and fairy

10. This is less true in Japan, where the more active roles are given to the humanoid *tengu* and *kappa*; see Figal, *Civilization and Monsters*, pp. 83–83, 144–45.

11. Silver, *Strange and Secret Peoples*, p. 10.

mounds. And all of them are primarily rural; they do not move into cities as the foxes do, although in both cultures gardens can be transitional spaces. In the Victorian era, it was left to poltergeists to be urban.

As we have seen, the late imperial fox traveled far from its animal roots. Such foxes are called *chusheng* 畜生, "animals," only in insults, usually by exorcists asking how a beast could have the gall to violate the order of the universe. When they refer to themselves, they sometimes use the term *yilei*.[12] *Yilei*, while more polite than "animal," is still an expression of distance: the true lover or friend of a fox does not regard his companion as of an alien kind, and the fox uses the term when imploring a human not to be estranged.[13] As the discussion in the previous chapters has shown, the animal body of the fox holds a different position in different parts of the fox tradition: glimpsing a hairy shape is part of coexisting with a haunting fox, but the fox body is not depicted in the images used in fox worship, and in long tales of intimate relations with foxes, it is used sparingly, to introduce moments of transition or revelation. The body of the beast is not indispensable in any case.

By late imperial times, foxes were more closely related to human culture than to anything outside it. This is not to say that there were no anecdotes placing foxes in the woods and wilderness, but the majority of stories placed them closer to human settlement. Ji Yun made the tie between foxes becoming monsters and Chinese culture overt when he observed that the foxes of Xinjiang do not become monsters. The project of self-improvement must be something they learned from men.[14] Those foxes that are the least cultured and the least human, the dark forms pressing down on sleeping humans or the ones clattering about in the rafters, are explained as being either responses to human flaws or creatures at the earliest stage of progress and civilization. What is most important here, once again, is transition: foxes are always in the process of attaining culture. The stories never hint of an independent existence, with the foxes burrowing

12. Qingfeng says *feilei* 非類, "not of the same kind," instead; see "Qingfeng," *LZ*, 1.112–18.

13. *YWCT*, 16.948, story 97.

14. *YWCT*, 6.263–64, story 264.

in the ground or hunting mice out of our sight; the foxes speak only of an anthropomorphized world of family and residence in various places. A simulacrum of human culture has become their only identity.

With fairies, there is more emphasis on their independent world, with its trappings of royalty. Moreover, fairies steal human beings to live with them in that world. Although men sometimes reside with the foxes, lingering in their glamorous mansions, there are only households, rather than an entire fairyland. Those who have already risen to become *xian* have a separate world, with its caves and peaks, more like the European fairyland, but most often the *xian* enters narrative by falling to this world for a liaison with a human. But, more important, the man who lingers with the vixen in her home does not stay permanently. The fox comes to her lover where he or she is more often than it takes him or her away; and when the encounter with the other proves fatal, the human dies in his own home.

The idea of the changeling child, so central to English fairylore, is absent in China.[15] The sickly child is explained instead as a ghost, reborn to collect a debt. With reincarnation, strangers can be directly born in one's household without any need for abduction and replacement. Although in older stories foxes occasionally substitute for family members, that theme had waned in popularity by late imperial times. More important, the fear in those stories was of false family members indistinguishable from the true, rather than of children or others who were obviously made strange. In late imperial China, it was the clever concubine, the fortuitously forward lover, or the lodgers in the next room who were suspected of being strange. Although in both cultures, ties, especially sexual ties, with another world were a way to explain physical and psychiatric afflictions in the young men and women of a family, the difference between the human who has "been away" and the one who remains at home, possessed by an alien force, is significant.

15. On the changeling, see *Strange and Secret Peoples*, chap. 2, pp. 59–87.

MIDDLENESS IN AUTHORITY AND MORALITY

Moral middleness in the European context is between two fixed points on a spectrum, with devils at one end and angels at the other; this establishes man in the middle and forces other peoples to be a secondary middle. To be between *xian* and *yao*, however, is to be between two paths rather than between two points. To some degree, humans can also choose these two paths, to refine themselves or to become sorcerers or rebels, but only a small minority go in either direction. Foxes are between these two paths in the sense that they can choose either one, not because they have a third path.

When European conceptions deny that fairies or elemental spirits have a soul, they create the possibility of an amoral but sentient species. Fairies can be a way of contemplating moral aliens, who do not share our sense of good and evil. Without the soul, fairies have caprices rather than emotions and only ape human passions.[16] Christian ideas situate individual moral choice and moral justice in the soul; moral obligations apply only to those with souls. But the Chinese system makes no such exclusions, since systems of moral justice must apply to all beings.[17] Interest in the moral alien can blend attraction with revulsion, especially when contemplating the amoral female. The Chinese case shares some of this as well: Yingning and Xiaocui are thought experiments, attempts to see how a woman who differed radically from the expectations for her sex could act as a wife.

In narrative practice, the fox can also seem to represent caprice without explicable human feelings or motivations, especially in cases of haunting or predatory sex. But once Chinese authors move out of individual anecdote to explanation, and thus from popular, shared narrative to intellectualizing, they are interested in two contradictory

---

16. Ibid., p. 12.

17. A *Yuewei caotang* anecdote describes a fox on trial in the infernal courts for killing his grandfather. One infernal official argues that animals should be judged by standards different from those applied to human beings; a second replies that since foxes are not like other animals, those who have improved themselves should be judged by human standards. A third argues that filial piety can be expected even of animals. See *YWCT* 7.311–12, story 21.

moral possibilities: either foxes are inherently morally inferior, repelled by good and attracted by evil; or they have the same moral choices as men. The one thing they cannot be is amoral. However, these possibilities also have their counterparts in the European arguments: Kirk envisioned the peoples of his "secret commonwealthes" as having the same range of virtues and vices as ourselves; yet at the same time they do the most harm to the barbarous and are defeated by Christian piety.[18]

Popular experience of foxes—their depredations, inscrutable apparitions, willful gifts, and harsh revenge—does create an impression of amoral torment. Perhaps on the ground, relations with the nearest alien were not very different in early modern China or Europe. Actual experience is the closest to chaos; narrative gives it shape, and explanation imposes a further level of order. Raw chaos seems the least culturally specific; it was in elite explanation that differences emerge.

Talk of moral middle ground evokes the image of the trickster of international folklore studies. The middle people and the trickster are not necessarily the same thing, although they overlap. The idea of the trickster has been defined by examples from folktales and myths, stories set in another plane of reality or another time, as opposed to the middle people who are most common in legends and reside on the margins of our world. The trickster is usually an individual (even if there is more than one, it is Coyote with a capital C, rather than coyotes). An entire tricky species is a different problem. Border-crossing and ambivalence are shared, but the difference is in the ordinariness of the middle people: borders keep being crossed, and the middle people beat a regular, if not predictable, path through our houses. Lewis Hyde's point about the male gender of nearly all tricksters is also relevant here.[19] A species in which both males and females cross boundaries, but each in distinct ways that usually keep the boundary between male and female clear, has a different structural function than a single male border-crosser: these are the

18. Kirk, *The Secret Commonwealthes of Elves, Fauns, and Fairies*, p. 73.

19. Hyde, *Trickster Made This World*, pp. 333–43. I agree with Hyde's selection of Sun Wukong as the Chinese representative of tricksters.

tricksters who provide a certain necessary element of chaos in a stable world rather than the single individual who remakes the world.[20]

GENRE AND SPECIES: FOLKLORE, DEMONOLOGY, LITERARY FAIRY TALES

Both the fox and the fairy are unorthodox, standing at the edges of the greater moral order of their respective universes. The difference between them is shaped, among other things, by the forms in which intellectual attention was paid to the unorthodox in their respective societies, which brings us back to the issue of genre. We have already seen the correlation between species and genre in the Chinese context: foxes dominate the classical tale, have a more marginal presence in the vernacular novel, and are almost absent in *chuanqi* drama. Any argument based on this correlation risks tautology: Are foxes most common in the classical tale because of their nature, or do they seem the way they are because of the genre that records them? I argue that species and genre are interdependent, with each shaping the other.

In looking at the relations of genre and species cross-culturally, I find the following distinctions useful: the difference between large and small stories; between stories set in other worlds and those set in this one; and between stories narrated as personal experience, as experience of named friends, and those held at a greater distance. Generally, the stories closest to personal experience are smaller tales, although not all small stories are close to personal experience. Different species find their ideal habitats at different points along this spectrum. Foxes thrive best in small, individual stories, which in China take the form of the classical tale, although they play their part in the larger stories of vernacular fiction. They are residents chiefly of this world and can be as close as personal experience or as distant as a nameless man at the end of a previous dynasty, the entire range of the classical tale itself.

In comparison, fairy tales or *Märchen* are tales of another world, held at a distance, and legends are tales of this world, sometimes closer to the teller. The creatures that resemble foxes the most, the sometimes mischievous, sometimes helpful, kobolds, are found in

20. Ibid., p. 188.

legends and written records, rather than *Märchen*.[21] In comparison with fairies, foxes are more like the regionally specific figures of legend than the beautiful but vague figures blessing cradles in the *Märchen*.

When foxes do appear in vernacular fiction, they are seldom central characters. Rather, they serve a functional role in a larger story: they are a source of demonic deception, but as in the Daji cycle or *Sanjiao kaimi*, the backstory of the fox provides an explanation for revenge or lust, or fox gratitude temporarily provides supernatural protection, as in *Qixia wuyi* 七俠五義 (Seven gallants and five heroes; 1889). (The exception is *Huli quanyuan.*) Foxes' acts of deception, possession, seduction, revenge, and reward do not make the entire narrative by themselves. The larger roles are usually reserved for exceptional beings who are individuals, further from common experience: the monkey Sun Wukong or even the white snake Bai Niangzi, who are never subsumed into their species the way a vixen is primarily a vixen. When a vixen becomes an individual, her audience is one appreciative lover or one fortunate or afflicted household.

In discussing narrative, I have neglected the obvious statement that, unlike *xian* and fairies who are subjects of poetry, foxes are primarily the subject of prose. After the Tang, when foxes were used as an image of deception, fox poems are rare. In contrast, *xian* and fairies are subjects of poetry. Although there are stories in which foxes compose poetry, such as Hu Shuzhen's cycle, these are scattered examples, and the poems make almost no reference to vulpine origins. There is no established tradition or set of imagery, as there is for the poetry of ghosts. This suggests that encounters with foxes are in some way a prosaic, in the sense of ordinary, experience. Poetry about vixen lovers uses the language of romance with a goddess, and from vixen lovers the language of the longing woman. The animal identity of the friend or lover is unpoetic, and the perspective of that alien species is not imagined clearly enough for poetry, in contrast to the once human ghost longing for life.

Partially as a consequence of the circumstances of folklore collection—folklorists collected someone else's lore, which was about to be

21. On kobold, see Müller and Wunderlich, *Dämonen, Monster, Fabelwese*, p. 370.

lost—fairies always seem to be drawing away from us. Carol Silver argues that departure is inherent to the nature of the species.[22] Fairies are native to a habitat threatened with loss as soon as men begin to cultivate it. The fox and the *zhiguai*, on the other hand, are not going anywhere. The men who collected *zhiguai* were collecting their own lore, and although individual stories might be lost, it was unthinkable that this kind of story itself might die out. Although the individual vixen departs, her species fills an ecological niche very similar to the starlings, Canada geese, and raccoons that thrive in American suburbia, stealing our garbage and roosting in our yards. Human habitat suits them very well.

The fox was not, within the timeframe of this book, the subject of systematic study in China, as the fairies were in England in the Victorian era.[23] Even Ji's theorizing is always in the context of narrative; narrative is never pressed into the service of treatises. Theoretical arguments about the supernatural do not take foxes as a central subject but focus instead on ghosts or human practices like divination and geomancy.[24] Perhaps the fox was too close and alive in contemporary conversation to become a subject of argument. I have already discussed the relation of this theoretical bent to the systematizing compulsions of demonology. What the Victorians and their contemporaries and predecessors in Qing China shared was the urge for documentation and voluminous publication of narrative and experience.

The Chinese case shows that the literary fantasy does not require distance from its creatures. The stuff of "ordinary" extraordinary experience, the thunks in the next room and the small space set aside for the fox, are part of the furniture of the truly extraordinary cases, the complex relationships with foxes. This overlap anchors weird experience and fantasy to each other: every abandoned room carries the possibility of marvel. But whereas the marvelous, *qi*, tends to shimmer in the distance, it is the weird, *guai*, that occasionally infests one's own garden or closets.

---

22. Silver, *Strange and Secret Peoples*, pp. 185–212. See also Briggs, *The Fairies in Tradition and Literature*, p. 210.

23. Silver, *Strange and Secret Peoples*, p. 4.

24. See the survey in Chan, *The Discourse of Foxes and Ghosts*, pp. 79–94.

Silver argues that the popularizing of fairies in moralistic and saccharine children's literature helped to bring about the fall of the tradition. As fairies lost their ambiguity, their power and attraction dwindled.[25] One can draw a parallel with the Guangxu-era fox romance, in which the vixen has lost her ambivalence and, in losing her ties to sex, often finds her claims to passion dulled as well. Satiation of desire becomes routine, and the strange becomes ordinary in the sense of market saturation. Yet precisely because the fox of close-hand experience was not going anywhere, the loss of ambivalence in one branch of the fox tradition did not dictate loss of ambivalence in the whole. Xu Feng'en 許奉恩, in a collection published in 1879, included—alongside a tale of a vixen as both lover and schoolmistress, good at eight-legged essays; and another of a man who requests a vixen lover and is rewarded with nine partners of both sexes,[26] until he nearly dies of debauchery; both illustrations of a late, self-conscious stage of the fox romance—an account of his own experience in a very different tone. He had gotten used to the footsteps of the fox transcendent who lived upstairs in the official residence in Zhejiang where he was temporarily lodging while grading exams. There had been one tense moment when a dog killed a fox, but he and his colleagues averted that disaster by burning incense and asking the foxes not to take their anger out on people. In the comment appended to this story, he related how one night his friends had been joking with him, since he was young and lodging alone, about the amorous ghosts and vixens recorded in books, just as young Sang's friends had joked with him in *Liaozhai*'s "Lianxiang." That night when he went to bed, a beautiful woman appeared. Terrified, he apologized for his friends' joking words, insisting he meant no disrespect. She vanished, but he could not think of the episode without the hair on the back of his neck standing up straight.[27] In contrast to his unnamed characters who long for a fox, he is terrified of the possibility. This vision is linked to reading and conversation, as opposed

25. Silver, *Strange and Secret Peoples*, pp. 186–89.

26. "Gu chuluan" 古雛鸞 and "Wuxiang mou taishi" 五鄉某太史, in Xu Feng'en, *Lantiaoguan waishi* 3.41b and 6.12b, respectively.

27. "Zhejiang xueshi shu hu" 浙江學使署狐, in ibid., 4.44b.

3. Japanese fox from *Dianshizhai huabao*

to the more immediate experience of foxes weeping for one of their own, but both reveal that the fox, when close at hand, had not lost its potential for threat. Whether this represents an account of experience or a parody of the suggestible *Liaozhai* reader, Xu chose to portray himself as a man who can coexist with foxes without assuming that they are benign.

Foxes as a presence in daily life and in narrative do eventually fade away, without entirely vanishing. The process of that fading is beyond the scope of this book. Foxes continue to appear in the pages of the newspaper *Shenbao* and the pictorial *Dianshizhai huabao* into the 1890s, and the odd fox story still attracts the attention of figures as important to modern literature as Lin Shu and Wu Jianren. When *Qingbai leichao* 清稗類鈔 (Categorized Qing fiction), published in 1916, keeps the fox stories in a group but places them within the larger category *mixin* 迷信, "superstition," this is a significant moment, with the genre intact, at least in retrospect, but one of its determinant topics renamed. The *zhiguai* and the fox tale had existed in the uneasily shared space between the supernatural ideas of their upper-class authors and those of their other informants and subjects. When the elite adopted new standards, strange tales were no longer potentially shared *yiwen* 異聞, "reports of the strange," but someone else's *mixin*, and a shared language was lost.[28] Gerald Figal has argued that in Meiji Japan theorizing on monsters was central to the modernizing project, as some parts of the supernatural were eliminated and others were made central to the Japanese spirit.[29] In China, in contrast, foxes and their kin were more unequivocally seen as backward.

HUMAN AND NON-HUMAN ALIENS

The overlap between the nonhuman alien and the human alien differs from culture to culture. In her work on fairies in Victorian consciousness, Silver examines the meaning of ideas about fairies in both ethnic and gender terms. As we have seen, gendered meanings of foxes were much more important than ethnic meanings. In both cultures, women themselves already straddled the boundary of humanity. During the witchcraft scares in early modern Europe, the demonological and judicial literature's interest in sexual relations between the human and the inhuman is the opposite of the Chinese case: women's ties with devils received more attention than men's relations with succubi. But in the Romantic and Victorian literature on fairies, the gender distribution is much more like the Chinese case, with focus on the fairy bride or *la belle dame sans merci*.[30] I believe this shift has to do with a shift in genre, from the regulation of social threats in judicial writings to the narration of individual experience in fictional accounts, which is closer to the world of *zhiguai* and *chuanqi*.

---

28. On the use of the term *mixin* in constructing *nongmin*, as opposed to elite, identity, see Dorfman, "The Spirits of Reform."
29. See Figal, *Civilization and Monsters*, p. 15.
30. See Silver, *Strange and Secret Peoples*, pp. 89–119, 178–83.

The conflation of ethnic others and the alien species seems more important in Victorian England than in Qing China.[31] I do not think that the ethnic implication of *hu*, "fox," as a pun for *hu* 胡, "northern barbarian," is alive in the Ming and Qing as it was in the Tang,[32] other than in a loose association of foxes with the north. At most, perhaps there is a parallel in the tales of literary fox friends to the relations between Han and Manchu men of similar status: one knew that the other was supposed to be distinct, yet they shared all the same elite cultural references and amusements. In the late Qing, there are occasional moments when foreignness and foxiness are overlaid: an anecdote in the pictorial *Dianshizhai huabao* about a Japanese fox opens, "In the world seductive women are called 'foxes,' because they are good at beguiling men. If a 'foxy' person can already beguile a man, how much more can a real fox, let alone a foreign fox?"[33] On an unnamed Japanese island known for its population of foxes, a Chinese traveler comes on shore desperate for something to eat. A beautiful woman invites him to her place for a meal. He follows her eagerly until the sound of Western troops doing military exercises nearby alarms her. As she flees, she reveals her true form as a fox. In the illustration, there seem to be a conflation of markers of ethnic identity and species identity as her obi and her tail are confounded. A simple tale of exorcism is reframed with international content. In another late Qing tale, a seductive vixen is clearly Westernized in dress, and she advises her lover to convert to Christianity to relieve his poverty.[34] But these remain momentary coincidences of different kinds of strangeness, rather than a sustained way of thinking about the alien.

However, the hope of advance, through study and proximity to humanity, has implications about sinification and inclusion. There are still limits to assimilation: a fox is never entirely human, and those who come closest are granted that status only as corpses. To phrase the question in ethnic terms: Does a "cooked" savage ever become well done enough that he dissolves into the mass of Han Chi-

31. See ibid., pp. 43–50, 117–47.
32. See Kang, "The Fox and the Barbarian."
33. "Yaohu xianmei" 妖狐獻媚, in *Dianshizhai huabao*, Zi 子 (2.1) 7, 56.
34. "Bai laochang" 白老長, in Xuan Ding, *Yeyu qiudeng lu*, 4.140.

nese? But the very question is a paradox: any story which recorded that transition would of necessity still preserve the label of "alien," at least in the beginning. Total assimilation, the barbarian who was no longer a barbarian, or the fox who was no longer a fox, could happen only outside of the narrative frame. Narrative instead traces an asymptotic approach. Although literary expectations of foxes as an entirely human-seeming species became routine, assimilation remained a matter for individuals: even in the late Qing, there remains an inexhaustible supply of unrefined foxes who are mysteries in a small sense—the noise in the attic.

FOX AND SOCIETY, FOX AND LITERATURE

To return to the Chinese case, what does the fox have to teach us about Chinese society in late imperial times? Fox haunting and the resident fox showed us that the home was a focus of intense attention, but at the same time there was a sense of a highly mobile, transient society. The competitive market in women clearly had a significant impact on the imaginary cosmos by creating a great need for women outside that market. Foxes were a means to think about all of women's roles other than the reproductive: they could either be depleting, barren sexual partners, the women one seeks out for entertainment, or they could provide for all of a man's other needs but let another woman bear the children.[35] Social mobility, which many argue is a distinguishing feature of late imperial society, was accepted in the fox story as a constant. Conversations about foxes' mobility seemed to serve to reassure humans that mobility is, in the end, inseparable from virtuous hard work, although wicked foxes dramatize the possibility of immoral, parasitic advance. The fox as a spirit of wealth dealt with similar anxieties about profit unrelated to production.

Interest in the horrible and monstrous is often read as a symptom of social discontent and instability.[36] How, then, is one to interpret interest in the alien in modes other than horror? Foxes were shown

35. See Bray, *Technology and Gender*, pp. 358–68.

36. Cf. the concern in Japan with *bakumatsu bakemono*, "the late Edo monstrosity"; Figal, *Civilization and Monsters*, pp. 21–37.

enduring the vicissitudes of history together with humans: chaste vixens sacrificed themselves when the Ming fell and again to the Taipings;[37] they fled human rebellions at least as often as they were involved in them; at least one late Qing vixen was addicted to opium,[38] and another dressed herself in imported fabrics. Rather than being a sign of anxiety about cultural change, foxes were a reassurance of cultural adaptability. Where they survive, we will, too. Foxes played out the great fantasies of satiation of desire and a just universe, but at the same time they filled an equally important appetite for the small, quotidian mischance or wonder. In the end, from an upper-class perspective at least, they were less frightening than other human beings.

TALKING ABOUT THE ALIEN

The different faces the fox shows in the classical tale and in the vernacular novel suggest that more comparisons between genres would be highly fruitful. Rather than simply tracing relationships of sources and variant versions, we need to pay attention to the ways in which different genres allow exploration of different ideas and issues. Genres that have been relatively neglected, like *biji*, much drama, especially regional drama, *baojuan* 寶眷 (precious scrolls), and *tanci* 彈詞 (plucking rhymes) would provide rich sources. Relations between genres as distinct ways of talking and thinking in constant interchange with one another are not restricted to a simple division of popular and elite. Some of the most interesting discoveries are likely to occur in the places where genres cross and in the gaps between them.

As for those genres that have been central to this project, Tak-hung Leo Chan closes his book by arguing that applying standards other than the aesthetic to Chinese literature will allow scholars to take on not only *zhiguai* but the vast oceans of *biji*.[39] I would second this. These genres contain a vast treasurehouse of the small stories of

---

37. "Lie hu zhuan" 烈狐傳, in Zhang Chao, *Yu chu xinzhi* 10.193; and Baiyi jushi, *Hutianlu*, *xia*, 46b–47a.

38. Xu Qiuzhai, *Wenjian yici*, in *BJXSDG*, 12: 2.7a.

39. Chan, *The Discourse of Foxes and Ghosts*, p. 250.

the late imperial tradition, including the popular, the whimsical, the personal, and the petty, which has barely been touched. Although the fox has provided a valuable glimpse into this world, in a future project I hope to go beyond a single topic and examine these works as a whole.

This discussion of foxes has revealed not so much the outer limits of the human imagination of the alien, as perhaps the inner limits, habits, and patterns of that imagination. Unlike contemporary authors of science fiction, the *zhiguai* authors did not deliberately set out to test those limits with the invention of species.[40] The fox in human form is a particular kind of alien: it is assumed that the alien, for good or ill, has placed us at the center, and the strange comes in a form that looks like us. The fox has two poles in the relatively known, a four-footed animal and a human shape; the strangeness lies in the link between the two.

Even in contemporary American and European science fiction, however, it is only the more literary end of the genre (like Stanislaw Lem's *Solaris*) which endeavors to test these boundaries.[41] Popular science fiction provides us with either monstrous ciphers, familiar as threats, or aliens much closer to ourselves. The former are often modeled on terrestrial non-mammalian species, either insects or reptiles; the latter come to us, like the fairies or the foxes, as humanoid bipeds.

As with the foxes, the contemporary popular tradition is obsessed with aliens who strive to become human: the heart of each successive *Star Trek* series had a creature striving toward, or struggling with, humanity. However, the pole opposite the human is the machine, not monster or animal, and the key to becoming human is emotion and release, rather than discipline or effort.

In the contemporary popular tradition, we are interested in both the alien that more purely represents some quality, be it logic or valor, than we do, and the one who is even more indeterminate and suspended between realms than we are. This same two possibilities were contained in the middle people, whether fairies or foxes. Either the mixed nature of the middle people is set up as a contrast to

---

40. Benford, "Effing the Ineffable," pp. 13–25.

41. Ibid., p. 14.

human purity, or humans themselves are the true mixed and middle beings. Foxes are both simpler than we are, and more indeterminate: they can focus on ascent, or lust, or mischief, to the exclusion of all other interests, but at the same time, they linger between categories.

Since he had the opening word, I give the last word again to Ji Yun. At the end of a story of a servant's wife seduced by a fox, who confounded all her husband's efforts to put a stop to it, Ji closed on a speculative note. It appeared the fox was able to change the shapes of other things with his tricks.

> The Song Confucians urged us to investigate things, but with matters like this, how can one extrapolate from principle? My father often said that when foxes live in a tomb and give it the illusory guise of a house and rooms, people see it as real, but what do the foxes see? Foxes have their fur and skin and transform it into rouge and mascara; people see it as real, but what do the foxes themselves see? And moreover, what does a fox see when it looks at another fox's illusion? There really is nowhere to start investigating this.[42]

Between the tomb and the red pelt and all the trappings of human fantasy was a third possibility, the true mystery of the perspective of the fox, the point where reason was exhausted. As much as he excelled at explaining the strange, Ji Yun gestured here toward his culture's limits in imagining the alien.

42. *YWCT,* 5.231, story 233.

Reference Matter

Bibliography

The following abbreviations are used in this bibliography:

BJXSDG *Biji xiaoshuo daguan* 筆記小說大觀
HJAS *Harvard Journal of Asiatic Studies*

Anagnost, Ann S. "Politics and Magic in Contemporary China." *Modern China* 13, no. 1 (Jan. 1987): 41–61.

Bai Juyi 白居易. *Bai Juyi ji* 白居易集. 4 vols. Beijing: Zhonghua shuju, 1975.

Baiyi jushi 百一居士. *Hutian lu* 壺天錄. 1885 Shenbao guan ed. In *Biji congbian* 筆記叢編. Taibei: Guangwen shuju, 1969.

Bargen, Doris. *A Woman's Weapon: Spirit Possession in the Tale of Genji*. Honolulu: University of Hawai'i Press, 1997.

Barr, Allan. "Pu Songling and *Liaozhai zhiyi*: A Study of Textual Transmission, Biographical Background, and Literary Antecedents." Ph.D. diss., Oxford University, 1983.

———. "A Comparative Study of Early and Late Tales in *Liaozhai zhiyi*." *HJAS*, 45, no. 1 (June 1985): 157–202.

———. "Disarming Intruders: Alien Women in *Liaozhai zhiyi*." *HJAS*, 49, no. 2 (Dec. 1989): 501–17.

Bascom, William. "The Forms of Folklore: Prose Narratives." In Alan Dundes, ed., *Sacred Narrative: Readings in the Theory of Myth*, pp. 5–29. Berkeley: University of California Press, 1984.

Biji xiaoshuo daguan 筆記小說大觀. Reprinted—Yangzhou: Jiangsu Guangling guji keyinshe, 1995.

Benford, Gregory. "Effing the Ineffable." In Slusser, George E. and Rabkin, Eric S., eds., *Aliens: the Anthropology of Science Fiction*, pp. 13–25. Carbondale: Southern Illinois University Press, 1987.

Birch, Cyril. *Scenes for Mandarins.* New York: Columbia University Press, 1995.

Bishan woqiao 碧山臥樵, pseud. *Youguai shitan* 幽怪詩談. Preface dated 1629. Copy in Beihai branch of Beijing Library.

Bol, Peter. "A Literati Miscellany and Sung Intellectual History: The Case of Chang Lei's *Ming-tao tsa-chih.*" *Journal of Song-Yuan Studies* 25 (1995), pp. 121–51.

Boltz, Judith. "Not by the Seal of Office Alone: New Weapons in Battles with the Supernatural." In Patricia Ebrey and Peter Gregory, eds., *Religion and Society in Tang and Sung China*, pp. 241–305. Honolulu: University of Hawai'i Press, 1993.

Bray, Francesca. *Technology and Gender: Fabrics of Power in Late Imperial China.* Berkeley: University of California Press, 1997.

Briggs, Katherine. *The Fairies in Tradition and Literature.* London: Routledge and Kegan Paul, 1967.

Brokaw, Cynthia. *The Ledgers of Merit and Demerit: Social Change and Moral Order in Late Imperial China.* Princeton: Princeton University Press, 1991.

Cai, Zongqi. *Configurations of Comparative Poetics: Three Perspectives on Western and Chinese Literary Criticism.* Honolulu: University of Hawai'i Press, 2002.

Campany, Robert Ford. *Strange Writing: Anomaly Accounts in Early Medieval China.* Albany: State University of New York Press, 1996.

Cao Xueqin 曹雪芹. *Honglou meng* 紅樓夢. Beijing: Renmin wenxue chubanshe, 1988.

Carlitz, Katherine. "The Social Uses of Feminine Virtue in Late Ming Editions of *Lienu zhuan.*" *Late Imperial China* 12, no. 2 (1991): 117–48.

Castle, Terry. *The Female Thermometer: Eighteenth-century Culture and the Invention of the Uncanny.* New York: Oxford University Press, 1995.

Chan, Leo Tak-hung. *The Discourse of Foxes and Ghosts: Ji Yun and Eighteenth-Century Chinese Storytelling.* Honolulu: University of Hawai'i Press, 1999.

Changbai haogezi 長白浩歌子, pseud. *Yingchuang yicao* 螢窗異草. Ji'nan: Qilu shushe, 1989.

Chen Ding 陳鼎. *Liuxi waizhuan* 留溪外傳. Two editions: one early Qing and one Guangxu.

Chen Guying 陳鼓應, ed. *Zhuangzi jinzhu jinyi* 莊子今注今譯. Beijing: Zhonghua shuju, 1988.

Chen Qiyuan 陳其元. *Yongxianzhai biji* 庸閑齋筆記. *BJXSDG*, vol. 10. Yangzhou: Jiangsu Guangling guji keyinshe, 1995.

Chen Wenxin 陳文新. *Zhongguo biji xiaoshuo shi* 中國筆記小說史. Taibei: Zhiyi chubanshe, 1995.

———. *Zhongguo wenyan xiaoshuo liupai yanjiu* 中國文言小說劉派研究. Wuhan: Wuhan University Press, 1994.

Cheng Zhixiang 程趾祥. *Ci zhong renyu* 此中人語. *Zhongguo jindai xiaoshuo shiliao huibian* 中國近代小說史料彙編, vol. 26. Taibei: Guangwen shuju, 1981.

Chu Renhuo 褚人穫. *Jianhu ji* 堅瓠集. Hangzhou: Zhejiang renmin chubanshe, 1986.

Cohen, Paul. *Between Tradition and Modernity: Wang Tao and Reform in Late Ch'ing China.* Cambridge, Mass.: Harvard University, Council on East Asian Studies, 1974.

Dai Lianfen 戴蓮芬. *Libian xuan zhiyan* 鸝砭軒質言. Shenbao guan ed.

Deng Xuan 鄧晅.*Yitan kexin lu* 異談可信錄. Preface dated 1796. In the Beihai branch of the Beijing Library.

Dewoskin, Kenneth J. "The *Sou shen chi* and the *chih-kuai* Tradition: A Bibliographic and Generic Survey." PhD. diss., Columbia University, 1974.

Dewoskin, Kenneth J., and J. I. Crump, Jr., trans. *In Search of the Supernatural: The Written Record.* Stanford: Stanford University Press,

Dianshizhai huabao 點石齋畫報. Reprinted—Guangzhou: Guangdong Renmin chubanshe, 1983.

Ding Bingren 丁秉仁. *Yaohua zhuan* 瑶華傳. *Zhongguo shenguai xiaoshuo daxi* 中國神怪小說大系, no. 5. Shenyang: Liaoshen sashe, 1992.

Dong Han 董含. *Zhuanxiang zhuibi* 專鄉贅筆. In Wu Zhenfang 吳震方, ed., *Shuoling* 說鈴. Preface dated 1702. 1825 ed.

Dongxuan zhuren 東軒主人, pseud. *Shuyi ji* 述異記. In Wu Zhenfang 吳震方, ed., *Shuoling* 說鈴. Preface dated 1702. 1799 ed.

Doré, Henri. *Researches into Chinese Superstitions,* vol. 5. Shanghai: T'usewei Printing Press, 1918.

Dorfman, Diane. "The Spirits of Reform: The Power of Belief in Northern China." *Positions* 4, no. 2 (1996): 253–89.

Dudbridge, Glen. *Religious Experience and Lay Society in T'ang China.* Cambridge, Eng.: Cambridge University Press, 1995.

———. *The Tale of Li Wa.* London: Ithaca Press, 1983.

Duxiang Yuyin 杜鄉漁隱, pseud. *Kejing ke'e ji* 可驚可愕集. Shanghai: Shanghai shuju, 1897. In the literature collection of the Chinese Institute of Social Sciences, Beijing.

Eberhard, Wolfram. *Die chinesische Novelle des 17.–19. Jahrhundert*. Ascona, Switzerland: Verlage Artibus Asiae, 1949.

Ebrey, Patricia. *The Inner Quarters: Marriage and the Lives of Chinese Women in the Song Period*. Berkeley: University of California Press, 1993.

Elman, Benjamin. *From Philosophy to Philology: Intellectual and Social Aspects of Change in Late Imperial China*. Cambridge, Mass.: Harvard University, Council on East Asian Studies, 1984.

Fang Ruhao 方汝浩. *Dongdu ji* 東度記. Beijing: Huaxia chubanshe, 1995.

Fang Yuankun 方元鶤. *Liangpeng yehua* 涼棚夜話. Preface dated 1799. Shuye tang 書業堂, 1839. In the literature collection of the Chinese Institute of Social Sciences, Beijing.

Fassbind-Eigenheer, Ruth. *Undine, oder, Die nasse Grenze zwischen mir und mir*. Stuttgart: Verlag Hans-Dieter Heinz, 1994.

Feng Menglong 馮夢龍. *Qingshi leilüe* 情史類略. In *Feng Menglong quanji* 馮夢全集龍, vol. 20. Shanghai: Shanghai guji chubanshe, 1993.

———. *Taiping guangji chao* 太平廣記鈔. In *Feng Menglong quanji* 馮夢全集龍, vol.18. Shanghai: Shanghai guji chubanshe, 1993.

———. *Xin pingyao zhuan* 新平妖傳. In *Feng Menglong quanji* 馮夢全集龍, vol 16. Shanghai: Shanghai guji chubanshe, 1993.

———. *Xingshi hengyan* 醒世恒言. Beijing: Renmin wenxue chubanshe, 1987.

———. *Yushi mingyan* 喻世明言. Beijing: Renmin wenxue chubanshe, 1987.

Figal, Gerald. *Civilization and Monsters: Spirits of Modernity in Meiji Japan*. Durham, N.C.: Duke University Press, 1999.

Finucane, R. C. *Appearances of the Dead: A Cultural History of Ghosts*. Buffalo: Prometheus Books, 1984.

Fishman, Olga. *Tri kitaiskii novelista*. Moscow: Nauka, 1980.

Fouqué, Friedrich Heinrich Karl de la Motte. *Undine*. New York: Rinehart, 1959.

Freud, Sigmund. "Das Unheimliche" in *Gesammelte Werke*, chronologisch geordnet 12:231 (Frankfurt am Main: S. Fischer, 1972).

Furth, Charlotte. "Concepts of Pregnancy, Childbirth, and Infancy in Qing China." *Journal of Asian Studies* 46 (1987): 7–35.

———. "Rethinking Van Gulik: Sexuality and Reproduction in Traditional Chinese Medicine." In Christina K. Gilmartin, Gail Hershatter, Lisa Rofel, and Tyrene White, eds., *Engendering China: Women, Culture, and the State*, pp. 125–46. Cambridge, Mass.: Harvard University Press, 1994.

———. *A Flourishing Yin*. Berkeley: University of California Press, 1999.

Gan Bao 干寶. *Soushen ji* 搜神記. Beijing: Zhonghua shuju, 1979.

Gauld, Alan, and A. D. Cornell. *Poltergeists*. London: Routledge and Kegan Paul, 1979.

Ge Hong 葛洪. *Baopu zi neipian jiaoshi* 抱朴子內篇校釋. Beijing: Zhonghua shuju, 1996.

Grambo, Rebecca L. *The World of the Fox*. San Francisco: Sierra Club Books, 1997.

Guhang yanyan sheng 古杭艷艷生, pseud. *Zhaoyang qushi* 昭陽趣史. *Si wu xie huibao* 思無邪匯報, vol. 3. Taibei: Taiwan daying baike, 1994.

Gu Meigao 辜美高. "Tan hu" 談狐. In Gu Meigao and Wang Zhizhong 王枝忠, eds., *Guoji liaozhai lunwen ji* 國際聊齋論文集, pp. 251–64. Beijing: Shifan xueyuan chubanshe, 1992.

Guy, R. Kent. *The Emperor's Four Treasuries: Scholars and the State in the Late Ch'ien-lung Era*. Cambridge, Mass.: Harvard University, Council on East Asian Studies, 1987.

Han Zhai and Dun'an 憨齋 鈍盦 .*Doupeng tanzu* 豆棚談助. Undated edition at the library of the Chinese Academy of Social Sciences, Beijing.

Hanan, Patrick, trans. *The Carnal Prayer Mat*. New York: Ballantine Books, 1990.

———. *The Chinese Vernacular Story*. Cambridge, Mass.: Harvard University Press, 1981.

———. "The Composition of the *P'ing yao zhuan*." *HJAS*, 31 (1971): 201–19.

———."The Making of The Pearl-Sewn Shirt and *The Courtesan's Jewel Box*." *HJAS*, 33 (1973): 124–53.

Hansen, Valerie. *The Changing Gods of Medieval China*. Princeton: Princeton University Press, 1990.

Hayashi Razan 林羅山 . *Gobi chō* 狐媚抄. In *Nishi Nihon kokugo kokubun gakkai hankaku shāho* 西日本國語國文學會翻刻雙書 1, no. 6. Fukuoka: Kankokai, 1964.

He Bang'e 和邦額. *Yetan suilu* 夜譚隨錄. Shanghai: Shanghai guji chubanshe, 1988.

———. *Yetan suilu* 夜譚隨錄. Hongbaozhai 鴻寶齋, 1884.

———. *Yetan suilu* 夜譚隨錄. 1789 ed.

Heine, Steven. *Shifting Shape, Shaping Text: Philosophy and Folklore in the Fox Koan*. Honolulu: University of Hawai'i Press, 1999.

Hershatter, Gail. "Modernizing Sex, Sexing Modernity: Prostitution in Early Twentieth-Century Shanghai." In Christina K. Gilmartin, Gail Hershatter, Lisa Rofel, and Tyrene White, eds., *Engendering China:*

Women, Culture, and State, pp. 147–74. Cambridge, Mass.: Harvard University Press, 1994.

Hong Mai 洪邁. *Yijian zhi* 夷堅志. Beijing: Zhonghua shuju, 1981.

Hou Zhongyi 候忠義. *Zhongguo wenyan xiaoshuo cankao ziliao* 中國文言小說參考資料. Beijing: Beijing daxue chubanshe, 1985.

Hou Zhongyi 候忠義 and Liu Shilin 劉世林. *Zhongguo wenyan xiaoshuo shigao* 中國文言小說史稿. Beijing: Beijing daxue chubanshe, 1993.

Hsieh, Daniel. "Man and Animal in Chinese Fox Stories." Unpublished manuscript.

Huli quanyuan 狐狸全緣. Wenyou tang 文酉堂 ed., 1888. Copy in the Harvard-Yenching Library, Cambridge, Mass.

Hu Kun 胡坤. "Zhongguo gudai hu xinyang yuanliu" 中國古代狐信仰源流. *Shehui kexue zhanxian* 社會科學戰線 (1989): 222–29.

Hu Yinglin 胡應麟. *Shaoshi shanfang bicong* 少室山房筆叢. Beijing: Zhonghua shuju, 1958.

Huang Zunsu 黃尊素. *Shuo lüe* 說略. In *Hanfenlou miji* 涵芬樓秘笈, vol. 8. Taibei: Shangwu yinshuguan, 1962.

Huntington, Rania. "Tigers, Foxes, and the Margins of Humanity in Tang *chuanqi* Fiction." *Harvard Papers on Chinese Literature* 1 (1993): 40–64.

Hyde, Lewis. *Trickster Made This World: Mischief, Myth, and Art*. New York: North Point Press, 1998.

Hymes, Robert. "Personal relations and bureaucratic hierarchy in Chinese religion: evidence from the Song dynasty." In Shahar, Meir and Weller, Robert P., eds., *Unruly Gods: Divinity and Society in China*. pp. 37–69. Honolulu: University of Hawai'i Press, 1996.

Jameson, R. D. *Three Lectures on Chinese Folklore delivered before the convocation of the North China Union Language School, March and April, 1932*. Beijing: North China Union Language School, 1932.

Jiwen leibian 記聞類編. 1877 ed. Copy in the Shoudu Library, Beijing.

Ji Yun 紀昀. *Ji xiaolan wenji* 紀曉嵐文集. Shijiazhuang: Hebei jiaoyu chubanshe, 1991.

———. *Yuewei caotang biji* 閱微草堂筆記. Shanghai: Shanghai guji chuban she, 1982.

———. *Yuewei caotang biji zhuyi* 閱微草堂筆記注譯. Beijing: Zhongguo huaqiao chubanshe, 1994.

Jiang Ruizao 蔣瑞藻. *Xiaoshuo kaozheng* 小說考證. Shanghai: Shanghai guji chubanshe, 1984.

Jiao ye pa 蕉葉帕. In Fu Xuancong 傅璇琮, ed., *Zhongguo gudai xiaoshuo zhenmi ben wenku* 中國古代小說珍秘本文庫. Xi'an: Sanqin chubanshe, 1998.

Jin Liang 金梁. *Guapu shuyi* 瓜圃述異. 1936 ed.

Jin Pengchang 金捧閶. *Shouyizhai kechuang biji* 守一齋客窗筆記 and *Kechuang erbi* 客窗二筆. *Suxiang shi congshu* 粟香室叢書, nos. 14–16. Reprinted—Guangzhou, 1890.

Johnson, David; Andrew Nathan; and Evelyn Rawski, eds. *Popular Culture in Late Imperial China*. Berkeley: University of California Press, 1985.

Kang, Xiaofei. "Power on the Margins: The Cult of the Fox in Late Imperial China." Ph.D. diss., Columbia University, 2000.

———. "The Fox and the Barbarian: Unraveling Representations of the Other in Late Tang Tales." *Journal of Chinese Religions* 27 (1999): 35–60.

Kao, Karl. *Classical Chinese Tales of the Supernatural and the Fantastic*. Bloomington: University of Indiana Press, 1985.

Karlgren, Bernard. *The Book of Odes*. Stockholm: Museum of Far Eastern Antiquities, 1950.

Katz, Paul. *Demon Hordes and Burning Boats: The Cult of Marshall Wen in Late Imperial Chekiang*. Albany: State University of New York Press, 1995.

———. "Enlightened Alchemist or Immoral Immortal?" In Shahar, Meir and Weller, Robert, eds. *Unruly Gods: Divinity and Society in China*, pp. 70–104. Honolulu: University of Hawai'i Press, 1996.

Keenan, David. *Shadows in a Chinese Landscape: The Notes of a Confucian Scholar*. Armonk, N.Y.: M. E. Sharpe, 1999.

Kida Teikichi 喜田貞吉. *Tsukimono* 憑物. Tokyo: Hōbunkan, 1988.

Kirk, Robert. *The Secret Commonwealthes of Elves, Fauns, and Fairies*. London: David Nutt, 1893.

Ko, Dorothy. *Teachers of the Inner Chambers: Women and Culture in Seventeenth-Century China*. Stanford: Stanford University Press, 1994.

Koizuga Minoru 戀塚稔. *Kitsune monogatai* 狐ものがたい. Tokyo: San'ichi shobō, 1982.

Kramer, Heinrich and James Sprenger. *Malleus Maleficarum*. Summers, Montague, trans. New York: Dover, 1971.

Kuhn, Phillip. *Soulstealers: The Chinese Sorcery Scare of 1768*. Cambridge, Mass.: Harvard University Press, 1990.

Lanling xiaoxiao sheng 蘭陵笑笑生, pseud. *Jin ping mei cihua* 金瓶梅詞話. Hong Kong: Taiping shuju, 1991.

Lang Ying 郎英. *Qixiu leigao* 七修類稿. 1776 re-edited ed. Copy in the Beihai branch of the Beijing Library.

"Laohu tan lidai meiren" 老狐談歷代美人. In *Xiangyan congshu* 香豔叢書, vol. 2, collection 3, 4.267–74. Shanghai: Shanghai shudian, 1991.

"Laohu tan lidai liren ji" 老狐談歷代麗人記. In *Yinghuan suoji* 瀛環瑣記, 8.4a–6a. Microfilm at the University of Heidelberg.

Leavy, Barbara Fass. *In Pursuit of the Swan Maiden.* New York: New York University Press, 1994.

Lewis, I. M. *Ecstastic Religion: A Study of Shamanism and Spirit Possession.* London and New York: Routledge, 1989.

Li Changqi 李昌祺. *Jiandeng yuhua* 剪燈余話. In *Jiandeng xinhua wai erzhong* 剪燈新話外二種. Beijing: Zhonghua shuju, 1962.

Li Fang 李昉 et al. *Taiping guangji* 太平廣記. Beijing: Zhonghua shuju, 1994.

Li Jianguo 李劍國. *Tangqian zhiguai xiaoshuo shi* 唐前志怪小說史. Tianjin: Nankai daxue chubanshe, 1984.

———. *Tang Wudai zhiguai chuanqi xulu* 唐五代志怪傳奇敘錄. Tianjin: Nankai University Press, 1994.

———. *Zhongguo hu wenhua* 中國狐文化. Beijing: Zhonghua shuju, 2001.

Li Jianguo 李劍國, ed. *Huli jing de gushi.* 狐狸精的故事. Tianjin: Nankai University Press, 1994.

Li Qingchen 李慶辰. *Zuicha zhiguai* 醉茶志怪. Tianjin: Tianjin guji chubanshe, 1990.

Li Shouju 李壽菊. *Huxian xinyang yu huli jing gushi* 狐仙信仰與狐狸精故事. Taibei: Xuesheng shushe, 1995.

Li Wai-yee. *Enchantment and Disenchantment.* Princeton: Princeton University Press, 1993.

Li Wei-tsu. "On the Cult of the Four Sacred Animals in the Neighborhood of Peking." *Folklore Studies* 7 (1948): 1–94.

Lin Shu 林紓. *Lin Shu xuanji xiaoshuo* 林紓選集小說. Chengdu: Sichuan Renmin chubanshe, 1988.

Ling Mengchu 凌濛初. *Erke pai'an jingqi* 二刻拍案警奇 1632. Reprinted—2 vols. Shanghai: Shanghai guji chubanshe, 1985.

Liu Fu 劉斧. *Qingsuo gaoyi* 青瑣高議. Shanghai: Shanghai guji chubanshe, 1983.

Liu Shide 劉世德, ed. *Zhongguo gudai xiaoshuo baike quanshu* 中國古代小說百科全書. Beijing: Zhongguo baike quanshu chubanshe, 1993.

Liu Shoumei 劉壽眉. *Chunquan jianwen lu* 春泉見聞錄. Preface dated 1800. Copy in the Beihai branch of the Beijing Library.

Liu Xiang 劉向. *Lie xian zhuan* 列仙傳. In *Daozang* 道藏, Dongzhen bu 洞真部, jizhuan lei 記傳類, hai 海 7.

———. *Zhan guo ce* 戰國策. Shanghai: Shanghai guji chubanshe, 1978.

Liu Yeqiu 劉葉秋. *Biji gailun* 筆記概論. Beijing: Zhonghua shuju, 1980.

Loudong yuyi ke 婁東羽衣客, pseud. *Jinghua shuiyue* 鏡花水月. Shenbao guan ed.

Louie, Kam, and Louise Edwards, trans. *Censored by Confucius: Ghost Stories by Yuan Mei.* Armonk, N.Y.: M. E. Sharpe, 1996.

Lu Can 陸粲. *Gengsi bian* 庚巳編. In Fan Qin 范欽, ed., *Yanxia xiaoshuo* 煙霞小說. 1590 ed. Copy in Beijing library; microfilm at Harvard-Yenching Library, Cambridge, Mass.

Lu Lin 陸林, ed. *Qingdai biji xiaoshuo leibian jingguai juan* 清代筆記小說類編精怪卷. Hefei: Huangshan shushe, 1994.

Lu, Sheldon Hsiao-Peng. *From Historicity to Fictionality: The Chinese Poetics of Narrative.* Stanford: Stanford University Press, 1994.

Lu Xun 魯迅. *Gudai xiaoshuo gouchen* 古代小說鉤沉. Ji'nan: Qilu shushe, 1997.

———. *Zhongguo xiaoshuo shilüe* 中國小說史略. Beijing: Beijing daxue xinchao she, 1924.

Lu Yanzhi 陸延枝. *Shuoting* 說聽. In Wang Wenru 王文濡, ed., *Shuo ku* 說庫. Shanghai: Shanghai wenming shuju, 1915.

Luo Guanzhong 羅貫中, attrib. *Sansui pingyao zhuan* 三遂平妖傳. Beijing: Beijing University Press, 1983.

Ma Guojun 麻國鈞, ed. *Lidai huxian chuanqi quanshu* 歷代狐仙傳奇全書. Hengshui: Nongcun duwu chubanshe, 1991.

Ma Xisha 馬西沙 and Han Bingfang 韓秉方. *Zhongguo minjian zongjiao shi* 中國民間宗教史. Shanghai: Shanghai Renmin chubanshe, 1992.

Maeno Naoaki 前野直彬. *Chūgoku shōsetsu shikō* 中國小說史考. Tokyo: Akiyama shoten, 1975.

Mair, Victor, and Dennis Mair, trans. *Strange Tales from a Make-do Studio.* Beijing: Foreign Languages Press, 1989.

Mann, Susan. *Precious Records: Women in China's Long Eighteenth Century.* Stanford: Stanford University Press, 1997.

McMahon, Keith. *Misers, Shrews, and Polygamists: Sexuality and Male-Female Relations in Eighteenth-Century Chinese Fiction.* Durham, N.C.: Duke University Press, 1995.

Mei Dingzuo 梅鼎祚. *Cai gui ji* 才鬼記. Zhengzhou: Zhongzhou guji chubanshe, 1989.

Meyer, Matthias, and Jens Tismar. *Kunstmärchen.* Stuttgart: J. B. Metzer, 1996.

Miao Zhuang 苗壯. *Biji xiaoshuo shi* 筆記小說史. Hangzhou: Zhejiang guji chubanshe, 1998.

Miao Zhuang 苗狀, ed. *Qinghu zhuan* 情狐傳. Shenyang: Liaoning guwu chubanshe, 1994.

Mo Chizi 墨屎子, pseud. *Humei congtan.* 狐媚叢談. Ming ed. Copy in Shanghai Library.

Monschein, Ylva. *Der Zauber der Fuchsfee: Entstehung und Wandel eines "Femme-Fatale" Motivs in der chinesischen Literatur.* Heidelberger Schriften zur Ostasienkunde, vol. 10. Frankfurt: Haag und Herchen, 1988.

Mowry, Hua-yuan Lin. *Chinese Love Stories from Ch'ing-shih.* Hamden, Conn.: Archon Books, 1983.

Müller, Ulrich, and Werner Wunderlich. *Dämonen, Monster, Fabelwesen.* St. Gallen, Switzerland: Fachverlage für Wissenschaft und Studien, 1999.

Nienhauser, William, ed. *The Indiana Companion to Traditional Chinese Literature.* Bloomington: Indiana University Press, 1985.

———, trans. "Miss Jen." In Y. W. Ma and Joseph S. M. Lau, eds., *Traditional Chinese Stories: Themes and Variations*, pp. 339–45. Boston: Cheng & Tsui, 1996.

Ning Jiayu 寧稼雨. *Zhongguo wenyan xiaoshuo zongmu tiyao* 中國文言小說總目提要. Ji'nan: Qilu shushe, 1996.

Nishioka Haruoka 西岡晴彥. "Jinshi to Einei no aida: koyō imēji no henyō" 任氏と嬰寧の間: 狐妖イメージの變容. *Tōyō bunka* 東洋文化 58 (1979): 101–26.

Niu Xiu 鈕琇. *Gu sheng* 觚賸. Shanghai: Shanghai guji chubanshe, 1986.

Ouyang Jian 歐陽健. *Zhongguo shenguai xiaoshuo tongshi* 中國神怪小說通史. Nanjing: Jiangsu jiaoyu chubanshe, 1997.

Owen, Alex. *The Darkened Room: Women, Power, and Spiritualism in Late Victorian England.* Philadelphia: University of Pennsylvania Press, 1990.

Owen, Stephen. *An Anthology of Chinese Literature.* New York: W. W. Norton, 1996.

Pan Jingruo 潘鏡若. *Sanjiao kaimi yanyi* 三教開迷演義. In *Guben xiaoshuo jicheng* 古本小說集成, series 1, vol. 65. Shanghai: Shanghai guji chubanshe, 1990.

Pan Lun'en 潘綸恩. *Daoting tushuo* 道聽途說. Hefei: Huangshan shushe, 1996.

Paracelsus (Theophrastus von Hohenheim). *Liber de nymphis, sylphis, pygmaeis et salamandris, et de caeteris spiritibus.* In *Altdeutsche Unbungstexte*, vol. 16. Bern: Francke Verlag, 1960.

Pinghua zhuren 評花主人. *Jiuwei hu* 九尾狐. In *Zhongguo jindai xiaoshuo shike huibian* 中國近代小說史料彙編, vol.4. Taibei: Guangwen shuju, 1981.

Plaks, Andrew. *Archetype and Allegory in Dream of the Red Chamber.* Princeton: Princeton University Press, 1976.

Pomeranz, Kenneth. "Power, Gender, and Pluralism: The Cult of the Goddess of Taishan." In Theodore Huters, Pauline Yu, and R. Bin Wong, eds., *Culture and State in Chinese History*, pp. 182–204. Stanford: Stanford University Press, 1997.

Propp, Vladimir. *Morphology of the Folktale*. Trans. Lawrence Scott. Austin: University of Texas Press, 1968.

Pu Songling 蒲松齡. *Liaozhai zhiyi (huijiao huihzu huiping ben)* 聊齋志異 (會校會註會評本). Ed. Zhang Youhe 張友鶴. Shanghai: Shanghai guji chubanshe, 1992 [1978].

———. *Pu Songling quanji* 蒲松齡全集. Ed. Sheng Wei 盛偉. Shanghai: Xuelin chubanshe, 1998.

Qi you ci li 豈有此理. Preface dated 1799. Copy in the Literature Institute of the Chinese Academy of Social Sciences, Beijing.

Qian Xiyan 錢希言. *Kuai yuan zhiyi* 獪園志異. 1614 ed. Microfilm in the van Gulik Collection, available in various libraries.

———. *Xixia* 戲瑕. Microfilm at the Library of Congress, Washington, D.C.

Qian Yong 錢泳. *Lüyuan conghua* 履園叢話. Beijing: Zhongguo shudian, 1991.

Qinhuai yuke 秦淮寓客, pseud. *Lüchuang nüshi* 綠窗女史. Beijing University Library microfilm of Ming ed.

Qing Chengzi 青成子, pseud. *Zhiyi xubian* 志異續編. *BJXSDG*, vol. 13. Yangzhou: Jiangsu Guangling guji keyinshe, 1995.

Robinet, Isabelle. *Taoism: The Growth of a Religion*. Trans. Phyllis Brooks. Stanford: Stanford University Press, 1997.

Roy, David. "A Confucian Interpretation of *Jin ping mei*." In *Guoji hanxue huiyi lunwen ji* 國際漢學會議論文集, pp. 39–61. Taibei: Academia Sinica, 1981.

Roy, David, trans. *Plum in the Golden Vase*, vol. 1. Princeton: Princeton University Press, 1993.

Schmitt, Jean-Claude. *Ghosts in the Middle Ages: The Living and the Dead in Medieval Society*. Chicago: University of Chicago Press, 1998.

Shahar, Meir, and Robert Weller, eds. *Unruly Gods: Divinity and Society in China*. Honolulu: University of Hawai'i Press, 1996.

Shan Ben 單本. *Jiaopa ji* 蕉帕記. In Mao Jin 毛晉, ed., *Liu shi zhong qu* 六十種曲, 9: 5243–370. Taibei: Kaiming shudian, 1970.

Shenbao 申報. Reprints of the 1872–87 issues. In *Zhongguo shixue congshu* 中國史學叢書. Taibei: Xuesheng shuju, 1965

Shen Defu 沈德符. *Wanli yehuo bian* 萬歷野獲編. Beijing: Zhonghua shuju, 1959.

Shen Qifeng 沈起風. *Xieduo* 諧鐸. In *Ming Qing shanben xiaoshuo congkan* 明清善本小說叢刊, vol. 85. Taibei: Tainyi chubanshe, 1985.

Silver, Carol. *Strange and Secret Peoples: Fairies and Victorian Consciousness*. Oxford: Oxford University Press, 1999.

Sima Qian 司馬遷. *Shi ji* 史記. Beijing: Zhonghua shuju, 1959.

Sleusser, George E., and Eric S. Rabkin, eds. *Aliens: The Anthropology of Science Fiction*. Carbondale: Southern Illinois University Press, 1987.

Smith, Richard. *Fortune-tellers and Philosophers: Divination in Chinese Society*. Boulder, Colo.: Westview Press, 1991.

Smyers, Karen. *The Fox and the Jewel: Shared and Private Meaning in Contemporary Japanese Inari Worship*. Honolulu: University of Hawai'i Press, 1999.

Sommer, Matthew. *Sex, Law, and Society in Late Imperial China*. Stanford: Stanford University Press, 2000.

Song Zhuxuan 松竹軒. *Yaohu yanshi* 妖狐艷史. In *Si wu xie* 思無邪, vol. 23. Taibei: Taiwan daying baike, 1995.

Tan Qian 談遷. *Bei you lu* 北游錄. In Shen Yunlong, 沈雲龍, ed., *Ming Qing shiliao huibian* 明清史料彙編 11, no. 67. Taibei: Tainyi chubanshe, 1985.

Tan Qian 談遷. *Zaolin zazu* 枣林雜俎. Preface dated 1626. *BJXSDG*, vol. 15. Reprinted—Yanzhou: Jiangsu Guangling guji keyinshe, 1995.

Tang Yongzhong 湯用中. *Yijiong baibian* 翼駉稗編. Preface dated 1849. *Biji xiaoshuo daguan congkan* 筆記小說大觀叢刊, vol. 32. Taibei: Xinxing shuju, 1973.

Tangherlini, Timothy. *Interpreting Legend: Danish Storytellers and Their Repertoires*. New York and London: Garland Publishing, 1994.

Terry, Patricia, trans. *Renard the Fox*. Boston: Northeastern University Press, 1983.

Tu Shen 屠紳. *Liuhe neiwai suoyan* 六合內外瑣言. Reprinted—Shanghai: Shenbao guan, 1876.

Unschuld, Paul. *Chinese Medicine: A History of Ideas*. Berkeley: University of California Press, 1985.

van Gulik, Robert. *Sexual Life in Ancient China*. Leiden: E. J. Brill, 1961.

von Glahn, Richard. "The Enchantment of Wealth: The God Wutong in the Social History of Jiangnan." *HJAS*, 51 (1991): 651–714.

Wan, Margaret Baptist. "Living What You Read: Meta-Fiction in the 19th-Century Popular Novel." Paper presented at the Meeting of the Association of Asian Studies, Spring 2000.

Wang Chong 王充. *Lunheng jiaoshi* 論衡校釋. Beijing: Zhonghua shuju, 1995.

Wang, David. *Fin-de-Siècle Splendor: Repressed Modernities of Late Qing Fiction, 1848–1911*. Stanford: Stanford University Press, 1997.

Wang Jian 王棫. *Qiudeng conghua* 秋燈叢話. Taibei: Guangwen shuju, 1968.

Wang Qishu 汪啓淑. *Shuicao qingxia lu* 水曹清暇錄. Preface dated 1797. Feihong tang 飛鴻堂.

Wang, Richard. "Creating Artifacts: The Ming Erotic Novella in Cultural Practice." Ph.D. diss., University of Chicago, 1999.

Wang Sanpin 王三聘. *Gujin shiwu kao* 古今事物考. In *Xu zhibuzu zhai congshu* 續知不足齋叢書, *Baibu congshu jicheng* 百部叢書集成, series 61, 4: 6.

Wang Tao 王韜. *Hou Liaozhai zhiyi quanyi xiangzhu* 後聊齋志異全譯詳注. Harbin: Heilongjiang Renmin chubanshe, 1988.

Wang Tonggui 王同軌. *Ertan* 耳談. 1602 ed. Microfilm in the Harvard-Yenching Library, Cambridge, Mass.

———. *Ertan leizeng* 耳談類增. 1603 ed. Microfilm in the Harvard-Yenching Library, Cambridge, Mass.

Watson, Burton, trans. *The Tso Chuan: Selections from China's Oldest Narrative History*. New York: Columbia University Press, 1989.

Widmer, Ellen. "Xiaoqing's Literary Legacy and the Place of the Woman Writer in Late Imperial China." *Late Imperial China* 13, no.1 (Jun 1992): 111–55.

Wile, Douglas. *Bedchamber Arts: The Chinese Sexual Yoga Classics Including Women's Sex Texts*. Albany: State University of New York Press, 1992.

Wilson, Colin. *Poltergeists: Cases of Destructive Haunting*. New York: Putnam, 1982.

Wu Changchi 吳昌熾. *Kechuang xianhua* 客窗閒話. *BJXSDG*, vol. 14. Yangzhou: Jiangsu Guangling guji keyinshe, 1995.

Wu Dazhen (fl. 1605) 吾大震. *Guang yanyi bian*. 廣艷異編. *Ming Qing shanben xiaoshuo congkan* 明清善本小說叢刊, vol. 34. Taibei: Tianyi chubanshe, 1985.

Wu, Fatima. "Foxes in Chinese Supernatural Tales." 2 pts. *Tamkang Review* 17, no. 2 (1986): 121–53; no. 3: 263–94.

Wu Qian 吳騫. *Fufeng qiao chuanxin lu* 扶風傳信錄. Preface dated 1807. In *Yugu congshu* 愚谷叢書 (also known as *Baijinglou congshu* 拜經婁叢書).

———. *Fufengqiao chuanxin lu* 扶風傳信錄. Manuscript ed. at the Shanghai Library.

Wu Woyao 吳沃堯. *Wo foshanren duanpian xiaoshuo ji, fu biji xiaoshuo wuzhong*. 我佛山人短篇小說集，附 筆記小說五種. Guangzhou: Huacheng chubanshe, 1984.

(*Xin kan quan xiang pinghua*) *Wuwang fa zhou shu* 新刊全相評話武王伐周書. In *Quan xiang pinghua si zhong* 全相評話四種. Shanghai: Shanghai gudian, 1955.

Wuyue chunqiu 吳越春秋. Taibei: Shijie shuju, 1967.

Xileng cike 西冷詞客, pseud. "Dian jindan" 點金丹. In *Liaozhai zhiyi xiqu ji* 聊齋志異戲曲集. Shanghai: Shanghai guji chubanshe, 1983.

Xia Jingqu 夏敬渠. *Yesou puyan* 野叟曝言. *Ming Qing shanben xiaoshuo congkan* 明清善本小說叢刊, vol. 186. Taibei: Tainyi chubanshe, 1985.

Xianhu qie bao lu 仙狐竊寶錄. *Zhongguo gudai zhenxi xiaoshuo* 中國古代珍稀小說, vol. 5. Shenyang: Chunfeng wenyi chubanshe, 1994.

Xie Zhaozhe 謝肇淛. *Wuza zu* 五雜俎. Shanghai: Zhongyang shudian, 1935.

Xu ? 徐 (pseud.: Qingliang daoren 清涼道人).*Ting yu xuan biji* 聽雨軒筆記. Preface dated 1806. *BJXSDG*, vol. 12. Yangzhou: Jiangsu Guangling guji keyinshe, 1995.

Xu Changzuo 徐昌祚. *Yanshan conglu* 燕山叢錄. Preface dated 1602. Copy of Wanli ed. at the Beijing Library.

Xu Chun 徐春. *Jishi jiayan* 紀氏嘉言. Copy of 1903 ed. in the Shoudu Library, Beijing.

Xu Feng'en 許奉恩. *Lisheng* 里乘. *BJXSDG*, vol. 15. Yangzhou: Jiangsu Guangling guji keyinshe, 1991.

———. *Lantiaoguan waishi* 蘭苕館外史 (also known as *Lisheng* 里乘). Baofang ge 抱芳閣, 1879.

Xu Ke 徐珂. *Qingbai leichao* 清稗類鈔. Taibei, 1966.

Xu Kun 徐昆. *Liuya waibian*. 柳崖外編. Preface dated 1791. In *Biji congkan* 筆記叢刊. Taibei: Guangwen shuju, 1969.

———. *Liuya waibian*. 柳崖外編. 1793 ed.

Xu Kunguo 徐昆國. *Dunzhai oubi* 遁齋偶筆. Preface dated 1753. 1880 ed.

Xu Qiucha 許秋垞. *Wenjian yici* 聞見異辭. *BJXSDG*, vol. 12. Yangzhou: Jiangsu Guangling guji keyinshe, 1995.

Xu Youchun 徐友春 et al., eds. *Minguo renwu da cidian* 民國人物大辭典. Shijiazhuang: Hebei Renmin chubanshe, 1991.

Xu Zhonglin 許仲琳. *Fengshen yanyi* 封神演義. Beijing: Renmin wenxue chubanshe, 1992.

Xuan Ding 宣鼎. *Yeyu qiudeng lu*. 夜雨秋燈錄. Harbin: Heilongjiang Renmin chubanshe, 1997.

Xue Fucheng 薛福成. *Yongan biji* 庸庵筆記. Shanghai: Shangwu yinshu guan, 1937.

Xue Zhuanyuan 薛傳源. *Jianggan congyu* 江干叢語. 1813 ed.

Yang Fenghui 楊鳳輝. *Nan'gao biji* 南皋筆記. *BJXSDG*, vol. 14. Yangzhou: Jiangsu Guangling guji keyinshe, 1995.

Yixing xian jiu zhi 宜興縣舊志. Preface dated ca. 1686.

Yongna jushi 慵納居士, pseud. *Zhi wen lu* 咫聞錄. Zhibuzu zhai 知不足齋, 1832.

Yoshino Hiroko 吉野裕子. *Kitsune: in'yō gogyō to inari shinkā* 狐: 陰陽五行と稲荷信仰. Tokyo: Hōsei daigaku shuppankyoku, 1980.

Yu Guolin 俞國林. *Jiaoxuan zhilu* 蕉軒摭錄. Shuanggui lou 雙桂樓, 1839.

Yu Jiao 俞蛟. *Meng'an zazhu* 夢厂雜著. *Zhongguo jindai xiaoshuo shike huibian* 中國近代小說史料彙編, vol. 22. Taibei: Guangwen shuju, 1980.

Yu, Kuang-hong. "Making a Malefactor a Benefactor." *Bulletin of the Institute of Ethnology, Academica Sinica* 70: 39–66 (Fall 1990).

Yu Rukang 余汝康. *Kuaixin xingshui lu* 快心醒睡錄. 1895 ed.

Yu Zongjun 俞宗駿. *Yanyi xinbian* 艷異新編. Preface dated 1882. In the library of the Chinese Academy of Social Sciences, Beijing.

Yushan zhuren 玉山主人, pseud. *Leifeng ta qizhuan* 雷鋒塔奇傳. In *Yiyao baishe quanzhuan* 義妖白蛇全傳. *Zhongguo shenguai xiaoshuo daxi* 中國神怪小說大系, vol. 2. Liaoning: Liaoshen shushe, 1991.

Yu Shaoyu 余邵魚. *Chunqiu lieguo zhi*. 春秋列國志. Two editions in *Ming Qing shanben xiaoshuo congkan* 明清善本小說叢刊, nos. 179 and 180. The edition in no. 180 is dated 1615. Taibei: Tainyi chubanshe, 1985.

Yu Yingshi 余英時. *Lun Dai Zhen yu Zhang Xuecheng* 論戴震與章學誠. Hong Kong: Longmen shudian, 1976.

Yu Yue 俞樾. *Qixia wuyi* 七俠五義. Beijing: Baowen tang, 1980.

———. *Youtai xianguan biji*. 右臺仙館筆記. Shanghai: Chaoji shuzhuang, 1910.

Yuan Haowen 元好問. *Xu Yijian zhi* 續夷堅志. Beijing: Zhonghua shuju, 1986.

Yuan Mei 袁枚. *Zi bu yu* 子不語. In *Yuan Mei quanji* 袁枚全集, vol. 4. Nanjing: Jiangsu guji chubanshe, 1993.

Yue Jun 樂鈞. *Ershi lu* 耳食錄. 1792 ed. Copy in the Harvard-Yenching Library, Cambridge, Mass.

Zamperini, Paola. "Lost Bodies: Images and Representations of Prostitution in Late Qing Fiction." Ph.D. diss., University of California, Berkeley, 1999.

Zeitlin, Judith. *Historian of the Strange: Pu Songling and the Chinese Classical Tale*. Stanford: Stanford University Press, 1993.

———. "Return of the Palace Lady: Historical Ghost Story and Dynastic Fall." In David Der-wei Wang and Wei Shang, eds., *From the Late Ming to the Late Qing: Dynastic Decline and Cultural Innovation.* Cambridge, Mass.: Harvard University Asia Center, forthcoming

Zeng Yandong 曾衍東. *Xiao doupeng* 小豆棚. Ji'nan: Qilu sushe, 1993.

Zhang Chao 張潮, ed. *Yu Chu xinzhi* 虞初新志. Shijiazhuang: Hebei Renmin chubanshe, 1985.

Zhang Jingyun 張景運. *Qiuping xinyu* 秋坪新語. Preface dated 1792. Copy in Harvard-Yenching Library, Cambridge, Mass.

Zhang Tao 張燾. *Jinmen zaji.* 津門雜記. Facsimile reprinting of the 1885 ed. In *Jindai Zhongguo shiliao congkan* 近代中國史料叢刊, no. 565. Taibei: Wenhai chubanshe, 1970.

Zhang Yun 張畇. *Suoshi xianlu* 瑣事閒錄. 1851 ed.

———. *Suoshi xian xulu* 瑣事閑續錄. Preface dated 1860.

Zhongguo tongsu xiaoshuo zongmu tiyao 中國通俗小說總目提要. Beijing: Zhongguo wenlian chuban gongsi, 1990.

Zhou sheng 周生. *Yangzhou meng* 揚州夢. Taibei: Shijie shuju, 1959.

Zhu Xi 朱熹. *Zhuzi yulei* 朱子語類. Kyoto: Chūbun shuppankai, 1979.

Zhu Yiqing 朱翊清. *Zhucun tanguai* 朱村談怪. Shanghai: Chongwen shuju, 1894.

Zong Li and Liu Qun. *Zhongguo minjian zhushen* 中國民間諸神. Shijiazhuang: Hebei Renmin chubanshe, 1987.

Zou Tao 鄒弢. *Sanjie lu bitan* 三借廬筆談. *BJXSDG*, vol. 13. Yangzhou: Jiangsu Guangling guji keyinshe, 1995.

Title and Author Index

Note: Most references are under titles, with authors cross-referenced only if they appear separately in the text. Stories referred to only in the notes are not indexed.

Subject Index

Note: This index includes historical figures who appear as characters in the narrative excerpts.

Harvard East Asian Monographs
(out-of-print)*

*1. Liang Fang-chung, *The Single-Whip Method of Taxation in China*
*2. Harold C. Hinton, *The Grain Tribute System of China, 1845-1911*
3. Ellsworth C. Carlson, *The Kaiping Mines, 1877-1912*
*4. Chao Kuo-chün, *Agrarian Policies of Mainland China: A Documentary Study, 1949-1956*
*5. Edgar Snow, *Random Notes on Red China, 1936-1945*
*6. Edwin George Beal, Jr., *The Origin of Likin, 1835-1864*
7. Chao Kuo-chün, *Economic Planning and Organization in Mainland China: A Documentary Study, 1949-1957*
*8. John K. Fairbank, *Ching Documents: An Introductory Syllabus*
*9. Helen Yin and Yi-chang Yin, *Economic Statistics of Mainland China, 1949-1957*
*10. Wolfgang Franke, *The Reform and Abolition of the Traditional Chinese Examination System*
11. Albert Feuerwerker and S. Cheng, *Chinese Communist Studies of Modern Chinese History*
12. C. John Stanley, *Late Ching Finance: Hu Kuang-yung as an Innovator*
13. S. M. Meng, *The Tsungli Yamen: Its Organization and Functions*
*14. Ssu-yü Teng, *Historiography of the Taiping Rebellion*
15. Chun-Jo Liu, *Controversies in Modern Chinese Intellectual History: An Analytic Bibliography of Periodical Articles, Mainly of the May Fourth and Post-May Fourth Era*
*16. Edward J. M. Rhoads, *The Chinese Red Army, 1927-1963: An Annotated Bibliography*
17. Andrew J. Nathan, *A History of the China International Famine Relief Commission*
*18. Frank H. H. King (ed.) and Prescott Clarke, *A Research Guide to China-Coast Newspapers, 1822-1911*
19. Ellis Joffe, *Party and Army: Professionalism and Political Control in the Chinese Officer Corps, 1949-1964*

*20. Toshio G. Tsukahira, *Feudal Control in Tokugawa Japan: The Sankin Kōtai System*
21. Kwang-Ching Liu, ed., *American Missionaries in China: Papers from Harvard Seminars*
22. George Moseley, *A Sino-Soviet Cultural Frontier: The Ili Kazakh Autonomous Chou*
23. Carl F. Nathan, *Plague Prevention and Politics in Manchuria*, 1910-1931
*24. Adrian Arthur Bennett, *John Fryer: The Introduction of Western Science and Technology into Nineteenth-Century China*
25. Donald J. Friedman, *The Road from Isolation: The Campaign of the American Committee for Non-Participation in Japanese Aggression*, 1938-1941
*26. Edward LeFevour, *Western Enterprise in Late Ching China: A Selective Survey of Jardine, Matheson and Company's Operations*, 1842-1895
27. Charles Neuhauser, *Third World Politics: China and the Afro-Asian People's Solidarity Organization*, 1957-1967
28. Kungtu C. Sun, assisted by Ralph W. Huenemann, *The Economic Development of Manchuria in the First Half of the Twentieth Century*
*29. Shahid Javed Burki, *A Study of Chinese Communes*, 1965
30. John Carter Vincent, *The Extraterritorial System in China: Final Phase*
31. Madeleine Chi, *China Diplomacy*, 1914-1918
*32. Clifton Jackson Phillips, *Protestant America and the Pagan World: The First Half Century of the American Board of Commissioners for Foreign Missions*, 1810-1860
33. James Pusey, *Wu Han: Attacking the Present through the Past*
34. Ying-wan Cheng, *Postal Communication in China and Its Modernization*, 1860-1896
35. Tuvia Blumenthal, *Saving in Postwar Japan*
36. Peter Frost, *The Bakumatsu Currency Crisis*
37. Stephen C. Lockwood, *Augustine Heard and Company*, 1858-1862
38. Robert R. Campbell, *James Duncan Campbell: A Memoir by His Son*
39. Jerome Alan Cohen, ed., *The Dynamics of China's Foreign Relations*
40. V. V. Vishnyakova-Akimova, *Two Years in Revolutionary China*, 1925-1927, tr. Steven L. Levine
*41. Meron Medzini, *French Policy in Japan during the Closing Years of the Tokugawa Regime*
42. Ezra Vogel, Margie Sargent, Vivienne B. Shue, Thomas Jay Mathews, and Deborah S. Davis, *The Cultural Revolution in the Provinces*
*43. Sidney A. Forsythe, *An American Missionary Community in China*, 1895-1905
*44. Benjamin I. Schwartz, ed., *Reflections on the May Fourth Movement.: A Symposium*

*45. Ching Young Choe, *The Rule of the Taewŏngun, 1864–1873: Restoration in Yi Korea*
46. W. P. J. Hall, *A Bibliographical Guide to Japanese Research on the Chinese Economy, 1958–1970*
47. Jack J. Gerson, *Horatio Nelson Lay and Sino-British Relations, 1854–1864*
48. Paul Richard Bohr, *Famine and the Missionary: Timothy Richard as Relief Administrator and Advocate of National Reform*
49. Endymion Wilkinson, *The History of Imperial China: A Research Guide*
50. Britten Dean, *China and Great Britain: The Diplomacy of Commercial Relations, 1860–1864*
51. Ellsworth C. Carlson, *The Foochow Missionaries, 1847–1880*
52. Yeh-chien Wang, *An Estimate of the Land-Tax Collection in China, 1753 and 1908*
53. Richard M. Pfeffer, *Understanding Business Contracts in China, 1949–1963*
54. Han-sheng Chuan and Richard Kraus, *Mid-Ching Rice Markets and Trade: An Essay in Price History*
55. Ranbir Vohra, *Lao She and the Chinese Revolution*
56. Liang-lin Hsiao, *China's Foreign Trade Statistics, 1864–1949*
*57. Lee-hsia Hsu Ting, *Government Control of the Press in Modern China, 1900–1949*
58. Edward W. Wagner, *The Literati Purges: Political Conflict in Early Yi Korea*
*59. Joungwon A. Kim, *Divided Korea: The Politics of Development, 1945–1972*
*60. Noriko Kamachi, John K. Fairbank, and Chūzō Ichiko, *Japanese Studies of Modern China Since 1953: A Bibliographical Guide to Historical and Social-Science Research on the Nineteenth and Twentieth Centuries, Supplementary Volume for 1953–1969*
61. Donald A. Gibbs and Yun-chen Li, *A Bibliography of Studies and Translations of Modern Chinese Literature, 1918–1942*
62. Robert H. Silin, *Leadership and Values: The Organization of Large-Scale Taiwanese Enterprises*
63. David Pong, *A Critical Guide to the Kwangtung Provincial Archives Deposited at the Public Record Office of London*
*64. Fred W. Drake, *China Charts the World: Hsu Chi-yü and His Geography of 1848*
*65. William A. Brown and Urgrunge Onon, translators and annotators, *History of the Mongolian People's Republic*
66. Edward L. Farmer, *Early Ming Government: The Evolution of Dual Capitals*
*67. Ralph C. Croizier, *Koxinga and Chinese Nationalism: History, Myth, and the Hero*
*68. William J. Tyler, tr., *The Psychological World of Natsume Sōseki*, by Doi Takeo

69. Eric Widmer, *The Russian Ecclesiastical Mission in Peking during the Eighteenth Century*
*70. Charlton M. Lewis, *Prologue to the Chinese Revolution: The Transformation of Ideas and Institutions in Hunan Province*, 1891–1907
71. Preston Torbert, *The Ch'ing Imperial Household Department: A Study of Its Organization and Principal Functions*, 1662–1796
72. Paul A. Cohen and John E. Schrecker, eds., *Reform in Nineteenth-Century China*
73. Jon Sigurdson, *Rural Industrialism in China*
74. Kang Chao, *The Development of Cotton Textile Production in China*
75. Valentin Rabe, *The Home Base of American China Missions*, 1880–1920
*76. Sarasin Viraphol, *Tribute and Profit: Sino-Siamese Trade*, 1652–1853
77. Ch'i-ch'ing Hsiao, *The Military Establishment of the Yuan Dynasty*
78. Meishi Tsai, *Contemporary Chinese Novels and Short Stories, 1949–1974: An Annotated Bibliography*
*79. Wellington K. K. Chan, *Merchants, Mandarins and Modern Enterprise in Late Ch'ing China*
80. Endymion Wilkinson, *Landlord and Labor in Late Imperial China: Case Studies from Shandong by Jing Su and Luo Lun*
*81. Barry Keenan, *The Dewey Experiment in China: Educational Reform and Political Power in the Early Republic*
*82. George A. Hayden, *Crime and Punishment in Medieval Chinese Drama: Three Judge Pao Plays*
*83. Sang-Chul Suh, *Growth and Structural Changes in the Korean Economy*, 1910–1940
84. J. W. Dower, *Empire and Aftermath: Yoshida Shigeru and the Japanese Experience*, 1878–1954
85. Martin Collcutt, *Five Mountains: The Rinzai Zen Monastic Institution in Medieval Japan*
86. Kwang Suk Kim and Michael Roemer, *Growth and Structural Transformation*
87. Anne O. Krueger, *The Developmental Role of the Foreign Sector and Aid*
*88. Edwin S. Mills and Byung-Nak Song, *Urbanization and Urban Problems*
89. Sung Hwan Ban, Pal Yong Moon, and Dwight H. Perkins, *Rural Development*
*90. Noel F. McGinn, Donald R. Snodgrass, Yung Bong Kim, Shin-Bok Kim, and Quee-Young Kim, *Education and Development in Korea*
91. Leroy P. Jones and Il SaKong, *Government, Business, and Entrepreneurship in Economic Development: The Korean Case*

92. Edward S. Mason, Dwight H. Perkins, Kwang Suk Kim, David C. Cole, Mahn Je Kim et al., *The Economic and Social Modernization of the Republic of Korea*
93. Robert Repetto, Tai Hwan Kwon, Son-Ung Kim, Dae Young Kim, John E. Sloboda, and Peter J. Donaldson, *Economic Development, Population Policy, and Demographic Transition in the Republic of Korea*
94. Parks M. Coble, Jr., *The Shanghai Capitalists and the Nationalist Government, 1927-1937*
95. Noriko Kamachi, *Reform in China: Huang Tsun-hsien and the Japanese Model*
96. Richard Wich, *Sino-Soviet Crisis Politics: A Study of Political Change and Communication*
97. Lillian M. Li, *China's Silk Trade: Traditional Industry in the Modern World, 1842-1937*
98. R. David Arkush, *Fei Xiaotong and Sociology in Revolutionary China*
*99. Kenneth Alan Grossberg, *Japan's Renaissance: The Politics of the Muromachi Bakufu*
100. James Reeve Pusey, *China and Charles Darwin*
101. Hoyt Cleveland Tillman, *Utilitarian Confucianism: Chen Liang's Challenge to Chu Hsi*
102. Thomas A. Stanley, *Ōsugi Sakae, Anarchist in Taishō Japan: The Creativity of the Ego*
103. Jonathan K. Ocko, *Bureaucratic Reform in Provincial China: Ting Jih-ch'ang in Restoration Kiangsu*, 1867-1870
104. James Reed, *The Missionary Mind and American East Asia Policy*, 1911-1915
105. Neil L. Waters, *Japan's Local Pragmatists: The Transition from Bakumatsu to Meiji in the Kawasaki Region*
106. David C. Cole and Yung Chul Park, *Financial Development in Korea*, 1945-1978
107. Roy Bahl, Chuk Kyo Kim, and Chong Kee Park, *Public Finances during the Korean Modernization Process*
108. William D. Wray, *Mitsubishi and the N.Y.K*, 1870-1914: *Business Strategy in the Japanese Shipping Industry*
109. Ralph William Huenemann, *The Dragon and the Iron Horse: The Economics of Railroads in China*, 1876-1937
110. Benjamin A. Elman, *From Philosophy to Philology: Intellectual and Social Aspects of Change in Late Imperial China*
111. Jane Kate Leonard, *Wei Yüan and China's Rediscovery of the Maritime World*
112. Luke S. K. Kwong, *A Mosaic of the Hundred Days:. Personalities, Politics, and Ideas of* 1898

Harvard East Asian Monographs

113. John E. Wills, Jr., *Embassies and Illusions: Dutch and Portuguese Envoys to K'ang-hsi, 1666–1687*
114. Joshua A. Fogel, *Politics and Sinology: The Case of Naitō Konan (1866–1934)*
*115. Jeffrey C. Kinkley, ed., *After Mao: Chinese Literature and Society, 1978–1981*
116. C. Andrew Gerstle, *Circles of Fantasy: Convention in the Plays of Chikamatsu*
117. Andrew Gordon, *The Evolution of Labor Relations in Japan: Heavy Industry, 1853–1955*
*118. Daniel K. Gardner, *Chu Hsi and the "Ta Hsueh": Neo-Confucian Reflection on the Confucian Canon*
119. Christine Guth Kanda, *Shinzō Hachiman Imagery and Its Development*
*120. Robert Borgen, *Sugawara no Michizane and the Early Heian Court*
121. Chang-tai Hung, *Going to the People: Chinese Intellectual and Folk Literature, 1918–1937*
*122. Michael A. Cusumano, *The Japanese Automobile Industry: Technology and Management at Nissan and Toyota*
123. Richard von Glahn, *The Country of Streams and Grottoes: Expansion, Settlement, and the Civilizing of the Sichuan Frontier in Song Times*
124. Steven D. Carter, *The Road to Komatsubara: A Classical Reading of the Renga Hyakuin*
125. Katherine F. Bruner, John K. Fairbank, and Richard T. Smith, *Entering China's Service: Robert Hart's Journals, 1854–1863*
126. Bob Tadashi Wakabayashi, *Anti-Foreignism and Western Learning in Early-Modern Japan: The "New Theses" of 1825*
127. Atsuko Hirai, *Individualism and Socialism: The Life and Thought of Kawai Eijirō (1891–1944)*
128. Ellen Widmer, *The Margins of Utopia: "Shui-hu hou-chuan" and the Literature of Ming Loyalism*
129. R. Kent Guy, *The Emperor's Four Treasuries: Scholars and the State in the Late Chien-lung Era*
130. Peter C. Perdue, *Exhausting the Earth: State and Peasant in Hunan, 1500–1850*
131. Susan Chan Egan, *A Latterday Confucian: Reminiscences of William Hung (1893–1980)*
132. James T. C. Liu, *China Turning Inward: Intellectual-Political Changes in the Early Twelfth Century*
133. Paul A. Cohen, *Between Tradition and Modernity: Wang T'ao and Reform in Late Ching China*
134. Kate Wildman Nakai, *Shogunal Politics: Arai Hakuseki and the Premises of Tokugawa Rule*

135. Parks M. Coble, *Facing Japan: Chinese Politics and Japanese Imperialism*, 1931–1937
136. Jon L. Saari, *Legacies of Childhood: Growing Up Chinese in a Time of Crisis*, 1890–1920
137. Susan Downing Videen, *Tales of Heichū*
138. Heinz Morioka and Miyoko Sasaki, *Rakugo: The Popular Narrative Art of Japan*
139. Joshua A. Fogel, *Nakae Ushikichi in China: The Mourning of Spirit*
140. Alexander Barton Woodside, *Vietnam and the Chinese Model.: A Comparative Study of Vietnamese and Chinese Government in the First Half of the Nineteenth Century*
141. George Elision, *Deus Destroyed: The Image of Christianity in Early Modern Japan*
142. William D. Wray, ed., *Managing Industrial Enterprise: Cases from Japan's Prewar Experience*
143. T'ung-tsu Ch'ü, *Local Government in China under the Ching*
144. Marie Anchordoguy, *Computers, Inc.: Japan's Challenge to IBM*
145. Barbara Molony, *Technology and Investment: The Prewar Japanese Chemical Industry*
146. Mary Elizabeth Berry, *Hideyoshi*
147. Laura E. Hein, *Fueling Growth: The Energy Revolution and Economic Policy in Postwar Japan*
148. Wen-hsin Yeh, *The Alienated Academy: Culture and Politics in Republican China*, 1919–1937
149. Dru C. Gladney, *Muslim Chinese: Ethnic Nationalism in the People's Republic*
150. Merle Goldman and Paul A. Cohen, eds., *Ideas Across Cultures: Essays on Chinese Thought in Honor of Benjamin L Schwartz*
151. James Polachek, *The Inner Opium War*
152. Gail Lee Bernstein, *Japanese Marxist: A Portrait of Kawakami Hajime*, 1879–1946
153. Lloyd E. Eastman, *The Abortive Revolution: China under Nationalist Rule*, 1927–1937
154. Mark Mason, *American Multinationals and Japan: The Political Economy of Japanese Capital Controls*, 1899–1980
155. Richard J. Smith, John K. Fairbank, and Katherine F. Bruner, *Robert Hart and China's Early Modernization: His Journals*, 1863–1866
156. George J. Tanabe, Jr., *Myōe the Dreamkeeper: Fantasy and Knowledge in Kamakura Buddhism*
157. William Wayne Farris, *Heavenly Warriors: The Evolution of Japan's Military*, 500–1300

158. Yu-ming Shaw, *An American Missionary in China: John Leighton Stuart and Chinese-American Relations*
159. James B. Palais, *Politics and Policy in Traditional Korea*
160. Douglas Reynolds, *China, 1898–1912: The Xinzheng Revolution and Japan*
161. Roger R. Thompson, *China's Local Councils in the Age of Constitutional Reform, 1898-1911*
162. William Johnston, *The Modern Epidemic: History of Tuberculosis in Japan*
163. Constantine Nomikos Vaporis, *Breaking Barriers: Travel and the State in Early Modern Japan*
164. Irmela Hijiya-Kirschnereit, *Rituals of Self-Revelation: Shishōsetsu as Literary Genre and Socio-Cultural Phenomenon*
165. James C. Baxter, *The Meiji Unification through the Lens of Ishikawa Prefecture*
166. Thomas R. H. Havens, *Architects of Affluence: The Tsutsumi Family and the Seibu-Saison Enterprises in Twentieth-Century Japan*
167. Anthony Hood Chambers, *The Secret Window: Ideal Worlds in Tanizaki's Fiction*
168. Steven J. Ericson, *The Sound of the Whistle: Railroads and the State in Meiji Japan*
169. Andrew Edmund Goble, *Kenmu: Go-Daigo's Revolution*
170. Denise Potrzeba Lett, *In Pursuit of Status: The Making of South Korea's "New" Urban Middle Class*
171. Mimi Hall Yiengpruksawan, *Hiraizumi: Buddhist Art and Regional Politics in Twelfth-Century Japan*
172. Charles Shirō Inouye, *The Similitude of Blossoms: A Critical Biography of Izumi Kyōka (1873-1939), Japanese Novelist and Playwright*
173. Aviad E. Raz, *Riding the Black Ship: Japan and Tokyo Disneyland*
174. Deborah J. Milly, *Poverty, Equality, and Growth: The Politics of Economic Need in Postwar Japan*
175. See Heng Teow, *Japan's Cultural Policy Toward China, 1918-1931: A Comparative Perspective*
176. Michael A. Fuller, *An Introduction to Literary Chinese*
177. Frederick R. Dickinson, *War and National Reinvention: Japan in the Great War, 1914-1919*
178. John Solt, *Shredding the Tapestry of Meaning: The Poetry and Poetics of Kitasono Katue (1902-1978)*
179. Edward Pratt, *Japan's Protoindustrial Elite: The Economic Foundations of the Gōnō*
180. Atsuko Sakaki, *Recontextualizing Texts: Narrative Performance in Modern Japanese Fiction*

181. Soon-Won Park, *Colonial Industrialization and Labor in Korea: The Onoda Cement Factory*
182. JaHyun Kim Haboush and Martina Deuchler, *Culture and the State in Late Chosŏn Korea*
183. John W. Chaffee, *Branches of Heaven: A History of the Imperial Clan of Sung China*
184. Gi-Wook Shin and Michael Robinson, eds., *Colonial Modernity in Korea*
185. Nam-lin Hur, *Prayer and Play in Late Tokugawa Japan: Asakusa Sensōji and Edo Society*
186. Kristin Stapleton, *Civilizing Chengdu: Chinese Urban Reform*, 1895–1937
187. Hyung Il Pai, *Constructing "Korean" Origins: A Critical Review of Archaeology, Historiography, and Racial Myth in Korean State-Formation Theories*
188. Brian D. Ruppert, *Jewel in the Ashes: Buddha Relics and Power in Early Medieval Japan*
189. Susan Daruvala, *Zhou Zuoren and an Alternative Chinese Response to Modernity*
190. James Z. Lee, *The Political Economy of a Frontier: Southwest China*, 1250–1850
191. Kerry Smith, *A Time of Crisis: Japan, the Great Depression, and Rural Revitalization*
192. Michael Lewis, *Becoming Apart: National Power and Local Politics in Toyama*, 1868–1945
193. William C. Kirby, Man-houng Lin, James Chin Shih, and David A. Pietz, eds., *State and Economy in Republican China: A Handbook for Scholars*
194. Timothy S. George, *Minamata: Pollution and the Struggle for Democracy in Postwar Japan*
195. Billy K. L. So, *Prosperity, Region, and Institutions in Maritime China: The South Fukien Pattern*, 946–1368
196. Yoshihisa Tak Matsusaka, *The Making of Japanese Manchuria*, 1904–1932
197. Maram Epstein, *Competing Discourses: Orthodoxy, Authenticity, and Engendered Meanings in Late Imperial Chinese Fiction*
198. Curtis J. Milhaupt, J. Mark Ramseyer, and Michael K. Young, eds. and comps., *Japanese Law in Context: Readings in Society, the Economy, and Politics*
199. Haruo Iguchi, *Unfinished Business: Ayukawa Yoshisuke and U.S.-Japan Relations*, 1937–1952
200. Scott Pearce, Audrey Spiro, and Patricia Ebrey, *Culture and Power in the Reconstitution of the Chinese Realm*, 200–600
201. Terry Kawashima, *Writing Margins: The Textual Construction of Gender in Heian and Kamakura Japan*
202. Martin W. Huang, *Desire and Fictional Narrative in Late Imperial China*

203. Robert S. Ross and Jiang Changbin, eds., *Re-examining the Cold War: U.S.-China Diplomacy*, 1954–1973
204. Guanhua Wang, *In Search of Justice: The* 1905–1906 *Chinese Anti-American Boycott*
205. David Schaberg, *A Patterned Past: Form and Thought in Early Chinese Historiography*
206. Christine Yano, *Tears of Longing: Nostalgia and the Nation in Japanese Popular Song*
207. Milena Doleželová-Velingerová and Oldřich Král, with Graham Sanders, eds., *The Appropriation of Cultural Capital: China's May Fourth Project*
208. Robert N. Huey, *The Making of 'Shinkokinshū'*
209. Lee Butler, *Emperor and Aristocracy in Japan*, 1467–1680*: Resilience and Renewal*
210. Suzanne Ogden, *Inklings of Democracy in China*
211. Kenneth J. Ruoff, *The People's Emperor: Democracy and the Japanese Monarchy*, 1945–1995
212. Haun Saussy, *Great Walls of Discourse and Other Adventures in Cultural China*
213. Aviad E. Raz, *Emotions at Work: Normative Control, Organizations, and Culture in Japan and America*
214. Rebecca E. Karl and Peter Zarrow, eds., *Rethinking the* 1898 *Reform Period: Political and Cultural Change in Late Qing China*
215. Kevin O'Rourke, *The Book of Korean Shijo*
216. Ezra F. Vogel, ed., *The Golden Age of the U.S.-China-Japan Triangle*, 1972–1989
217. Thomas A Wilson, ed., *On Sacred Grounds: Culture, Society, Politics, and the Formation of the Cult of Confucius*
218. Donald S. Sutton, *Steps of Perfection: Exorcistic Performers and Chinese Religion in Twentieth-Century Taiwan*
219. Daqing Yang, *Technology of Empire: Telecommunications and Japanese Imperialism*, 1930–1945
220. Qianshen Bai, *Fu Shan's World: The Transformation of Chinese Calligraphy in the Seventeenth Century*
221. Paul Jakov Smith and Richard von Glahn, eds., *The Song-Yuan-Ming Transition in Chinese History*
222. Rania Huntington, *Alien Kind: Foxes and Late Imperial Chinese Narrative*
223. Jordan Sand, *House and Home in Modern Japan: Architecture, Domestic Space, and Bourgeois Culture*, 1880–1930
224. Karl Gerth, *China Made: Consumer Culture and the Creation of the Nation*
225. Xiaoshan Yang, *Metamorphosis of the Private Sphere: Gardens and Objects in Tang-Song Poetry*

Harvard East Asian Monographs

226. Barbara Mittler, *A Newspaper for China? Power, Identity, and Change in Shanghai's News Media*, 1872–1912
227. Joyce Madancy, *The Troublesome Legacy of Commissioner Lin: The Opium Trade and Opium Suppression in Fujian Province, 1820s to 1920s*
228. John Makeham, *Transmitters and Creators: Chinese Commentators and Commentaries on the Analects*
229. Elizabeth Köll, *From Cotton Mill to Business Empire: The Emergence of Regional Enterprises in Modern China*